S0-BSN-725

THE IMAGE OF THE BLACK IN WESTERN ART

PUBLICATIONS OF MENIL FOUNDATION, INC.

THE IMAGE OF THE BLACK IN WESTERN ART

I
FROM THE PHARAOHS TO THE FALL OF THE ROMAN EMPIRE

II
FROM THE EARLY CHRISTIAN ERA TO THE "AGE OF DISCOVERY"

1
FROM THE DEMONIC THREAT
TO THE INCARNATION OF SAINTHOOD

2
AFRICANS IN THE CHRISTIAN ORDINANCE
OF THE WORLD
(FOURTEENTH TO THE SIXTEENTH CENTURY)

III
FROM EUROPE TO AMERICA
(SIXTEENTH TO THE TWENTIETH CENTURY)

LADISLAS BUGNER General Editor

THE IMAGE OF THE BLACK IN WESTERN ART

II

FROM THE EARLY CHRISTIAN ERA TO THE "AGE OF DISCOVERY"

1
FROM THE DEMONIC THREAT
TO THE INCARNATION OF SAINTHOOD

JEAN DEVISSE

With a preliminary essay by JEAN MARIE COURTÈS

Translation by William Granger Ryan

WILLIAM MORROW AND COMPANY, INC.
New York 1979

Designed by Hanspeter Schmidt.
Studio S + T, Lausanne

Inquiries should be addressed to
William Morrow and Company, Inc.,
105 Madison Ave., New York, N.Y. 10016.

Printed in Switzerland.

ISBN 0-688-03543-4 Part 1
0-688-03548-5 Part 2
LC 76-25772

TABLE OF CONTENTS

NOTICE

When we embarked, years ago, on this investigation of the iconography of the blacks in Western medieval art, we had no idea of the unforeseen byways and unexpected depths to which it would lead us. The abundance and diversity of themes encountered necessitated the presentation of this volume in two parts. Were one to leaf through this book and sample the rich harvest of images without carefully reading the text we have built around the illustrations, one's dominant impression would be the lack of coherence of the material.

As soon, however, as one looks at these iconographic documents not only as works of art but as cultural signals that must be classified, decoded, and arranged in logical sequences, the information they contain appears extremely rich and often very new. Who would have suspected that St. Maurice could turn black in the middle of the thirteenth century? Who would have imagined how long it took for the black King to be accepted among the Magi? Who would have supposed that the *Cántigas* of Alfonso the Wise would supply a series of illustrations so indicative of the preconceptions and phantasms of a society? Surprise awaited us at every turn. A new image modified our understanding of ten others previously brought together; a text threw light on the image, and this, in turn, clarified the meaning of another text. The force of circumstances launched us upon a historical inquiry, although at the start our intention was simply to comment on a selection of interesting images: the images themselves often constituted historical series.

We want to say here how valuable, unhesitating, and painstaking has been the collaboration of those who gathered and classified the documents and of all the others whom the Foundation engaged to aid us. And we cannot fail to note how much our discussions with Monique and Ladislas Bugner, a thousand times renewed, have helped us to enrich and give depth to this text.

The study, ten times rewritten and restructured, still fails to satisfy those who have conducted it, because at every step secondary investigations seemed needed in order to understand images that proved to be more significant than we had suspected at the outset. One simple example: in the second part of this volume will be found a brief discussion of paintings relating to medieval astrology. We know very little about them, and months of patient work would have been necessary to interpret them and make them intelligible to the reader. In cases like this we often felt discouraged. If we were ever to get the book out, then many details had to be left unexamined. Such further studies are indispensable to the pursuit of the inquiry into the reasons that impelled the peoples of the West to look upon blacks and their color as they did for so many centuries.

May readers and researchers not forget this Notice, which is in effect a warning and which applies to both parts of the second volume. Indeed, Jean Devisse, Michel Mollat, and Jean Marie Courtès wish to state clearly that this book is a beginning, a groundbreaking, an invitation to look further, to be curious: it is not the soft pillow on which the hasty certitudes of hurried civilizations too often fall asleep.

THE THEME OF "ETHIOPIA" AND "ETHIOPIANS" IN PATRISTIC LITERATURE

To anyone seeking information about the black, the reading of the Greek and Latin patristic writings, which span almost the entire Imperial period, is quite as disappointing as research in the iconography of that time and culture. Explicit mention of persons of color is extremely rare and not very significant. The concept of the black hardly goes beyond that of skin coloration, which seems to be the only racial characteristic taken into account by Christian writers. It can be said without exaggeration that blackness is not regarded as a specific racial difference, but simply as the darkest of the various shades of color found among the peoples of the Mediterranean Basin and the East.

From this it would be tempting to infer that there was an absence of "race consciousness," and that this in turn was a corollary of the vocation of the Church to universality; but the silence of the sources does not justify such a conclusion. It would be equally specious to dismiss the problem on the basis of certain assumptions. It might be thought, for instance, that the spread of the new religion, beginning as it did among the servile and lower classes and reaching great numbers of foreigners and exotic groups, inevitably included some blacks without creating any special problem. But is it not just as plausible to suppose that their race itself isolated the blacks, or that their tribal cohesiveness kept them from any contact with Christianity? For the present no sure conclusions can be drawn on this question. Further discoveries may be made, but at best they will bring to light only individual or limited examples.

The substance of our theme and the manner of its treatment in this abundant literature, with its great variety of genres, must therefore be studied together. A preliminary inventory, not intended to be definitive, suggests certain lines of research once we establish the contexts in which the topic of the blacks is likely to emerge.

It is apparent that the greater number of references to "Ethiopians" can be divided into two groupings. The first, a very broad one, draws on works of exegetical interpretation. The second and more limited one constitutes a demonology of the black. The first grouping includes all the Judaeo-Christian definitions of Ethiopians and Ethiopia which appear by way of coincidence in commentaries on Scripture: this forms a fairly coherent body of doctrine. The "demonological" texts, on the other hand, resolutely avoid any contact with the realities of anthropology (here understood in the broadest sense to include myth and symbol insofar as they have a concrete foundation). These texts will be considered here only as a metaphorical complement to our main theme and as a measure of its acceptability.

We must emphasize the coincidental and dependent character of these references to Ethiopians: they occur only in connection with a formal explication of the sacred text, or as called for by a fixed topic such as found in eremitic literature. On the other hand, such allusions are lacking precisely where the modern reader would expect them, for instance in the numerous explanations of the creation of man, the dispersion of the races, or the reunification of mankind in the Church. These observations seem to indicate a certain lack of interest in the black as such, even among those of our authors who lived in geographical and cultural proximity to black peoples. By way of compensation, however, the terms *Ethiopia* and *Ethiopian*, being used in an abstract rather than a concrete sense, serve in many ways as means of definition and limitation, and of marking the opposition between good and evil, between the graced and the ungraced. A selection of texts will give an idea of the similarity and variety of ways in which these quasi-symbolic terms are used.

ETHIOPIA: THE SYMBOLISM OF THE PLACE ITSELF

The Book of Genesis, after telling how man was created and brought to life, mentions (Gen. 2:8-14)* the planting of a garden in Eden, to the East. A river flowed out of Eden and divided into four branches, of which the second, Gihon, surrounded the whole land of Chus, i.e., Ethiopia. Origen echoes a "Phrygian" tradition according to which Eden represents the brain and the four rivers the senses whose center is in the head: Pishon stands for sight, Gihon for hearing, Tigris for the sense of smell, and Euphrates for that of taste. Gihon hems in the almost inaccessible land of Ethiopia like a labyrinth: it resembles an ear, and this leads naturally to the implication that the Ethiopians will in the future give ear to the message of the Gospel.[1] Another example: Caesarius notes that the Egyptians went up the river (the Nile) to make their way to Paradise, but were stopped by the heat of the equatorial zone and had to turn back—a circumstance which made them aware of the limitations of human knowledge.[2]

Augustine, on the contrary, rejects any allegorical interpretation:[3] Pishon is the Ganges, Gihon the Nile, and so on. But then how could such figurative interpretations as going by water to Eden be justified? With the exception of the Nile, all the rivers mentioned rise from known sources and therefore cannot be the rivers of Genesis. Augustine offers an ingenious solution to this problem: the known sources are only the places where the

* The biblical quotations in this essay are taken from the Latin Vulgate. The only English version based solely on the Vulgate is the Douay-Rheims (1582-1609), and the translator has followed the Douay-Rheims. It is to be noted, however, that references to the Psalms include the number of the Psalm as given in the Latin Vulgate and the Douay-Rheims, followed in parentheses by the number found in modern versions: e.g., Psalm 67(68). — Trans.

rivers return to the surface after following underground channels. This leaves Ethiopia where it was before, somewhere at the edge of the other world; but could not the frontiers to be reached by the Gospel be pushed back farther and farther by pointing to the Ethiopians, who live "beyond the river" and are not yet evangelized?[4]

DIVISION BY COLOR

The Ethiopians' black pigmentation provides a principle of inversion in anthropological structuralism. Xenophon, whom Clement of Alexandria follows,[5] had observed that the gods the blacks made for themselves were black with simian features, in accordance with the principle of anthropomorphic likeness. But if the regressive comparison thus led to denying the universality of the gods, the whole perspective might just as easily be reversed. Three significant examples will show how these positions are opposed.

Origen uses the following argument against astrology. We are told that those born under the sign of Virgo have fair skin and smooth hair. No Ethiopian, therefore, can be born under this sign unless he takes on the characteristics proper to it—in other words, ceases to be an Ethiopian. But it is known that Ethiopians are born the year round, a fact which, assuming the unity of the human race and the universal influence of an astral determinism independent of cultures and geographical situation, prompts some skepticism about astrology:[6] the zodiac, seen from the tropics in the vertical plane, does not necessarily look the same as when it is seen obliquely from the extratropical zones. The monk Meletios, writing about the nature of man,[7] sees the diversity of racial colors as a mark of the Creator's loving care: once skin color is seen as an accidental property like the other differences between men, the notion of similitude, which is not accidental, can be extended to constitute a new principle of genetic equality in God. Athanasius[8] distinguishes the 'proper' (ἰδίωμα, i.e., the composite of mortal and immortal natures) from the 'subordinate' (ὑποτακτικόν — whiteness, blackness, height, etc.), and says that after the Resurrection men will not recognize each other because all the signs by which they are recognizable belong to the nature that perishes. They will recover the first man's oneness of form, with no distinction due to 'accidents'—no tall ones or short ones, no whites or blacks, no flat noses, etc. This is a handy solution to otherwise insoluble difficulties, such as recognizing the child who died young and will rise with the glorious body of a thirty-year-old or the Ethiopian who rises a white man.[9] The discriminating racial characteristic goes the way of the individuality which will no longer exist.

Arnobius, writing about the pagan sacrifices in the seventh book of his *Adversus nationes*,[10] tries to determine the reason behind the separation of the gods to right and left, noting that the ones to the right claim white victims while the others demand black ones, and that the two groups preside over the upper and lower regions of the world respectively. Black goes with the idea of sadness and death, white with that of joy. But then there arises a line of thought derived from the well-known syllogism of the Ethiopian: it is true that the sacrificial victims' fleece is black, but their flesh, bones, and brains are white; if therefore the logic of chromatic and theological partition were followed, the proper procedure would be to sacrifice only the fleece, or else to color the incense, fruit, milk, blood, and oil of the libations. Arnobius is being playful—*stolide ludamus*—but here displays a curiosity common in his day concerning such notional contrasts and dichotomies. In a more serious passage[11] he goes so far as to deny that the souls of men are of divine or heavenly origin. All men, he asserts (to bolster his thesis, of course), have "dark bodies."

THE BLACK BODIES OF THE DAMNED

Origen proposes the hypothesis that the "outer darkness" into which the damned will be cast after the Resurrection means that these souls will then be clothed in black bodies. Their outward appearance in the world to come will thus correspond to the darkness of ignorance that filled their inward being in this world and will make it visibly manifest.[12] Nevertheless the Resurrection will reestablish man in the image and likeness of God by abolishing the diversity and mutability of the body. Origen makes no reference whatever to racial differences, either in the sense of a reuniting of mankind or in that of a continuation of diversity.[13] In fact there is no need to raise the question, since God has neither form nor color, and all his human creatures bear the same likeness to him in their essence, independently of racial or other peculiarities.[14] The transformation of the damned is related rather to the symbolism of light and darkness: any mention of bodily elements in God is allegorical. Origen reaffirms the definition found in the First Epistle of John: "God is light and in him there is no darkness" (1 John 1:5).[15] Moreover, a simple analysis of the way an artist portrays a body gives an idea of the contingent nature of the factors that create visual resemblance: the painter produces a likeness solely by the use of colors without a third dimension, the sculptor uses relief without color.[16] The damned in their blackness are in reality those who have been judged unworthy of the brightness of the glorified body: they certainly are not to be thought of as Ethiopians.

Augustine declares firmly that whatever men's shape or color may be now, they all trace their origin to a single human form. His definition of man, "a rational and mortal being,"[17] simply ignores external marks of classification or differentiation. It also affords a solution to the problem raised by deformities and monstrosities, realities which fit neither a literal interpretation of likeness nor the teleological views implied or expressed in Christian thought on the *sacramentum hominis*.[18] The concept of man therefore embraces the most surprising peculiarities found in ethnological fable, compared to which racial characteristics seem negligible since they have no effect on the essential relationship of likeness. This relationship not only exists between the Creator and his creature: it is also the conformity of the body with the rational soul. This latter aspect of likeness is manifested not through *liniamenta figurasque membrorum* ("the features and shape of the body"), but through the disposition of the human composite in relation to the *superna* ("the things above"). The heavens are spread out before the only animal that stands up straight and is built conformably with the spiritual destiny of the soul. This explains why the Genesis story of the formation of man does not include the *secundum genus* which accompanies the account of the creation of plants and animals. "Man was made one: even woman was made from him. There are not several races of men as there are species of herbs and trees, fishes and winged creatures, serpents, wild beasts and grazing animals."[19]

Augustine tends to minimize anything that might seem an intrusion of the bodily into the spiritual, and thus (given the nimbleness of the imagination) might cause the appearances of the body to be taken for the properties of the spirit. He denounces the illusion—produced by fantasy or by the Devil—suffered by those who attribute form, shape, or color to the soul, and conceive it, without always being aware of so doing, as a body. Before refuting the theses of Vincentius Victor[20] he takes issue with Tertullian's *De anima.* Tertullian ascribed to the soul "a color of air and light": quite gratuitously he gave it senses and members of a like nature. Augustine observes that an Ethiopian almost always sees himself as black, even in dreams. Were he to see himself as being of another color he would be astonished. As for the "color of air and light," no one has ever seen his soul thus adorned, unless in dream, and that would be an illusion anyway. The Ethiopian would never have such an idea unless he got it from some source outside himself.[21]

Obviously this does not mean that the soul of a white man is different from that of a black, but it does mean that consciousness of skin color affects the deceptive images one forms to represent one's own being. The *De Trinitate* gives the ultimate analysis and general philosophical formulation: "Color, which has in itself no proper substance, resides in a colored subject; the colored body is the substance, the color is in the substance."[22] It is no contradiction, therefore (provided the terms are understood allegorically), to say on the one hand that after the Resurrection the just will have the beauty of the sun's brilliance as a perfection of their nature, and on the other that each one's beauty "consists in the symmetry of the parts of the body and a pleasing color."[23] This metaphysical assumption is probably responsible for the absence of blacks in Augustine's works. The oft cited eunuch of Queen Candace does not appear as an Ethiopian in these writings,[24] and Moses' Ethiopian wife becomes a Midianite.[25]

THE QUALITY OF BLACKNESS: "NIGER ... DICITUR IN QUO NIGREDO PERMANSERIT"[26]

In patristic thought all speculation on the origin of man leads to a debate on the Trinity and a theology of the image. Didymus the Blind had shown that the Word had no qualities, and that even if for convenience of thought the Word was assumed to be the prototype of man, its *image* had no more than a nominal relationship to the images of *mimesis* of form and color.[27] But it was Boethius (the commentator of Aristotle as interpreted by Porphyry) who, anticipating medieval thought, turned his attention to the study of 'accidents', basing his analysis on the data accessible to the human mind. The modern reader may be tempted to smile at the dialectical and verbal gymnastics which he finds so hard to fathom, but if he follows their permutations and combinations he will have to admire the freedom of mind acquired through the device of syllogistic reasoning.

An example: if a 'proper' applies to an individual it applies also to the 'accidents' of the individual. Man is an animal capable of reason and laughter: if I say "black Ethiopian," it follows that I can say "black rational" or "black capable of laughter" or "black individual."[28] Now let us consider a crow and an Ethiopian, both black, and let us imagine that both of them lose their blackness: the crow will then be white but will still be a crow, whereas the Ethiopian will lose his quality as an Ethiopian and will simply be a man like other men. His natural identity with them becomes apparent once the 'accident' is eliminated, but the detour would have been unnecessary if a 'proper' (*rationale* or *risibile*) had been taken into consideration.[29] "Est igitur accidens quod adest et abest praeter subjecti corruptionem" ("An accident is that which may be present or absent without corruption of the subject").[30]

Of course it could be argued that blackness is not the only distinguishing characteristic of the Ethiopian.[31] Boethius remarks moreover that there are many degrees of blackness, from *fuscis proxima* ("swarthy") to *nigerrima* ("pitch-black"), and that as much could be said of other 'accidents': like blackness they are subject to quantity and therefore to uncertainty (how dark must one be before he is black?—a difficulty coming from the chain-of-syllogisms type of argument). The 'proper', on the other hand, does not lead to this difficulty. It is absolute, it either is or is not: be he black, tan, or white, or even an albinic Negro, a man laughs and reasons.[32] The *Commentary on the Categories* states: "When it is said of a man that he is a man of color, it is not said of the man himself, because man as man is not color. It is because he *has* a color that he is called a man of color."[33] Blackness is simply the permanence of a condition that can be fortuitous. "When heat has cooked the blood that comes to the surface of the face, the glow of the burnt blood produces a black color. If the same phenomenon is caused by something that happens to the face of a newborn child, it is probable that its body will be colored in the same way."[34]

It is also probable that when he wrote these and many similar lines Boethius had no concrete image of a black in mind. The point of view he adopts, like Augustine's, excludes such a possibility. Both authors put the emphasis on the unity of mankind; but whereas Augustine bases this unity on the undifferentiated and transcendent archetype, Boethius sees it *in se* beneath the diversity of 'accidents'.

EXEGETICAL TREATMENT

Origen's commentary on the Song of Songs contains an anthology of scriptural texts and a cluster of interpretations on the theme of nigritude which set the tone of all later exegesis, both Greek and Latin. (We note that the Greek original and a large part of the works of Origen have disappeared, and that we read him in a Latin translation.)[35] The text he is commenting is the following:

> I am black but beautiful, O ye daughters of Jerusalem, as the tents of Kedar, as the curtains of Solomon. Do not consider me that I am brown, because the sun hath altered my colour. . . . Who is she that cometh forth as the morning rising, fair as the moon, bright as the sun . . . ? [Song of Songs 1:4-5, 6:9]

With the exception of Theodore of Mopsuestia,[36] who considered the Song of Songs a very realistic poem written by Solomon with the Queen of Sheba in mind, the entire Christian tradition accepts Origen's exegesis, according to which the Bride represents the Church of the Gentiles. Yet it should be remembered that Origen saw in the Song of Songs a sort of sacred drama, a mystical play.[37] Attention must therefore be given to the concrete terms of the allegory as well as to what they signify.

The Church is black "with regard to her color," beautiful "due to the internal ordering of her members." She is black by reason of the obscurity of her origins (thus differing from the Synagogue), although Kedar connects her with Ishmael and the curtains of Solomon relate her to the tabernacle of God: black also because she is the Ethiopian bride of Moses. Origen reviews the Old Testament texts which may be cited in support of this interpretation, referring to the story of Moses' marriage in the Book of Numbers, the episode of the Queen of Sheba in 1 Kings, Psalm 67(68), the prophecy of Zephaniah, and Ebed-melech's intervention on behalf of Jeremiah.[38]

Moses, as the twelfth chapter of Numbers tells us, had taken an Ethiopian woman to wife, and because of this Miriam and Aaron spoke against him. In this symbolic event Origen sees the union of the spiritual Law with the Gentile nations, which in turn foreshadowed the universal Church. Miriam expresses the resentment of the Synagogue abandoned and soon to be stricken with a leprosy white as snow, Aaron the carnal priesthood's failure to understand the significance of the event. To this caste also belonged the priests who condemned Jeremiah before he was saved by Ebed-melech, the Ethiopian eunuch (Jer. 38:7-13). Thus everything is directed to the spread of the truth, from the Queen of Sheba's visit to Solomon to consult his wisdom (1 Kings 10), to the final repetition of this visit on the Day of Judgment, when the Church will come to hear the new Solomon.

Psalm 67(68) conveys the same meaning, since the disqualification of Israel opens the way of salvation to Ethiopia. The rivers beyond which lies Ethiopia symbolize the "fullness of the peoples"—in other words, the whole of mankind including Israel, which had been subjected to the "dark coloring of wickedness" and had become "black and darkened." Origen's general theory of salvation thus takes this passage of the Psalm to be the image of a spiritual land of passage and, since the ultimate goal is salvation, a metamorphosis of Egypt bathed and inundated by the saving waters.

Coming back to the Bride, Origen explains the words of the Song of Songs. Neither Nature nor the Creator made the Bride black. She got her color *ex accidentibus*, through exposure to the sun, but by a process which was the reverse of that undergone by the Ethiopians.[39] Her blackness is not a transmissible characteristic acquired by genetic inheritance; it is a sign of neglect: *despexit me sol*.[40] Here we discern between the lines the typological opposition between Scythian and Ethiopian, which is linked in a way with the opposition of the visible and the spiritual. The visible sun burns those who are directly beneath it while those whom its rays touch obliquely are left white. Contrariwise, the spiritual sun sheds light on the former and leaves the latter in darkness. The Bride in her dark beauty can say that she has "drawn near to him who is the image of God, the first-born of all creation, the radiance of God's glory and the perfect copy of his nature," and that she has "been made beautiful." But there is more to this than mystical allegory. In both weddings—that of Moses and that of the Bride of the Song of Songs—an actual whitening takes place. The initial subjective statement "I am black but beautiful" is replaced by the objective judgment of the virgins, queens, and concubines, based on the color transformation interpreted as a sign. This visible passage from potency to act is one of the keys to the "Ethiopian" symbolism of the Christian tradition.

THE CONVERSION OF THE ETHIOPIANS, SONS OF THE DEVIL

Didymus the Blind, in his *Commentary on Zechariah*, turns his attention to the ways in which the Ethiopians may be brought into the economy of salvation. Quoting Ps. 86 (87):3-4, where they are named with the people of Tyre, Didymus makes the point that "[these] foreigners . . . have a place in the glorious city of God only after they have turned away from impiety and the worship of demons."[41] This conversion follows the trial announced by the prophet Zephaniah (2:12): "You Ethiopians, also shall be slain with my sword." Through this wound they lose their sonship with the Devil and in God become white as snow. "Once they have been wounded by Him who says these words and have given up their Ethiopian way of life, they will receive immortality, and, filled with thankfulness, will say, 'Let the brightness of the Lord our God be upon us' (Ps. 89 [90]:17). Washed by the Author of all good we have emerged clean and white, according to the word of him who said with confidence, 'Thou shalt wash me, and I shall be made whiter than snow' (Ps. 50 [51]:9)." "What was it therefore," Didymus continues, "that made them Ethiopians—these people who are wounded for their own good in order to die to impiety? It was that they were born of the Devil and wished to serve his evil designs. He is assumed to be black because of the darkness in which his ignorance of God and his perversity establish him." The *Epistle of Barnabas* and *The Shepherd* of Hermas are cited as authorities on this same point.[42] Further on, and still referring to Zeph. 2:12, Didymus substitutes the notion of participation in the original fall of Satan for that of sonship: "Those who fall beneath the stroke of God's sword are the Ethiopians, because they all share in the malice and sin of the Devil, from whose blackness they take their name." The Devil is black "because he fell from the splendor, virtue, and spiritual whiteness which only those who have been whitened by God can possess."[43]

Jerome's ideas are like those of Origen and Didymus. Yet, although he adds nothing that would indicate a particular interest in the Ethiopian theme, his treatment of it has some originality. Only when the City of God (the Church) has been built will it be possible to count those who are born in it: "Behold the foreigners, and Tyre, and the people of the Ethiopians, these were [born] there [in Zion]" (Ps. 86 [87]:4), says the Psalmist. Citizenship is acquired by the offering that confers a birthright, even if the one who offers it comes from the remote regions *trans flumina* (cf. Zeph.

2:12 and Ps. 67 [68]:31-32). Here a spiritual meaning is projected into the reality of earthly space.[44] Zechariah's vision confirms the character of Jerusalem as an open city which the heavenly surveyor is measuring. The Eternal will be its "wall of fire" (cf. Zech. 2:1-5; Ps. 67 [68]:32), as he is also the *gladius fortium* ("sword of the strong"). The Ethiopians, wounded by this sword, will then be admitted to the city and will be on the same footing as those born there. At that time they will lose their blackness and will rejoice as David did after he repented (Ps. 50:9-10 [51:7-8]).

Considered from the standpoint of language and material reality, such a transformation can hardly be thought of as possible. Jeremiah says: "If the Ethiopian can change his skin, or the leopard his spots: you also may do well, when you have learned evil" (Jer. 13:23). Here the Manichaeans had seen a weighty argument for the dual nature of man and the impossibility of passing from blackness to whiteness, from the polychrome of guilt to the single color of repentance. Jerome answers that nothing is impossible "to him who acts in the Ethiopian and the leopard."[45] The nature of a being can be changed not by the being itself but by the One who is its principle of existence and action.

Ambrose of Milan, the northernmost of our authors, is aware of the many possible allegorical meanings of nigritude. Origen's exegesis of the Song of Songs often provides Ambrose with a hermeneutical key for his own interpretations, which he supplements with large collections of biblical texts. The various and original ways in which he uses this key will be seen from a remarkable example, the *Exposition of Psalm 118*, where it appears in a number of contexts. Here are some examples of the way he applies it.

John the Apostle: Soul and Body. The Gospel narrative of the Last Supper shows John reclining on the Lord's breast (John 13:23). In this Ambrose sees the visible, historical development of the mysteries of the Song of Songs. The "slave" leaning on the Master should cause no surprise: this is the flesh of sin resting upon the temple of the Word, or again the soul caught in the bonds of flesh and gazing into the fullness of God. Like the Bride, John's soul is both black and beautiful, due to the double effect of sin and grace. The flesh is also black and yet beautiful, but its blackness comes from the dust of the world picked up in the struggle, while its beauty comes from the spiritual oil which washes away that stain. The spiritual combat thus takes on a sacramental aspect. By the absolution it confers, Baptism removes the blackness of sin and consecrates the reconciliation of the flesh, exiled in Eve and assumed into heaven in Mary.[46]

The Synagogue. Jesus, Peter, John, and James were Jews, dissident heirs of the Synagogue, the *prima congregatio Dei*, which also was both black and beautiful, since in it were associated the refusal to believe and the transmission of the Law, the Fall, and the first assembly of believers. Its blackness, like that of the Ethiopians, is due to the Sun, but this time to the lack of it in the darkness of abandonment: "I am black because the Sun of Justice, which shone upon me in the past, has abandoned me; my face has lost its color; the keenness of my eyes is dulled . . . I wander in the darkness." Yet the Sun that now shines on the Gentiles will rise again upon Israel when this people opens itself to the Light.[47]

The Church. The Church includes saints, who are comparable to heavenly creatures, and men of the earth. She is earth and heaven, darkness and light. She has the black color of the Bride just as the winter world is dark, far from the sun's brightness. Henceforth she receives the Light, and the Light also shines on Greeks, Barbarians, and Scythians, following upon the darkness of the centuries of the Law.[48] The moral and spiritual division of her members prolongs and illustrates her history, which is that of the truth at first hidden and then revealed.

The Desert of Life. The soul is the Spouse who comes up pure white from the desert (cf. Song of Songs 8:5), or again (according to some versions of the Song of Songs) who is whitened, "as she comes up from the desert," by accumulated merits that wipe away the blackness of worldly folly.[49] The thing to do, then, is to cast off the earthly and put on the heavenly image of man, which no shadow nor any color can express, and in which Christ recognizes himself.[50]

Morality and Mysticism. The Church sees men, to whom she is guide and teacher, in a double light. Therefore she has two eyes, of which the "doves washed with milk" (Song of Songs 5:12) are a figure. The doves also suggest the black and whitened Bride, as well as those sincere souls whom the Lord baptizes in milk. Their whiteness fits them morally for spiritual knowledge. Leaving behind the *maculosa confusio* of nigritude, and thanks to the rational milk, they acquire the purity of mystical sight.[51]

Orthodoxy. The Church was formerly "black in broad daylight," but later "shone brightly in the night." Now she is white, being cleansed of the Manichaean and Arian heresies: she receives the dual illumination of the Old and New Testaments, which she unites and fulfills. The daughters of Jerusalem who wonder at the coming up of the Bride, now whitened *(dealbata)*, represent the Old Law contemplating the new sacrament.[52]

These themes and some few others are closely connected with the speculations about the sun that were so dear to the contemporaries of Macrobius, and just as closely with the various light symbolisms of the Neoplatonists. Ambrose borrows from Philo when he interprets Ethiopia in moralistic terms indicative of disdain (the outsider, the thing of small value)—an interpretation which he extends to the body, symbolized by the earth burnt by the passions. The river Gihon, which is a figure of chastity, purifies the body as it bathes the land of Ethiopia.[53] Indeed, if the conscience is darkened by sin its night spreads to the body, the *corpus tenebrosum*[54] imprisoned in its materiality. This dark side of human nature is personified in Nimrod the hunter, who was black like his father Chus. Forced by his nature to live and act more like an animal than a creature of reason, Nimrod is an image of the guilty soul, "Ethiopian, enemy of the light, deprived of brightness."[55]

Gregory the Great, in his *Moralia*,[56] sketches a little synthesis on our theme. Commenting on Job 28:19 ("The topaz of Ethiopia shall not be equal to [wisdom]"), he explains that Ethiopia signifies the present world whose blackness is the sign of a sinful people, although he does not exclude the narrower interpretation according to which Ethiopia is the symbol of "the Gentiles, black with the sins of infidelity." As such, Ethiopia will feel God's might: "I saw the tents of Ethiopia for their iniquity" (Hab. 3:7); but Ps. 67(68):32 intimates that the Ethiopians will accept the faith before the Jews do. The black world of the Gentiles presents itself to the Lord in order to be saved. The topaz *(topantium)* also expresses totality (τὸ πᾶν!), and the multiplicity of colors bestowed on the ex-Ethiopians by the practice of virtues. Yet they must not go too far: they must practice humility, which subordinates the brilliance of the gem coming from "the blackness of the world" to the radiance of Wisdom—that by way of response to the pride of the Nestorians! Conversely, the Lamentations of Jeremiah describes the metamorphosis of the Nazirites: "Her Nazirites were whiter than snow, purer than milk . . . [now] their face is made blacker than coals" (Lam. 4:7-8). Gregory comments: "They had been white and became black because having lost God's justice they trust in themselves and fall into sins that they do not even understand."[57]

In either case nigritude is identified with an inferior level of knowledge. This inferiority, consisting of a lack of knowledge from which sins proceed, has its origin in the relativity of everything in this world, including human righteousness.

ETHIOPIAN DEMONS

The literature of edification, such as the lives of the saints and the passions of the martyrs, often introduces the demons, who try to tempt saintly persons or appear to them in the dreams and visions visited upon them. These evil spirits, adjutants of the Prince of Darkness (called "the Black" from the beginning, according to the *Epistle of Barnabas*),[58] are soon likened to "Ethiopians." This comparison, however, does not seem to go beyond an indication of color, and no text refers explicitly to other racial characteristics, nor to any resemblance to real Ethiopians. The visible appearance of the devils who carry on in this wealth of tales is a mark of identity, an element of symmetry, in the diptychs of darkness and light. By way of exception we get a glimpse of an Ethiopian hermit who possesses all the virtues,[59] but the theme of the false hermit, which enjoyed such popularity throughout the Middle Ages, makes no use of the disguise of nigritude. It can be said that every black is the incarnation of evil and of danger to the soul.

A limited selection of examples will suffice to give an idea of the range of this colorful theme.[60] A monk is tempted by the sensuous vision of an Ethiopian girl gathering ears of corn.[61] Another sees two crows or a black dancer.[62] Antony sees himself being brought into a theater and forced to wrestle with a huge Ethiopian before an audience comprising whites and blacks.[63] Melania the Younger argues theology with the Devil disguised as a young black (he takes the side of the Nestorians): she routs him by calling upon Christ, and for six days suffers a pain that returns regularly at the hour of her encounter with the demon.[64] Liturgical offices are sometimes disrupted, although here we are not sure whether we are dealing with "facts" or visions. In a monastery, at the time when the brethren are about to receive the Eucharist, Ethiopians put burning coals into their hands, whereas they should have been holding palm branches.[65] Macarius is awakened by a demon and goes to the church, to find it filled with little black Ethiopians who run hither and thither and seem to flit through the air. Then a psalm is read, the assistants being seated as they listen or make the responses. The black imps make a game of putting the brothers to sleep by rubbing their eyelids, or making them yawn by sticking a finger into their mouths. They walk back and forth on the backs of those who lie prostrate in prayer, making them see tempting visions of women and journeys and houses.[66]

More grandiose are the scenes related to the Last Judgment. A giant Ethiopian does the winnowing of souls:[67] others load the scales of the Judgment with lists of accusations.[68] More immediate are the premonitions experienced in time of trial. Perpetua in a dream finds herself face-to-face with an Ethiopian.[69] Much later, but again in Africa, Victor of Vita reports that the Vandal persecution had been foreshadowed in this way: a brightly lighted church is suddenly plunged into darkness and filled with a foul stench, while Ethiopians drive out the crowd of the blessed.[70]

Antony encounters an ugly black youth who makes himself known as the spirit of fornication[71] and boasts about his conquests of young men. He has to admit his failure to break down the hermit's constancy. Modestly, Antony observes that his age and color are signs of weakness; then he bursts into a chant, and the specter vanishes. The aged abbot Apollo is worried about his tendency to take pride in his work, which threatens to undermine his last monastic foundation. A voice from on high orders him to reach back and to bury in the sand whatever he finds on his shoulders. He reaches back and seizes a tiny Ethiopian, the spirit of vanity, which he buries alive.[72] Still more involved is the story of a troubled monk who makes a retreat before abandoning the religious life. An ugly, evil-smelling Ethiopian woman appears to him and declares, "I am she who seems so sweet to the hearts of men; but because of your obedience and the trials you have borne, God would not allow me to lead you astray. All I can do is to let you smell my foul odor."[73]

These disdainful descriptions certainly denote the secondary importance of these poor, powerless beings, but a certain racism is also discernible, and this was to furnish themes—the ugliness or bad odor of the Negro, for instance—which were destined for a long life. At best the demons fail in their efforts, like the little black dancer who jumps through the window into the cell where a holy man is chanting the Psalms.[74] Having tried in vain to distract him by dancing around him, the demon denounces him for a fraud because he has made three mistakes in his psalmody. Having scored this cheap victory he can only take himself off, which he does. In all this picturesque gallimaufry the only anecdote with any real significance is that of a "black Ethiopian" who is cutting wood. Having cut an armful he tries to lift it, and finding that he cannot, goes on cutting more and more wood, thus sinking deeper into futility and failure, like the unrepentant sinner.[75]

We are further informed that the Thebaid, and more specifically the city of Hermopolis, was visited by the Christ Child on the flight into Egypt (cf. Matt. 2:13-20), this being a sign of the future evangelization of these distant lands. Thus we are not surprised to find there certain persons unnamed, who, three centuries later, give proof of the fulfillment of the sign. "We saw there a number of men of the Ethiopian race who lived with the monks and far outdid many of them in virtue and religious observance, so much so that in them the Scripture seemed fulfilled wherein it says that 'Ethiopia shall soon stretch out her hands to God' (Ps. 67[68]:32)."[76]

Should we take this for actual fact? The possibility is there, but it seems more likely that at the same time the narrator is expressing repentance for his antiracial feelings by a kind of rhetorical paradox. This is not uncommon in this type of literature: thus we find theatrical performers converted, persecutors touched by grace, etc. At any rate it is certain that while the Ethiopians were in no sense relegated to spiritual ostracism, they suffered nonetheless by their metaphorical relationship with the demons, and their small number in the midst of white society kept more favorable evidence from making itself felt. They were not excluded but remained on the outside: for instance we are told that the Ethiopians themselves knew Simeon Stylites, the renowned ascetic, but they are not mentioned among the pilgrims who swarmed at the foot of his pillar.[77] No less worthy of note is the tale handed on by Augustine in the *City of God*:[78] In Carthage a physician who suffers from gout has a dream in which he sees woolly-haired black children who try to keep him from being baptized, and who, to lend authenticity to the vision, stamp on his aching feet. He perseveres despite all this and is cured as he receives the Sacrament.

THE BAPTISM OF THE ETHIOPIAN EUNUCH, MINISTER OF QUEEN CANDACE (ACTS 8:26-40)

An angel orders the disciple Philip to take the road toward the south, and Philip meets the Ethiopian eunuch, who is reading Isaiah as he rides along in his chariot. Philip asks him, "Do you understand what you are reading?" The Ethiopian has him climb up and ride beside him and asks him to explain the meaning of the text, which refers to Christ. Philip thereupon announces the Good News to the eunuch, and at his request baptizes him as they come to a wayside pond.

This anecdote, which is richly illustrated in iconography from the third century on, attracted the attention of the early exegetes for a multitude of converging reasons. This is the first instance of the baptism of a non-Jew, and the only mention of an Ethiopian in the New Testament: the evangelization of the world at large has its beginning here. So we find the episode mentioned many times in the early doctrinal writings, notably those on Baptism, as well as in the speculations on the end of the world, which would take place, it was generally thought, when the spread of the Gospel message was completed (cf. Matt. 28:19-20).

The eunuch is a man of power, since he controls the treasures of the heiress of the Queen of Sheba. Yet he reads, and gives proof of his humility when he finds the text hard going. He is on his way home from Jerusalem, where he had gone to worship in the Temple. All these touches identify him with the attitude of the Gentiles, in contrast to the spiritual arrogance and poverty of Israel. The treasures are the mass of souls to be saved as well as the riches of human learning contained in the books of the profane world.[79] The call of the eunuch to Christianity lifts the curse that hung over the race of Chus and Nimrod, a stain washed away by baptism voluntarily received as a right due to faith alone. "See, here is water! What doth hinder me from being baptized?" Philip answers, "If thou believest with all thy heart, thou mayest," and baptized him forthwith (cf. Acts 8:36-37).[80] This faith therefore demonstrates the active presence of Christ the Light everywhere in the world—in Jerusalem, in Babylon, in Ethiopia[81]—enlightening by the gift of faith "every man that cometh into the world" and is willing to receive the gift, just as Christ is present everywhere in the continuous act of creation (cf. John 1:9-12).

Athanasius marvels at the posthumous power of Christ, who can send his messengers as far as Ethiopia.[82] They go north, south, east, and west: they penetrate regions where the primary qualities of the elements (dryness, humidity, cold, and heat) prevail, and the great masses of men live. "Let us imitate the Ethiopian eunuch, who, by receiving baptism on the road, himself became a road for the Ethiopians who believed."[83] In the eunuch the farthest outpost of the world is potentially attained.[84]

But the realists see things somewhat differently. Epiphanius may celebrate the unity of the Church beneath the diversity of tongues, including those of the peoples who dwell in the southern region of the world,[85] but the various commentators of Matthew hesitate to affirm the evangelization of the future kingdom of Prester John. Origen says forthrightly[86] that all the Ethiopians, "particularly those who are beyond the river," have not yet been touched by the Gospel. At the other end of our period Theodoret puts them in the second phase of the spread of the truth, along with Persians, Scythians, Massagetes, Sarmatians, and Indians.[87] This confirms the exegesis of Hab. 3:7, where "the iniquity of the tents of Ethiopia" signifies the defeat of the demons.[88]

SEXUALITY

In contrast to the "racial image," widespread in antiquity, which represented the black as possessed of a kind of hypersexuality, the Ethiopians of our texts present an image of continence and dignity that reminds us of the respect paid them in the Homeric poems. We might, however, record a few less edifying tidbits. Epiphanius asserts that Origen was said to have been forced to choose between an act signifying apostasy and an act of sodomy with an Ethiopian.[89] A hermit is tempted by a pretty, black, peasant woman.[90] Ennodius recommends virginity in the following terms:

> Sic tua non maculent nigrantis membra puellae,
> Nec jaceas propter Tartaream faciem.[91]
> (Don't let the body of a black girl soil yours, nor lie with her for her Hell-black face.)

Here, however, there can scarcely be an allusion to a real person. What we find in the main are the usual pious conventions such as the chaste visit of the Queen of Sheba to Solomon, her sole interest being the quest of wisdom,[92] and the *decor Aethiopicus*, the beauty of nigritude assumed by the Bride in the 'metanoia' of absolution.[93] The eunuch baptized by Philip exemplifies the defeat of libido. "The chaste take the kingdom of heaven by force,"[94] Arator, the last link in the chain of exegesis that began with Origen, exclaims at the end of a charming synopsis. The image of Ethiopia, the dark region, is rich in implications. It confirms the symbolic marriage of Moses (the man who met God face-to-face) representing the Law, with the eternal Bride, the Church, which, like the comely maiden of the Song of Songs, came out of the scorched land at the end of the road to the South, the road on which the studious eunuch met the disciple guided by the angel.[95]

TROPOLOGICAL SYNTHESIS: THE CONTINUED COMMENTARY ON THE BLACK

The extensive exegetical treatment of our topic certainly merits attention for its thematic detail, although this is on the whole fairly limited. Perhaps even more interesting is the way the authors, one after another, go back over the same material, thus adding link upon link to a long chain of exegetical development. Before examining a noteworthy specimen, it will be useful, with regard to the texts themselves, to make a few observations on scriptural commentaries as a literary genre.

This genre virtually reached its finished form in the writings of Origen, before being introduced to Western Europe by Rufinus, Jerome, and Augustine. The real intent of these profuse monuments of erudition and subtlety is anything but clear, and their preliminary statements and dedicatory formulas throw but little light on the authors' purpose in writing them. We need hardly say that no useful mention of a critical reading, aside from a few discussions of points of doctrine, has come down to us. We therefore do not know whether they were conceived, or received, as comprehensive and coherent wholes. Were they intended to be merely hermeneutical repertories following the order of the Bible, or the Book itself explicated and deciphered for a relatively intelligent and cultured readership?

Comparison with the exegetical homilies actually delivered to an audience makes possible an analytical approach, though rarely in connection with our present study. Such an approach, moreover, must be undertaken with due caution because sacred orators like Athanasius, Hilary of Poitiers, and Ambrose are also difficult writers, who, it would seem, were not afraid to leave the clarification of Scripture buried under layer upon layer of "explanations," however much these might agree or disagree. We follow their unpredictable lead down countless trails of exegesis, which successive authors either abandoned or returned to with the fundamental conviction that the full meaning of the sacred writings is beyond human ken. To delve into it was for these commentators an exercise of faith or the fulfillment of a pastoral obligation; they felt it a duty to comment the Scriptures, thus putting to use the charismatic insight bestowed on them. The interpreter said all he knew, all he had read, all the meanings and nonmeanings dug out by others before him. Of course he did not bother to give references: the "scholarship" of antiquity did not demand them, and the inadequate authority of mere men rendered them of little use when applied to the word of God. So when a theme is pursued or broken off, this may be due to the chance information available, but it may just as well be due to a deliberate choice or to a latent interest coming to light in this way.

Thus, when Cyprian tries to establish an irrefutable basis for his position on Baptism, he falls back on Philip's procedure in conferring the sacrament on the Ethiopian eunuch; but, using it for his particular purpose, he omits any allusion to its racial connotation, which elsewhere is determinative when the episode in the Acts of the Apostles is discussed.[96] Jerome uses the event in an entirely different way, in a highly complex sequence of his commentary on the prophet Zephaniah.[97] Zephaniah is the son of Chusi, and *Chusi* means either 'humility' or 'my Ethiopian'. Naturally no explanation of this baffling ambiguity is given. There is not even an attempt to furnish the semantic explanation which the context leads one to expect: "After such merits are enumerated, how could the name Ethiopian sound like praise?" In fact, Jerome suggests, this is a false problem, and he eliminates it with a morphological note to the effect that the text reads *Chusi*, not *Chus*. If it read *Chus* the difficulty would be insoluble, since Chus was born of Ham the accursed, and his name is equivalent to *Ethiopian*, which is equivalent to *sinner*. On the other hand *Chusi* means 'my Ethiopian', and this touches on a mystery—that of the Ethiopian restored to God's favor by penance. Besides the Psalmist's testimony,[98] the Bride of the Song of Songs and the Ethiopian eunuch Ebedmelech (mentioned in Jer. 39:15-18 as having pleased God) help to introduce the baptism of the eunuch by Philip, and this completes the *exempla* that prove the point. Scrutinizing the letter of the text (like the eunuch himself, whose attachment to Holy Scripture made him read the Book of Isaiah as he rode in his chariot though he could not understand it), Jerome points to the surprising formula *vir Aethiops eunuchus*—a man, a eunuch, and an Ethiopian to boot! He was, then, a eunuch of Christ, who had made himself a eunuch for the kingdom of heaven, and so could still be called a man. That is why Zephaniah, son of Chusi, had a right as the son of an Ethiopian to speak of the Ethiopians' penance—this being the natural explanation of Zeph. 3:10: "From beyond the rivers of Ethiopia, shall my suppliants the children of my dispersed people bring me an offering."

Needless to say, these unconvincing verbal acrobatics make sense only in the language of allegory: it would be futile to destroy the eunuch's virility, even if it were spiritual like his mutilation, by a stylistic observation. It would be equally fruitless to ask why all the particular Ethiopians met in connection with our topic lack the aggressive sexuality generally attributed to the black: they are so few that no plausible conclusion can be drawn. It is possible, however, to suggest Jerome's implicit reasoning. Zephaniah is one of the redeemed Ethiopians—allegorically at least, for he certainly is not black. His penance has left him a whole man, a man who has subjugated his sexual nature, like the eunuch of Queen Candace—a disciple of Paul without knowing it. He belongs to the glorious lineage of his fathers, in accordance with a pattern as dear to Jewish tradition as to Hellenistic and Roman sensitivity. One might almost say that by penance he loses his distinctive color, the anthropological reality of which becomes merely a symbolic coloration, a metaphor. The Scriptures use the name *Ethiopian* for those who are deeply sunken in vice, as we read in Jer. 13:23: "If the Ethiopian can change his skin ...." If what is impossible can nevertheless be brought about by conversion, then there is hope that no man who does penance will be denied salvation.

This optimistic view, which seems tinged with a certain Pelagianism,[99] is based on the personage of the Bride of the Song of Songs, who is black but beautiful, as well as on another figure, the Ethiopian wife of Moses. Maintaining their own characteristics as they confront the daughters of Jerusalem and the jealous personification of the Synagogue, they show that the "washing away of the color of darkness" is possible.

Some pages further on, Jerome talks about the time when all peoples will call upon the name of the Lord and will bring offerings from beyond the rivers of Ethiopia, whence came the Queen of Sheba to listen to

Solomon's wisdom. That is when the Ethiopian woman marries the truth-speaking Lawgiver who inflicted the ten plagues upon Egypt. The Synagogue, of yore the beloved daughter but now tormented by jealousy, will have to resign herself to seeing the sacrificial victims sent by Ethiopia, in other words by the Gentiles. The blackness of the soul, the dragon's poison and his dark color—the color of sin and vice—can disappear as soon as the teachers of false doctrines are left in the rivers of Ethiopia.[100] The mystical frontier of these rivers—they were crossed in many ways in the historical events of the economy of salvation—must therefore be understood as an exemplary and, in a way, necessary passage. The journey of the soul coordinates and completes these narratives. The Queen of Sheba was satisfied by the teaching of her host, but the eunuch, servant of her distant successor, started back from Jerusalem still beset by uncertainty. His meeting with Philip on the road toward the south was of more benefit to him than his pilgrimage, which could no longer serve its purpose. The significance of the wife of Moses is explained by the scandal of the evangelization of the Gentiles more clearly than by a comparison with the black but beautiful Bride.

Inevitably there are still questions which we shall mention without attempting to answer them. What part does the concrete image of the black play in the setting of the theme, and more especially in conveying the author's meaning? In other words, is the strangeness of the Ethiopian so strongly felt that he will be understood as the equivalent of the "old man" which is the body of sin (cf. Rom. 6:6)? On the other hand, how should we interpret the unfavorable judgment contained in the analysis which questions it even while making it the basis of the argument? The prophet admits being the son of an Ethiopian only after revision and appropriation of the relationship. The eunuch is not what he appears to be. And the salvation of the black people, real or symbolic, supposes a mutation, a return to whiteness.

NIGRITUDE: REFUSAL AND ACCEPTANCE

The adventures of one Ethiopian, explicitly described as black, are significant. This is a certain Moses.[101] He begins as a brigand who is able to perform astonishing feats of strength. We see him swimming the Nile at night to steal four rams, which he kills and carries back across the river. He eats some of the meat, trades the rest for wine, then walks fifty miles to rejoin his comrades. Later he does penance and becomes a monk. We shall hold on to this truculent character as a possible document—no more than a possible one, since his saintly actions are a little too close a counterpoint to his misdeeds which, after all, were not so heinous. At any rate he stands guarantee for the universality of monasticism, and especially for the fact of 'metanoia', the change of heart, illustrated by his race.

Some pointers will help to understand the complexity, and even the contradictions, of the theme. In his treatise on the theater[102] Tertullian writes: "When God threatens Egypt and Ethiopia with extinction, he pronounces sentence on every sinful nation. Thus every sinful nation is called Egypt or Ethiopia (Isa. 11:11, 14:24-27) *a specie ad genus.*" In the context this is given as an example of rhetorical style, the rhetorical figure here being the reverse of the one that includes every theatrical spectacle in the expression "council of the wicked"—*a genere ad speciem.* But the introduction of this example is not purely accidental. The typology of the fundamental fault turns up again in connection with the interpretation of a verse of Jeremiah (13:23): "If the Ethiopian can change his skin, or the leopard his spots: . . . ." Peter, bishop of Alexandria, who had reason to know what he was talking about,[103] teaches that Ethiopians are the men who have reached the limit of despair. The blackness caused by sin is identical with the black pigment of the skin, as indelible as the fig tree cursed by Christ is sterile. Naturally the leopard's spots are cited not only as a physiological feature but as an image of the stains borne by the guilty soul. But here again the proliferation and contamination of the directive images make it impossible to extract a relatively simple syntax of the theme.

Theodoret starts from the note in the Song of Songs "I am black . . ." but emphasizes the symbolic connotations. The Bride is black, like Moses' Ethiopian wife: she herself is Ethiopian, and is also the spouse of the great Lawgiver in the marriage of the Church and the New Law. Where does her color come from? From looking too fixedly at the things of earth, at the sun here below, neglecting the Sun of Justice.[104] Justus of Urgel echoes this, but with a nuance that deserves our attention as bearing on the sixth-century Spanish context. The Bride represents in particular the first Church, that of Jerusalem, made up of converted Jews, which was black by the confession of its sins, beautiful by the grace of the sacrament.[105] This interpretation runs counter to the tradition which sees in the wife of Moses the image of the Church of the Gentiles. This tradition was firmly established by Isidore of Seville in his *Allegories of Holy Scripture*, a work that served for centuries as a compendium of exegesis.[106]

Might we mention the romantic little story drawn from Josephus, about the military campaign conducted by Moses in Ethiopia? His troops were besieging the enemy city. A princess saw him from the towers of the beleaguered town and fell in love with him. Moses made her his wife in exchange for the surrender of the place. An embellishment of the tale added that he got out of this union by a stratagem as ambiguous as it is worthy of courtly literature: he fashioned two gems, identical in appearance, of which one caused forgetfulness and the other memory. He kept the second and left the first to the princess, and when she forgot all about him he made his way back to Egypt.[107]

The Cappadocian Fathers left an immense store of writings, but the black is rarely mentioned in them. It is certainly possible to hold that this relative silence can be explained by the fact that despite the picturesque motley of their mixed populations, the great metropolises of the Eastern Empire—Constantinople, Antioch, and the rest—"ignored" the Negro as such, just as the cities of the West did. John Chrysostom works him into vast historical intuitions. In a homily on St. John's Gospel[108] he says that Pythagoras and Plato had deceived mankind with a false philosophy that time had exposed for what it was. On the other hand, the apostle's message (the exegetes of the New Testament generally considered John as the evangelist who flew high and far)[109] went beyond the geographical boundaries of the Greek world and the temporal boundaries of human thought and taught the Ethiopians, among other exotic peoples, to philosophize in their own language. In short, this was a second Pentecost with long-lasting perspectives: it was foreshadowed in an inverted figure by the eunuch, a privileged personage among "those who came from East and West to be crowned with Abraham, Isaac, and Jacob."[110] The narrative in the Acts of the Apostles is explained along the same lines.[111] If Philip did not stay with the eunuch in his chariot to give him a long and leisurely lesson as they rode through the desert, it was because he was not on an apostolic mission, but was there to do a one-time demonstration. The eunuch, for his part, neither asked for nor received such instruction as a catechumen would require. He only asks a negative question: "What doth hinder me from being baptized?" Once the ceremony is over, Philip is snatched away by the Spirit, who does not show himself to the new Christian. What had taken place, then, was a spiritual demonstration which any supernatural occurrence would have made more disturbing than convincing to the eunuch, who, suddenly finding himself alone, went his way rejoicing.

Gregory of Nazianzus may have been thinking of the eunuch when he wrote, in a moral poem, that it is sweet to see a white form among the Ethiopians.[112] He certainly had him in mind when he exhorts the hesitant to ask for baptism: "I am Philip, be thou Candace"[113]—a hardy, inexact formula that probably evoked a familiar image implying no assimilation.

WE ARE ALL ETHIOPIANS

In a treatise on Psalm 67(68) intended for direct pastoral use—a fairly rare thing in his work—Jerome gives a kind of personalized aspect to the equation color = sin. His exegesis is an original one. "*Ambassadors shall come out of Egypt: Egypt* is interpreted as meaning 'darkness', so the ambassadors come out of the darkness of this world. *Ethiopia shall take the lead, with her hands, before God:* since we were black because of our sins and passions, we have taken the lead over the people of Israel and we believe in the Savior, as the woman with the issue of blood came ahead of the daughter of the ruler of the synagogue and recovered her health (Matt. 9:20-22)."[114] In another treatise in the same series[115] Jerome goes still further: "*People of the Ethiopians* means those who are black, being covered with the stain of sin. In the past we were Ethiopians, being made so by our sins and vices. How? Because sin had made us black. But then we heeded Isaiah (Isa. 1:16)—'Wash yourselves, be clean'—and we said, 'Thou shalt wash me, and I shall be made whiter than snow' (Ps. 50[51]:9). Thus we, Ethiopians that we were, transformed ourselves and became white."

In contrast to these professions of optimistic humility, probably called for because the treatise was intended for a "popular" audience, Paulinus of Nola furnishes a remarkable restatement of the question. In one of his long, meditative poems the soul, though enlightened by grace, is still conscious of spiritual danger and on guard against it: "The dragon devours the peoples of Ethiopia, *who are not burnt by the sun* but are black with vice, sin giving them the color of night. These are the Ethiopians the serpent devours, being condemned to make them his food, for God used the single word *earth* to designate both the sinner and the food of the serpent."[116]

In the passages just referred to we find two rather infrequent connotations of our theme, both with a feminine allusion—the woman suffering from hemorrhage, and the Marian image of the serpent crushed to the earth. Also worth noting is the departure from the traditional explanation of blackness. In the same spirit, Augustine declares that Moses' Ethiopian wife was a Midianite, "a people almost no one now calls Ethiopians"; he regards this as a common enough example of onomastic development, which has no effect on the symbolic value of the names.[117]

A timid rehabilitation of blackness appears even in certain tropological contexts. Commenting on 1 Kings 5:8, Paulinus of Nola speaks of "good, black, fir trees" needed for the building of the Temple, and refers to the Bride of the Song of Songs, black and beautiful, as well as to palm trees and cedars, which are just as dark and yet can have a place in the hull of the ship of the Church. "Even now souls instructed in the faith of the apostles are fir trees black and good: no longer, in my opinion, black because of sin, but by reason of their bodily dwelling-place, or else blackened by the dust of battle and the sweat mixed with sand of spiritual discipline."[118]

About six centuries later, Simeon the New Theologian, in a very beautiful hymn, went so far as to allow that blackness could persist after the Resurrection: "The bodies of sinners will rise ... as black as they can be, for having done the works of darkness. . . . They too, however, will arise immortal and spiritual, but like to darkness; and the unhappy souls united to them, dark and impure also, will become like to the devil because they imitated his works."[119] This is not much of a rehabilitation, but it makes room for a distinctive character which most of the testimonies refer to only to abolish it. May we see here a hesitant advance toward a human type hitherto rejected?

DARKNESS AND GRACE

The theme of *obscuratio*, the darkening of the heart by sin (cf. Rom. 1:21), bears a close relationship to the allegorical interpretations of blackness, especially in the Pelagian controversy. According to Pelagius's optimistic view, it simply would not do to admit that such a punishment could be meted out by God as would inevitably beget other sins and thus close off any possibility of salvation. Are the *contenebrati* inexorably doomed to *opera tenebrarum*? The strictly orthodox answer[120] was that sin is a deliberate choice of that will which Pelagius was so anxious to exalt, and not something imposed by God. Prosper of Aquitaine, in his *Carmen de ingratis*, put this thesis very well: "Thus, the soul which possessed light of the greatest brilliance enveloped the will in darkness, and, when the light had been abandoned, the will chose to be darkened by the counsel of the foul night."[121] It is no longer a matter of the hard night preceding the preaching of the Gospel, which the dawn of truth could brighten, but of a process *(nigrescere)* and of envelopment in a dark mantle *(caligine tetra induitur)*. This picturesque connotation may imply a reference to circus games and their exotic personnel; the pitiable darkness of the soul appears in the paradox of the man able to tame lions but unable to govern his own conduct.[122]

A later illustration of similar ideas is found in Cassiodorus's explication of Ps. 73(74):14: "Thou hast given him [the dragon] to be meat for the people of the Ethiopians." Satan (i.e., the dragon) darkened himself by a perverse act of the will. That God gives him as food to repentant sinners (i.e., the Ethiopians, now enlightened and converted) shows that the Devil's machinations contribute, in fact, to the progress of the saints.[123]

We cannot resist quoting a lovely text (little known, probably because written in Syriac), Ephraem Syrus's *The Pearl, or Seven Rhythms on the Faith*:

> Very glistening are the pearls of Ethiopia, as it is written, Who gave thee to Ethiopia [the land] of black men. He that gave light to the Gentiles, both to the Ethiopians and unto the Indians did His bright beams reach. The eunuch of Ethiopia upon his chariot saw Philip: the Lamb of Light met the dark man from out of the bath. While he was reading, the Ethiopian was baptized and glistened with joy, and journeyed on! He made disciples and taught, and out of black men he made men white [as snow]. And the dark Ethiopic women became pearls for the Son; He offered them up to the Father, as a glistening crown from the Ethiopians.
>
> The Queen of Sheba was a sheep that had come into the place of wolves; the lamp of truth did Solomon give her, who also married her when he fell away. She was enlightened and went away, but they were dark as their manner was. The bright spark which went down home with that blessed [Queen], held on its shining amid the darkness, till the new Day-spring came. The bright spark met with this shining, and illumined the place.[124]

The virtuosity of the changes rung on the theme of light savors of a preciosity attributable, no doubt, to the poetic style of Eastern hymnody. But the Occident did not lag behind, even if it preferred the nacreous iridescence of words and formulas. Thus Peter Chrysologus: "Nec minus animat me illius spadonis exemplum quem fides ante rapuit ad gratiam quam currus ad Indiam domumque revocaret" ("Nor am I less heartened by the example of that eunuch, whom faith snatched up unto grace before his chariot bore him away to India and home")[125]—an image of sovereign speed, or even of a spiritual leap and return, as in this from the same author: "Aethiops spado arcanum vitalis lavacari praeteriens invenit in via, rapuit in transitu" ("As he passed by on the road, the Ethiopian eunuch found the secret of the life-giving bath, and snatched it up on the run").[126]

RIDDLES VS. CLEAR SPEECH

Origen gives the Ethiopian marriage of Moses a double prophetic dimension: it is prophetic both in the general economy of Redemption, which it prefigures, and by the definition of a new mode of transmission of the Word, which it inaugurates. Moses is the Law of the Lord. He allies himself by marriage to Ethiopia, the "assemblage drawn from the Nations." The marriage is confirmed by God, who generously allows his people's guide to live in peace with the foreign woman, in order to leave time for the Synagogue, personified by Miriam the leper, to purify itself and join the one flock of reconciled mankind.[127] This interpretation not only means that the historic condemnation of the Gentiles is lifted by their receiving the Gospel; it also is based on a subtle analysis of the text of Numbers, in which Origen notes that it is only after Moses had taken the black woman to wife that God declared: "For I speak to him mouth to mouth: and plainly, and not by riddles . . ." (Num. 12:8). It is therefore "when Moses came to us, was united with our Ethiopian, that the Law of God is henceforth made manifest no longer in figures and images but in its true and open form."[128] Thus the baptism of regeneration "in water and the Holy Spirit" replaces the ambiguities of the cloud and the passage through the Red Sea, as the Eucharist replaces the manna, and the clear language of the New Testament the riddles of the Old. The reconciliation resolves what was only an apparent historical conflict, an interval of adaptation to an immediate understanding that frightened and scandalized Israel, temporarily unable to accept the simplicity of the offer proposed through the Ethiopian woman.

This definitely does not mean that the spiritual Ethiopia received special treatment. On the contrary, Ethiopia's character as exceptionally "other" is precisely what reveals God's infinite solicitude for mankind. For instance, when Ezekiel foretells the devastation of Egypt by Nebuchadnezzar, he makes it clear that the terror over the event will spread to Ethiopia; and Origen explains[129] that this means to those beyond Egypt who live in the night of error and in the dark, and whose blackness does not become white, or does so only with difficulty. The prophet even adds that the Ethiopians living in Egypt will also be struck down, but the invader will halt at Syene, at the utmost limits of Egypt. He will not go to the land of the black men, the Blemmyes, where the Nile is no longer navigable and the roar of the cataracts resounds, where no road is carved out and snakes and poisonous beasts are everywhere. In this hostile world, beneath the overpowering sun that blackens the laborers who work all day long and at day's end receive no more than the promised wage,[130] it is the stricken conscience of the sinner that makes him fear God's punishment.

Here the hermeneutical bond is assured by Augustine in a sermon on Psalm 67(68), in which he marshals Ethiopia to the defense of his thesis on the necessity of faith for salvation. The problem is to explain the difficult expression in verse 32, which, depending on the Latin translation, can mean either "Ethiopia will forestall the vengeance of God" or "Ethiopia will precede her own works before God." The two interpretations, needless to say, complete without excluding each other, even if it takes some philological sleight of hand to make them do it.[131] For Augustine the question raised by the verse concerns justification by faith, and the text, in its ambivalent obscurity, answers the question: "Behold Ethiopia, which appears to be the farthest of the nations, justified by faith without the works of the law. . . . She does not put her merits before her faith, but by faith precedes her own works." The bishop-theologian may get a little ahead of the exegete here, but in his view the *doctrina christiana* needed every possible support. Augustine's rival Jerome, faced with a similar obscure passage in Isaiah,[132] also gives two versions of his text. One of them throws the Marcionites back "beyond the rivers of Ethiopia." The heretics, he says, are busy launching fragile papyrus boats, bearing their erroneous doctrine, upon the sea of this world, but they are doomed to founder.

If we try to grasp the general idea behind these contrived and unavoidably heterogeneous elaborations, a strong bond can be seen between the explication of the faith and the Ethiopian theme, the equivocal nature of which lends itself to paradoxical word games; but these are intended to extend the promise and possibility of salvation to all mankind.

Here and there we find insistence on the scandal provoked by some Old Testament figures. Moses' Ethiopian is the paradoxical vehicle of salvation, and she arouses the hostility of Miriam, in whom we must see prophecy enslaved to the letter. Here again the fundamental question of understanding arises. The scandalous wife is black and beautiful; her opponent turns white with leprosy and then is restored to her original color; but when the black woman is baptized, she changes color and goes from black to white. Her blackness therefore is strictly paradigmatic and vanishes in the flood of light imparted by the truth.[133] More bluntly, Gregory of Elvira declares: "I admit to being confused. How can the Church say she is black and beautiful, whereas she who is black cannot be beautiful? How can she be black if she is beautiful, or beautiful if she is black? But ponder the mystery of the word, and see with what depth of meaning the Holy Spirit speaks."[134] Not until the acceptance of the faith is imminent is the trait of blackness brought in, like a shadow to throw the event into high relief. Moreover, blackness undergoes some strange metaphorical transformations. It can result from the smoke of idolatry and the fires of sacrifices; the sun, contrary to the traditional cliché, can make it disappear, either by illuminating what is only a lack of light or by taking away the color altogether. In these circumstances the process is reversible. Israel, having escaped from Egypt, risks being brought back there by its love of pleasure and can find itself in Ethiopia, beyond the land of captivity, the captive of a color of skin that cannot again be changed until Christ grants the change. To state the case more generally, the Ethiopians put on the raiment of the children of God if they have done penance, and the children of God become Ethiopians if they plunge into the abyss of sin.[135] Throughout the entire history of the city of God, morality and sin re-create the alternation of white and black, a fitting metaphor for the vicissitudes of the faith.

ETHIOPIA AND GOD'S PROMISES

The *Book of God's Promises and Predictions*, written by the African bishop Quodvultdeus in the middle of the fifth century, brings together the historical facts that demonstrate the truth of the prophecies and prophetic events of the Old Testament. Moses' marriage and the harsh criticisms it drew find their counterpart in the reproaches aimed at Jesus for consorting with publicans and sinners.[136] Christ "took as his bride an Ethiopian, the Church of the Nations, which exclaims: 'I am black but beautiful, daughters of Jerusalem'." Another promise "believed and seen" was contained in the visit of the Queen of Sheba to Solomon. The queen of the South is the antitype of the Jews who scorned wisdom when it came to them and the type of the Church, which from the East to the West runs to listen to the Lord, as she will do at the Last Judgment.[137] The type, however, is only partially representative, since not just one queen but the whole company of kings of the earth will crowd around the One who is greater than Solomon.[138] The Old Testament, the Gospels, and the Sibylline Oracles foretell the progress of the spread of the Gospel, an observable fact when Quodvultdeus wrote.[139] On the other hand, an event foretold and believed in, but awaiting its accomplishment in the future, is the final defeat of the dragon—the Devil or the pharaoh—which is given as fodder to the Ethiopians (Ps. 73 [74]: 13-14).[140]

The diversity of the sources labeled "patristic" dictates a large measure of caution when we come to draw conclusions, partial though these may be. Different milieus, literary genres, and doctrinal currents are less clearly distinguishable in secondary or exotic themes—a common phenomenon closely connected with the methods of ancient scholarship. From the point of view of Christian literature as from that of profane science, the black was essentially "other"—the borderline case, situated in every sense at the outside limit of humanity. It must be said that there is no question here of a hierarchical classification of the races, nor of the superiority of one to the other, but we should also note that their equality was only theoretical, metaphysical, notional. The tenet that all peoples are equally called to eternal salvation led to no corollary such as the equality or inequality of their earthly cultures.

That may well be due to the fact that there was so little contact between the white world and black Africa, but the further and perhaps more important fact is that to the white world "black" stood for "Ethiopian," meaning "inhabitant of Ethiopia," not simply "burnt face."[141] Now Ethiopia, as we have stated before in these pages, is a land bathed by a river (the Nile), the source of which is unknown and, like the land itself, cannot be reached or investigated.[142] Is this to be taken as a convenient cloak for ignorance or lack of interest, or was it simply the usual substitution of fable for knowledge about the frontiers of the known world?

To that question we have no final answer, but one thing is certain: when the Church Fathers came across the few scriptural allusions that forced them to recognize the existence of their colored fellowmen, they read the texts as white men. The symbolism of the color black, of light and darkness, was so strong an influence that the theology of the divine image and likeness in man could do no better, all things considered, than to try to play down nigritude—to pretend it did not exist. The opening of the Gospel of salvation to the world, illustrated by Moses' Ethiopian wife, by the flight into Egypt, or by the conversion of the eunuch, was primarily an argument against the closed Jewish mentality, limited as this was by inbreeding and spiritual exclusivism.[143] The Gospel therefore was to reach the most unusual kinds of people, and this signifies the unity of mankind in the new Adam and in the totality of the Church.

Once given that principle, which restores all races to their original status as sons of light made in the likeness of a Creator who has no color of his own, but also in the likeness of Christ who took a white body, the triumphant post-Constantinian Church and her historians showed no interest in the progress of the faith *trans flumina Aethiopiae*, and still less in its advance among other black peoples.[144] We shall not propose the unkind surmise that behind this lack of interest was the thought of delaying the end of the world, which, as Jesus had foretold, would come when all men had been evangelized. Yet it does seem clear that the Establishment mentality and the pomp and circumstance of the Christian empire shrouded the final catastrophe in the vagueness of signs and figures, and that this vagueness affected realities which also served as symbols, among them Ethiopia and its dark inhabitants.

Jean Marie Courtès

FROM THE DEMONIC THREAT TO THE INCARNATION OF SAINTHOOD

INTRODUCTION

The place occupied by the black man and the color black in the imagination and imagery of the Western world between the fourth and the fourteenth century gives us much essential information about the Christian mentality with its contradictions, its dreads and fears, its enthusiams and uncertainties. To judge from the comparisons brought out in preparatory conferences held by the authors contributing to this series of volumes, there was probably no time when the image of the black and of his color was so insistently, intimately, and essentially present to the Christians of the Occident as it was in the centuries during which they were cut off from Africa.

Until the first European expansion, which we still too restrictively call "the Crusades," imagination superseded contact with reality to an ever increasing degree. Isolated from Africa, then from the Orient, even prevented for a short time from sailing the Mediterranean, Western Europe distorted the image of the black to fit its own ideas. Beginning in the eleventh century, however, Italian expansion and new contacts in the Iberian Peninsula brought insights quite different from those the West had been living on two centuries earlier. Western thought patterns in every domain were profoundly shaken by renewal of contact with the Byzantine and Muslim East, and there is no doubt that this led to heightened interest in the exotic and the marvelous. Europeans, now realizing that the world was a lot wider than they had envisioned it, also saw the black's place in it differently. The new vision was not only more contradictory, it was also a great deal richer, and as early as the twelfth century it prepared the burgeoning of themes that came to full bloom later on, such as Prester John and his kingdom, the black Wise Man, and many others less important in appearance at least. A general change in tone took place, and the black was no longer merely a synonym and symbol of sin and ill omen. For those given to thought and reflection, the optimism of the universal call to salvation overcame the habit of identifying "Christian" and "Occidental."

At the same time one personage was given a truly exceptional prominence, at least by the iconography of which he was the subject. This was Maurice, a more or less legendary saint, who in the thirteenth century became, in the West, the first incarnation of the sanctity of a black man.

I

CHRISTIANS AND BLACK

The civilization of Western Europe, like that of Byzantium and Islam, is at least in part a heritage from antiquity, but between the fifth and the ninth century Europe did not put this inheritance to use in the same way its neighbors did. As we shall see, differences in the total historical situation explain in large measure the wide range of attitudes with regard to the problems we are about to take up.

Our first endeavor will be to see clearly how Western European man thought about and pictured Africa and Africans, extricating these representations from the intermixtures that make them difficult to distinguish. This effort is necessary if we are to understand the iconography that has come down to us from these centuries. It will also help us to understand and root out prejudices handed down to us from that distant time.

Christian Africa, and Egypt especially, far from ignoring the black, spontaneously granted him a place in the Christian fold. But the direct effect of this in later times was very limited in the rest of the Mediterranean world, and almost nonexistent in Western Europe.

Separated as they were from the land of Africa, and being part of a world whose norms were the Mediterranean climate, the values of the white man, and the intellectual thought patterns of the Greeks, Christians had to face up to the heritage of ancient knowledge and reconcile it with the demands of their faith. Their choices were, to say the least, little short of disastrous for Africa and its peoples. The idea that sin is black leads implicitly to the notion that "God is white," and it has taken twenty centuries for Christianity to put this dangerously anthropocentric point of view behind it. For a long, long time the Occident was satisfied with the very abstract, rudimentary principle of the equality of all men as regards salvation. For five or six centuries Western man had no direct contact with men of other colors to force him to consider the concrete question of their humanity and their spiritual vocation. The result was that writers at every level bogged down in a morass of clichés and prejudices—and more so in the West than elsewhere. From the simplistic but readily accepted idea that black is the sign of death and therefore of sin, it was easy to go on to the more dangerous idea that the man whose color was black was a menace, a temptation, a creature of the Devil. A whole imagery, conscious or unconscious, grew up in the minds of Western Europeans during the centuries of their physical and cultural isolation from the African world. What is needed now is an intense and continuous critical effort to modify this imagery, which had become consubstantial with the cultural life of the Christian West.

AN AMBIGUOUS ICONOGRAPHY: THE PLACE OF THE BLACK IN THE CHRISTIAN COMMUNITIES OF AFRICA IN THE EARLY CENTURIES OF THE MIDDLE AGES

In Egypt, prior to the seventh century, a large number of black people lived side by side with the "white" population. This is a fact for which there is substantial evidence, although it has not yet been thoroughly studied.[1] Now Egypt, or more broadly the Nile Valley, was at the center of international traffic, particularly after the Sassanid barrier rose to the east of the Roman world, blocking the access routes to Asia.

Byzantine international policy, aimed at maintaining the relations with the Far East and India that were so vital throughout the Middle Ages,[2] required a tight control of the Nile Valley and the Red Sea.[3] The evangelization of the Nubians[4] and the entente with the Ethiopians, who were officially Christian from the fourth century on, formed a logical part of general Byzantine policy, as did the effort to Christianize the Ghassanid Arabs of Petra.

Another factor increased the geographical importance of the Nile Delta during the early Christian centuries. From the fourth to the sixth century at least, the pilgrimage to the Holy Places where Christ lived and died[5] became traditional for Western and Eastern Christians alike: indeed, this pilgrimage was gradually integrated into a journey of expiation imposed on Western Christians for sins judged to be the most serious. On the overland pilgrimage maps Edessa was one of the stops, and we shall treat of that later on. On the sea journey to the East the Nile Delta was a much frequented passage point for part of the trip.

Everything in Egyptian life was conducive to a mixing of the races and to a very open-minded concept of Christianity in the matter of interracial relations. But colonial pressure from the Byzantine authorities, which took both religious and economic forms, caused the secession of Egypt. Falling back first on a "national" and anti-Byzantine Monophysitism, that country offered no resistance to conquest by Persia in the sixth century and by the Muslims in the seventh, and thus got free of Byzantium. From the seventh century onward the relations between Egypt—first Coptic but under Muslim domination, then gradually converted to Islam, and finally conquered by the Fatimids—and the Nubian countries changed both in content and in significance.[6] We must not forget these basic facts if we are to try to estimate the importance of the iconographic remains that will be discussed in this essay.

The Monastery of St. Menas,[7] not far from Alexandria, became an important passage point for travelers and pilgrims coming from overseas, from the Libyan Desert, or from the southern Nile area. Situated on the shore of Lake Mareotis at the place where the route to the western desert opened, and built over the tomb of St. Menas,[8] which was venerated from the fourth century on, the monastery began to attract pilgrims in the fifth century. A whole town sprang up in response to this movement of pilgrims and caravans. In the eighth century and thereafter the pilgrimage lost much of its importance and was on its way to extinction in the ninth. Here we see the effect of the Muslim conquest, but also, more broadly, that of the dwindling traffic on the western route, noted by Ibn Ḥawqal in the tenth century.[9] A voluminous sea traffic from the Ifrikiyan coast to Alexandria replaced the old itinerary.

St. Menas—Mina in Coptic—is the patron saint of Alexandria.[10] For centuries he played a prime role in the Christian community there: the patronymic "Mina" has been favored by the Copts throughout the centuries.[11] Research bearing on St. Menas leads to the impression that the monks were shrewd enough to take advantage of circumstances in order to "meet the demand" of the different types of Christian believers who frequented the saint's tomb or who lived in the vicinity.[12] What is needed is a comprehensive study of the saint's miracles, attributes of clothing, and functions. Particular attention should be given to comparing the corpus of materials attached to St. Menas's name with those concerning all the more or less military saints, all legendary, whom the East honored.[13] In this general and inadequately known context the representations of St. Menas in our possession stand out as particularly interesting and raise questions to which only long future studies, based on sound statistics and exact geography, will give answers.

C.M. Kaufmann's excavations revealed[14]—and later discoveries confirmed the fact—that when the pilgrims set out again from the Monastery of St. Menas they sometimes took with them ampullae of various sizes containing water or oil reputed to have miraculous powers.[15] This was nothing new. In the fifth century Theodoret was already emphasizing the help that possession of an "ampulla containing the oil of the martyrs" afforded in battle.[16] Earlier, in the Saïtic period, ampullae of this kind bearing New Year's wishes were exchanged among close friends.[17] The Attic, white-ground alabastra dating from the fifth century B.C., decorated with drawings of an "Ethiopian" warrior,[18] may be the remote ancestors of the Saïtic flasks, the Christian ampullae, and the Muslim *kulla*.[19]

It is possible, therefore, that the St. Menas ampullae fit into an uninterrupted Egyptian tradition. The devotion in which St. Menas was held might likewise be connected with ancient Nilotic modes of veneration. As early as 1910[20] Kaufmann called attention to the fact that Menas had succeeded Osiris as a healer, and noted also the saint's role as protector against crocodiles, in which role he is the descendant of Horus.[21] It is true that J. Doresse[22] rejects all such comparisons out of hand. Unfortunately he does not base his stand on convincing evidence, and it remains simply the hypothetical negation of earlier hypotheses. The matter therefore calls for a thorough reexamination.

The iconography of this "saint of all work" may well contain some interesting surprises. Obviously it must be compared with the iconography

2 3

1

1. Eulogia ampulla: St. Menas between two camels. From Egypt. V-VII century. Marseilles, Musée Borély.

2, 3. Eulogia ampulla. Side A: profile of St. Menas; side B: invocation formula. From Alexandria. V-VI century. Paris, Musée du Louvre.

of St. George the dragon killer.[23] The St. George legend was repudiated as apocryphal by a council in the fifth century, but the condemnation did not materially affect the cult of this "pseudo-saint."[24] We may note immediately that an image of Menas, to which we shall return further on, bears a singular resemblance to that of St. George.[25]

The devotion to St. Menas spread widely, at least from the fifth to the ninth century. Kaufmann fixes numerous centers of the cult in the Nile Valley,[26] several of them south of Luxor; but others were in Cyprus, Constantinople, Mauretania, Rome, Solin, Arles, Trier, and finally at Dongola in the heart of Nubia.[27] He refers to the visits of numbers of foreigners, identifiable by the graffiti they sometimes left in the monastery: there were Greeks, Cypriots, and people from Smyrna.[28] Extremely interesting Nubian texts and others, more recent, from Ethiopia,[29] speak of Menas. Given the character of the patron saint of Alexandria and his popularity outside of Egypt, his iconography promises to be of great interest.

Long ago E. Quatremère furnished the translation of a Coptic text which in our view is of considerable importance:

> From there one proceeds to the church of St. Mina, a huge building decorated with statues and paintings of the greatest beauty. Candles burn there day and night without interruption. At the end of this edifice is a large tomb and *two marble camels on which a man is standing* [italics ours], with one foot resting on either animal. He has one hand open and the other closed.[30] It is said that this figure, which is also of marble, represents St. Mina.[31]

This theme also appears on reliefs,[32] frescoes,[33] and many ampullae.[34] fig. 1

What we have here, therefore, is an official representation of the saint. It is sometimes regarded as being connected with his role as protector of caravans,[35] but other explanations are possible. Kaufmann himself, moreover, suggests comparisons with Asian themes.[36] In any event the figuration of Menas described above was the one most widely accepted for a long time and over wide areas.[37] But in it there is never any indication that the saint belonged to the world of the blacks. Our visit to the Greco-Roman Museum in Alexandria convinced us that while the image on certain ampullae (we shall see more about them) looks somewhat like a black, the great majority, and especially those that seem to correspond to the "official portrait," represent Menas as white except when they have no decoration at all.[38]

On the ampullae that show a "Negroid" type[39] the style is conventional: the thick-lipped profile and the hair done in tight curls to indicate the kinky hair of the black came from the Hellenistic world. The small number of such ampullae made us doubt, early in our investigation, that Menas was the personage represented, but a series of ampullae in the Louvre[40] figs. 2, 3 compelled us to abandon this first hypothesis. One side has an epigraph and refers explicitly to the saint, while the other side has the profile of a black as just described. Hence it must be admitted that in a certain number of cases Menas is represented with "Negroid" features, although *nothing* in the

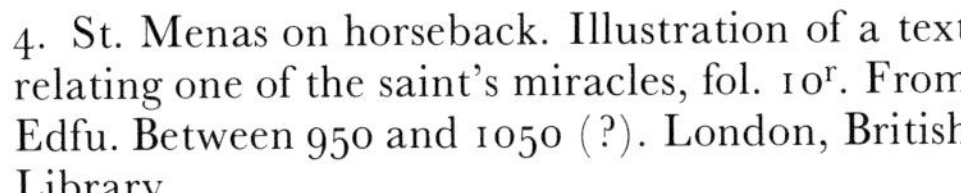

4. St. Menas on horseback. Illustration of a text relating one of the saint's miracles, fol. 10r. From Edfu. Between 950 and 1050 (?). London, British Library.

4

texts concerning him supports the supposition that he was of black origin or even that he was connected with Nubia in any way whatever.[41]

So there is reason to raise questions about the purpose and meaning of these apparently haphazard representations. The answer is perhaps to be sought in Nubia. A text referred to by Kaufmann,[42] but published before him,[43] opens an important avenue of research and makes new hypotheses possible. A manuscript in the British Library, which contains a text dating between 950 and 1050[44] referring to St. Menas (the text is in the Nubian language but is written in Greek characters), gives us an interesting image of the saint:[45] he is shown riding a horse, his cape flying behind him, a lance in his hand. On his head, woolly-haired, he wears three crowns—a detail explained in the texts relating to the saint himself.[46] What interests us here is that, taking into account the graphic stylization of the work, it unquestionably represents Menas as a black man. fig. 4

Kaufmann tried to sketch the evolution of the saint as protector of the Nubians.[47] He thought that the first to have this role was St. Mark, borrowed from the Delta and adopted by the Nubians,[48] and that in the Delta, around the sixth century, Menas took Mark's place. Are we to suppose that the same thing happened in Nubia three centuries later? It would be risky to draw conclusions on the basis of the sole example we have at present. At least this idea of a sainted protector borrowed from the Delta and then "blackened" seems to us to throw some light on what caused ampullae bearing the profile of a black to be sold at the monastery: there is reason to assume that the buyers thought this was St. Menas.

So we must return to the catalogue drawn up by Kaufmann. We see that the ampullae fall into a certain number of broad types. One is the "official portrait" already discussed. It is probably not foolhardy to match this type with the concerns of occasional purchasers coming over the desert routes. Thus the "dromedary" type could have contributed to the spread of the Menas cult toward Libya and probably beyond.

Another type may be related to travel by sea. In Kaufmann's inventory there are few such examples,[49] but the type gains in interest when put in relation to an episode of the Menas legend.[50] This suggests the likelihood that the monks of the Egyptian monastery found it convenient to adapt their saint's miracles to their visitors' wishes. May they not have done likewise with regard to iconography? With this hypothesis as a starting point it would be easy to understand that there was no conflict between the black Menas, produced for the Nubians, and the other representations of the saint manufactured at the same time.[51]

Needless to say, we must move cautiously along a trail of research like this one. At the outset we are deprived of a decisive set of clues: Kaufmann's excavations were so badly conducted that we will never know whether the ampullae were simply thrown together pell-mell or were stocked according to type or size. Clearly it would also be helpful to be able to establish the chronology of the manufacture, sale, and changing styles of these objects. Moreover, we see how a critical study of the narrative layers that progressively embellished the Menas legend would lead to more exact dating. All these preliminary questions must be answered as far as possible if the study we are undertaking is to lead to sound conclusions. Furthermore, it is important to remind those engaged in the search that it would be highly useful to know the geographical distribution of the ampullae they discover. If by any chance it turned out that they were localized by types, our hypothesis would be strengthened.

At any rate it would seem that the Byzantine Empire did not think of Menas as black, any more than the people of Western Europe did. So we are brought back to the idea that the canny monks "met the need" manifested by their black clientele by giving their saint, as occasion demanded, a black face exportable all through the Nile Valley toward the south. Nubia might thereupon have readily adopted the saint coming from Egypt.[52]

Another thing to be explained is why Menas as a black saint disappeared from Nubia after the tenth century, apparently leaving hardly a trace, whereas he survived for a long time in Ethiopia as a white saint. The information now available makes it possible only to explore some avenues of research. Menas, we know, was very closely connected with the businessmen of Alexandria, who in turn were hand-in-glove with the Muslim masters of Egypt. Is it not possible that the Nubians came to consider him a poor protector against the traders and masters from the north, who exacted from them the heavy annual tribute of *baḳṭ*?[53] Did they finally prefer a saint more warlike, yet with a sufficient resemblance to Menas—viz., St. George[54]—to the Alexandrian saint who was so far away and so tied up with the traffickers of the Lower Nile Valley?

At this point the inquiry turns to St. George's appearance in Nubia. Unquestionably the saint was born of the imagination of the Orientals,[55] not of the Nubians. But no less certainly he was in favor in Nubia from the ninth century onward: paintings as well as patronymics prove it.[56] But when and why did a white George replace a black Menas? Was it due to a desire to break with the Delta and to be fully a part of the diplomatic life of the Near East, dealing directly with the rulers of Baghdad? Or was it merely a fad? The answer can be found only in the history of Nubia itself, and of this we have but little knowledge. It is at least worth noting that Menas, "naturalized" as a black in Nubia, did not long hold out against the submergence of his cult in Egypt, nor against the break between Nubians and Copts, and that from Faras to Dongola a saint who was white but not compromised by involvement in Egyptian politics won out over him. Thus Menas, who picked up traits coming from other more or less legendary saints, may have seen his own persona "go to pieces" somewhere about the tenth century, ceding some of his characteristics to Mark, to George, and perhaps even to St. Maurice,[57] while his following was confined to Egypt alone. And the black Menas, symbol of a Christianization opening widely to the south,[58] thus seems to have disappeared, the victim of the breach between the black Christians in the Upper Nile Valley and the Egyptians, whether Muslims, Jews, or Christians, farther to the north.

Egypt, which was Byzantine before being converted to Islam, included blacks among her more or less temporary and more or less voluntary inhabitants. It may be that this fact influenced the attitude of the Byzantines: did they not have among them people who, like the rest of men, were called by Christ to eternal salvation?[59]

5

6

7

5. Marriage of Isaac (detail): meeting of Eliezer and Rebecca. *Ashburnham Pentateuch*, fol. 21r. VI-VII century (?). Paris, Bibliothèque nationale.

6. Joseph receives his brothers in Egypt (detail): Hebrews and Egyptians at table. *Ashburnham Pentateuch*, fol. 44r. VI-VII century (?). Paris, Bibliothèque nationale.

7. Crossing the Red Sea (detail): the pharaoh's army. *Ashburnham Pentateuch*, fol. 68r. VI-VII century (?). Paris, Bibliothèque nationale.

8. Tenth plague on Egypt and the deliverance of the children of Israel. *Ashburnham Pentateuch*, fol. 65v. VI-VII century (?). Paris, Bibliothèque nationale.

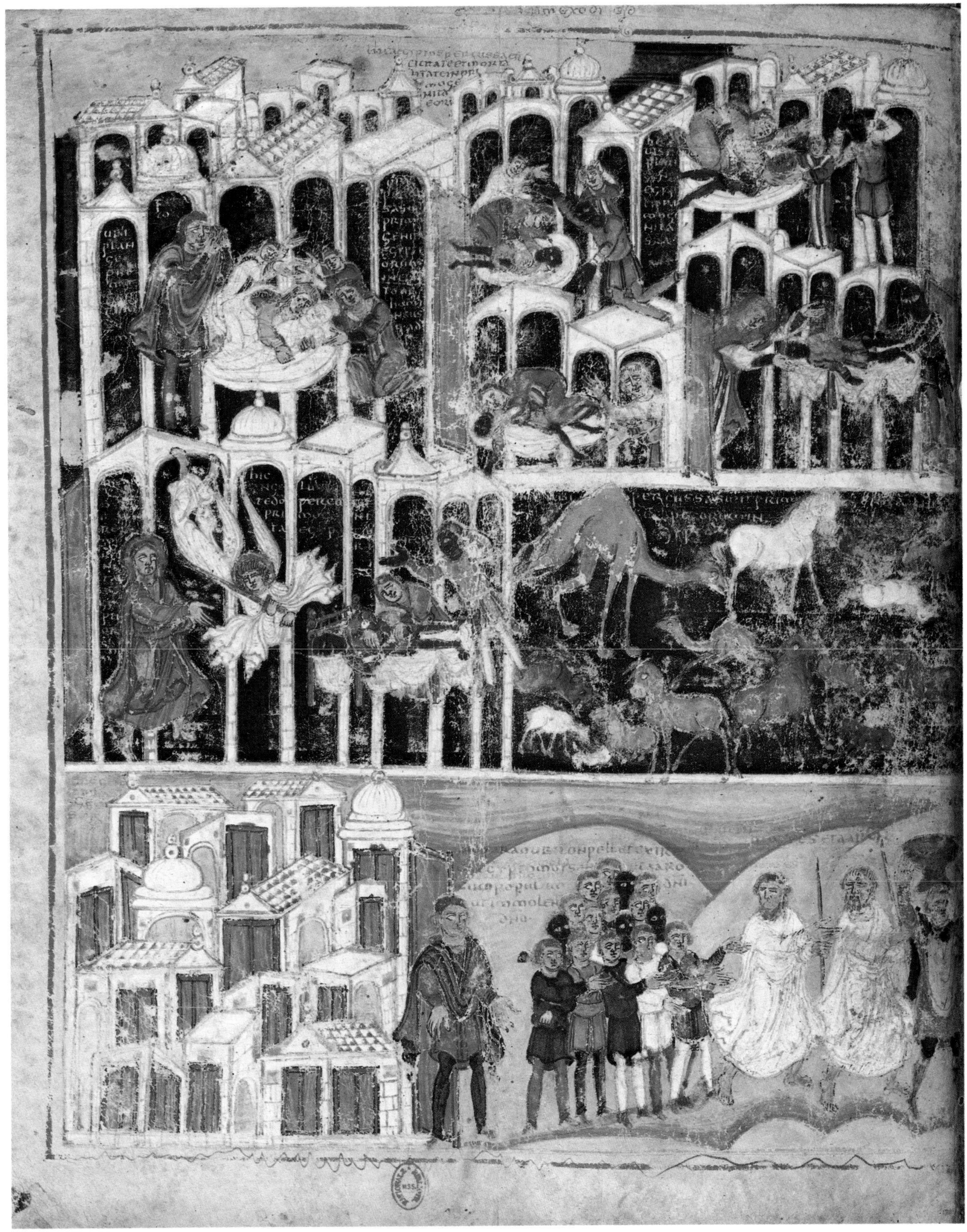

8

9. *Oikoumenē* of Strabo. Reprinted from E. H. Bunbury, *A History of Ancient Geography* (London, 1879).

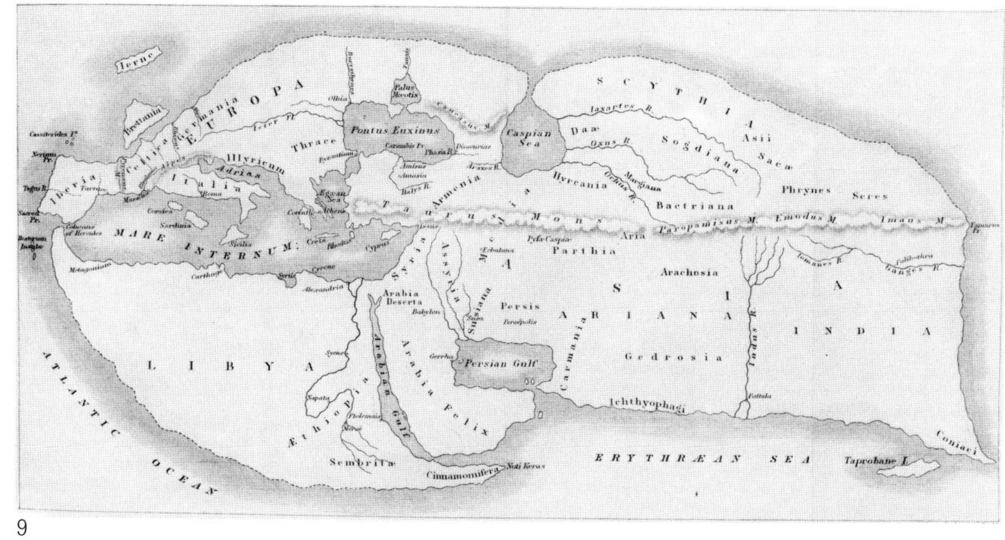

9

As seen by manuscript painters, at least from the fifth to the twelfth century, Egypt was populated in part by blacks. In itself this fact deserves attention, and we shall come back to it later, because more than one iconographic problem will have to be examined in light of it. In one of the oldest illuminated manuscripts of Western Europe, the magnificent *Ashburnham Pentateuch* (also called the *Pentateuque de Tours*),[60] Africa[61] and the blacks are much in evidence. Black camel drivers appear in the scene of the marriage of Isaac;[62] other blacks, usually clothed in white, sit at table (fig. 5) among the Egyptians or busy themselves as servers in the episode of Joseph's repast with his brothers.[63] This pictorial description of pharaonic (fig. 6) Egypt shows blacks both as servants and as the equals of Joseph and counselors to the pharaoh, as victims of the tenth plague,[64] and horsemen in (fig. 8) the army that perished in the Red Sea.[65] Therefore, the painter of the (fig. 7) *Pentateuch* thought of the Egyptian population as including a certain proportion of blacks, even in the highest posts of authority and in the army: but is this an index by which we can date the manuscript or determine its origin? Does it indicate an attitude of mind? It would be hard to say, since what we have here is pure illustration without any very explicit significance. What we do know is that these rare signs of a heritage from African Christianity and from the current of optimism that Christianity appropriated from antiquity rapidly gave way before the triumphant pessimism that was born of ignorance and fear.

THE BLACK UNKNOWN, THE BLACK DISHONORED

For a Byzantine, at least before the seventh century, and for a Muslim after that, Africa, or at least eastern Africa, was a concrete reality. Ethiopia was a power to be reckoned with. The blacks were real people, known although not very well, even though Galen's prejudices still influenced the minds of all the heirs of ancient cultures. Byzantine diplomats and merchants often needed an alliance with Ethiopia and an understanding with the Nubians in order to control the trade routes to the rich Far East, so they were well aware of the importance of these regions. Yet it was essentially as allies, and in the case of the Ethiopians as maritime allies, that these Eastern Christians were known and kept in mind.[66] Yet even the Byzantines, businesslike realists that they were, thought of Africa as a land with limits that could not be crossed: as they saw it, no man could live in a hypothetical expanse situated south of the Equator.[67] Ancient knowledge (or lack of it) as summarized by existing maps[68] also influenced their thinking. The regions south of the parallel of Meroë were unknown and ignored: this was the rule of a tradition accepted by Christians and Muslims alike and taught without criticism, at least by the Christians, for a long period of time. fig. 9

The Christians of Nubia and Ethiopia might have promulgated a favorable image of the African of color, and even of their own saints, but they themselves were cut off from the north, first by the intolerance of the Byzantine Empire and then by the installation of the Muslims in the Lower Nile Valley. Isolated from the south, Byzantium seems to have remembered only the physical fact that Egypt comprised a relatively mixed population, without giving much thought to the religious and theological consequences of the existence of the blacks. What is still more remarkable is the fact that the Coptic Christians of Egypt and Ethiopia made no effort to stand up for African solidarity. Both of these Christian societies[69] remained "colonial" for centuries, blindly accepting the Mediterranean point of view with regard to the genealogy of the sons of Noah and practically giving up the black saints.[70] Meanwhile Nubia, frustrated, seems to have withdrawn into its own brand of Christianity, having found no real support or contact either among the Copts to the north or in Ethiopia to the southeast. Most likely these difficult problems will have to be restudied *in toto*: at present, we repeat, it is impossible to do more than make learned guesses.

As for Western Europe, it did not have the same "historical" reasons as Byzantium for retaining a kindly interest in African Christianity.[71] Particularly between the sixth and the eleventh century the Occident fashioned an entire imagery based on prejudice and errors which "cultivated" minds substituted, century after century, for objective thinking about Africa and the blacks.[72] This situation sprang primarily from lack of knowledge which was sustained by the absence of physical contact between Africa and Europe. But the poorly assimilated heritage of antiquity on the one hand, and a quite astonishing interpretation of the Christian texts on the other, are the direct forebears of this tragic aberration.

Africa, the third and smallest of the known continents,[73] the largest being Asia,[74] had no uniformly and universally accepted name in the cultural heritage of antiquity. *Africa* and *Libya* were used interchangeably.[75] After 600, however, *Africa* became more common, *Libya* progressively less so. But this choice led to new difficulties: toward the end of antiquity *Africa* had two different meanings. The continent lying south of the Mediterranean was called Africa, but the name was also applied, more restrictively, to the northeastern part of northern Africa,[76] which for this reason the Arabs later called Ifrikiya. Cosmographers, encyclopedists, and priests found the first designation more suitable, while practical men—the Mediterraneans who were used to Roman administrative categories—preferred the second.

There was just as much vagueness when it came to fixing the limits of the African continent or describing its internal subdivisions. Roman antiquity regarded Africa as bound by the Nile,[77] and, of course, by the

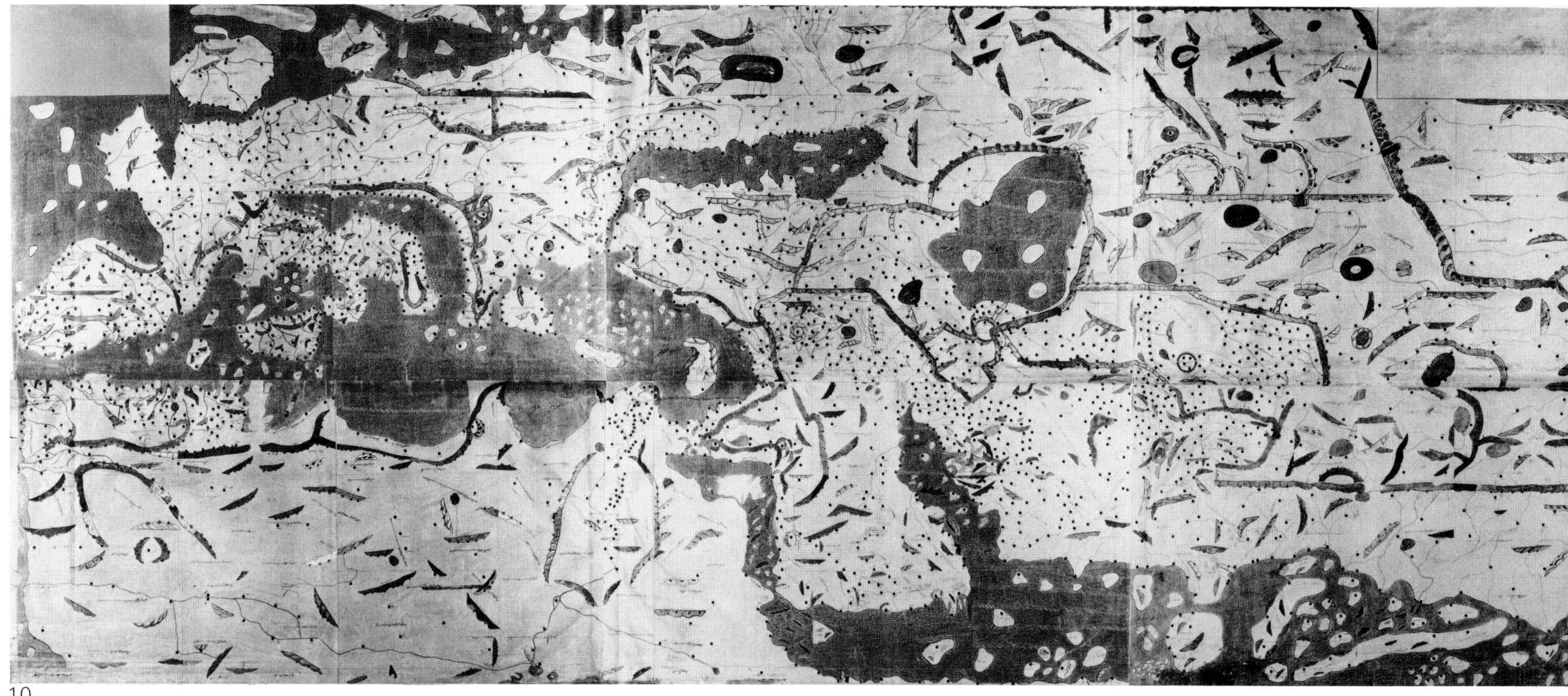

10

10. Facsimile reconstruction of al-Idrisi's planisphere, 1140-50, after a thirteenth-century copy (inverted: north at the top). Paris, Bibliothèque nationale.

western ocean; but Ptolemy's heirs,[78] and particularly the Muslims, thought that it stretched far out to the east. Their tendency was to picture Africa as extending eastward opposite Asia, south of an immensely prolonged Mediterranean Sea that was open at its eastern extremity.[79] As to the southern part of the continent, it was the complete Unknown, and even more so toward the west than toward the east; by that very fact the imagination, unhampered by the fetters of rationality, could conjure up a boundless land of sunbaked sand, filled with marvels quite abnormal,[80] rich in gold and precious stones,[81] and bounded by a fearsome ocean. Little by little the Muslims came to know a part of these irritating and enticing, dangerous and fascinating lands. Western Europe knew nothing about them before the fifteenth century except from indirect sources,[82] yet expected much of them, beginning with such wondrous plants as cinnamon.[83] In ancient times and thereafter, when exploration, exploitation, colonization, or evangelization was concerned, the Africa of the Nile and the Red Sea and the Africa of the north and west were thought of in entirely different ways: there was no common measure between the already extensive knowledge of the former and the lack of knowledge with regard to the latter. This imbalance shows through in every representation of the African continent conceived by the Christians of Western Europe. The Muslim geographers also distinguished between these regions of the vast African continent. The eastern part, peopled by Nūba (Nubians), Bujja (Bejas), Ḥabash (Ethiopians), and Zanj (blacks), is clearly recognizable, and divided into well-defined areas, in their writings. West of the Nile things are less clear. The Maghreb sometimes begins at Tripoli, sometimes at Cyrenaica. The African west, often called *Bilād al-Sūdān* ("land of the blacks"), was for a long time less well known than the east. So, for the medieval man, and especially for the Western European, there were two Africas or two Libyas.[84]

fig. 10

To further complicate matters, there was Ethiopia. Pliny the Elder, followed by his Mediterranean readers including Isidore of Seville, locates it south of Africa-Libya,[85] in an arc stretching from the southern part of Egypt, from which the "Island" of Meroë[86] separates it, all the way to the ocean. Isidore divides Ethiopia (as he does Africa) into two sections with different populations: one, south of Egypt, corresponds to the land we now call Ethiopia; the other, farther west, covers about the same territory as the present Libya.[87] Both the eastern and western limits of Ethiopia are even vaguer than those of Africa. The Nile "girds" it to the east:[88] sometimes it extends to the land of the Sabaeans,[89] or, still farther, to the Indus.[90] Little is known about the perilous ocean that bathes its western coast.[91]

When, by recourse to the Latin documents, we try to arrive at a more exact geographic image of the continent, confusion is worse confounded. Isidore of Seville bequeathed to his innumerable readers and copiers a definition of Africa that clouded the vision of medieval men. As he described it, Africa began south of Egypt and extended in an arc to the ocean and the Pillars of Hercules. Thus it was to a large degree coextensive with Ethiopia. It included the following provinces: Libya, Cyrenaica, Pentapolis, Tripolitania, Byzacena, Carthaginiensis, Numidia, Mauretania Tingitana, and, "in the area where the ardor of the sun is great," Ethiopia.[92] What we have here is administrative geography crossed with imagination.

As if these bits of information were not confused enough, another and final element contributed its share of disorder. For the geographers of the Low Latin period, India was part of Asia.[93] But with the help of "biblical" geography and, later on, of Muslim tradition, and with the area of black population in view, India was thought of as being divided into three zones on the "two coasts" of the Indian Mediterranean.[94] Thus parcelled out between Asia and present Africa, the three Indias do not facilitate the determination of landmarks in a delirious geographical landscape.[95] The Western European Middle Ages lived entirely on this heritage, enriched with Oriental legends that proliferated beginning in the eleventh century.[96]

To the Mediterranean man, who thought of himself as the measure of all things, the climate of Africa was exceptional[97] in that it was dominated by a relentless sun which darkened men's skin and parched the earth, thus making impossible the production of "normal" crops.[98] Men and beasts were no less affected by these extreme conditions than the earth itself. Of old, Africa had been full of the monsters known as elephants:[99] it was still the habitat of an exceptional fauna. Rhinoceroses,[100] giraffes,[101] scorpions, ostriches, and dromedaries were known to the people of the Occident through the medium of exegetical commentaries inspired by the outlandish shapes of these animals. But the "existence" of gigantic dragons[102] in whose brains gems were embedded,[103] of giant ants,[104] and of sphinxes, was also "known." Africa was reputed to abound in serpents,[105] the most fearsome being the basilisk.[106]

The Nile,[107] the Atlas,[108] and the hills of the Rif[109] concealed mysteries as dangerous as those of the rest of this scorched land. Was it not known that Libya, of which there was more knowledge, had a spring that was abnormal, since the water flowed hot at night and cold in the daytime? True, many of these fables, contaminated as they were with ancient paganism, were not preserved in the official teaching of the Christian West. We scarcely find Satyrs and Aegypans except in certain poets and "imprudent" encyclopedists.

F. M. Snowden, Jr., came to the highly optimistic conclusion that among the men of antiquity there existed not a trace of antiblack racism, nor was there even a consciousness of racial differences.[110] His view is that it was simply a matter of climate and that climatic differences, a mere 'accident', could not beget a sense of inequality in human relations.

We have to look closely at the facts in order to analyze the heritage of antiquity and to understand what medieval Christians made of it. We find that the said Christians displayed none of the optimistic open-mindedness that Snowden attributes to the man of antiquity. Three explanations are possible. The first—obviously a wrongheaded one—would be based on the perversity characteristic of the medieval man; the second would hold that the ancient optimism was perverted by Islam and Christianity; the third would lead one to think that the heritage of antiquity was less unilaterally favorable than Snowden says it was. The question must be dealt with on three distinct levels, and the answers come out quite different.

On the ideological level it is true that antiquity showed no *racism*[111] vis-à-vis the blacks, nor even a sense of racial inequality.[112] The ancient tradition of neutrality with regard to the "Ethiopians" was followed in Western Europe in a certain number of instances, as the illustration of an eleventh-century English manuscript shows.[113] It is also true that the cli- fig. 11
mate theory explained ethnic differences without leading to value judgments, and that the qualities of the blacks were brought out clearly by more than one ancient author. On all these points Snowden's conclusions are well founded and abundantly set forth. Moreover, on the level of principles, both Christianity and Islam are called to proclaim the absolute equality of the races of men and to repudiate the idea of inequality in all its forms, along with racism and the exploitation of "inferiors" by self-styled "superiors." Snowden, once again, explains this very well for Christianity in its beginnings, although he has passed over some few serious dissonances.

Examined at the level of daily life and concrete social relationships, the scene changes remarkably. It is quite true—and J. Desanges is right in stressing this—that slavery was never exclusively racial and that it lumped blacks and whites together in a common status: the Middle Ages, both Christian and Muslim, inherited this situation. It is quite true that the murderous, ninth-century revolt of the Zanj in the Abbassid area was not exclusively racial: whites and blacks took part in it side by side. Its root cause was the working conditions—that long ago!—in the sugarcane plantations. And it is quite true that in theory both Christianity and Islam condemned slavery.

But, sad to say, it is no less true that the Western European Christian strove first to save Christians from slavery, and for a long time was content to leave the non-Christian slaves to their fate;[114] and it is a fact that the Muslim considered it the normal thing to enslave the distant Slav or the black after he had enslaved the Turk, so long as they were set free once they were converted. In the last analysis the condemnation of slavery, in the monotheistic religions as well as in the Greek and Roman worlds, was at the discretion of the group that possessed privileged status: it was not the

11

11. Ethiopians. *De rebus ex Oriente mirabilibus*, fol. 86^{r} (detail). Winchester, second quarter XI century (?). London, British Library.

result of a universally respected principle, and in day-to-day affairs the generosity of proclaimed principles gave way to *de facto* inequality. Everything shows that from ancient times this is the way life was, and that we must not allow ourselves to be misled by the texts. This social inequality bred prejudice and raised barriers.

The element that does not seem to have been present in antiquity, but which developed in later civilizations, is a marked antipathy toward blackness itself, and, as a consequence, toward black people. It is true that eleventh-century Christendom in Western Europe allowed upward social movement: there were many men of "ministerial" rank whose origins were servile and who grew rich and powerful. Islam, more open than the West, permitted the social promotion of the freed slave. Even though *'abīd* and *blacks* were often used synonymously in Arabic, blacks were not excluded from this theoretically generous possibility any more than Turks were.[115] Yet we are convinced that Islam itself was not of one mind on this subject. The people of Basra, whose prosperity certainly depended in part on the traffic in black slaves brought in from the African coasts by Iranian mariners, were locked in basic argument on the matter: traces of this survive in al-Jāḥiẓ's treatise on the superiority of the blacks. In Western Europe, at least until the twelfth century, there were simply no black people except in some very limited areas. Hostility to blackness as a color was therefore given free rein since blackness was associated with human beings only in a very abstract manner. It is certain that as far back as antiquity, and in any case for the medieval civilizations, the view of the black and his color was considerably more ambiguous at the level of social life than it was at the ideological level.

Turning finally to the level of intellectual reactions and of accepted definitions of "normality," we find that the situation of Africa and its inhabitants was still more clearly unfavorable. For the peoples around the Mediterranean[116] the area of "normal" phenomena was the area in which they lived, although they might allow that some of the Asian territory visited by Alexander the Great was part of it, since this, to their way of thinking, had long belonged to the economic world they knew. Since the days of the Roman Empire, indeed, the Mediterranean man saw the routes of economic and cultural contact as running west and east, from Spain and northern Morocco to China and southern Asia. Africa, for all its size, was unknown except along its fringes, the northern part being known due to military occupation and economic exploitation, the eastern section around the Nile by reason of its prestige and its wealth. In the Byzantine period the need to open new routes to Asia through the Red Sea gave the Ethiopians a place of importance. Byzantium, like the Muslim civilizations of Arabia and the Nile Valley, remembered this after the victory of Islam: the Christian West, even along the Mediterranean, speedily forgot Ethiopia. The brief experience of the evangelization of Nubia, and the remoteness of Ethiopia after the year 700, diminished the importance of these African regions so far as Byzantium was concerned. The memory of whatever brief contact there had been was replaced by the ideas inherited from the cosmographers and geographers of antiquity, who were chiefly interested in the "reasonable" space of the Mediterranean coastal areas.

Ibn Khaldūn[117] is unequivocal on the subject of "normality": the *normal* universe is the balanced universe that corresponds to the temperate zone reaching from France to China. It would be hard to imagine a more ethnocentric idea of the world of travel and exchange, of interests, and of intellectual speculation, than that in which Mediterranean man has lived from the days of antiquity until recently—if indeed, as we should like to think, that time has passed. This ethnocentrism made "others" so *abnormal* that no effort was made to understand them, even if they had been cleansed of all "malediction."[118] In the tenth century Mas 'ūdī visited the east coast of Africa, and witnessed and recorded some very interesting observances of the traditional religious life without understanding a bit of it.[119] Ibn Baṭṭūṭa repeated the experience in western Africa in the fourteenth century.[120] What we see here is the effect of an intellectual conditioning that bred strong prejudices and a spirit of white superiority. The Mediterranean people absorbed these attitudes; but we must remember that their culture was transplanted, along with Christianity, to northwest Europe—the "North" that Ibn Khaldūn thought to be abnormal and dangerous. The people of this area were more remote from Africa and Africans than those farther south, and we need not be surprised that the Carolingian period, on the intellectual plane, marks the widest separation between Europe and Africa as well as the liveliest hostility to blackness. Thus his cultural heritage built up in the white man a more or less deeply felt antipathy against Africa.[121]

The "climate theory" comes from Macrobius, an author whose writings date from around A.D. 400. Before him Galen, a learned physician revered in the Middle Ages as much as in antiquity, circulated some regrettably foolish opinions about the African man and the effect of his exposure to the unbearable heat of the sun, and Latin and Arab authors repeated and enlarged upon these ideas. If Islam at times contributed to this harmful nonsense, it was because Islam, too, was "Mediterranean," and because its human standards, like Christian Europe's were those of the white man. Mas 'ūdī, using al-Kindī as a source,[122] went still further: according to him the Zanj, burnt by the sun and subject to the influence of Saturn,[123] which rules everything black, was scarcely a man at all. Another tenth-century text puts the matter even more bluntly: "What is south of the Equator is occupied in part by the sea, and the rest is extremely hot. The inhabitants are hardly human." For al-Bīrūnī, in the eleventh century, the men who live near the horrible Equator "are burnt as to their color, their hair, their nature, and their reason." Avicenna—the great Avicenna himself—is caught in the same bind: he says that the skin of the black man's skull is very tough and does not let the hair come through easily, so they are less subject to baldness than other men.[124] Popular preachers adopted this theme; scholars quickly rejected it. It took the erudite Ibn Khaldūn, in the fourteenth century, to refute these inanities, which were accepted by almost all authors for centuries on end.[125]

Western European writers were equally zealous in copying Galen. From the seventh to the fourteenth century they handed on (explicitly or implicitly) this vision of Africa, according to which it was a land of geographic, physiological, and intellectual abnormality. The cultural heritage of antiquity, distorted and amplified by its heirs, predisposed those latter to regard Africa as dangerous[126] and the African as subhuman.

It will be understood that in writing these lines we have no intention of drawing up an indictment: we would not put ourselves in the ridiculous position of making a facile and pharisaical value judgment. On the whole, given the conditions that surrounded them, it was just about impossible for the men of the Middle Ages to react otherwise than they did. We simply wanted to tone down what seemed to us to be the excessive optimism of Snowden's overall analysis; and besides, we have drawn upon facts that were outside the scope of his study. Even if we are to maintain an optimistic estimate of the attitude of antiquity, we find it noteworthy that the "man of the Middle Ages" was so much less open-minded and tolerant than his predecessors.

Let us focus our attention on the Europeans, who in their western pale were also heirs of the Mediterranean culture, which came to them foreshortened, distorted, often confused. Ancient texts were at hand to inform them that in the land of Africa, so strange, so foreign, lived beings more or less comparable to other men. The Greco-Latin tradition furnished, at least for the northern section of that continent, an abundant list of peoples with very curious names, mostly derived from and descriptive of their supposed diet. The Pamphagi[127] (who ate anything the body could absorb) and the Ichthyophagi[128] soon disappeared from the medieval memory, as did the Anthropophagi,[129] however strong the impression they made on the imagination; and we still wonder what exactly the Istophagi were supposed to live on. The Troglodytes enjoyed a more durable renown[130] than their neighbors the Marsi and the Psylli, who quickly disappeared.[131] The fame of the Garamantes lasted even longer: the favor they enjoy with historians, even in our own day, probably stems from our almost complete lack of knowledge of their real role in middle Africa up to the ninth century.[132] The Sciapodes,[133] who were more abnormal and lived farther to the south, provided, along with many others, a fine pictorial theme for the Vézelay tympanum.[134] Neither Solinus nor Pomponius Mela nor yet Martianus Capella could save the Atlantes,[135] the Gamphasantes,[136] and the Amantes[137] from oblivion. The story is different for the Pygmies,[138] already dear to Herodotus (the cranes associated with their memory stalk through a poem by Theodulf[139]): they were still alive, as a literary topic, in the twelfth and thirteenth centuries.[140] Some peoples in the west of Africa were mixed up with the Satyrs and Aegypans of mythology: Isidore of Seville,[141] and after him Theodulf,[142] record their names. Interesting myths were already taking shape regarding these peoples.[143] These themes were ephemeral in literature. The lovely, difficult tympanum at Vézelay makes room for a few of these peoples, in a context that does not concern us here.[144]

For most Europeans, even those who were fairly well educated, Africa harbored a much smaller number of peoples. Little by little, moreover, one name—that of the Ethiopians[145]—stands out over all the others. For Isidore of Seville this name designates all blacks; for Solinus and Gregory of Tours it applies essentially to the Nubians, whose queen was a Candace. To all of them *Aethiops* meant 'the black'[146]—so much so that they had to coin an absurd neologism, *Leucoaethiopes*,[147] to designate the white inhabitants of northern Africa. The *Aethiopes* themselves do not often appear in Occidental iconography. At most their presence is noted at Souvigny[148] and at Nevers,[149] but there is no connection with the theme we are considering. Gradually, moreover, they came to be designated by the name "Mauri,"[150] which also comes from the ancient vocabulary. Yet this did not clarify the situation, since on the one hand Mauri (Moors) and Saracens[151] were all too often confused, and on the other a distinction was made between white Moors and black Moors.[152] *Maurus*, says the inevitable Isidore, means 'black' in Greek.[153]

Fables, myths, and prejudices[154]—such was the heritage relative to Africa and its peoples that the culture of antiquity, distorted by the doughty compilers whose boast was that they were preserving it from oblivion, passed on to the medieval man. And he, being Christian, could not be satisfied with it.[155]

"Varro says that there are monsters born contrary to nature. This is not so, since they were created by the will of God. ... The monster's existence therefore is not contrary to nature but contrary to known nature."[156] This is a ninth-century Christian writer's way of reassuring himself before tackling the subject of Satyrs, Cynocephali, and Sciapodes.[157]

Christianity very early strove to put some coherence into the heritage we have been discussing, within its own vision of the world, and created for itself a biblical geography in which Africa and the blacks had an important place. Everything pertinent to the life of man and that of creation as a whole had to be fitted into a metaphysical-historical perspective. The relations between the creature and his Creator, highlighted by episodes of far-reaching significance, could no longer remain outside the logic of the new belief.[158] This perspective, as we shall see later, raised some very difficult theological problems: the destiny of the blacks was less easy to put in focus than that of the antipodes. Islam also proceeded, though less rigorously, to attempt a metaphysical reordering of the cultural legacy of antiquity.

It is assumed, of course, that all men are descended from Adam.[159] This fact calls for emphasis because of one very positive consequence: the blacks are men and have souls, like the whites. So at one stroke the ancient fables regarding the "marginals," half man and half beast, that haunt the solitudes of Africa, are swept away. Except for the dealings between God and man, the long period from Adam to Noah is characterized only by the incredible fecundity and exceptional longevity of our remote ancestors. Things took a turn for the worse after the Deluge (worldwide, of course), which reduced the human species to Noah and his descendants. Filaster[160] considered it heretical to think that the Greeks, Egyptians, and Persians might have partitioned the known earth before Noah: the parceling out of the globe was his doing and his alone—after the Deluge—and this made it possible to trace Greeks, Egyptians, and Persians to one of Noah's sons. It follows that the blacks, like all men, were descendants of Noah. The inevitable consequence of this is one of the traps into which, even in our own times, historians have fallen: the African continent could have been peopled and civilized only from the northeast, in other words from the area where Africa touches the Middle East, the "historic theater" of the Deluge. "Oriental origin" runs like an inevitable leitmotiv through all questions relative to the ancient inhabitants of Africa, bringing nothing but confusion to the subject.

A long series of texts, most of them anonymous, dating from the fourth to the ninth century, bear such titles as *Book of Generations*, *Genealogical Book*, etc.[161] All these texts go back to Genesis;[162] all of them give detailed accounts of the imaginary ways in which the post-Deluge dispersion came about. Among Noah's sons Shem and Japheth do not concern us here. To Ham and his descendants was allotted a vast territory extending from southern Syria to the Strait of Gades.[163] With variations upon which later centuries loved to ring the changes, the basic chord is always the same. Ham had four sons. Chus, the eldest, was the father of the Ethiopians: among his children Nimrod, a man of extraordinary height, had a special destiny.[164] Ham's second son begot the Egyptians. The third, Phut, was father to the Troglodytes. From Canaan, the last son, sprang the *Afri* and the *Phoenices*: his posterity was the most numerous, and Isidore of Seville took it upon himself to straighten out their lines of descendance. So a rather incongruous catalogue of the peoples descended from Chus is drawn up, and into it are introduced ancient names that could not be totally ignored if the subject were to be adequately treated. We even have a list of the peoples issuing from Chus who knew how to write,[165] and in addition a certain number of localizations[166] that represent a laborious effort to synthesize the information we have been reviewing. This common fund of data was used by poets and commentators of all kinds.

To these genealogies Isidore of Seville added etymological commentaries that were not helpful.[167] When a difficulty arises in his classification, he declares that, due to the Ethiopian wars, certain of Ham's descendants had simply been forgotten entirely; and since some explanation of *Afri* and *Africa* must be found, Isidore invokes a distant descendant of Abraham, Afer by name, who had conquered the Libyans and then given them his name. If there seems to be no evident relationship between Chus and the Ethiopians whose ancestor he is supposed to be, he explains that in Hebrew *Chus* means 'Aethiops'! Moreover, these Ethiopians divide into three peoples who are not connected with Chus at all—Hesperians in the west, Garamantes in the middle, and ... Indians. Orthodox considerations thus give way to ancient "culture." Besides all this, a convenient excuse for errors and omissions is at hand. After the Deluge, at the time of the Tower of Babel, came the total confusion of tongues, and after that there were problems that just could not be figured out.[168] Isidore's successors adopted and improved upon these fantasies.[169]

The Fathers of the Church made a capital contribution to this theme. Augustine ponders the question: how to admit that a certain number of monstrous creatures mentioned in history descend from Noah or even from Adam? Nobody has to believe in the Sciapodes, but the Pygmies—their small size poses a delicate problem.[170] Should we infer from this that for Augustine such anomalies, by comparison with the usual characteristics of Mediterranean man, raise metaphysical questions?

Ambrose adds the theme of malediction to the earlier distortions. Ham laughed at his father's nakedness; his fault fell on his son Chus, and all of this latter's posterity were condemned.[171] Out of this came a current of exegesis that quickly sought a basis in certain biblical texts. Poets,[172] hagiographers,[173] chroniclers,[174] encyclopedists,[175] and various authors of the Carolingian period[176] repeat, without giving it further thought, the theme of the curse of the sons of Ham: Chus and the *Aethiopes* were the Devil's predestined share of Noah's progeny.[177] It was reassuring to have such a scapegoat to abandon to the ancient Enemy of mankind. This lamentable assumption,[178] based on geneaology, spawned many another error[179] and prompted a hostile, "segregationist" attitude.

Western European Christianity was not alone in accepting the genealogical tradition that connected the blacks with Ham: Byzantium may have invented and certainly promulgated it. The Christian communities in Muslim territory[180] and Ethiopia[181] did likewise, most often without any pejorative connotations. Islam also adopted these genealogical explanations in its own way. The Islamic tradition has the descendants of Chus, son of Canaan, crossing the Nile and moving westward. They separated into groups thereafter distinct from one another. Nūba, Bujja, and Zanj went toward the south and southeast;[182] the others fared to the west. It was only in Western Europe, however, that the theme of the inherited curse laid upon the descendants of Ham was fully developed. What remains to be seen is whether this curse fell upon the blacks: this is not clear either in Ambrose or in the other authors we have cited. We shall return to this topic.

In any event the mechanical application of simplistic explanations to problems of the geographical and ethnic origin of Africans, and the theme of the collective curse transmitted to the descendants of Ham, persisted for centuries and introduced inexhaustible elements of distortion into the effort, already fraught with difficulty, to reconstruct the African past. More than that, it bred the germs of racism—a word we must use this time. These trends did not inevitably give rise to antiblack racism. Neither Islam nor Christianity is intrinsically responsible for the conclusions that *certain* Christians and certain Muslims, from medieval times to our own day, have drawn from the conceptions we have noted. Yet these conceptions contained the elements of a "white superiority" complex of which we ought to be aware even today.

Christianity and Islam have also dealt with the problems raised for their metaphysics by the nature of the earth, the shape and limits of the continents, and the creatures living in them. At the edges of the "normal" world, living conditions, adversely affected by cold, by heat, by the immensity of the ocean, or the height of the mountains, begin to be abnormal. God wills it so. The "limits" of Creation, according to ancient tradition, encompass extraordinary kinds of people, and Christianity revived these myths. The West is of little interest to us at this point. The Fortunate Isles and the Isle of Apples dear to King Arthur are in no way related to Africa, notwithstanding the fact that the western ocean had many an enduring legend attached to it.[183] The North concerns us only indirectly, as Alexander, the wonder-hero of Christians and Muslims, heads that way in search of new adventures.

On the other hand, the East includes two localizations which for the medieval man were contradictory but nonetheless essential. During the centuries with which we are dealing, the Paradise out of which Adam was driven was commonly situated in the East by Muslims and Christians alike;[184] but Gog and Magog and the peoples of the Apocalypse also lived there, poised to pounce on guilty mankind.[185] To the man of the tenth and eleventh centuries such presences were not romantic fancies but potential realities made possible by divine omnipotence. Anything in the East or coming from the East could perfectly well lie outside the apparently normal rules of human life as established by God for the Mediterranean world. Moreover, it must be evident that God himself gives man proof of the existence of this Paradise, since it was there that he caused four rivers that water the earth to rise.[186] The proof of the extraordinary origin of the rivers themselves lies in the wondrous products borne along by their waters, as well as in the abnormal and uncertain character of their flow.

The Nile[187] is of course one of these rivers. The ancient Gihon was easily Christianized in this way.[188] In this world of wonders it matters little that authors confused the Nile with the Indus and at times with the Ganges.[189] Isidore of Seville summed up this purely imaginary geography. The Gihon, he reports, rises in Paradise; it girdles the land of the Egyptians, who called it the Nile because of the silt it carried down to them; it is not the same as the Ganges and the Indus.[190] Bede holds that the four rivers have a single source:[191] they symbolize the four Gospels.[192] The Carolingian exegetes simply repeat all this.[193] In the eleventh century Honorius of Autun keeps to the same line except for one detail: the Nile has at least one source in the west of Africa and goes underground for a long way before resurfacing in the east and encircling Ethiopia.[194] For the Muslims, moreover, the East was also the vast ocean, which the imagination filled with terrors: the most dangerous myths took root there in such faraway places as the island of Waqwāq, from which mariners had a hard time getting back alive. All thought of the Orient as an area abounding in rare products, gold,[195] and precious stones.

But while the Muslims saw Africa as the land of gold and were quick to exploit it, Christian Europe, at least until the thirteenth century, saw it as a dangerous, far-off land[196] which awakened far less curiosity or cupidity than fabulous Asia. It was simply unknown to the European; its land and its people were part of a distorted vision of the world. Ultimately it was reserved for sinners, and so for centuries Africa occupied an oddly unfavorable place in Occidental consciousness.

As Mediterranean men viewed them, black people, being "primitives," were by nature slaves. Yet they were allowed to move upward in society, on two conditions: they had to become converts to one of the monotheistic religions, and they had to get rich or demonstrate some ability entitling them to upward movement. The influx of black slaves into the Muslim world, and, though probably in much smaller numbers, into Byzantium, had the effect of maintaining this image of the black, more benign and in appearance less discouraging than the one taking shape in Western Europe, which no longer had any contact with blacks. All that was known about them was an abstraction—blackness itself. As human beings, the black and the African in general presented no direct problem, physical or metaphysical, to the Western European. Hence a total hostility to blackness could take root, apparently, without jeopardizing the fundamental idea of the vocation of all men to salvation. The fears and terrors of the Occidental were centered on blackness itself.[197] It was easy enough to let the black *Aethiops* stand in as a contrast, both physical and religious, and so to make the white man look better; this involved no concrete, routine social situation. F. M. Snowden, Jr., while noting the favorable attitude toward black people that emerges from the reading of ancient sources, nevertheless also points out the appearance of less positive tendencies.[198] He shows, with good reason, that some Christian authors—and not the least eminent ones—were open to the ideas of the redemption of the blacks and of their equality with whites on earth;[199] but his area of research did not extend beyond the fourth or fifth century, or he would have found some markedly different texts to deal with.

A preliminary question may usefully be looked into here: how did the Bible treat the *color* black, and, more importantly, how did the commentators of Holy Writ interpret that color?[200] Unless we are mistaken, the word *niger* appears twelve times in the ancient Latin versions of the Bible.[201] Nine of these loci need no comment: three have stirred up more or less lively debates. When the Apocalypse describes a black horse,[202] this prompts Jerome, Caesarius, archbishop of Arles, Bede, and Beatus of Liébana to take this color for a symbol of the damned.[203] Equally prejudicial to the color black are all the interpretations we have collected relating to Song of Songs 5:11.[204] But the well-known verse, "I am black but beautiful,"[205] is the one that brings out the really interesting exegeses. All the commentators hold, more or less firmly, that blackness here is attached to sin, and must be "washed" if man is to recover the whiteness that assures his salvation.[206] Reciprocally, sin causes the soul to lose its whiteness, as Gregory the Great declares.[207] Finally, analysis of the commentaries relative to the Ethiopian wife of Moses[208] shows us, first, that all of them condemn the hostile attitude of Miriam and Aaron toward this woman. But, more notably, we see that according to Augustine she was not Ethiopian at all: she was, he says, a woman from the region inhabited by the Midianites, and these people were now called Saracens; no one, or almost no one, called them Ethiopians any longer.[209]

As for Africa itself, it is hardly mentioned in the Scriptures:[210] the designation of places is very vague. Jerome's commentary on Isaiah is worth examining here, as it is of prime importance for the understanding of the Christian attitude toward Africa and Africans. Among the books of the Old Testament, Isaiah is surely one of the most difficult for a Christian to interpret. It is at once a profound chant of loving rebuke against Israel and a foretelling of the final triumph after the Chosen People turns again to doing the will of its Lord; but this long book is also one of the most clearly historical in the entire Old Testament. First of all—and here we emphasize a point that we will not discuss further—the Book of Isaiah shows the way the image of evil and its punishment operate. But this way is not identical with the one that Christianity made traditional, for, if fire and flames signify both punishment and purification in this book, the color of sin is not black but red.[211] Here we see a rivalry between red and black that runs through all Oriental, Jewish, Christian, and Muslim exegesis and symbology. This play of colors has more to tell us; other surprises await the reader. Isaiah lived and prophesied in a difficult period of Israel's history—a period we are coming to know more about[212]—and he hammers on the real dangers, namely Egypt and Assyria, that weighed on the people of Yahweh.[213] Neither Jerome nor the other medieval commentators knew enough about the political geography of the lands between the cataracts and Asia Minor to understand Isaiah's allusions: this is clear from the considerable differences appearing in the translations of the Isaian verses that speak of the Kushites. What is more, the prophet proclaims—and this is the basis of all his prophecies—that like it or not, Israel, purified by fire, would bow to the will of Yahweh. Then the other peoples will gather around Israel, "the inheritance of God," and Yahweh will give them the knowledge that he and he alone is God.[214] Nothing in the Old Testament comes so close to the idea that the peoples of the earth could be united in one religion, that of Yahweh (Judaism);[215] the blacks of Kush, symbolized by the name "Put," are included in this call. Such a vision could seem to Jerome to be in direct conflict with Matthew's "Go and teach all nations," which called all men to the Christian religion. It would therefore betray the whole spirit of Christianity, descended from but then opposed to Judaism, and Jerome could not assume responsibility for promoting it.[216]

The Byzantines took a different tack. Intent on sustaining their rivalry with their Semitic neighbors—Jews and Arabs, "descendants of Shem"—the Byzantines took care to steal from Isaiah the idea of the universal vocation of all peoples to salvation: they eclipsed the Old Testament theme by developing that of Pentecost, as we shall see. More concretely, they made it their business to find allies in Africa against the hostile Semites, and also looked for them among the Slavs to the north. For the Byzantines Africa and Egypt were not lands unknown and unimportant, and their tradition diverged sharply from the Latin. The latter, originating in its broad lines with Jerome, was encumbered with the notion that black was the color of sin and death and was troubled by the reaction against Origen's liberalism, which threw the doors of salvation wide open to all peoples. Jerome, determined to make no concession to the Old Testament or to the Jews who had refused to recognize the divinity of Jesus, simply abandoned Africa, a land foreign to Judaism as well as to Christianity. Here is a symptomatic fact: when Jerome, heir to a complex exegesis regarding the Antichrist, tried to identify historical incarnations of this theological "type," he never thought of Africa or the Africans.[217] This situation looks favorable to the blacks, but what it really did was to leave them completely outside of the Fathers' profound exegesis. On the other hand, the same Fathers, and Jerome in particular, could never resist a real fascination with the children of Shem, enemies but brothers, monotheists to whom salvation was open once they acknowledged the divinity of Christ. Augustine is more optimistic, explaining that Isa. 66:19 must be interpreted as a sign that God wills the eternal beatitude of all men.

Blacks and Africa—only marginally and incidentally do they come into exegetical commentaries on the rare biblical passages that evoke them. (Neither Byzantium nor Islam, for different reasons, adopted that attitude.) The Latinized Bible shows little awareness of Africa, and reading it with the commentaries suggests that blackness is at best the sign of a redeemable state of sin and at worst a sign of damnation. Christian exegesis and popular prejudice[218] put together a stable image in which blackness was a sign of evil. While this was not a matter of conscious hostility to black people, the picture impressed upon the Western European mind was added to the ancient tradition, with the result that the black and his land were thought of as abnormal elements in creation. Egypt and the Egyptian, rather rarely India and the Indian,[219] Ethiopia and the Ethiopian,[220] all allegorically represented the proper domain of sin. The Hebrew term *ṣiyyīm*,[221] the Greek *Aithiops*, the Latin *Aethiops*, the Geez *habašūt*, and the Arabic *Ḥabash*[222] all designate a part of the posterity of Chus. Because this particular group was black, it was identified by some as a symbol of sin, and by others—worse yet—as the Devil's portion on earth. Thus the disfavor with which blackness and blacks were regarded varied in degree. A considerable section of Western exegesis emphasized the idea that a curse accompanied the black descendants of Chus. Noah, with prophetic insight, had foreseen this.[223] Here we find a link with ancient tradition to which we have thus far given little attention.[224]

Concomitant to the curse was a forced migration toward the most unwholesome regions of the earth, and there the *Aethiopes* turned black. As descendants of Adam through Noah, they could have had only a white as original ancestor, and therefore it was *by their own fault* that they became black. Flodoard, in the tenth century, speaks very simply of "the people of the Ethiopians, black in sin and in body."[225] Hence to be black was to share, through Chus, in a collective sin. Of course no theologian went so far as to make such a theory explicit: this would have amounted to inventing a new Original Sin inhering in the *Aethiopes* alone. But the marvel is that no one thought to explore the grave consequences of this prejudice, which had come down through the centuries without occasioning discussion or criticism, nor even a second look. It fastened itself upon the popular unconscious without ever becoming a subject of theological discussion—or doing so very late indeed.

The history of events of the fourth and fifth centuries furnished some unusual arguments to the above preposterous themes. The marginal zones of the human world provided refuge to all sorts of dissenters. Jews of the Diaspora who may have had some notion of converting their hosts,[226] Monophysites with whom the Nubians and Ethiopians aligned themselves, Nestorians who settled in western and central Asia, all were regarded as sources of temporal and spiritual peril by the "Romans" and the Orthodox Christians. We in our day no longer have any idea of the violence of the ideological confrontations that accompanied the political upheavals occurring, from the Near East to the Nile, between the third and the seventh centuries. Yet one has only to turn once again to the Bible to see that these disturbances had an ancient historical dimension.

The text of the Acts of the Apostles relative to the baptism of the Ethiopian eunuch, minister to Queen Candace, by Philip the Deacon[227] has, in our opinion, a considerable importance.[228] The *Aethiops*, already a sinner born, is also liable to rally to the "error of Judaism" and, soon enough, to that of Islam. It would be long before such patterns of thought faded away. For the time being, *Aethiopes*, Jews, and heretics of every stripe ate the flesh of the dragon—so says the Psalm—and not that of the pure Lamb, which was reserved to Christians.[229] This marginal world east and south of the Mediterranean absorbed the world of antiquity, and in it Alexander the intemperate,[230] Nimrod,[231] the Queen of Sheba,[232] and the Candaces[233] were more or less interchangeable. The story of Philip also served as prototype for all later themes of conversion of the peoples remote from the Mediterranean. Matthew very early became the apostle responsible for the redemption of the Ethiopians,[234] and later on we shall come to the mission of St. Thomas to India.

On the theme of the *Aethiops*-sinner, a verse of Psalm 67(68)[235] furnished a pretext for some fairly divergent interpretations. One current, clearly unfavorable to the Ethiopians, is at first represented by Jerome. The barbarous, bloody ways of the Ethiopians earned them their name;[236] their land, like the Egyptians', symbolizes all the earthly attachments that chain men to the blackness of sin.[237] While he admits in theory that they are called to salvation through the gift of grace,[238] Jerome's comments regarding them are generally harsh.[239] His texts were repeated again and again, and it is undeniable that they inspired the later interpretations that invariably identified blackness with sin,[240] Ethiopia with the land of sin,[241] and the Ethiopian with the collective sin of a people. Yet a far more optimistic interpretation of the same Psalm was possible. Granted that black is a symbol of sin, the fact that Ethiopians are black is incidental, and they may be named simply to provide an *exemplum* intended to make other men take thought of themselves. Are not all men called to salvation, as a text of Prosper of Aquitaine,[242] restating and enlarging upon Augustine's doctrine,[243] roundly affirms? The Middle Ages show some signs of sympathy with this teaching, and here and there the literature sounds notes that hearten the reader.[244] The relatively few partisans of this optimistic exegesis see Ethiopia as a symbol of humanity in quest of salvation. By her effort to reach out to Christ she proves her will to be saved by grace and can therefore be likened in merit to the sinner who strives to free himself from his sin. Thenceforth God helps her to shed the blackness of her skin and to "whiten herself."[245] The waters of Baptism wash away the blackness of sin; the light of Christ's teaching enlightens the conscience. For the theologians, Ethiopia thereupon becomes only the symbol of attachment to the world, but the Ethiopian can turn away from the world and attach himself to God.[246]

The fact remains that as the great majority of Western Christians felt about it, black meant sin, and with this color went sadness, death, and danger. When the Ethiopian goes to the baths, says Gregory the Great,[247] he cannot blame the proprietor if he comes out as black as he went in. The analogy limps badly, but, we are told, it is interesting to the extent that it reflects a proverb popular in the sixth century. As early as Victor of Vita,[248] a suddenly spreading darkness and fetid smells were associated with the arrival of *Aethiopes*. The Carolingian world went further still. The little known *Aethiops* disappears, but the color black is more than ever a symbol of sin. Audradus Modicus[249] imagines himself being led into the darkness of Hell by the wicked people of the *Aethiopes*: the image is poetic, not exegetical. Hincmar describes sinful bishops as blackened and in tatters after their death.[250] A well in Purgatory contains water as black as pitch, out of which issue huge flames and demons. A count whose body was blackened by sin recovers his original color through the power of prayer.[251] The linking together of the four ideas—black, other, sinner, dangerous—runs throughout all the manifestations of medieval Western Christian thought. The Saracen, the "enemy" in the epic poems,[252] and the bird that distracts the saint at prayer[253] are black.

12

12. *Exultet* roll (detail). South Italy, late XII century. Troia, cathedral, Archivio capitolare.

Dissident though it was, the Christian East gave evidence of agreeing with this association of ideas. As early as the sixth century the *Life of Severus* by Zacharias Scholasticus assimilates sin and blackness.[254] The *Nestorian History*[255] tells of the conversion of al-Nu‘mān, son of al-Mundhir, by Christ: he fell asleep, and two figures seen in vision assailed him, one of them being that of a black man whose physiognomy struck terror and whose odor was repulsive. A little known example, the legend of Abba Moses gives us a gauge of the depth to which these ideas had penetrated Christian thought. He was a monk of Ethiopian origin, who apparently lived in Egypt in the desert of Scete and died a martyr in the fourth century.[256] Interesting details were tacked onto this simple theme from time to time. The *Historia Lausiaca* firmly asserts that Moses was "Ethiopian and black."[257] Greek and Ethiopian sources (the Ethiopian being much later than the others) affirm that he, a man of unusual physical strength, had been a libertine given to every excess. The first monk whom Moses, in quest of God, met in the desert was terrified by his physical appearance.[258] Becoming a monk himself, the future saint was beset by violent temptations, particularly of a sexual nature.[259] The *Apophthegmata*,[260] which are of Greek origin, introduce two episodes of conclusive significance. The monks, gathered together at Scete, treat Moses with open contempt and ask why this Ethiopian has come among them. We cannot suppose that the Egyptians shunned and despised the blacks, whose lives were so closely intertwined with their own: iconography, and notably the *Ashburnham Pentateuch*, have shown us the contrary. Therefore we must resort to an allegorical interpretation, as we see from the second episode. Moses becomes a cleric, and the ordaining bishop says to him, "Now, Abba Moses, you are whitened wholly." Moses answers, "May I be whitened inside as well as out!" The story continues as Moses allows himself to be driven out of the chapel by his brethren and exclaims, "They are right about thee, thy skin is as black as coal. Since thou are not a man, why goest thou among men?"[261] cf. fig. 87 Thus the person of Abba Moses seems to epitomize the *Aethiops*-sinner's symbolic road from the darkness of sin to the light of grace as the Greek, and especially the Western European Christian, would have thought of it.

In Western Europe this preconception, which ambiguously linked blackness with sin—at once repulsive and alluring, like temptation itself—sometimes occasioned the creation of works of high quality. On a fragment from an eleventh-century mosaic, now in Vercelli,[262] two men-at-arms, Fel fig. 13 and Fol, confront each other. The difficulty lies in the interpretation of these names. According to Dionysius of Tell-Mahrē, who took his information from an *Epitome*, Alexander had met Phol, king of India, in mortal combat, in which the king lost his life.[263] The Pseudo-Methodius of Patara[264]—a Syrian author who wrote in the last third of the seventh century and was translated into Latin in a Frankish region in the eighth—has it that Phol was a king of Ethiopia whose daughter Chuseth became the wife of Philip of Macedonia. In other versions Phol is identified with Porus, king of India. But it is much more interesting to note that Isaiah uses this name to designate the third son of Ham or Africa, *Fūl* or *Pūl*, which later became *Pūt* or *Fūt*.[265] All the ancient versions have *Ful* or *Pul*, the Syriac and Arabic versions have *Pul*, and the Septuagint made it *Phut*, the form

13

13. Combat between Fel and Fol. Mosaic fragment. From the Collegiate Church of Sta. Maria Maggiore in Vercelli. XI century. Vercelli, Museo Camillo Leone.

we know. Whichever version is adopted, Fol or Ful is supposed to be an "Oriental" or "African" warrior-king. But in our mosaic it is the white warrior who is called Fol, and not the black, as we might have expected. Fel, the name given to the black, may come from the allegorical use of the Latin word *fel*, meaning bile, to designate choler and the color black.[266] The fact remains that it is hard to understand the supposed fight between a king from the East and this allegorical black. The puzzle remains unsolved.

Much clearer in its meaning is an Italian *Exultet* roll on parchment, figs. 12, 16 executed late in the twelfth century.[267] On the theme of the Easter Night liturgy the painter introduced, among the scenes of pardon and reconciliation, the illumination of the Night—symbol of the darkness of sin—by the light of Christ. But here we are already in the twelfth century and in an area of Europe where important developments were taking place.

14. Forces of evil and the "second death." *Apocalypse*, fol. 37r (detail). IX century. Valenciennes, Bibliothèque municipale.

15. Satan unbound goes to tempt the Nations, Gog and Magog. Beatus of Liébana, *Commentary on the Apocalypse*, fol. 155v. 1086. Burgo de Osma, Cathedral Museum.

16. Detail of figure 12: Allegory of Easter Night. *Exultet* roll. South Italy, late XII century. Troia, cathedral, Archivio capitolare.

17. Parable of the Rich Man and Lazarus (detail): Hell. *Codex Aureus*, fol. 117v. Echternach, 1043-46. Escorial, Real Monasterio, Biblioteca.

14

15

WHITE GOD AND DARK DEVIL[268]

Where did the Christians' Devil and his demons get their dark color?[269] A fascinating question, but one that we shall not probe here: for us the fact is a basic assumption. The iconography of the High Middle Ages represented the Devil and his minions in dark colors ranging from dark brown to purple.[270] This fact ties in with all the allegories of human fears that we find as far back as we may go into the past,[271] but it does not mean that the Devil or demons were represented with the features of a *black man*. Yet this symbolism, devoid though it may have been of any judgment unfavorable to Africans, nevertheless fitted into the pattern of the *Aethiops*-sinner whose color signified commitment to evil. It also harmonized with the convention, to be considered further on, by which the figure of an executioner was normally that of a black. Thus the dark-color symbolism once again conveyed an ambiguous typology that impressed itself upon the unconscious of the Western Christian. To judge by the iconography of the Devil that we have managed to examine, it seems to us that in the period when Europe was again coming face-to-face with blacks, the demon lost his explicitly dark character and took on a more fantastic appearance.[272] This is something that would be worth studying statistically, area by area, throughout Europe.

As early as the eight century, a fresco in Sta. Maria Antiqua in Rome[273] shows Christ, as he descends into Limbo, trampling a dark figure underfoot. In the same period a black demon also appears in a manuscript executed in Italy and now kept in Patmos:[274] it is in very poor condition, but there are unmistakable traces of black paint on the demon's body, which is that of a man. The example of the fresco in Rome not being absolutely certain, the Patmos manuscript must be considered the oldest testimony of the blackening of the demon at present known to us, but the field is wide open for further discoveries. In fact, what we have found so

16

17

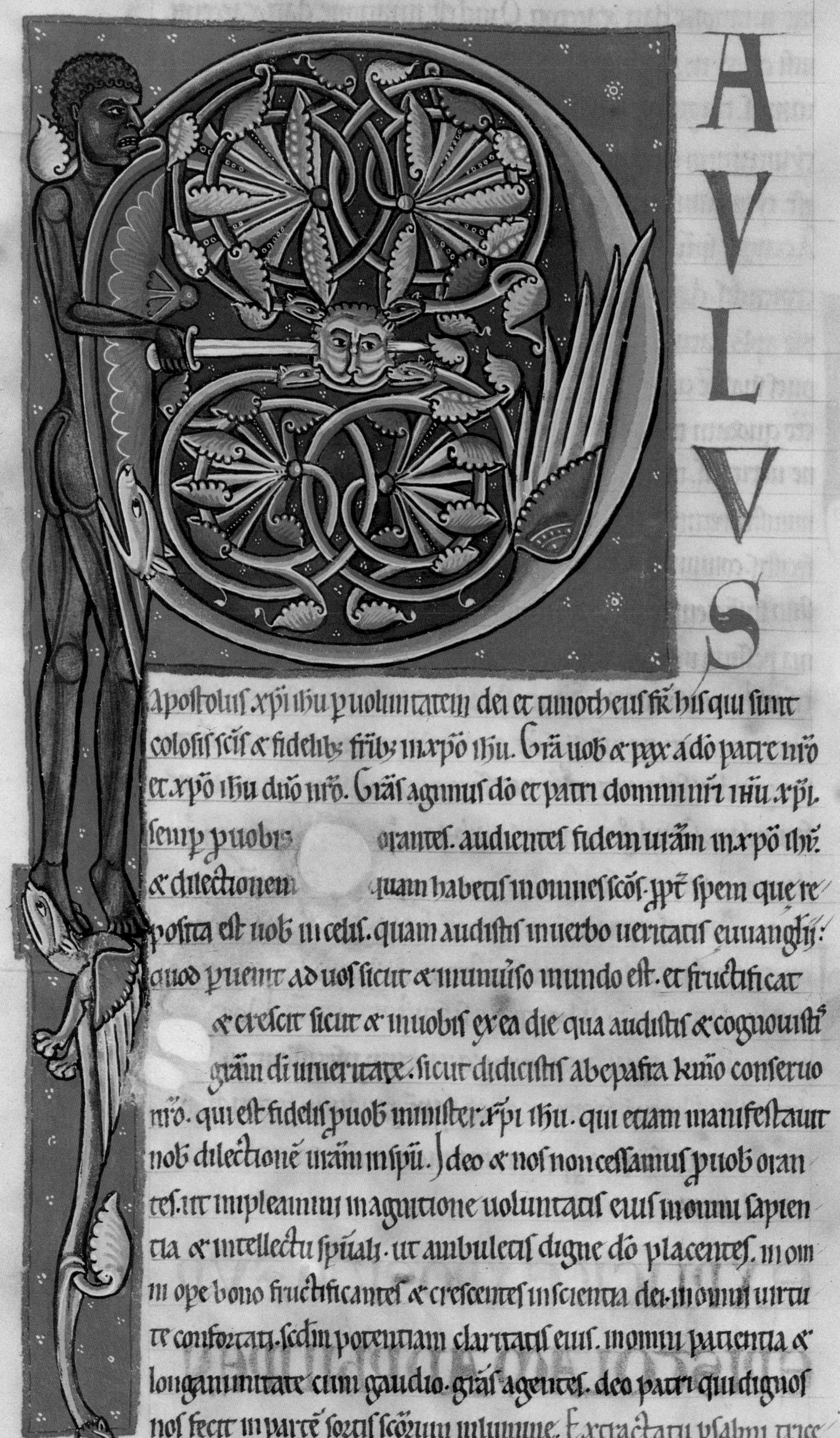

18

18. Decorated initial. Florus, *Expositio in epistolas Pauli*, vol. II, fol. 67v. From Corbie Abbey. 1164. Paris, Bibliothèque nationale.

19. Christ delivering the Gospel to St. John. Beatus of Liébana, *Commentary on the Apocalypse*, fol. 4v. From the Abbey of Saint-Sever. 1028-72. Paris, Bibliothèque nationale.

far, especially in the Carolingian geographic area, are completely conventional representations, and they could probably be multiplied without adding much of value to our inquiry. Until Asian influences modified his image, the dark demon reigned over medieval illumination.

The Apocalypse brings us far more numerous and more interesting illustrations of this subject than all the other books of the Bible. A ninth-century manuscript[275] shows how deeply this text inspired the artists: the throne of Christ is put in contrast to the dark dynamism of the forces of evil and the "second death." When a systematic study of the incomparable series of manuscripts related to the *Commentary on the Apocalypse* by Beatus of Liébana is made, it will probably bring out some astonishing images. For the moment it is good to show the rather spectacular black Satan in the manuscript at Burgo de Osma that treats of Gog and Magog.[276] Yet all the dark-hued individuals represented are not supposed to be demons. We have an example in the *Commentary on the Apocalypse* from the Abbey of Saint-Sever,[277] dating from the eleventh century, showing the slightly caricatured head of a black that has nothing diabolic about it, and is, for the time being, one of our oldest European figurations of a black.

fig. 14
fig. 15
fig. 19

We find the incarnation of evil in more or less fantastic and outlandish forms in a considerable number of manuscripts. We may mention, among

19

20

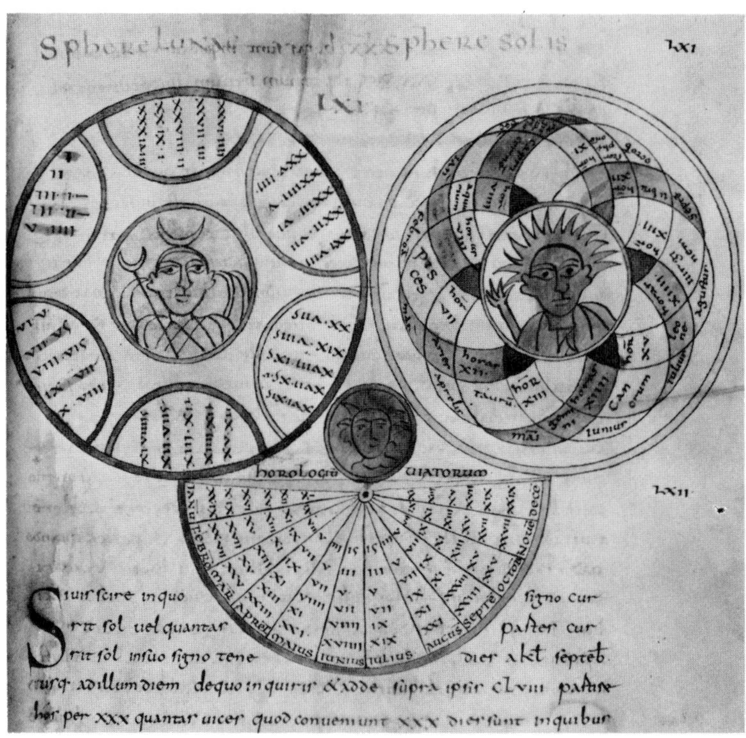

21

20. Temptation of Christ. Historiated initial. *Otbert Psalter*, fol. 101ʳ. From Saint-Bertin Abbey in Saint-Omer. About 1000. Boulogne-sur-Mer, Bibliothèque municipale.

21. "Sphere Lunae-Sphere Solis." Isidore of Seville, *De natura rerum*, fol. 53ʳ (detail). North France, IX century. Laon, Bibliothèque municipale.

others, the *Codex Aureus* in the Escorial:[278] a huge devil, in chains, lies in fig. 17
Hell (symbolized by tongues of flame), ready to gather in the soul of the Wicked Rich Man. These flames appear as symbols in the hair of certain demons, whether Satan himself in the *Commentary on the Apocalypse* in Gerona Cathedral[279] or the Tempter of Christ in a historiated initial in the *Otbert Psalter*[280] (about 1000). O. A. Erich noted eight other examples of this fig. 20
iconographic treatment of demon figures,[281] and brought out the fact that the Western representation differs from the Byzantine, especially from the Carolingian period onward.[282] In his opinion the origin of the radiating hair arrangement goes back to the serpentine style of antiquity,[283] but we think it more likely that we are dealing with a solar theme connected with cults condemned by Christianity.

A celebrated impost at Quintanilla de las Viñas[284] represents a sun with hair standing out like rays, waited upon by two angels; that was enough to make some historians associate this particular church with a heretical cult.[285] The same theme, but Christianized and lacking the radiating hair arrangement, is repeated on another impost in the same chapel. The recurrence of this image interests us: for instance, the mythology of the African sun led the artist who illustrated a manuscript of Isidore of Seville
in the ninth century[286] to represent the sun as a personage with radiating fig. 21
tresses of light brown hair. This type of hair arrangement is worth an overall study, which should lead to some rewarding insights regarding artistic exchanges.

Given the present state of our knowledge, it is very hard to find a place in this study for a series of decorated initials dating from the twelfth century, in which the figures of partially or totally nude men with more or less clearly marked "black" characteristics form the stem of the capital letter *P*. These initials appear in a group of manuscripts executed in

22

22. Decorated initial introducing St. Paul's Epistle to the Colossians. *New Testament and Psalter*, fol. 91v. Second half XII century. Bourg-en-Bresse, Bibliothèque municipale.

northern France, and they include one common trait: they are all connected with St. Paul's Epistles,[287] or, at times, with the commentaries on the Epistles written by Florus in the ninth century.[288] Neither the text of the Epistles nor Florus's text furnishes a reason for the presence of these dark blue figures. One of the most "Negroid" in appearance, if only because of the hair done in tight curls, is in the Corbie manuscript.[289] More exotic is fig. 18 the figure wearing an odd-looking, short garment, seen in a manuscript of the New Testament now in Bourg-en-Bresse:[290] unfortunately its prov- fig. 22 enance is not known. The reason for the appearance of this type in northern France is still not clear to us.[291] In 1959 J. Porcher proposed a Byzantine influence to explain this exoticism;[292] but we are far from the Byzantine world and very late in time. Recently C. de Mérindol[293] has come up with some new and impressive conclusions apropos of the manuscript from Corbie:[294] this manuscript was transcribed at Corbie in 1164 by Jean d'Amiens, a professional copyist, and decorated by a painter named Felix, who came from England.[295] Regarding Felix's treatment of this sort of initial the author writes, "The shape of the initial is that of a dragon,[296] or a lion, the body stretched out with one paw lifted,[297] or a lion or animal flattened out,[298] . . . or a nude man."[299] These observations are arresting. A painter comes over from England and introduces at Corbie a style of ornament known in his native surroundings, and in this style there is a strong trace of exoticism. Comparing the manuscripts he attributes to Felix in England and France, C. de Mérindol studied the blue color so characteristic of MS. lat. 11576: it is a technique peculiar to this painter, or, in any case, to the school that trained him.[300] So we are brought back to the uncertainties we started with. If the connection with a chance Anglo-Saxon source gives more coherence to this group of letters, it is still no easier to see in them any intention to allude to Africa and the blacks.

The demon whom we have seen in fantastic forms is more interesting when, in order to tempt men, he assumes a human shape.[301] We wish we had a number of representations comparable to the one in the Collegiate Church of San Isidoro in León,[302] which shows St. Martin at grips with a fig. 23 demon in the shape of a black child. For this theme Gregory the Great furnished a prototype which, one would think, should have been of more inspiration to artists. A monk is unable to keep his mind on his prayers. The abbot is watching him, and "he noticed that a little Negro was tugging at the cloak of the monk who could not stay at prayer. ..." The monk receives the treatment prescribed by the Rule and is beaten with rods, whereupon his black tempter leaves him in peace, and, says Gregory, "thus the ancient Enemy, as if he himself had been whipped, no longer dared to disturb [the monk's] thoughts."[303]

The Ethiopian Synaxarion[304] describes how the Devil appeared as an old man to two men in order to distract them from their duty; but their holiness, and the help they had from Christ, unmasked him, and he resumed his "normal" shape. "'O Being filled with evil, father of lies,' the two men exclaim, 'begone from us, for you are going against the way of God!' Immediately his appearance was transformed and he became like a black slave." Thus the Ethiopians themselves adopted this image! The Byzantines, in the twelfth century, used the same sort of images to evoke

23. St. Martin resisting a demon. Mural painting. XII century. León, Collegiate Church of San Isidoro.

24. Healing of the Gadarene demoniacs. *Psalter*, fol. 3v (detail). From Canterbury. About 1200. Paris, Bibliothèque nationale.

25. Beheading of John the Baptist. *Psalter*, fol. 2v (detail). From Canterbury. About 1200. Paris, Bibliothèque nationale.

26. St. Peter confounds Simon Magus by reviving a dead man. Stained-glass window (detail). About 1215. Troyes, Cathedral of SS. Peter and Paul, absidal chapel.

23

the intervention of the demon. A sorcerer is bathing with some other people and falls to quarreling with them. He calls for the demon. Very soon the bathers hurry out of the water, pursued by beings blacker than pitch.[305]

Most frequently the Devil acts without letting himself be seen. He intervenes particularly in cases of possession, and it takes all the exorcists' skill to drive him out. Such a scene of triumph was often used by painters. We shall mention only one example, the illustration of an English Psalter dating from the early thirteenth century,[306] in which the healing of the men of Gadara possessed by the Devil is included.[307] Here the "possessed" are as black as the demons driven out of them, and the painter has faithfully rendered the miracle by showing the swine plunging headlong into the sea once the evil spirits have gone into them. Byzantium also represented the demons in dark colors[308]—but how early, or under what influences, we do not know. On this subject there is much research to be done: here we simply point out the interest such a study would have. fig. 24

24

25

26

27

27, 28. Scenes from the Passion of Christ. Details of a painted panel. Late XII century. Barcelona, Museo de Bellas Artes de Cataluña.

Lucifer, the fallen angel of light, occupies a complex position in our inquiry. As the Devil he is almost never represented with the physical traits of a Negro, and we rarely find him colored black. It is true that purely technical considerations may explain this peculiarity. In fact it seems to us that the painters were reluctant to represent Satan, that angelic creature, in the form of a man, even an *Aethiops*, because they were afraid of erring on the side of anthropomorphism. Hence, perhaps, the adoption of "exceptional" characteristics—the solar hair arrangement, suitable to an "angel of light," and the horns, which, with the passage of time, came to distinguish the Devil more and more clearly from the Negro. Conversely, when the Evil One crossed into the created order of the natural world and appeared as a man in order to tempt men, artists seem to have been no more hesitant than writers about introducing "Negroid" characteristics.

The executioner or torturer, as an agent directly involved in the Devil's work, is sometimes portrayed as black. Here color and ethnic connection are joined, and in many cases such personages are carefully depicted with the physical traits of the Negro.

Although the text does not describe the details of color that concern us, the *Passion of Perpetua* written by Tertullian in the second century constitutes our earliest witness of the presence of an "African" headsman.[309] Yet it was not until the twelfth century that iconography began to portray the type. Thereafter we cannot dispel the thought that once contact with areas where there were blacks was renewed, artists who chose the black as the type of the executioner knew exactly what they were doing. The date explains why we find personages whose features are "Negroid" rather than simply dark in color. It was the time when, as we shall soon see, contacts of all kinds were reestablished between Western Europe and Africa and the Africans, and also when some sectors of European Christianity raised again, and in very positive terms, the problem of the possible sainthood of a black; and at this very time the menace represented by "the black" was brought into sharper focus by an iconography thenceforth no longer subject to change. The executioner with "Negroid" features survived for a long period as the negative countertype of the saved and sainted Negro who made his

28

29

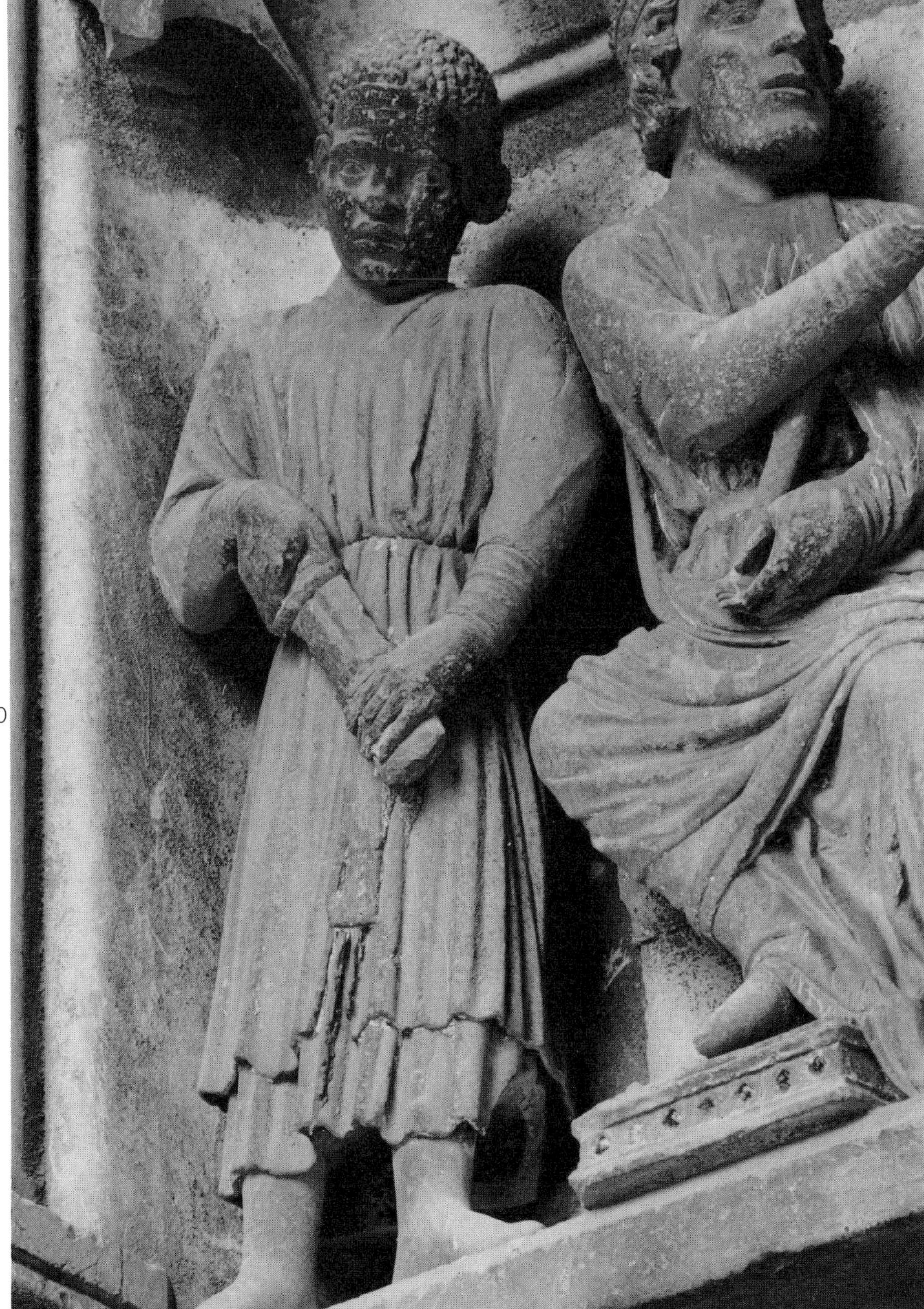

30

29. Scourging. Historiated initial. *Evangelistary*, fol. 6r. From Marbach-Schwarzenthann. Late XII century. Laon, Bibliothèque municipale.

30. Black executioner in the Judgment of Solomon. Carved tympanum (detail). About 1220. Chartres, Cathedral of Notre-Dame, portal of the north transept.

31

32

33

31. Beheading of John the Baptist. Carved tympanum (detail). About 1260. Rouen, Cathedral of Notre-Dame, north portal of the west façade.

32. St. Stephen led before the judge. Carved tympanum (detail). After 1257. Paris, Cathedral of Notre-Dame, portal of the south transept.

33. Judgment of Solomon. Relief. Late XIII or early XIV century. Auxerre, Cathedral of St-Etienne, west façade.

appearance in the thirteenth and fourteenth centuries. By then we are in a realistic world of ideas quite different from that of the Carolingian era, but the descriptions written by Carolingian authors directly prepared their successors to give admittance to the image of the black executioner.

Spain probably provides the oldest examples, even though the value of the evidence we are about to discuss is highly questionable. On a panel in the Barcelona museum,[310] the original destination of which is the subject of several hypotheses,[311] are painted several scenes from the Passion of Christ. The scenes include some strange, dark individuals, and it is clear that the painter intended to set them apart. They are the only ones whose faces and hands are dark in color, and their clothing is distinctive: a light-colored cloth, knotted under the chin, covers their heads, and the same cloth is wrapped around their waists in the form of a fringed sash.[312] Probably they are kindred to the Saracens (whom the Reconquest had taught Spaniards to hate, whereas they had coexisted without problems for two or three centuries), quite as much as to Negroes. And yet in Spain, both Muslim[313] and Christian,[314] blacks were a familiar sight. We may ask whether the

figs. 27, 28

34. Stoning of St. Stephen. *Images de la vie du Christ et des saints*, fol. 76r. Hainaut (?), about 1280-90. Paris, Bibliothèque nationale.

35. Betrayal of Judas. *Sarum Missal*, fol. 150v. Salisbury, XIII century. Manchester, John Rylands Library.

36. Carrying of the Cross. *Images de la vie du Christ et des saints*, fol. 37v. Hainaut (?), about 1280-90. Paris, Bibliothèque nationale.

painter was deliberately presenting a hateful image, or at least a very unfriendly one, of a nonwhite executioner. To answer the question we would first have to know the whole composition of which this panel was only a segment. The scenes measure about twenty centimeters (5 ½ in.) in height. Set before the gaze of Christians they might well be an incitement, poignant to us, to hate "the other."

If the Barcelona painters do not reveal all their secrets, there are other more explicit witnesses. A manuscript dating from the end of the twelfth century and probably executed in Alsace[315] leaves us still in doubt: the torturer who scourges Christ here is simply a "foreigner," as his costume and particularly his headdress indicate. In the same northern areas, however, the black executioner—black in the purest ethnic sense of the word—eventually took over. What is the origin of this iconography? One might

fig. 29

34

35

37

37. Executioner's head. Fragment from Rheims Cathedral. 1247-55. Rheims, Palais du Tau.

38, 39. Scenes from the life of St. Catherine (detail): executioner near Emperor Maxentius (before and after restoration). Stained-glass window. XII century. Angers, Cathedral of St-Maurice, nave.

38

39

hold Guibert of Nogent[316] responsible by reason of his story about Baudry, bishop of Laon, and his "black" laboring man, who terrified those who saw him;[317] but to be convinced of this we would have to know by whom and how widely Guibert was read. Here at any rate we come upon a widespread theme. There is the black man beheading John the Baptist, as we find him both in a Canterbury Psalter (early thirteenth century)[318] and in the tympanum at Rouen (about 1260), in which the sculptor impressed upon his subject an undeniable stamp of truth and plastic beauty.[319] The same description fits the young black about to draw his sword in the scene of the Judgment of Solomon on the north portal of Chartres Cathedral.[320] This theme is used a little later on the west façade of the Cathedral of Auxerre,[321] where the executioner, again with "Negroid" features, wears the cuirass of a man-at-arms. We find him again on the Cathedral of Notre-Dame in Paris, dressed the same way, leading St. Stephen before his judge.[322] He also appears, clad in chain mail, in a manuscript (end of the thirteenth century) that may have been done in Hainaut, notably in the illustration of the Carrying of the Cross.[323] In other paintings in the same manuscript depicting scenes of martyrdom—the Stoning of St. Stephen, for instance[324]—the executioners are dark-skinned, their features are "Negroid" or else caricatured, and they wear tunics belted at the waist.

fig. 25 fig. 31 fig. 30 fig. 33 fig. 32 fig. 36 fig. 34

Thus the tradition, so prejudicial to the *Aethiopes* ever since Bede, was firmly maintained. A Rhemish sculpture done in mid-thirteenth century shows two extremes. This is a head attributed to one of Christ's executioners,[325] but it is hard to imagine how so lovely a work of art could be intended to illustrate a theme so dishonorable: the sculptor kept the unmistakable "Negroid" facial traits but rejected the "traditional," crimped-curl

fig. 37

hair style. This type of representation is seen in stained-glass windows, but there the black color is rendered by a bluish tint, following the accepted convention: this is the way a servingman, thick-lipped and kinky-haired, fig. 26 appears in several medallions of a window illustrating the life of St. Peter, in the Cathedral of Troyes.[326]

The black, menacing personage is seen several times in a thirteenth-century Betrayal of Judas:[327] here religious hostility toward the Jews led to fig. 35 a curious "surcharge" of black or dark colors on their figures. This deliberately contrasting image—Judas is not blackened, which would be "anti-historical"—looks very important to us, since it shows the combining of two essentially religious hostilities directed toward two human groups, the Jews and the blacks.

Rather unrewarding as the study of the executioner may be in its iconographic findings, it is nonetheless worth pursuing, since it provides the historian with first-rate statistical evidence pertinent to the history of thought and social attitudes. How many generations of Christians have been conditioned by looking at a grimacing black man torturing Christ or his saints? The mental set was so tenacious that in the twentieth century a window restorer working on the image of a white headsman in the service figs. 38, 3 of the Emperor Maxentius thought nothing of transforming him into a black by doing his hair in tight little curls, totally unlike the original.[328]

Ignorance and prejudices arising from many sources created an assortment of clichés on Africa and its peoples, clichés that were reinforced by the extraordinarily crude equivalence imagined by Christians between a color and the most disturbing aspects of the Christian world. A whole mental structure, unconscious for the most part, was erected to the detriment of the blacks,[329] although in some cases and to some degree other facts and other experiences could, as we shall see, modify this state of mind.

II

THE BLACK AND HIS COLOR: FROM SYMBOLS TO REALITIES

The second half of the eleventh century was a period during which the types of relations that had existed between Western Europe and the Mediterranean and Eastern world were profoundly modified. The peoples of the West had lived in a closed economy. They had been sure of being *right* in religion and culture, in the midst of a world awash in error. All this gave way to a prolonged phase of expansion. In various forms and with varying degrees of rapidity and violence, this expansion, beginning after 1050, went on to its imperialistic climax in the nineteenth century. The long adventure, which across the centuries took the shape of an illusory Westernization of the rest of the world and a prideful reinforcement of white ethnocentrism, was underway.

The expansion of the West, many-sided as it was, did not proceed without checks and surprises. Social groupings whose levels of culture and whose deep concerns were widely diversified came into contact with the Byzantine East and the lands of Islam, and the reaction to this contact varied in the different segments of European society. Rome and its bishop, the Germanic emperor and his court, the retinue of the kings of Sicily, the Venetian traders and the Genoese, the feudal lordlings who were the blood and bone of the Crusades, the monks of Cluny—to take a few examples—did not look upon relations with Byzantium and Islam in the same way. We must be on our guard against thinking too quickly of a sort of "one West," and we shall have to make many careful analyses before abandoning ourselves to the abstract joys of generalization.

Bonds more numerous than one would think had often continued to exist, at least between the Ottonian Empire and Byzantium: now there was a coherent renewal of economic relations, soon to be followed by clashes of various kinds with the Eastern Christian world. There the men of the West, as we shall see, found a "Byzantine outlook" on black people, to which we cannot remain indifferent. There was a cleft between Western and Byzan-

40. Yaḥyā al-Wasītī. Ship crossing the Persian Gulf. Al-Harīrī, *Maḳāmāt*, fol. 119ᵛ. 1236-37. Paris, Bibliothèque nationale.

tine mental attitudes, and the military expeditions of the Crusades deepened it beyond repair in 1204. After that date the "Orthodox" world was more foreign to the "Roman" than it had ever been before. Yet the least that can be said is that the Byzantines certainly had an influence on the image which Western Europeans formed of the East[1] and of the blacks, whether the Europeans were conscious of it or not.

In Spain and Sicily, on the African coast, and in the Near East, the Christian warriors from the West, in the name of their Church and its values, came into more or less violent contact with the lands of Islam; and in these regions *physical* contact with blacks began again. Blacks were present in the Islamic lands in greater or lesser numbers. Their complex social situation was disconcerting to the European, accustomed as he was to the simplified cultural distinctions of an earlier period. Blacks might be hired soldiers or Muslims fighting for their faith, slaves clinging to their traditional religion or servants converted to Islam and treated with respect, advisors who were listened to and sometimes powerful, as in Fatimid Egypt,[2] or the whipping boys of masters whose idiosyncracies were not always different—particularly in Spain—from those of Christians.

The partitioning of society masked conflicts of ideology. This is particularly true of Castile, due to the marked convergence of interests and lifestyles within the Muslim and Christian aristocracies. For Western Europeans the renewal of contact with Islam and the blacks who lived in Muslim territory provoked complex reactions which varied according to region, time, and type of society. It would be a serious mistake to try to determine a single direction, or a single and characteristic attitude, even within one region. Castilians, for instance, were at first acutely aware of the power of black fighting men, and in time transferred the old feelings of hostility from the *Aethiops* to the "black Moor," who thereupon, being caught up in the wave of anti-Muslim intolerance stimulated by the Cluniacs,[3] particularly in Spain, was hated and damned like any other Muslim warrior. At the same time Castilians saw blacks serving in the houses of wealthy Muslims, who had begun to buy them. Lastly—and here was a vital question that could not be dodged—the black was a man created by God and capable of being redeemed by baptism. But the dominant attitude, in the lands of Castile, was for a long time one of hostility. In Aragon, on the other hand, the situation was less clear, and it seems that the fact that blacks, like other men, were called to salvation very soon prevailed over unfriendly attitudes toward them. Similar analyses must be undertaken with regard to each case, each zone, and each period of contact, but the different positions taken by the Castilians and the Aragonese show us how dangerous hasty generalizations can be. With these reservations regarding caution and methodology in mind, we can try to define certain overall attitudes and certain important problems. We can be sure, for instance, that the case of the Iberian Peninsula is one most worthy of study, due to the contradictory elements of religious and social tolerance and ideological intolerance there manifest, the intolerance having been brought in mainly by the Cluniacs and the "Romanization" of the Church in Castile during the twelfth century.

In the same Mediterranean area the attitudes of the Byzantines and the Italians in the eleventh and twelfth centuries deserve equal attention. The

القرآن ثم قرأ بعد أساطير تلاها وزخارف جلاها وقال اركبوا فيها بسم الله مجراها
ومرساها ثم تنفس تنفس المغرمين أو عباد الله المكرمين وقال أما أنا

problem of the Crusaders' reactions and their possible contacts with blacks should also be looked at; on this point the evidence in art is very disappointing, and much more extensive research, especially in the texts, is called for. It already is clear that the attitude of the Crusaders, most of whom were "French," toward Islam and eventually toward blacks was—particularly when they were from the North—far more abstract and less complex than that of the Castilians. When the sense of defeat took hold of the Crusaders after Hattin, they put no limit to their rigid hostility toward Islam,[4] and it is likely enough that at times this attitude included the blacks.

In imperial circles the fall of Edessa in 1144 symbolized the failure of the Crusades, and the imperial army's inability to recapture the city gave rise, in the empire, to reactions of a totally different kind. Here there was little or no direct contact with blacks; yet ideology would eventually seize upon them as major characters in a worldwide reshuffle in which they, over and above the Muslims and the Jews, might foretoken the hope of an expansion of Christendom. All this came out in the realm of imagination and imagery, but the consequences are of capital importance for our purpose, since it was in the lands of the empire that the most remarkable transformations in the iconography of the blacks took place. Favorable attitudes toward them had a continuous flowering, in our opinion, from the twelfth to the fifteenth century. Then the Germanic Empire was forcefully recalled to a sense of the Muslim peril by the Ottoman invasions deep into Balkan Europe; and this clearly shows that the idealized image of the black had no hold on reality, and that facts impose a revision of dreams.

At any rate the black, for the Italians and also for the French, especially in the South, was now a being of flesh and blood whose presence prompted questions. Of course his image—more accurate now that one could see him—could still be used to represent the demon or the executioner,[5] as before, but one could no longer imagine without some nuances that blackness, as a color, was symbolic of sin and damnation. The old stereotypes needed revision. Furthermore, the occasional conversion of black people raised the concrete problem of the liberation of these "captives of the Muslims" at the social level and of their call to salvation on the spiritual plane. The thirteenth century—the century of the Mendicants and the Friars Preachers—could not escape the question that rose out of the depths of the Christian ages: are not the blacks, like all the descendants of Adam and Noah, called to salvation? And perhaps this new Mediterranean insight was also to reach the empire, reinforcing the favorable images of the black that were developing there since the twelfth century.

Europe, officially unified in its Christianity, was made up of sections unevenly developed from every point of view, and each section saw the black in its own way. We shall try, in the pages that follow, to discern the contrasting image that emerges from this mosaic of contradictions and convergences.

MEDITERRANEAN CHRISTIANS IN CONTACT WITH BLACKS AND MUSLIMS

Before presenting the artistic testimony of the Christians along the Mediterranean, it is important to ask, briefly, whether Islam had its own way of

41

42

41. Yaḥyā al-Wasiṭī. Slave market. Al-Harīrī, *Maḳāmāt*, fol. 105^r (detail). 1236-37. Paris, Bibliothèque nationale.

42. Abū Sa'īd a guest at supper with a group of savants. Al-Harīrī, *Maḳāmāt*, fol. 16^r (detail). Syria or Mesopotamia, 1222-23. Paris, Bibliothèque nationale.

43

regarding the blacks. (This short note must be seen as a very tentative first step in a field of investigation hitherto untouched.) For reasons that are known though often misinterpreted, the medieval Muslim world did not readily resort to the representation of the human figure, black or white. We do, however, have some few examples of paintings of blacks: slaves[6] and fig. 41 servants,[7] but also laborers,[8] appear in two Arabic manuscripts now in figs. 42, 4 Paris. Of course Western Europe had no knowledge of these images, but (if further research bears out early surmises) they still have a value, which lies in the fact that they show the place allotted to the black, at least in the Near East, by those who portrayed him. On this subject we shall have to broaden our investigation. Our first findings regarding the Muslim world prove again that the topic is of real importance.[9]

Muslim Spain, as we see it reflected in paintings in Christian manuscripts, presents a conception of relations between whites and blacks that denotes economic and social inequality. This is the case at least in the twelfth and thirteenth centuries, following the Almoravid episode that probably improved the situation of blacks then directly connected with the ruling powers and the army. The Muslim aristocracy openly treated their black serving people as inferiors, even though ideologically they acknowledged the religious equality and personal freedom of the blacks when these were Muslims. Spain therefore naturally becomes our first area of observation. According to the Arabic sources blacks were numerous in Spain: they came there at least from the tenth century onward,[10] under different auspices and with varying status, although their social level was stabilized during the Almohad period.

The Christians' first impression of the black was probably the one based upon their encounter on the battlefield. It is likely that the image of the "black Moor" derives directly from clashes, at the end of the eleventh century, with the Almoravid armies in which there were black contingents. In the thirteenth century we find the black Moor in the enemy camp, as we see from a mural painting, preserved in Barcelona, illustrating the conquest figs. 43, 4 of Majorca by James I of Aragon.[11] For the second half of the thirteenth century we gather a rich harvest of precise information regarding the Castilian territory from the work of Alfonso X of Castile. Under this

43. Conquest of Majorca by James I of Aragon. Mural painting. From Barcelona, Palacio Aguilar. XIII century. Barcelona, Museo de Bellas Artes de Cataluña.

44. Detail of figure 43: defending the ramparts.

44

sovereign Castile developed a real phobia for Islam. Cluny's influence was strong, and iconographic themes were increasingly drawn from the common French source, notably from Peter Comestor. Alfonso X thought of himself as "European": he spent years trying to secure the imperial crown. The immense *oeuvre* brought to completion around him is studded with contradictions. On one side, it reflects the specifically Hispanic character of this heir to the preceding centuries and of the mixed Islamic-Christian society which had developed over four or five hundred years in the south of Spain; on the other side, it shows his desire to establish his connection with the beliefs and images of Western Europe,[12] even if this effort came somewhat late.

The paintings in a manuscript dating from 1283[13] show us how realistically the people of this mixed world of Spain were depicted after the Reconquest.[14] Certain Muslim "noblemen" are sometimes dark-skinned, but servants are always distinguished by their dress from personages of quality, who wear turbans. Among the servants there are a few blacks. One is playing a harp,[15] another is engaged in a game of chess:[16] he does not wear a headcloth but a bandeau on the forehead.[17] figs. 47, 45

What we have here, then, are no longer allegorical scenes or metaphysical probings into the black's place in the Creation or in the economy of redemption, or a hostile symbolism in which black color is an omen of danger. The present pictures are done with a very high degree of precision in the details, perhaps based on Muslim manuscripts in some instances. The blacks in them (seldom in the foreground) are painted with great care for exactness by artists who unquestionably have rubbed elbows with these Africans who were brought to the Iberian Peninsula by the Muslims.

45. *Chessbook* of Alfonso X the Wise, fol. 55ʳ. 1283. Escorial, Real Monasterio, Biblioteca.

46. Astrological symbol for the stone *Zebech. Lapidario* of Alfonso X the Wise, fol. 95ᵛ (detail). XIII century. Escorial, Real Monasterio, Biblioteca.

47. *Chessbook* of Alfonso X the Wise, fol 22ʳ. 1283. Escorial, Real Monasterio, Biblioteca.

45

Between 1252 and 1284 Alfonso X directed the compilation of a book of songs in honor of Our Lady.[18] The text formed the basis for a very important series of illustrations, executed in Spain by local painters who probably were inspired in large part by French models,[19] but who based their pictures on their immediate surroundings, as J. Guerrero Lovillo's detailed study of the architectural elements and costumes clearly shows.[20] We must therefore carefully observe the ways in which blacks are inserted into this panorama of Spanish life in the thirteenth century.

In *Las Cántigas de Santa Maria* the image of the demon has undergone a marked transformation. As elsewhere in Western Europe at this time, he is most often represented here with the grotesque features of a dark but not black figure fitted out with wings like those of a bat.[21] In only one instance is he anthropologically black, recognizable by his profile and hair; moreover, the text of the *Cantiga* describes him as a black.[22]

Thus (with rare exceptions) blacks are lifted out of the metaphysical realm and are physically very present indeed. We see them first of all in the Muslim armies, where generally[23] they appear in lowly positions, on foot, bareheaded,[24] identifiable by the profile and hair. There are few of them fig. 48
and they only have "bit parts" in the big scenes.[25]

Sometimes one or two blacks are involved in an anecdote: for instance, two "Moors" are kidnapping a Christian count:[26] one of them is fig. 49
dark-skinned, the other black,[27] both bareheaded. While they lay hold of their victim, the noble Moors, turbaned, sit waiting in the boat that will carry the captive away. The next episode shows the same two "Moors" as rowers aboard the boat,[28] striving in vain to pull away from the bank, against the will of God, who protects the Christian.

So in this Spanish world the Christian painter associated the black with the Saracens, assigning him a minor place both as to numbers and as to social status. The representations of blacks are realistic in the portrayal of their roughhewn features and poor dress, and project a sharp contrast with the rich Moors, all of them "white."

46

47

48

48. Muslim expedition on Christian soil and taking booty. *Las Cántigas de Santa Maria, Cantiga* XLVI (detail). Second half XIII century. Escorial, Real Monasterio, Biblioteca.

The most astonishing of these "pictured strips" has a very different bearing: it gives us a new example of the black slave, christened "servitor" in the text. This is the illustration of *Cantiga* CLXXXVI, in six scenes.[29] fig. 50
We give here a translation of the legends that appear under each of the scenes.

> How a lady was asleep and her mother-in-law sent one of her Moors to dally with her
>
> How the old mother showed her son how his wife was bedded
>
> How they went to call upon the Justice and surprised the two of them sleeping
>
> How the Justice took the lady and the Moor and led them away to be burnt
>
> How the traitorous Moor was burnt and Our Lady protected the lady whom the fire did not touch
>
> How the lady told of her mother-in-law's deception and all were loud in their praise of Our Lady

49

49. Expedition at sea: kidnapping a Christian count. *Las Cántigas, Cantiga* XCV (detail). Second half XIII century. Escorial, Real Monasterio, Biblioteca.

50. Story of a woman accused of committing adultery with a Moor. *Las Cántigas, Cantiga* CLXXXVI. Second half XIII century. Escorial, Real Monasterio, Biblioteca.

51. Story of a Moor's conversion. *Las Cántigas, Cantiga* CXCII. Second half XIII century. Escorial, Real Monasterio, Biblioteca.

The significance of these images[30] is confirmed by a contemporary text: a girl guilty of fornication with a Moor is liable to the loss of half her goods for a first offense, and of all she has for a second one; the Moor is arrested and is liable to the death penalty.[31] This juridical text also explains that the Latin word *Sarracenus* is translated by *Moro* ("Moor") in the Romance tongue.[32] Our illustrator has therefore respected the conventions in force around him. Even if the woman is innocent—the necessary condition for the "happy ending"—it is hard to imagine a clearer intimation of interracial and interreligious sexual relations in Spain, or a more violently expressive taboo intended to foreclose the possibility of such goings-on. Here the image confirms the law, and how powerfully! And this time the Moor is black, so it is simply undeniable that in this particular case the horror of miscegenation redoubles the prohibition of sexual relations between persons of different religions. It is true that the text itself suggests another interpretation: the black is "one of *her* Moors," therefore a slave belonging to the mother-in-law. The social taboo is added to the others, but "honor is saved" so far as color is concerned. It probably was painful, in the thirteenth century, to portray a white man reduced to slavery, although, as we

CXCII

know, whites were in fact so reduced. The painter was completely untouched by the monstrous idea of the burning of the black man, whom his owner, the mother-in-law, led into a trap of which he was the sole victim, and who from all appearances got no pleasure out of the entrapment. Adopt whatever interpretation you please, in our view this image is one of the most remarkable racial-social manifestos produced by medieval Western Europe.

The most telling group of paintings, however, is that found at *Cantiga* CXCII;[33] its significance in our opinion, is due to the change of attitude it indicates. Here six pictures have to do with the conversion of a black Moor. In the first a Christian is urging him on; next he is struggling with a demon; then the Virgin comes to his assistance and encourages him to turn Christian. The Moor accepts her advice and is baptized, and the last picture shows him determined to be a faithful Christian throughout his life. The social key to the situation is found in the fourth scene: before he is baptized he informs his lord of his desire to be converted. The posture of the characters in this scene leaves no doubt about the status of the black: he is a slave, and his conversion[34] threatens to involve a change in his social position. This observation should be kept in mind, and we shall find its echo later on. Was the introduction of this thematic material due to the preaching of the Mendicants, who applied themselves so wholeheartedly to the conversion of the Infidel that during the thirteenth century several of them suffered martyrdom in northern Africa? A recent study[35] shows us how deeply the Catalan Raymond Lull was engaged in the effort to convert Infidels and pagans, and how optimistically and favorably he regarded them. Did such a change of attitude make itself felt among the people around Alfonso X,[36] as it did among those around the kings of Aragon? Was baptism about to wash out the color black? Here we touch on a fundamental point of discussion, especially as regards Spain: was the ideological change of community effected by baptism of a nature to eliminate the anthropological differences that previously had been signs indicating that blacks were under a curse? Herein lies the whole debate between, on the one hand, the Muslim and Christian position, according to which conversion and baptism made the new believers equal to other men in every respect, and, on the other, nineteenth- and twentieth-century racism, which makes anthropological characteristics paramount over ideological adherence. But during the Visigothic period the laws of the late seventh century in Spain spoke of "converted Jews," thereby maintaining a plainly ambiguous position of ethnic and cultural hostility toward the new Christians. When our research has been carried a good deal further, we shall have to look closely into the attitudes of the people of the thirteenth and later centuries toward blacks and Muslims who had accepted Christianity. At present we do not know enough to come to a conclusion.

fig. 51

At any rate the baptism theme spread after 1250 in Aragon as well as in Castile. An Aragonese *fuero* ("statute") issued in the second half of the thirteenth century indicates the will to facilitate such conversion:[37] baptism, and with it the social and moral rights attaching to it, was to be granted to any Jew or Muslim who sincerely desired to convert to Christianity. In this instance the text is less interesting than the images illustrating it. Historiated initials twice include black Muslims. In one, two blacks

52

are on trial before a king; the other, which is more explicit, shows us a black in the baptismal basin.[38] figs. 52, 53

The voluminous *Lapidario*[39] compiled by order of Alfonso X is entirely different in its inspiration. The Castilian king was interested in astronomy and astrology.[40] In his thought Saturn, whose effigy is in lead, corresponds to the color black and is the master of hard, black stones. (In general, he is considered to be the god of heathendom.)[41] We shall find an echo of these studies and syntheses in Bohemia during the fourteenth and fifteenth centuries. The *Lapidario* is a complex work and calls for a detailed study, which could not be undertaken here. Based on the astrological signs, the text consists of a catalogue of about six hundred stones; to each is appended a statement giving its physical description, origin, medical properties, and relation to the heavenly bodies. This work, as the introduction makes clear, is a compilation of ancient sources handed down through Arab traditions, translated from Arabic into Latin by a Jew who was Alfonso's physician, and from Latin into Old Castilian. The manuscript is abundantly illustrated with ornamental initials and with figures inscribed in the circles that alternate with the text, which is set out in two columns on each folio. The number of stones, the relative abundance of black-colored ones, and some few allusions to the Country of the Blacks, gave hope of finding images relevant to our subject.[42] Regrettably, the result is disappointing. At folio 4^{r}, two blacks are standing on the bank of a river. One of them is holding the stone called *Milititaz*, but the stone described as black in the left-hand column of the text is *Telliminuz*, whereas *Milititaz* is bright red. *Telliminuz* is

53

52. Two black captives on trial. Historiated initial. *Fueros del Reino de Aragon*, fol. 244^{r}. From Barcelona (?). About 1260-80. Aachen, Dr. Peter and Irene Ludwig Collection.

53. Baptism of a black man. Historiated initial (detail). *Fueros del Reino de Aragon*, fol. 242^{v}. From Barcelona (?). About 1260-80. Aachen, Dr. Peter and Irene Ludwig Collection.

54

55

54. Astrological symbol for the stone *Sanguina. Lapidario* of Alfonso X the Wise, fol. 94ᵛ (detail). XIII century. Escorial, Real Monasterio, Biblioteca.

55. Astrological symbol for the stone *Almagnitaz. Lapidario*, fol. 97ᵛ (detail). XIII century. Escorial, Real Monasterio, Biblioteca.

also the stone found in the Country of the Blacks, so it seems that the painter reversed the two images. At folio 19ᵛ, in a small circle at the bottom of the page, appear an Arab and a figure whose face has been blackened; the green stone described is called *Aliaza* and comes from Arabia. It is therefore hard to explain the presence of a black, unless we choose to find a social implication here and suppose that the black man is the Arab's servant. At folio 73ᵛ, two men with blackened faces appear in the head letter of the left-hand column: the stone in question is *Muruquid* and comes from a place called *Zurin*, near a city named *Aterbuliz* in the Country of the Blacks, but the stone is grey. The end of the manuscript sums up and completes some of the information. Here the illustration is haphazard: some circles were left empty, others enclose only line drawings, and in some cases the painter, hampered by the complexity of the descriptions given in the text, simply reproduced in series the related astrological signs. It is all the more important to call attention to the exceptional character of certain folios in which fantastic illustrations appear:[43] these fig. 46
seem to have influenced a number of fourteenth-century Bohemian manuscripts, to which we shall turn later. Moreover, in two instances the black silhouette corresponds directly to the text.[44] One of these concerns the stone called *Sanguina*, the efficacy of which is greatest when "the strength of the fig. 54
image of a black man" falls upon it; the second concerns the stone called *Almagnitaz*, which is subject to the same effects. Hence the paintings in this fig. 55
manuscript are rather disconcerting. The figures of blacks are not linked systematically with black stones,[45] nor with African origin, nor with the symbolism of color. All this is very disappointing, and it seems unlikely that a detailed study would bring out further information on this precise point. We should, however, note that Alfonso X's interest in astrological and astronomical questions, and in the signification and nature of stones, fits into a very broad European current, which had its beginnings in the eleventh century and involved South Italy and Sicily—and, by way of consequence, England.[46] The study cannot therefore be fully effective unless it is pursued within this general framework and the translations and interpretations made between the eleventh century and the late thirteenth are taken into account. In the case of Spain it must be noted that the twofold pull in the direction of Arab science and the Jewish input that prolonged it probably explains the simultaneous reaction of Roman religious orthodoxy, which clearly marks the works executed for Alfonso X. This fundamental contradiction was certainly very fruitful.

Thus Spain offers us a wide spectrum of attitudes with regard to black people, especially in the thirteenth century. The blacks found themselves in highly diverse situations—in the Muslim army, where they were associated with the type of the "hated Moor," in service to the Moorish lords, where their status began to be more ambiguous, and lastly in the perspective of redemption by baptism.

Byzantium, it seems, offers more nuances in its vision of the black than we find in that of the Western Europeans. Our research, moreover, is still in progress,[47] and most of our information bears on the period from the ninth to the twelfth century: obviously these dates must be kept in mind when estimating the scope of the reflections that follow. A general remark is

56. Nestor. Conversion of the Ethiopian eunuch. *Menologion of Basil II*, p. 107. From Constantinople. Between 976 and 1025. Vatican, Biblioteca Apostolica Vaticana.

56

57. Michael of Blachernae. Martyrdom of the Holy Fathers of the Sinai by the Blemmyes. *Menologion of Basil II*, p. 315. From Constantinople. Between 976 and 1025. Vatican, Biblioteca Apostolica Vaticana.

58. Pantoleon. Martyrdom of the thirty Fathers of Raïthu in the Sinai by the Blemmyes. *Menologion of Basil II*, p. 317. From Constantinople. Between 976 and 1025. Vatican, Biblioteca Apostolica Vaticana.

called for: the illuminated manuscripts are very rare.[48] To judge by those we have been able to study, it seems that Byzantine civilization, which kept a closer contact with Africa and its peoples, represented the latter in forms more varied than those common in the West.

In the *Menologion of Basil II*,[49] the Blemmyes, a people whose ancient habitat lay between the Nile and the Red Sea,[50] are shown three times torturing and putting to death the holy Fathers of the Sinai desert.[51] They figs. 57, 5 are identified by their conventional dress and by their boots, which in one of the pictures are inscribed with Arabic characters: the "Negroid" features are not strongly marked, being limited to the skin color of several individuals. On the other hand, the eunuch of Queen Candace, depicted as clearly fig. 56 African, compensates for these derogatory portrayals and is a reminder of the black people's call to salvation.[52]

In the eleventh century small black figures illustrated some manuscripts

57

58

59, 60. Scenes of hunting and playing. Margin decorations. Gregory of Nazianzus, *Homilies*, fols. 94^{v} and 251^{r}. Greece, XII century. Paris, Bibliothèque nationale.

61. Canon Tables. *Tetraevangelion*, fol. 4^{v}. From Greece. Early XI century. Paris, Bibliothèque nationale.

62. Lion hunt in Libya. Pseudo-Oppian, *Cynegetica*, fol. 41^{r} (detail). Constantinople, X-XI century. Venice, Biblioteca Nazionale Marciana.

63. Camel drivers. Pseudo-Oppian, *Cynegetica*, fol. 53^{v} (detail). Constantinople,X-XI century. Venice, Biblioteca Nazionale Marciana.

59

61

62

60

63

64. Sarah returning to Abraham. *Octateuch*, fol. 65[r], lower scene. Constantinople, XII century. Vatican, Biblioteca Apostolica Vaticana.

65. Descendants of the sons of Noah. *Octateuch*, fol. 60[v] (detail). Constantinople, XII century. Vatican, Biblioteca Apostolica Vaticana.

66. Destruction of the Tower of Babel and dispersion of the nations. *Octateuch*, fol. 61[v] (detail). Constantinople, XII century. Vatican, Biblioteca Apostolica Vaticana.

67. Apostles teaching the nations. *Tetraevangelion*, fol. 20[v] (detail). Constantinople, mid-XI century. Paris, Bibliothèque nationale.

in a purely decorative way, with elements of the African fauna and flora.[53] figs. 59-6
This is simply a survival of ornamental traditions applied to the mosaics of the distant past. An illuminated manuscript of Pseudo-Oppian's *Cynegetica (On Hunting)* dates from the same period. In it we see paintings which are rather naïve but realistic and fresh, showing a black struggling with a lion, figs. 62, 6
or again two blacks accompanied by camels.[54] At this stage of our research we know of no other examples of this kind of anecdotal illustration done between the twelfth century and the fourteenth. At the latter date we find it again in Greek manuscripts which are more or less copies of earlier works.[55]

The place assigned to blacks in Byzantine works of art has a far different import in three series of illustrations. In these we see, first of all, the reflection of the Byzantines' theoretical, general idea of the blacks; second, a certain number of significant evidences of concrete relations with the blacks of Africa; and lastly, a large eschatological perspective, peculiar to Byzantium, in the conception of Pentecost.

The theme of the descendants of Noah was rarely illustrated in Western Europe. This was not true of Byzantium, as we see in the two Octateuchs in the Vatican library (one from the eleventh century, the other from the twelfth, and both seemingly originating in Constantinople or the region thereabout[56]) and in the Istanbul Octateuch. In these manuscripts the Byzantines put the blacks on a footing of complete equality among the descendants of the sons of Noah, in the scene of the destruction of the Tower of Babel, and the dispersion of the nations.[57] There is no suggestion figs. 65, 6
of culpability of any kind attaching to the blacks. If we stay with the illustrations and leave the texts aside, it is safe to say that Byzantium did not see in the dispersion of the sons of Noah all the tragic consequences that certain Latin Fathers, and more especially their commentators in the Middle Ages, drew from that event. Here the black is not typed as a sinner, and still less as potentially damned. He is shown as black from the moment

64

65

66

67

68

69

70

71

72

68. Isaac and Rebecca before Abimelech. *Octateuch*, fol. 47^{v}, upper scene. Constantinople, XI century. Vatican, Biblioteca Apostolica Vaticana.

69. Moses and Aaron summoned before Pharaoh and his magicians. *Octateuch*, fol. 82^{v}, upper scene. Constantinople, XI century. Vatican, Biblioteca Apostolica Vaticana.

70. Joseph sold to Putiphar by the Ishmaelites. *Octateuch*, fol. 59^{v}, lower scene. Constantinople, XI century. Vatican, Biblioteca Apostolica Vaticana.

71. Sixth plague on Egypt: boils. *Octateuch*, fol. 82^{r}, upper scene. Constantinople, XI century. Vatican, Biblioteca Apostolica Vaticana.

72. Sarah is brought to Pharaoh; Pharaoh gives Sarah back to Abraham. *Octateuch*, fol. 35^{r}, two upper scenes. Constantinople, XI century. Vatican, Biblioteca Apostolica Vaticana.

of the dispersion; there is no hint of the interpretation that made his blackness a result of exile in the hot lands of sin.

The iconography of the two Vatican Octateuchs brings us many other interesting images; it is complex and it mixes traditions, following one in one manuscript and a different and sometimes contradictory one in the other.[58] All we can do at this time is to describe what we see: we cannot offer a thorough study, nor, *a fortiori*, can we arrive at conclusions. The two manuscripts, and no doubt some others, call for a fundamental study, which will, we hope, deliver the key to the puzzling details we are about to examine. In both manuscripts the old *allegorical* tradition is maintained. Hades[59] and Night[60] are represented by black-colored figures. As might be expected, black servants[61] and soldiers,[62] socially dependent or inferior, are figs. 72, 68, 64 also in evidence. The pictures in MS. Vat. gr. 747, painted on better material than that of MS. Vat. gr. 746 and very carefully done, call for close examination. Here the blacks are armed with lances, an image that occurs frequently. cf. fig. 78 Some of them wear a costume which leaves the right shoulder free and is decorated with circles.[63] fig. 71 This costume often reappears in various forms on blacks represented by the Byzantines.

Already, therefore, despite the evident convergence of ancient biblical and allegorical traditions, we find unusual details in the realistic observation of the dress and weaponry of "genuine" blacks. Admittedly this realism did not exclude pejorative intentions.[64] fig. 69 But a noteworthy array of representations leads us to think that their basis, for the painters of the time, was an ethnic contact that implied no value judgment. The realism comes out first of all in the depiction of personages and the "stage setting": even if the scenes were drawn from Scripture there was no compelling reason to include blacks.[65] It may be that the portrayal of black pharaohs[66] betrays an allegorizing tendency to "blacken" the enemy of the Israelites. It may be that the same intention led to representing the master who has just bought Joseph and the master's companion as blacks,[67] or to giving the same treatment to the Ishmaelites who sold him to Putiphar.[68] fig. 70

But the realism extends even to details. Everted lips are hardly visible, but the costumes are often characteristic: in two instances, the garment is made of narrow colored strips sewn together, as is still done today in more than one region of the black world. So these paintings appear to reflect a new way of looking upon a perfectly real Egypt where turbaned Muslims[69] and blacks[70] lived side by side, which grew upon the Byzantines and is important to us on more than one count. The Byzantines regarded as *dark* all the peoples in the East and across the Mediterranean. This may explain both the images they left us and those in the *Ashburnham Pentateuch.* The Nile Valley was home to a mixture of peoples, from those whose light brown skin was like that of other Mediterraneans to those whose features clearly indicated their kinship with the black world. The manuscript painters tried to represent this mixture in ways which were both realistic and subtle and which must be studied more thoroughly. So far as we know, the Occident knew nothing of these subtleties: in comparable scenes only whites are depicted.

Byzantine ecumenism was so much criticized by Rome that we have still to rediscover it in its deepest dimensions. The Byzantines may have learned a lesson from the bitter experience of violent anticolonialism which led to the secession of Asian and African peoples who in the past had been subjects of the Roman Empire and whom the Byzantines themselves had tried to unite in an authoritarian and readily suspicious Christianity. What we see in their art prompts us to believe that after the iconoclast crisis they thought of the spreading of Christianity not as an armed mission of conquest carried on by a chosen people,[71] but as a calling to the Gospel of men who were equal by the fact of that vocation. The illustrations of the New Testament are convincing evidence of this. In a ninth-century manuscript of the *Homilies* of Gregory of Nazianzus a full-page painting shows us, in small scenes arranged in three registers, each of the apostles baptizing;[72] in the last scene both apostle and neophyte are black. In an eleventh-century Tetraevangelion, among the peoples called to Christianity, we see blacks figs. 73, 6 presented without any sort of discrimination—barefoot, clothed in red, blue, and gold tunics tied at the shoulder—grouped around an apostle who was sent to convert them.[73] We may also mention an eleventh-century Psalter coming from Studion, in which two folios[74] are devoted to illustrat- fig. 75 ing the theme of the preaching of the Apostles, two of whom, James and Thomas, are teaching black people.

Still more noteworthy is the fact that the theme of Pentecost, which suddenly emerged in the thirteenth century and was to have a direct influence on Western Europe, confirms our view that the Byzantines had a conception of the blacks that differed from that of the Occidentals, the latter having taken form in the Carolingian period.[75] We must ask ourselves immediately whether or not the adoption of this position influenced the German imperial court, which had close relations with Byzantium as early as the eleventh century, and still more so in the thirteenth. The black is deliberately inserted in the Byzantine iconography of Pentecost, although the text of the Acts of the Apostles furnishes no ground for this interpretation.[76] The illustration of the theme quickly became stereotyped, a fact that emphasizes the intention to make it the rule. In monumental art[77] the black again symbolizes one of the "nations" called to accept the Gospel:[78]

73

73. Apostles teaching the nations. *Tetraevangelion*, fol. 20r (detail). Constantinople, mid-XI century. Paris, Bibliothèque nationale.

74. Pentecost (detail). Mural painting. Early XIV century. Peć, Church of St. Demetrius.

75. Preaching of the Apostles. *Psalter*, fol. 20r. From Constantinople, Studion Monastery. 1066. London, British Library.

74

75

we see this in a mural painting in the fourteenth century, in the church at Peć.[79] In manuscript paintings the same scene illustrates the Pentecost event every time. The Apostles, with St. Peter and St. Paul presiding in the upper part, are seated in a semicircle that appears to symbolize the open door of the Upper Room: the rays of the Holy Spirit shine down on them. Two or more personages face each other within the semicircle: these may be whites,[80] but turbaned blacks, one dressed in red, the other in blue, figure in the illumination of one of Gregory of Nazianzus's homilies for Pentecost.[81] Two enameled plaques on the Pala d'Oro in Venice[82] repeat the Pentecost theme. The larger one, executed in Constantinople in the twelfth century, presents a harmonious and serene interpretation. The

fig. 74

fig. 77

fig. 76

76. Pentecost. Enameled plaque. From Constantinople. XII century. Pala d'Oro. Venice, Basilica of St. Mark.

77. Pentecost. Gregory of Nazianzus, *Homilies*, fol. 28r (detail). Constantinople, XII century. Paris, Bibliothèque nationale.

78. Pentecost. Enameled plaque. Before 1105. Pala d'Oro. Venice, Basilica of St. Mark.

second plaque, which dates from before 1105 and is older than the first, interests us more because of the freshness of its inspiration. In it a black is represented bare above the waist and wears a garment that directly recalls the decorated loincloths in Byzantine manuscripts; he stands facing a white man beneath a semicircle. The Pentecost theme appears again with the same structure in a Syriac manuscript,[83] but with a curious innovation. Below the central arc are seen two rather disconcerting groups of people: one of these wears a cuirass and a red cloak, and has the head of a fantastic animal, while another wears a turban, and a third a pointed cap (the Muslim and the Jew?). It is hard to regard these men as belonging to the elect: the picture may represent a vision of those "called," whom the Apostles are to convert. The ecumenical significance is potent. fig. 78 cf. figs. 70-72

Yet Byzantium itself did not completely omit pejorative representations. As in the West, its art frequently included imps depicted in dark colors. A survey of the manuscripts in Paris reveals that they are most often found in connection with verses of Psalm 104(105)[84] and with the temptation of Jesus in the desert.[85] In every instance what we find are dark colors, not ethnic traits.[86] The illustration of the healing of the sick and the possessed furnished opportunities to multiply these demons.[87] The Last Judgment, which after the fourteenth century became a fairly frequent iconographic

76

77

78

theme in mural paintings and icons, was seldom used in the manuscripts, and in them the devils are discreetly tinted.[88] One eleventh-century example, the only one we have so far, illustrates the sentence, "I saw Satan fall . . . from heaven."[89] Here the artist simply painted winged shadows descending in a vertical fall. We could continue the enumeration at length,[90] but actually it is just as dull as that of the Western items, and gives us little of interest to this study. During the period of Byzantine greatness, therefore, the demon was never *a black*, and he was completely distinguished from human beings by his wings. To conclude: the Byzantine world gives us both more realistic images and a more favorable way of looking at black people than that of the West. Probably the manuscripts had relatively little influence on their rare readers, but the same cannot be said of such deliberately designed iconographic programs as that of the Pentecost, and Western Europe could not have been totally unaware of this different view of the blacks. fig. 79

79. Satan's fall. Margin decoration. *Tetraevangelion*, fol. 131r. Constantinople, mid-XI century. Paris, Bibliothèque nationale.

Southern Italy was an area deeply penetrated by Byzantine culture, in regular contact with Egypt and the eastern Mediterranean, yet conquered by the "men of the North": like Byzantium, the region merits our attention. The three characteristics just mentioned give us a ready insight into the complexity of the artistic evidence we are about to study, and into the difficulty of interpreting it. In this region, which historians have too often neglected in favor of the glamorous achievements of Venice, Genoa, and Florence, the cities, over a long span of time, had no such brilliant success as those farther to the north. Yet we should keep in mind the remarkable composite civilization of the Normans as well as the rise of shipping out of Trani and Bari that began in the second half of the eleventh century. The works of art still visible today tell us much about the activity that went on for some time along the coasts of Apulia.

At first this activity was directed toward Byzantium. A considerable volume of traffic moved there by sea from Bari[91] and Trani as far as Dyrrhachium, and from there over a land route, the importance of which is not generally recognized. South Italy was also in contact with North Africa: Sicily particularly played a preponderant role in the Mediterranean area during the twelfth century. And, as the texts show, trade was extended to the Near East, though not regularly, especially by the seafarers of Bari. Local tradition also retains a vivid memory of the presence of the Muslims, who controlled Bari in the ninth century and Sicily until the end of the eleventh. Norman policy toward them, however, was liberal only in appearance; actually its aim was to eliminate the Muslim problem as rapidly as possible. In that social context the local view of black people, known as domestic servants, mercenaries, slaves, or believing Muslims,[92] was not a friendly one. Yet on the cultural level—and here we see the originality of southern Italy—the Normans completely absorbed the various Mediterranean traditions, Byzantine, Islamic, and Latin, thus preparing the way for the eclecticism of Frederick II Hohenstaufen in the thirteenth century. So, despite an unfavorable background, blacks found themselves situated in an open, complex social setting.

A curious illuminated manuscript dating from 1195-97[93] gives a reasonably clear idea of the general state of mind in twelfth-century Sicily, and

80

80. Chancellor Matthew of Ajello treating his gout in a black man's blood. Peter of Eboli, *Liber ad honorem Augusti*, fol. 127ʳ. Palermo (?), between 1195 and 1197. Berne, Burgerbibliothek.

of the confrontations taking place there; and it is a striking fact that in this document blacks play no role at all. Peter, bishop of Eboli, the author of this polemical poem,[94] was a relentless supporter of the imperial aim to take over South Italy and Sicily.[95] He puts Matthew of Ajello, chancellor of the Norman kings, who had no wish to fall under the rod of the feudal lords from the north, in the front rank of the opponents. From the opening lines of the *carmen* Matthew is presented as a grotesque, fantastic character: he was, in any case, a "bigamous" cleric whom the author compares to Judas.[96] The chancellor, who suffered from gout, is accused in the text of all sorts of crimes.[97] The image says more than the text and more than the legend accompanying the image itself.[98] The legend relates that to relieve fig. 80 his gout, the chancellor was accustomed to bathe his feet in the blood of young men whose throats had been cut. The young men are not further specified, but what we see here is the blood of a black who had just been beheaded. Obviously this is pure calumny on the part of the bishop. Nothing history tells us about the chancellor supports this infamous slander, which comes straight out of the author's hatred.[99] The image we were looking at is so violent that we consulted medical sources to see if by chance a treatment for gout might have called for bathing in blood or the use of black-colored substances. We found nothing of the sort in the course of our reading.[100] So we are forced to return to the only possible explanation—a gratuitous calumny coming from the disordered imagination of Peter of Eboli. But why is the victim a young black?

Bari, a port of embarkation for pilgrims, kept up its relations with the East.[101] In their own way the Christian mariners of Bari,[102] before the Crusades began, imitated the Venetians, who had stolen the relics of St. Mark from Egypt. In 1087 a bold exploit won them the remains of St. Nicholas, a more or less legendary bishop of Myra.[103] The arrival of the relic at Bari[104] did not go unnoticed—indeed it provoked some violent incidents. The archbishop wanted to seize the precious remains for the cathedral, but the mariners[105] and the populace turned them over to Elias, the venerable abbot of a Benedictine monastery. Work began at once on the building of a shrine worthy of the saint whom Bari had adopted as its protector, and in whose honor the city inaugurated two annual feasts. In 1089 the lower part of the edifice was ready, and Urban II consecrated it on 9 May. The initial plan was modified and amplified century after century, and this marvelous stone reliquary became the thing of rare beauty that it still is.[106] As remarkable as the architecture of St. Nicholas of Bari and other churches of Apulia is, we are directly concerned with the decoration created by this "Norman" art and its successors. And this decoration brings us back to Africa and the Africans, at the same time adding new themes.

At Bari, Trani, and Otranto some mosaic pavements have survived more or less intact. Only the one in Otranto is almost entire:[107] it was executed between 1163 and 1165 by Pantaleone, a learned priest, at the request of the local archbishop, for the cathedral recently completed at the behest of the Norman rulers. The whole pavement covers four areas—the entire length of the central nave, part of each of the lateral naves,[108] and the choir. Here we shall give little attention to the pavements in the choir[109] and the south nave,[110] which are rather disorderly in appearance

81

and may have been restored here and there. In them we find only anecdotal elements: the overall plan is hard to interpret and there are no figures of blacks. The pavement in the lower part of the choir comprises sixteen medallions, each enclosing a human figure or a more or less fantastic animal: at least two of them have a border decorated with stylized Kufic characters. The Queen of Sheba—*Regina Austri*, the inscription says— figs. 82, 8
represented as white and with human feet, appears in the upper register, followed by Solomon, a siren with a double tail, and a griffin. Lower down we note particularly a centaur with a "black" profile—diabolic?—dragging a stag—Christ?—and a unicorn. The other figures are drawn from the Oriental bestiary, with the exception of the two central medallions in the lower register, in which Eve, tempted by the serpent, is next to Adam. None of the human figures or animals is black in color. Paradise and Hell share the surface of the north nave, which, like the two others, is divided into two halves, from east to west, by a tree trunk.[111] In Hell a black demon is placed at the bottom of the composition: other black personages, not easily identifiable, are located at various planes.

The central nave is of greater interest, although it shows almost no black figures. Here we seem to have one of the earliest systematic representations of the evolution of mankind, read "according to the Bible." At the top, near the choir, the story of the fall of Adam and Eve and the loss of Paradise constitutes the first age of man. It ends with Abel's murder and the allegorizing evocation of King Arthur. Arthur, coming from France with the Normans, symbolizes lack of purity in a dignitary who is attacked and conquered by the cat (diabolical), and finally killed. Beside Arthur the pure hero of the Grail—Percival or Galahad—represents the humanity of the future, redeemed by Christ.[112] This first episode of human history is interrupted by a decorative ensemble—the astrological and agricultural calendar—which seems to have no logical connection with what precedes.

82

83

81. Pantaleone. "Ascension" of Alexander. Mosaic (detail). 1163-65. Otranto, cathedral, central nave.

82, 83. Pantaleone. Queen of Sheba and Solomon. Mosaic (details). 1163-65. Otranto, cathedral, lower part of the choir.

In fact, however, to understand this intrusion of the "rhythm of the years" we have only to recall that man, becoming mortal, was thenceforth subject to the dual law of time and therefore of death and labor. We note that the borders of the medallions contain stylized graphic characters, which here seem to be Greek. Then comes the second age of man, which comes to no better end than the first, since God, despite Noah's docility, wipes out his disobedient subjects and saves only the "prototypes" of the second alliance in the Ark. There is no allusion here to a malediction laid upon Ham and his descendants, nor to the dispersion of the peoples after the Tower of Babel, looming proud and gigantic, is destroyed. There is one noteworthy feature, however, in the episode of the Ark: a crow turns its back on the vessel and holds a severed human leg in its claw.[113] A long hiatus separates the Tower of Babel sequence from the one the artist represented in the north nave. There, in the setting of Paradise, appear Abraham and Jacob,[114] whose posterity is symbolized by the children standing in front of the two Patriarchs.

Returning to the central nave, we find that there is no image concerning the history of man between the building of the Tower of Babel and the fanciful ascension of Alexander. Half of the surface of the central nave is fig. 81
covered with figures connected by no apparent logical bond:[115] among the fantastic animals we note a lion with one head and four bodies,[116] an image we shall see again, transposed, in sculpture. "King Alexander," raised aloft by two griffins,[117] has only a figurative role here: but does he not evoke, above and beyond the already famous person of the Macedonian emperor,[118] the first epoch in which "the Occident dominated the Orient," the first great empire, the first unification of the known world of which Western European Christendom was dreaming in the twelfth century? All this perhaps sends us back to the relations maintained by Otranto with the East and to the ambitions of that busy commercial city.[119] The realistic

representation of exotic fauna—lions, dromedaries, serpents—here runs along with the most fantastic transpositions. This need not surprise us.[120] Muslim Sicily was certainly familiar with the dromedary, and probably with other animals, imported from nearby Africa. Moreover, we know that Frederick II Hohenstaufen, leaving southern Italy for Germany, had in his train a part of his menagerie, notably including dromedaries.[121] An elephant, given by the Egyptians to the same emperor, lived in Cremona from 1235 to 1248.

A quite different sort of evidence is furnished by a series of episcopal thrones.[122] One of these thrones, still in St. Nicholas of Bari, is of special figs. 85, 8 interest to us.[123] The seat is supported by the figures of three men, while the step in front of it rests upon two lions. The theme of the conquered man who is forced to bear the weight of the conqueror is a very old one. In Egypt the pharaoh planted his foot on the captives taken by his armies, and A. Grabar furnishes a series of references to the Hittites, Babylonians, Persians, and Byzantines: H. Stern, whom he quotes, shows that prisoners as caryatids were known to the Romans.[124] The Bari throne therefore takes its place in a long tradition, but the original upon which it may have been modeled is still not clearly identifiable. Whatever its origin was, the work is important for us if it be admitted that one of the prisoners is a black, following conventions of Hellenistic origin. The meaning of his presence, however, is still an open question. A. Grabar thinks that the general cultural practice of borrowing from earlier models answers the question sufficiently. F. Schettini puts forward a different and very attractive interpretation: he sees in this representation the symbol of the triumph of civil order over rebels thrown to the wild beasts. In that case the question of the origin and date of the throne is left intact and fundamental. If the piece is Islamic, as Schettini holds, it would suggest the suppression of a slave uprising in which blacks had taken part; if its origin is Christian and post-1080, as Grabar proposes, it would constitute an allusion to a rebellion of Muslims, including some blacks, suppressed by the new masters of South Italy, and would refer to the well-known riots that shook Sicily until the time of Frederick II. In either case there are serious chronological and logical difficulties. Whatever the answer may be, the fact remains that the first "black" we find in this region is a conquered man upon whom weigh the recent events in the central Mediterranean. Our investigation is still too incomplete for us to make a unilateral interpretation of the evidence.

We must be all the more careful in view of the fact that during the thirteenth century this same region produced works of art in which the "black" is represented without hostility, with a degree of realism and unquestionable formal quality. Was this due to the ambiguity of the then current view of the black? We do not think so. First of all, as regards form, the black headsman and the black servingman were not consistently portrayed as ugly or deformed: we have pointed out several remarkable examples. We remember, moreover, that it was Norman Italy that gave us the most beautiful aesthetic expression of Easter Night in the *Exultet* scroll cf. figs. already mentioned. South Italy was an area of intense artistic creativity, 12, 16 where three cultures met and fused, and which produced artistic treasures still unknown or not well known. However unfriendly the *social* view of the

84

84. Abba Moses swimming across the Nile. *Vitae Patrum*, fol. 54v (detail). Italy, XIV century. Vatican, Biblioteca Apostolica Vaticana.

black may have been there, he was not mocked or caricatured in art. We also have remarked in the preceding pages—and we shall see this more clearly further on—that beginning in the thirteenth century a real change occurred, especially in the Mediterranean lands, in the way "others" were regarded. In the iconographic examples we are about to present there is no evidence of a prejudicial value judgment. It may have been in this climate of thought that a manuscript of the *Vitae Patrum* was painted, in which the story of Abba Moses,[125] already commented upon above, was related—for the first time, so far as we know. Not once is this converted Ethiopian given any pejorative treatment. Short scenes illustrate the text;[126] the best executed is the one that shows Moses, before his conversion, swimming across figs. 87, 84

85. Episcopal throne. 1098. Bari, Church of St. Nicholas.

86. Detail of figure 85: an atlas.

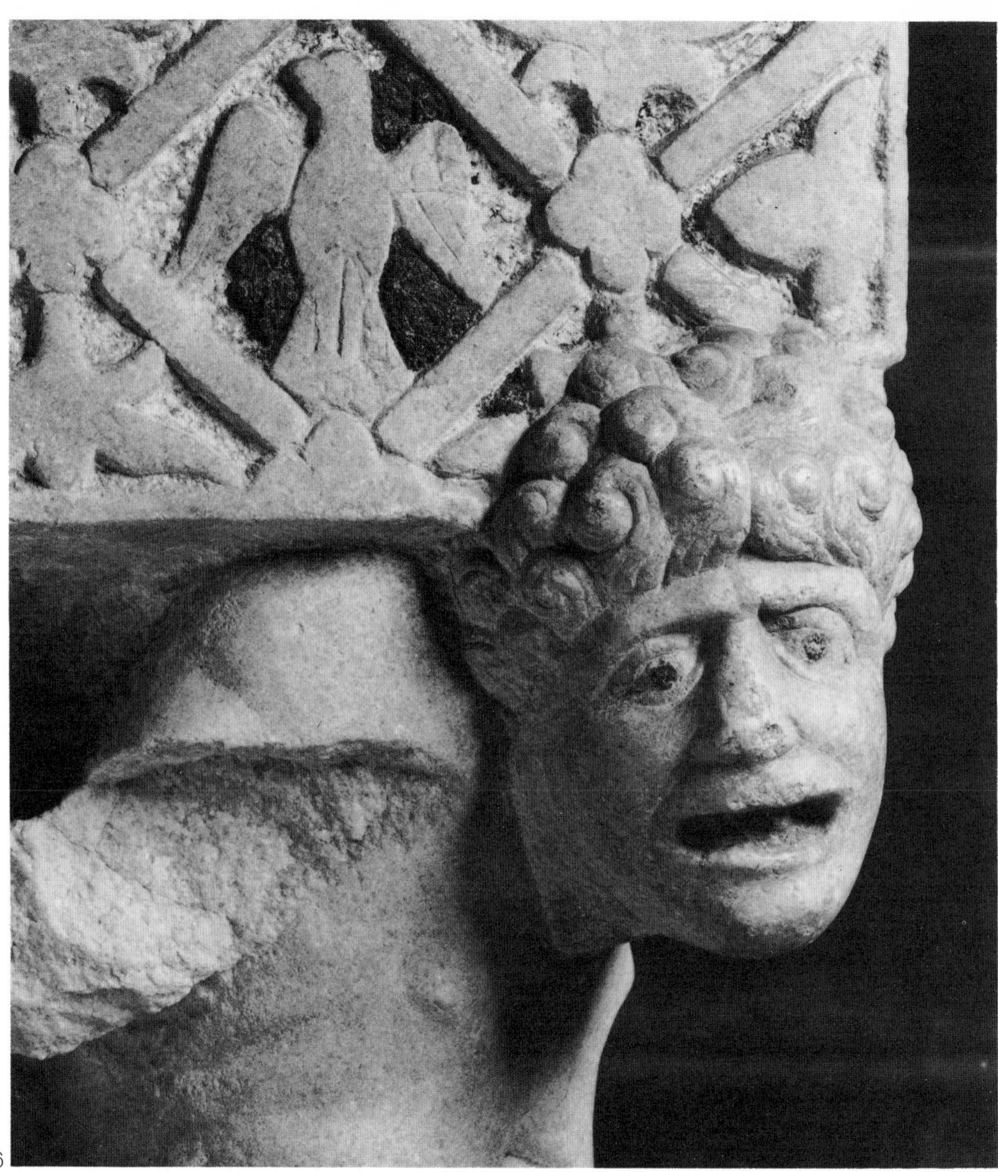

86

85

the Nile, wearing nothing but a turban, and pulling four stolen sheep after him.[127]

A capital from Troia,[128] of great plastic beauty, is composed of four heads at the corners emerging from a setting of leaves and flowers. One of the heads, a particularly realistic piece, is that of a black. In New York[129] there is a version of this same capital, very close in style and period and in a better state of preservation: this fine head of a black is joined by that of a turbaned Muslim. The origin of the style of these capitals has been sought outside of Italy, but their inspiration, in our opinion, belongs entirely to the Mediterranean world we have been talking about.[130] fig. 91 figs. 89,

These representations multiplied, and the geography of their diffusion is important. About 1250 a Norman sculptor placed three heads under the abacus of a pillar in Rouen Cathedral: a Delilah, identified by the scissors under her neck, next to a bearded Samson, and unexpectedly, a black with strongly marked features.[131] The meaning of this escapes us, but we feel that we have here an echo of the Italian theme. The relations between the different "Norman" areas were extremely close in the twelfth and thirteenth centuries, and such occasional borrowings are not surprising. Still it fig. 93

87. Scenes from the life of Abba Moses. *Vitae Patrum*, fol. 55^{r} (detail). Italy, XIV century. Vatican, Biblioteca Apostolica Vaticana.

88. Ethiopian cutting wood. Historiated initial. *Vitae Patrum*, fol. 112^{v} (detail). Italy, XIV century. Vatican, Biblioteca Apostolica Vaticana.

89. Head of a black. Detail of a capital. From South Italy. About 1212-20. New York, Metropolitan Museum of Art, The Cloisters.

will be necessary to dig much deeper to see whether there are facts or texts that confirm our hypothesis.

Still more puzzling is a keystone in the Abbey of Saint-Wandrille.[132] fig. 92 Four figures face each other in pairs: a winged, bearded king wearing a coat of mail is opposite a queen, also with wings, her head covered with a veil but her upper body bare, ringing a small bell; a winged dragon with a crown faces a lion covered with a drapery. In the center four heads are clearly visible: a bearded man faces a woman, a black wearing a sort of turban with a flap faces a satyr. Could this represent, as M. Aubert suggests, the allegory of wisdom and folly? It would be presumptuous on our part to propose any kind of interpretation. What connects the piece with our subject is the presence of a head with "Negroid" features whose headdress recalls that of the Muslims.

Among the Christians of the Mediterranean world who were in contact with the Muslims and perhaps with blacks, there were also the Crusaders. When these knights were not from the empire or the Anglo-Norman kingdom, they often came from a feudal society whose culture was rather rudimentary. Moreover, their contact with Muslims was for the most part "simple," mainly military, and the splits quickly widened between their descendants in the Holy Land and their family roots, which were still in

87

88

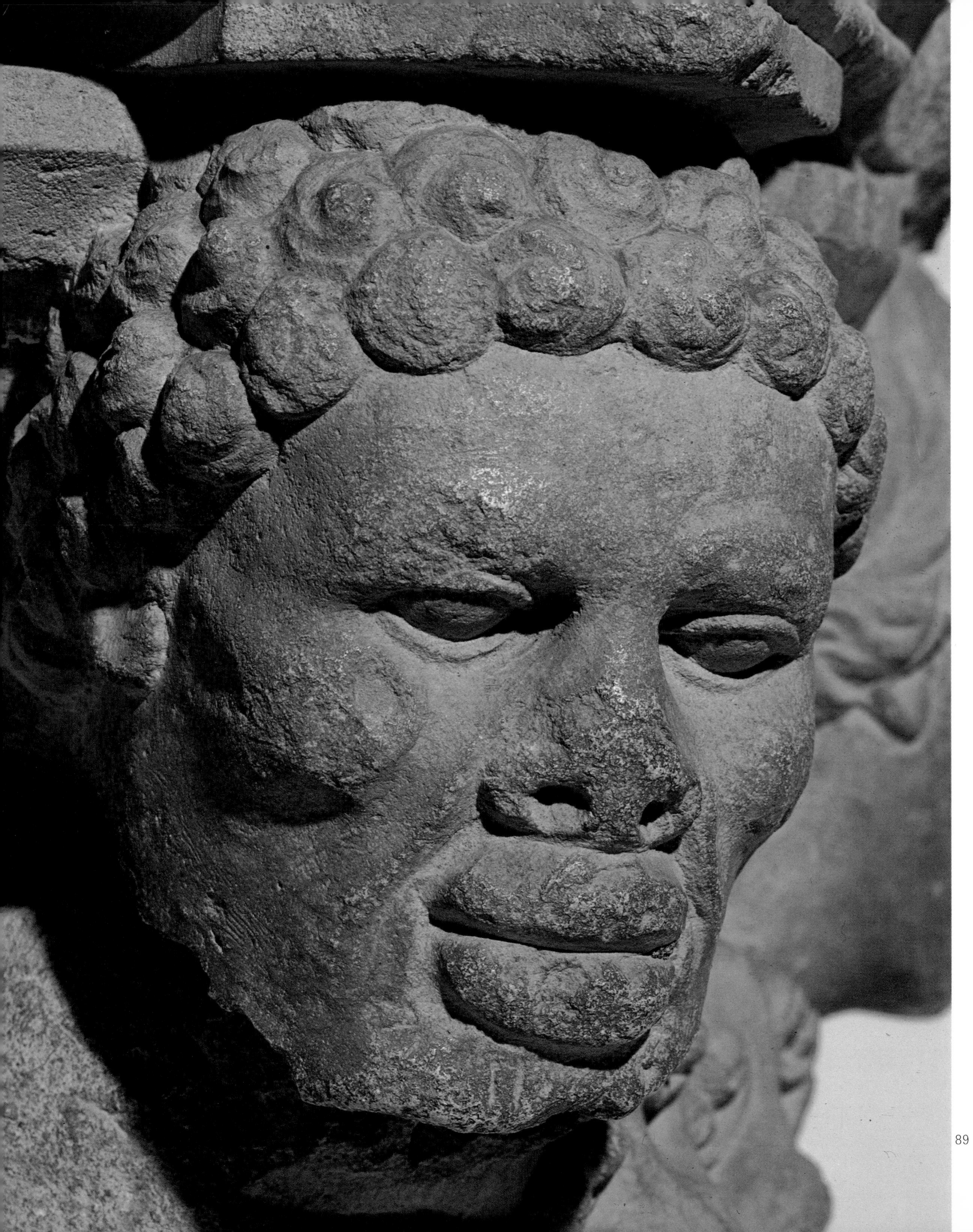

90. Capital decorated with four heads. Overall view of figure 89.

91. Capital decorated with four heads (detail). From the cathedral in Troia. About 1212-20. Troia, bishop's palace.

90

Europe. We are dealing here not with a society in day-to-day, peaceful contact with blacks, nor with an intellectually developed class, but on the contrary with a group of people among whom survived clichés and prejudices inherited from the Carolingian period. To these preconceptions were added those inculcated by the Cluniacs, the Cistercians, and the French aristocracy, and when some openness of mind was manifested, for instance by the people of Toulouse, the attempt at dialogue with Islam and the Eastern cultures was labeled "heresy." The rude barons of the North were going to make sure that their social and cultural structure held firm: curiosity about other cultures and other men was, in and of itself, a danger to the faith and the certainties one needed in order to live.

The Crusaders could not therefore be expected to have a favorable point of view with regard to blacks. In fact, the first evidences we discover[133] are hostile. The texts are unmerciful where Muslims of color are concerned. To kill a Saracen was the dream of every knight: if he was black, the pleasure and the glory grew. Besides, the term *Aethiops* no longer designated the vague inhabitant of a nebulous land;[134] to the Crusaders it meant a black Muslim. Coming closer and closer to them, eastern Africa began to be better known, and the grosser misjudgments were fading away, at least among Europeans living in Syria and Palestine. On the other hand,

91

92. Keystone representing an unidentified subject. Early XIV century. Abbey of Saint-Wandrille, cloister.

92

the assumption of superiority over the Muslims, and even over the Byzantines, was as strong as ever.[135]

As early as the twelfth century the evocation of the Crusades provided a reason for representing battles between Frankish and Saracen cavalrymen. To be sure, much of the evidence is lost or known to us only through restorations.[136] It is nevertheless interesting to note that we have not found a scene of this type, where blacks are included among the combatants, before the fourteenth century; we shall see that after that date the documents are plentiful.[137] It seems, therefore, that the presence of the black in the Muslim armies was exploited only after the end of the Crusades, at which time the representation acquired, in a way, a retrospective value: the Occident, its knighthood in defeat, may have found some consolation in it. This hypothesis is supported by the fact that the scene which is considered to be the first of these duels between cavalrymen—white against black—does not illustrate a historical Crusade cycle but rather a chivalric romance. The fight between William of Orange and Ysore, the black Saracen giant, at Pernes,[138] derives from a theme already firmly anchored in epic literature:[139] its iconographic exploitation developed gradually in the fourteenth century as the military feats of the Crusaders became legend. fig. 94

To sum up: direct contacts with black Muslims did not improve the European view of the black. They even strengthened the feeling—social as

93

well as ethnic—that black people belonged in menial positions and should be kept in total isolation when they came into the white community.

It is worth noting, however, that the artists of Western Europe did not simply leave this rediscovered black out of their works entirely. These extraordinary creatures, upon whom the light of day played so differently than on white skins, exerted a kind of enduring fascination, complex and contradictory indeed, upon the European consciousness. The evidence before us seems to indicate that artists were the first to feel it. Moreover, the time was at hand when Western imagery, moving by tortuous ways, was about to prepare a spectacular change in the vision it projected.

NEW VISION FROM THE EAST: THE BLACK IN THE EMPIRE

The capture of Edessa[140] by the Muslims in 1144 is certainly an event of major importance for the subject with which we are dealing. In the realm of ideas it was the turning point between the illusions then current in Western Europe and the first stage of a progressive military defeat for which the West consoled itself with wild flights of fancy. For Islam it meant a move toward concerted action following fifty years of weakness.[141] The Muslims of the time made no mistake in seeing the taking of the city as the start of a new effort—a *jihad*, a holy war—against the Christian presence.[142] The Armenian population of the city, while not very friendly to the

93. Heads of Delilah, Samson, and a black carved under the abacus of a pillar. About 1250. Rouen, Cathedral of Notre-Dame.

94. Combat between William of Orange and the giant Ysore (detail). Mural painting. Late XIII century. Pernes, Tour Ferrande.

94

Crusaders, deeply felt the fall of Edessa.[143] In Western Europe the event was not much talked about nor commented upon at the time. Edessa was, of course, a strategic point, but it was far inland and far from Jerusalem. At such a distance no one pointed out the importance of holding or losing it.

Otto of Freising, however, was one man who intuitively grasped the significance of its loss. He emerges, as we shall see, as a major figure in the history of his time. As bishop of Freising from 1138 to 1158, he occupied an exceptional place in twelfth-century society.[144] The fifth son of Margrave Leopold III of Austria and of Agnes, daughter of Emperor Henry IV, he was, due to interlocking family alliances, the uncle of Emperor Frederick Barbarossa.[145] His father sent him, already an erudite clerk, to Paris for further study. He entered the Cistercian order at Morimond, and when he became the first Cistercian bishop in Germany, he had already had long experience as abbot of his monastery and was a man of broad culture. In 1143 he began the composition of his *Chronicle*, an ample and ambitious work to which we shall make frequent references; it was completed in 1146, and he reworked it before dedicating it to Frederick Barbarossa in 1157. The news of the fall of Edessa reached him as he was putting the *Chronicle* in shape: he considered the event a disaster, of which there are important echoes in his book. Subsequently Otto took part in the Second Crusade with Conrad III; the footsoldiery beside which he rode was cut to pieces by the Turks. His family continued to be concerned with the fortunes of the East.[146] These few biographical notes will suffice, for the moment, to indicate the measure of the man and his role.

In Otto's eyes the fall of Edessa was due to the Christians' lack of faith.

The city, he notes, succumbed beneath the overwhelming mass of the assailants, whereupon the Muslims proceeded to massacre the Christians from the West,[147] and the conqueror—what was graver still—defiled the churches, "principally the basilica of Blessed Mary ever Virgin and the church in which the body of the apostle Thomas was enshrined."[148] This fact considerably enhanced the popularity of the saint.

For the people of the East, Edessa was a center of great importance.[149] After the middle of the fifth century the Nestorians, whose doctrine had been condemned by the Council of Ephesus in 431, left the Eastern Roman Empire, where they were being pursued and hounded down. In particular they abandoned Edessa, where numbers of them had been studying in the still active schools of the city. They first settled in numbers in the Sassanid Persian Empire, and toward the end of the fifth century the Christian church existing there adopted Nestorianism.[150] From then on the spread of the Nestorians toward Asia continued without interruption,[151] at least until the fourteenth century. They left their mark particularly between Lake Balkhash and the Himalayas, and in India—a fact which has a bearing on the legends that the West was to welcome and propagate.[152]

The Nestorians traced the conversion of their areas to two disciples of St. Thomas, Thaddaeus and Addai. According to the tradition their successor, Aggai, appointed the first bishops,[153] whose authority reached from Persia to the borders of India and the land of Gog and Magog. The Gospel came to them from Edessa. The Nestorian Church was firmly based on its own traditions and was not in contact with the Mediterranean Christianity which had condemned it. Although another group of dissident Christians, the Monophysites,[154] showed less concern about a direct connection with Edessa, they nonetheless gave much prominence to St. Thomas. His commemoration has an important place, though by no means a fixed one,[155] in the liturgies of the various churches—at times in unexpected association with Abraham in October or with the whole company of the saints in July. In Ethiopia the cult of St. Bartholomew was closely connected with that of St. Thomas.[156] It would be interesting to know the forms of this cult and the iconography which may occasionally have accompanied it.

The Syrian churches also held the memory of St. Thomas in veneration, even after they came under Muslim control. One of the most thought-provoking mentions of the Thomas traditions is found in the writings of a tenth-century Arabic Christian author, Agapius.[157] The apostle recognized the risen Christ, and by him was sent to Edessa. There he brought King Abgar back to the faith, which the king had abandoned, whereupon he had forthwith turned black. After Thomas's death the apostles chose Addai to succeed him. Also at this time the emir of Ethiopia, who was none other than the eunuch of the Acts of the Apostles, was baptized by Philip. Thus several diverse traditions eventually came together.

The Byzantine sector of Eastern Christianity also had built its own image of St. Thomas before the upheavals of the sixth and seventh centuries engulfed his memory in silence for a while. Gregory of Nazianzus was the first to weave a theme which in time gave rise to story elements of significance both for Western Christendom and for the blacks. Thomas was sent to evangelize the Indians.[158] Previous to that the unbelieving apostle had had little notice either in the Scriptures[159] or in the Apocrypha.[160] The historians Socrates and Sozomen[161] make Thomas the preacher to the Parthians, while Matthew brought the word to Ethiopia and Bartholomew to India. According to these authors,[162] as also for Rufinus,[163] Thomas was buried at Edessa.[164] St. Jerome seems to be the one responsible for confusing the traditions:[165] according to him Thomas reposes in India—and that is the version the West preserved. Toward the end of the tenth century the *Menologion of Basil II* showed that St. Thomas had not been forgotten. Among the paintings in the manuscript—we have already seen something about them—is one illustrating the saint's martyrdom.[166] In a mountainous landscape, near a temple, the apostle, erect and haloed, is set upon by two men with black skin, wearing short tunics and boots and armed with lances.[167] Furthermore the legends keep growing. To the central theme of the apostle's mission each church adds details adapted to its own needs, whether they concerned his stay in Edessa, his martyrdom in India, or the return of his remains to Edessa.[168] The place where he was put to death and that of his burial vary, but this does not matter to us; what is important is not the details, but the major themes that crystallized in the twelfth century, forming a vast fresco of legend which was adopted by Western Europe. fig. 95

The Occident, indeed, knew about Edessa and welcomed Thomas long before the Crusades. In the fourth century Etheria, a renowned traveler, had given a fairly exact description of the city in her account of her journey, although it is already embroidered with wonders.[169] An anonymous *Passion* from the middle of the fifth century, which became very popular,[170] straightened out the apparent paradox of the two locations of the apostle's relics: his body was brought back from India, where it had been preserved; the silver casket used for its translation now hung in the church at Edessa. Since its arrival there no heretic, no Jew, no worshiper of idols, could live in Edessa. Gregory of Tours, perhaps carried away by the enthusiasm of pilgrims back from the Orient,[171] added his own embellishments to Jerome's version of the matter.[172] Thomas was buried in India following his martyrdom, and later was transported to Edessa, but his former tomb in India continued to be the scene of edifying marvels. A temple and a monastery were built there, and a lamp burns perpetually before the former sepulchre, due entirely to the power of the apostle, there being no need to renew the oil in the lamp. For the saint's feast days in Edessa[173] great crowds of pilgrims and merchants converge on the city.[174] For weeks there is not a sign of disorder, a miracle obviously attributable to St. Thomas, and—what is still more wonderful—no flies come to spoil the meat and no one suffers from thirst.

What fertile soil for the growth of myths! The huge, strange temple, the miraculous tomb, the lamp that burned without renewal of its oil, the water that rose in the wells around the saint's feast day and receded afterwards, the abundance of food that tradesmen and pilgrims were sure of[175]—all these were themes which the twelfth and thirteenth centuries took up and elaborated with inexhaustible inventiveness.

Like St. Jerome, Gregory of Tours associates Bartholomew with Thomas,[176] but Bartholomew, also martyred in India, was unable to match the marvels wrought by his fellow apostle. His leaden coffin was thrown into the sea and floated about for a long time, until it came ashore in the

95. Nestor. Martyrdom of St. Thomas. *Menologion of Basil II*, p. 93. From Constantinople. Between 976 and 1025. Vatican, Biblioteca Apostolica Vaticana.

95

Lipari Islands. And there, so far as the West was concerned, Bartholomew's wondrous career came to an end.

Isidore of Seville merely handed on (complicating them, as was his wont) the legends that had probably spread around the Mediterranean and which Gregory of Tours had used.[177] He also dwells on the miraculous power of St. Thomas in the matter of food supply. The popes in their correspondence[178] and the Fathers in their commentaries[179] touch upon the subject of the incredulous apostle only lightly and in passing. He finds a place, however, in the liturgical calendars.[180] In the ninth century Carolingian poets[181] and synods[182] established long-lasting stereotypes relative to Thomas and Bartholomew, to whom two apocryphal Passions[183] were attributed. In England[184] Bede was the first to include Thomas in his Martyrology.[185] Aldhelm[186] stresses only his failure to believe. During the twelfth century the influence of the mixed culture which developed in Sicily and was readily accepted, and even encouraged, by the kings, made it possible for Norman England to obtain a remarkable body of information about the East.[187] Before the fall of Edessa a strictly British tradition relating to St. Thomas made its appearance. Florence of Worcester mentions in his *Chronicle*[188] that in 883 Alfred the Great sent large gifts to the saint's tomb in India. A little later, William of Malmesbury[189] added some choice details: the king's legate had brought back precious stones and perfumes from the Orient.

These Western themes were but a pale reflection of the luxuriant crop of Oriental texts dedicated to the "apostle of the Indias." On the other hand, shortly before the fall of Edessa and perhaps because the city had been occupied at the time of the First Crusade,[190] the West gave a hearty welcome, heightened by curiosity, to the flood of legends about St. Thomas that came in from the Oriental Christian communities.[191] At that time new details, which amplified and even distorted Gregory of Tours[192] and Wil-

96. Land of the Indians. *Life of Barlaam and Joasaph*, fol. 3r (detail). Byzantine, late XII-early XIII century. Mount Athos, Monastery of Iveron.

liam of Malmesbury, spread abroad. The travelers guaranteed their authenticity.[193] The most remarkable novelty, which was to attain a lightning success, concerned the annual distribution of the Eucharist at the saint's tomb. According to this bit of legend the arm that had touched Christ's side enjoyed the privilege of continued life: this arm gave Communion once a year and punished the "insincere" on the spot. That was surely enough to make Thomas, in the eyes of the victory-starved Occident, eager for marvels, the most remarkable—and too long neglected—of the Apostles.[194]

When Edessa fell, the event stirred a wave of emotion that lent to Thomas's missionary activities in the East a dramatic dimension previously absent. Only its salient aspects, however, were retained.[195] The tomb and the lost city were left in shadow and the temple in India exalted. India, moreover, included blacks[196] (the illustration of the *Life of Barlaam and Joasaph* in a Mount Athos manuscript of the late twelfth or early thirteenth century[197] shows that the Greeks shared this point of view); India, like Ethiopia, thereafter represented a "beyond Islam" that greatly interested the Christians of Western Europe. Brother Eliseus's account of the saint's tomb, which located it at the top of a mountain, made it seem almost unreal. The old theme of the mountain where Thomas met his end was about to be transformed and to fill an essential role in the story of the Magi and, to a lesser degree, in that of Prester John. fig. 96

Research on the iconography of St. Thomas is still to be done: it is difficult, because for that period significant information can come only from manuscripts, especially the calendars.[198] As things stand now, it seems risky to posit a connection between Thomas's feast day on 21 December and the figure of a black, painted alongside that date on a folio of the Lunel Psalter covering the month of December.[199] The young black man who is opening the door of winter evokes the period of the longest nights accompanying the solstice: he appears in like manner, but reduced in size, at the summer solstice.[200] A very fine thirteenth-century relief, now in Avignon, confirms our impression:[201] two half-naked young men face each other in symmetrical postures. Their features are clearly defined, and one of them shows definitely "Negroid" characteristics: they personify Gemini, one of the signs of the zodiac, which covers the period of the year just before the summer solstice. It is hard to interpret these images, and only extensive study of the sources may perhaps throw some light on them. fig. 97 fig. 98

96

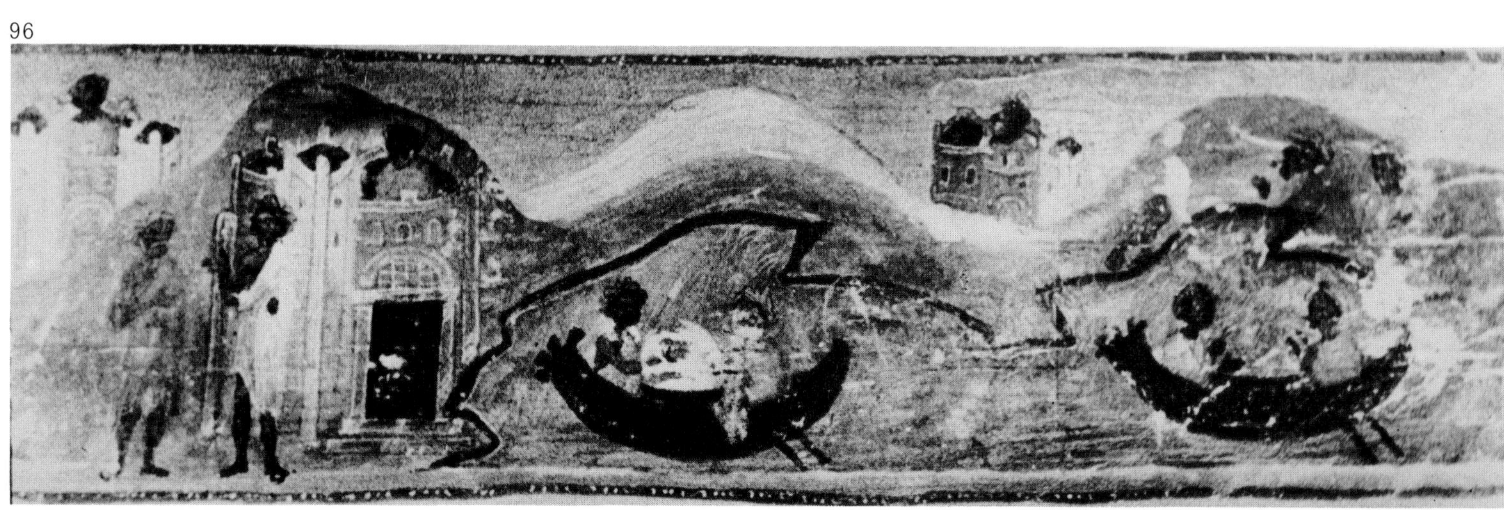

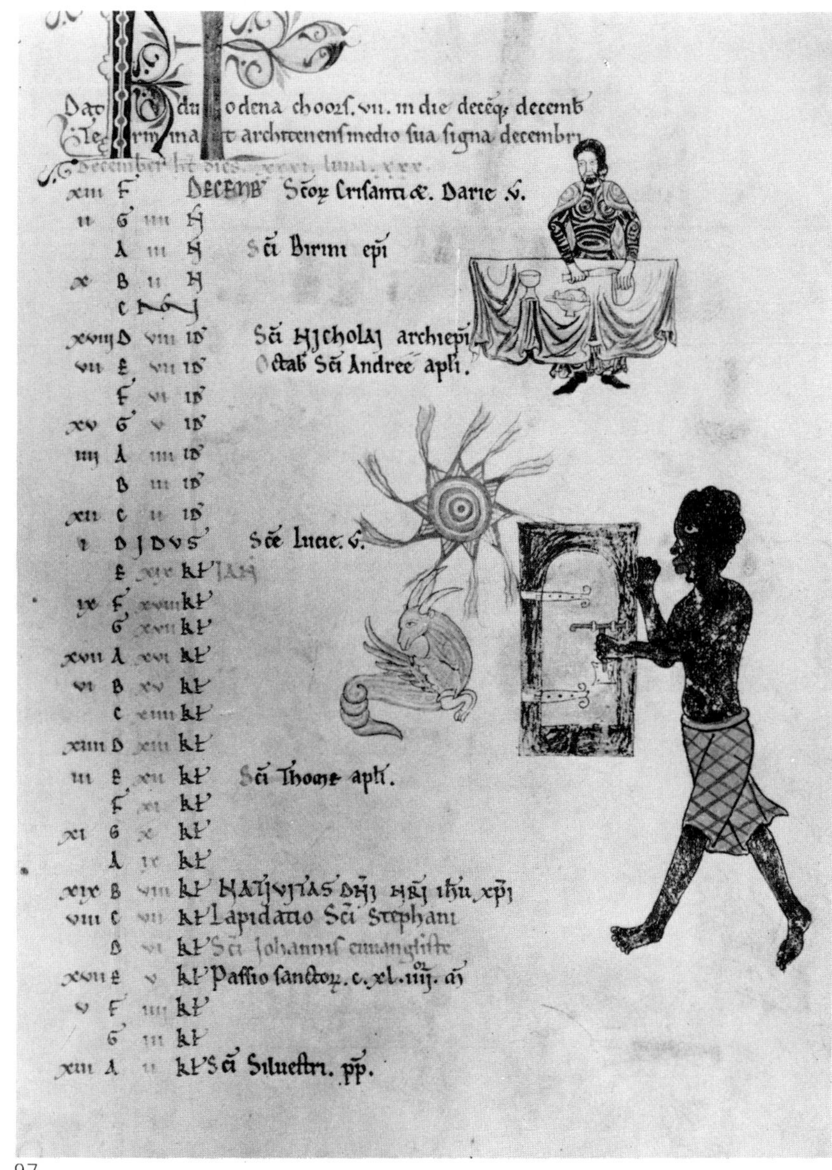

97. Calendar, month of December. *Psalter*, fol. 5r. From the Abbey of Gellone. England, first half XII century. Lunel, Bibliothèque municipale.

97

We have already seen something of Otto of Freising, and must now devote considerable further attention to his activity in the empire. In the middle of the twelfth century the humiliation of the imperial powers vis-à-vis the Church, as well as the defeats suffered in the Near East, brought the theoreticians and the agents of the regime to a spectacular hardening of position. Nostalgia for lost power at first took the form, at the existential level, of oft-repeated reaffirmation of universal obedience to the emperor.[202] There existed a dream of empire that aimed not at territorial hegemony over the Occident but at a world-wide vocation. In 1144 when Edessa was lost, Conrad III, for all his courage, was not the perfect embodiment of this dream, which, on the contrary, acquired substance in 1152 in the person and reign of Frederick I. Frederick had made repeated efforts to bring about the reconciliation of the two warring families in Germany, and Otto of Freising saw in his accession to power "the cornerstone that could seal together the two walls that were falling asunder."[203] In 1157, not long before his uncle's death and perhaps on the advice of Rainald of Dassel, Frederick I, at the Diet of Fulda, proclaimed that he had received "the government of the City and the world" from the divine clemency.[204] From

98. Gemini. Fragment of a carved zodiac. From Caissargues. XIII century. Avignon, Musée Calvet.

then on all the sycophants of power extolled the emperor above every other human being.[205] Peter of Eboli joined them at the end of the century.[206] This empire, like its remote Byzantine model, has a sort of ecumenical vocation that must not be confused with purely territorial imperialism. If the empire did not enter into direct conflict with Byzantium, it gave rise to difficulties for Rome that came into clear view in the middle of the twelfth century.

Otto was aware of the problems that faced his country, but he transposed them to the level of History, and, in his *Chronicle*, to lift the debate into the realm of metaphysics and philosophy. As the heir of Augustine and Orosius,[207] he describes the ages of the world,[208] as did Rupert of Deutz, his contemporary, and distinguishes six major phases. One of the most glorious is the era of the Roman Empire, since it was then that Christ became man and gave History a new meaning.[209] His view is that the eternal conflict between the city of salvation—the City of God—and the city of damnation, is continually waged on earth, the two cities being intimately and inextricably intertwined; and the empire is no stranger to this conflict. Otto was deeply pessimistic,[210] and, at the end of the first version of the *Chronicle*, announced the early coming of the Antichrist and the end of the world. When he reworked his text before presenting it to Frederick, the new hope of the empire, he softened somewhat the mechanical rigor of his vision. Yet the fact remains that for him, as for many thinkers of his time, the end of the world was at hand, and the emperor's duty was to take care to keep Christianity on the road of salvation and to bring Infidels and pagans into the Christian fold. Thus the approach of Doomsday[211] added new gravity to the duty of extending the Church. But, as Otto sees and deplores, the rivalry between the empire and Rome threatened to weaken the effort needed.[212] At the level of action the bishop of Freising achieved little enough[213] in the contest that was brewing, and he died without having witnessed its somber developments.

As a studious and faithful disciple of Gilbert de la Porrée, Otto contrasts the *genuinum*—divine, unique, solitary, *uncreated*—with the *nativum*—the *created*—which is common to all human beings. Only the *nativa* are accessible to human reason, and Otto deduces that the essential identity among men thus justifies the term "human race."[214] So here was a mind capable of understanding and appreciating the rigorous monotheism of Islam, yet for all sorts of reasons[215] he ignored it. Here was a "universalist" who could have done justice to Africa and its people, yet of both he has no more than the rudimentary image that came to him through his intellectual inheritance. Granted, Egypt, so suspect to some of his contemporaries, seemed to him worthy of consideration, since she had given thousands of saints to the Church;[216] granted, too, that this watchful diplomat took note of Egypt's offer of an alliance against the Turks when Antioch was besieged during the First Crusade.[217] As for the rest of the continent,[218] which he knew only from Orosius, it received slight notice in the *Chronicle* and appears as little more than the ancient Roman province.[219] Ethiopia is mentioned:[220] it had been ruled by Semiramis simultaneously with India and had escaped the Deluge, but a terrible plague had decimated it:[221] its inhabitants' bodies were blackened.[222] For Otto the only real problem was what the shape and color of these people's bodies would be on Resurrection Day.[223] But at least

98

he does not classify Ethiopians with monsters. Otto, neither hostile nor sympathetic, opines that black is their normal color, and that the fact that they have white teeth is not important.[224]

Although both logic and experience made him pessimistic, Otto still hoped that the empire would recover, faithful to its destiny, which was to lead the Christian people to the final confrontation with Antichrist. His education and his convictions turned him against the Muslims, and he was heir to the long Occidental tradition of philosophical and ideological introversion; but the bishop of Freising was also the intelligent student of the new Parisian philosophers and of the "new Aristotle" coming from Muslim Spain. His view of the universe was such that he could not help wishing that the whole world would come to Christ: far-off peoples became an objective worthy of interest. In a subsidiary and more immediate way they could lend military aid against the Turks and could open a breach in the as yet impenetrable wall of Muslim encirclement. But among these peoples he does not include the Africans. At best—and this remark is not without importance—he knows that a Theban named Maurice conducted himself admirably as a Christian, and that he submitted to martyrdom along with 6,666 of his comrades, some few of whom, escaping that massacre, had in turn been martyred at Cologne with St. Gereon.[225] On the other hand the Orient and Asia, as he sees them, offer possible recourse. Islam appears to be Asiatic, the Turks are Asiatic; but probably he also had much older historical reasons in mind, reasons founded in Christian culture. Asia, after all, was the lost Paradise, Gog and Magog, the very origin of the human race if one followed the Bible.

"Prester John" is the first to come in view. Let us follow Otto's recital. In 1145 certain Armenians came from the East: they were sent by their catholicos—so-called because of the great number of bishops who were subordinate to him[226]—to find out how their religious rites compared with those of the Greeks and the Latins. During their meeting with the pope they were the astonished witnesses of a miracle: two doves flew up and down above the pontiff's head. The consultations continued for a long time, and the Armenians related all sorts of extraordinary things that happened where they came from, while their hearers listened with amazement.[227]

But now, without any transition, Otto turns to another item with a promising future. Hugh, bishop of Jabala[228] in Syria, arrives in Rome. In tears he describes to the pope the desolation of the churches after the fall of Edessa: he wants to cross the Alps to seek help from the king of the Romans and the Franks, i.e., the emperor.[229] He is the first to speak of a certain John, king and priest,[230] who lives in the farthest reaches of the Orient. This Prester John,[231] Nestorian like his people and a prodigious conqueror, desires to hasten to the aid of Jerusalem.[232] His plans had been held up for a long time because he could not get his forces across the Tigris: the valorous and all-powerful warrior had been waiting for the river to freeze over. Had he not been forced to return to his own land to restore peace and order, he certainly would have marched westward. And finally—feeding manna to the myth-makers—the bishop of Jabala adds that Prester John is a descendant of the Magi, the Wise Men of whom the Gospel speaks.[233] We probably will never know how much of this useful and wonderful information should be credited to the bishop of Jabala and how much to the bishop of Freising. One may well think that even if Otto is faithful to his sources—which he took care to correct upon occasion—he had no dislike for the marvelous, the only gleam of hope in the sorry world around him. His picture of the "Asiatic background" promised rich future developments.[234] It is surprising to note that it was only a few years before his allusion to Prester John took form in one of the most widely circulated forgeries of the Middle Ages, the so-called Letter of Prester John.[235] The extent to which this text, with variants,[236] was disseminated shows that at various times and for various reasons the entire Christian West felt that it had a bearing on its interests, as late as the sixteenth century.[237] Prester John is the key personage of the whole Oriental mythology, to whom Thomas[238] and the Magi in particular were gradually to be attached. As such he took root in the period we are studying, but it was not until the fifteenth century that we have pictorial evidence of this.[239]

Not long after him the Queen of Sheba makes her appearance in a manner that differs oddly as compared with older tradition. In 1181 Wernher, provost of the chapter of Canons Regular at Klosterneuburg, gave an order to Nicolas of Verdun for an ambo[240] on which salvation history was to be represented.[241] Following the new exegetical procedures prefigured by Suger at Saint-Denis,[242] Nicolas used images from the Old Testament to forecast those of the New and clarify their meaning, in a group of enameled panels. Two of these are of special interest to us. In one, the Three Magi, all of whom are white, bring "to the true God three mysterious gifts," as the accompanying legend says; in the other, the Queen of Sheba, whose skin is black and whose hair is blond, stands before fig. 103 Solomon, putting a protective arm over a kneeling servitor who presents gifts: "In the mystery of her gifts the queen reveals the faith to Solomon." This image is not understandable unless one refers to the new exegesis. Previously the queen had not been so prominent; she is an incidental personage in the Bible; her genealogy is uncertain and her place of residence variable. As late as the sixth century Cosmas Indicopleustes treats of her as a sovereign who had really existed, but the exegesis he applies to her is anything but favorable.[243] At the end of the twelfth century, however, the tendency is reversed. The road leading to the reversal is marked by exceedingly clear texts. Very early, with Origen, the image of the lovely pagan, whose faith could be her salvation, haunted certain "optimistic" theologians. Isidore of Seville already saw the queen as symbolizing those who pass from paganism to Christianity by their own volition.[244] In the twelfth century the idea was further developed by French interpreters of the Scripture, of whom the most noteworthy in this respect was Hugh of St.-Victor. Rupert of Deutz,[245] drawing his inspiration from the same principles upon which the Parisian teaching was based, but being especially careful about a precise exegesis founded on the Bible text itself, took the decisive step.[246] For him the queen symbolizes *the Gentiles* who desire to follow Christ—or, still more exactly, she stands as the symbol of the *nations of the whole world*, the Jews excepted.

On this point German exegesis differed from the French, being more allegorical, and adopted a typological orientation which for two or three centuries was to follow a new line of development. What else, indeed, was the symbolic Gentile world but the Asian and European nations which the empire, a new "chosen people,"[247] was called to convert? So Otto of Freising's thought was completed and illustrated. The influence of Rupert of Deutz was immediately and lastingly effective: the manuscripts and the Klosterneuburg ambo are evidence of this. The new theme of the Queen of Sheba as symbol of the pagan world was to spread and beget an original iconography.[248] Sometimes the queen is white, and her entourage is the only sign of her African origin. In a stained-glass window in Canterbury Cathedral, dating from the end of the twelfth century,[249] the queen moves fig. 99 forward toward Solomon, followed by two servitors mounted on dromedaries, one of whom wears a turban, while the other is a black recognizable by his facial traits, his woolly hair and his blue-tinted face—a convention followed in thirteenth-century windows to render black color. Thus the queen's attendants symbolize the Gentiles and relate directly to Rupert of Deutz's thought.[250] The same inspiration is expressed at Chartres, though less explicitly and at a slightly later date:[251] on the north portal a black figs. 100, 101 menial crouches under the feet of the queen, holding a cup filled with gold: the realism of the figure is striking.

Toward the end of the thirteenth century the black queen of Klosterneuburg reappears in the imperial area and in the lands of the empire's allies. At Strasbourg a medallion in a window dated about 1270 shows her fig. 102

99

99. Meeting of Solomon and the Queen of Sheba. Stained-glass window (detail). Late XII century. Canterbury, cathedral.

100. Queen of Sheba between Balaam and Solomon. About 1230. Chartres, Cathedral of Notre-Dame, portal of the north transept.

101. Detail of figure 100: black man crouching beneath the feet of the Queen of Sheba.

100

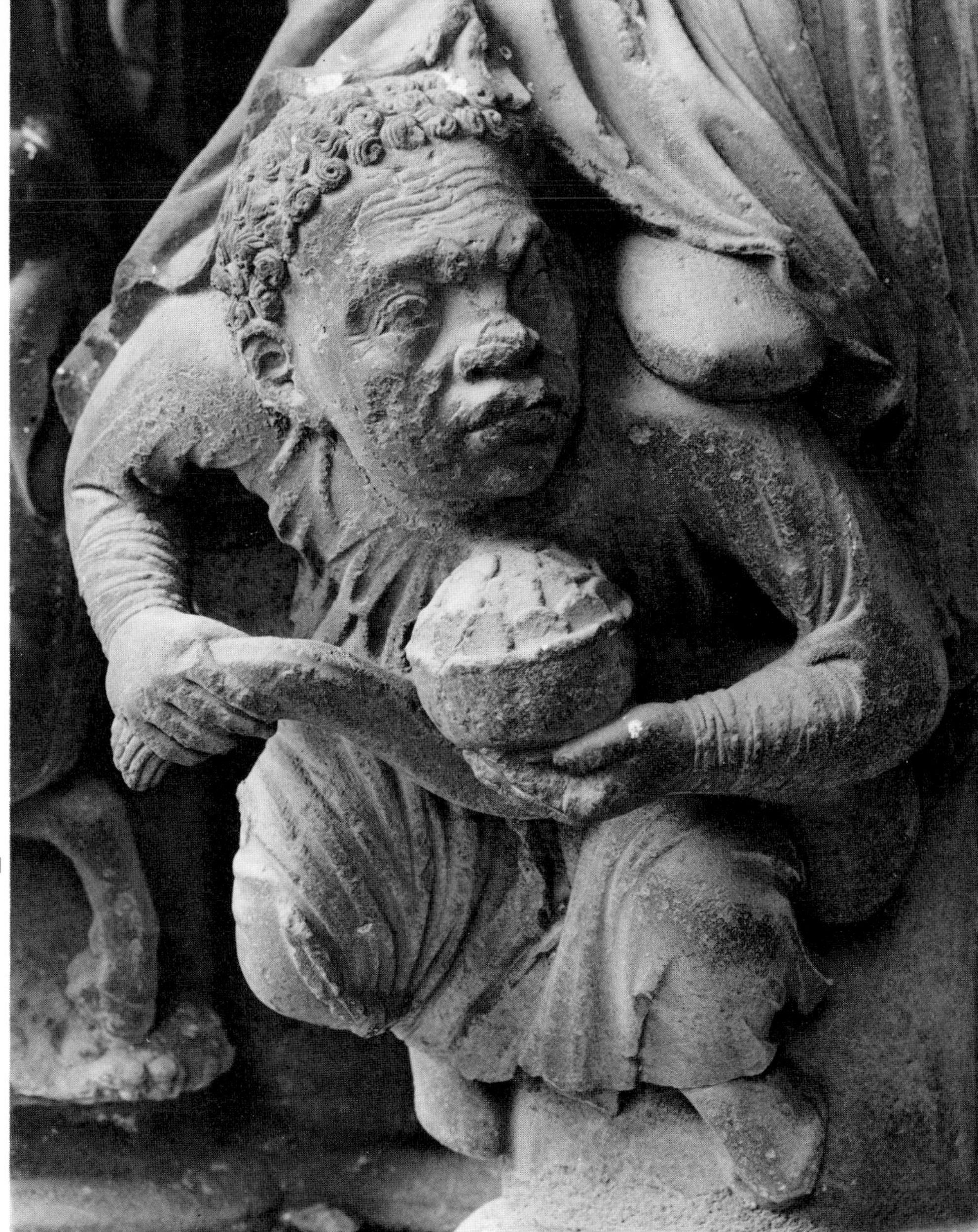

101

before Solomon, followed by a servingwoman; her bluish gray face and long hair of the same color clearly indicate the artist's intention to blacken the queen.[252] Nor is this an isolated case, since in the same period we find her again with the same blue-tinted face (here the servant is treated the same way) in the Cathedral of Cologne, in the typological stained-glass windows of the Chapels of the Three Kings and of St. Stephen.[253] Despite the restorations there seems to be no doubt that the artist was carrying out Rupert of Deutz's idea.

We have already touched on the Magi.[254] Coming from the depths of the Christian era, they appear in a new light in the lands of the empire during the second half of the twelfth century. In these years an outstanding personage, Rainald of Dassel,[255] chancellor to Frederick Barbarossa, played a leading role. Rainald, like Otto of Freising, belonged to a great German family and was a man of culture, educated at Hildesheim. In the course of his studies he came in contact with a certain Eckbert, whom we shall meet again shortly,[256] and probably received further instruction in Paris. In 1153 he became provost of the Cathedral of Hildesheim, and after 1156, as archchancellor of Italy, he was one of Frederick Barbarossa's closest and

102

most trusted associates, instigating, in particular, the ruthless policy that set the emperor against the Italians and against Rome. Frederick imposed him on Cologne as archbishop in 1159, but he did not succeed in taking full possession of the see until after 1162. He played a cautious game in ecclesiastical affairs, notably refusing to ask the antipope, whom the emperor supported, for episcopal ordination. Contrariwise he was very aggressive in Italy. The Milanese having received him ungraciously in 1159, he got his revenge three years later, when his master sacked the city. It was then that he "encountered" the Magi. In 1158, in the Church of S. Eustorgio outside the walls of Milan, three bodies had been discovered in a remarkable state of preservation, and tradition had it that they had come from Greece: the idea sprang up that they were the bodies of the Wise Men-Kings. Rainald, familiar with the emperor's custom of sharing relics among his bishops, seems to have lost no time in winning over, by a bold stroke, both the emperor and the bishopric of Liège.[257] On 12 June 1164 (the dates are important) he sent an embassy from Pavia to Cologne to announce the arrival of the precious relics, which he convoyed by slow stages, making a long detour through Burgundy.[258] His aim was to support the claim of the antipope Paschal III, whom he had acknowledged as successor to Victor IV:[259] for this reason he met general resistance, in the course of his journey, from the supporters of Alexander III, the legitimate pope since 1159.[260] Rainald passed through Salins, Besançon, Breisach, and Mainz, and reached Cologne on 23 July.[261] His welcome—well planned, as we shall see—was obviously a triumph. Two pages of the register of the *Acts* of the archbishops of Cologne[262] are devoted to the ceremonies organized by Rainald of Dassel, the letters he wrote and received, the parts of the holy bodies which he sent to other churches in Germany. How, after all that, could Cologne refuse him the enthronement so long deferred? On 2 October 1165, Rainald was finally installed as metropolitan archbishop. It was the Magi's first miracle.

Who are these Magi, these Wise Men whom everyone coveted? More especially, what place in the life of the Church does exegesis assign to them? M. Elissagaray's excellent book, coming after G. Vezin's work,[263] makes it unnecessary to go into detail for the old periods. Although the Magi had neither cult nor iconography of any importance in Western Europe, an impressive cluster of apocryphal tales, which still continue to mislead more than one historian, grew up around their persons. For a long time they were objects of suspicion—*magus* is a word with a pagan connotation, as is the Arabic *maǧus*—but in the twelfth century, as we have stated, they took on a new character which calls for our attention. In that period, and not until then, ideas carried over for centuries in sermons and manuscripts sprouted once again. Prudentius,[264] Tertullian, and Pope Leo the Great[265] had pointed to their allegorical importance. But in the Occident[266] Leo the Great was the first to go much further: "The blindness of the Jews makes us realize how grateful we must be to the Lord for having enlightened the Gentiles. . . . Thus the prophetic text already instructed the Gentiles: foreigners learned to recognize Christ foretold by the ancient oracles, while the faithless Jews had the truth on their lips but kept the lie in their hearts. . . . Let us, beloved sons, acknowledge in the Magi who worshiped Christ the first fruits of our vocation and our faith. . . . The truth

102. Solomon and the Queen of Sheba (detail). Fragment of a stained-glass window. From Strasbourg, Church of St-Thomas. About 1270. Strasbourg, Musée de l'Œuvre Notre-Dame.

103. Nicolas of Verdun. Solomon and the Queen of Sheba. Enameled plaque of an ambo. 1181. Klosterneuburg, Museum des Chorherrenstiftes Klosterneuburg.

103

which the Jews in their blindness refused to accept has shed its light over all nations."[267] In another sermon the same author gives the theoretic universal explanation: God had promised Abraham posterity in numbers beyond counting, and he became the father of the nations. The Jews, blinded by earthly goods, allowed their heritage to be perverted even in the sphere of politics and rejected the luminous signs that forecast the coming of Christ. There is no anti-Semitism in these texts, but the position taken against the "blind" Jews is very harsh, and medieval iconography perpetuated it in the image of the Synagogue blindfolded. Leo I draws the conclusion which seems to have been forgotten until the twelfth century—with some rare exceptions—just as the "bodies of the Three Kings" had been: "Come in, then, O fulness of the nations, come into the family of the patriarchs. Receive, O sons of the promise, the blessing of the race of Abraham, since the sons of his blood renounce it. Let all peoples, in the person of the Three Magi, adore the Creator of the universe, and let God no longer be known in Judea alone, but throughout the whole world."[268] Explicit as these texts are, it must be emphasized that they found few echoes among twelfth-century French exegetes. St. Bernard seems not to have heeded them:[269] no more did Hugh of St.-Victor.[270] Abelard, while he retained the image of their universal vocation, established no contrast between the Magi thus exalted and the blind Jews:[271] he may question their royal status, but grants them some value as being the first fruits of the Christian nations.[272] Some of his sermons show that the legendary content connected with the Magi was known again after centuries of silence: according to him these sages lived in a cavern on a mountain, which they climbed every year in expectation of the sign.[273] French exegesis, both allegorical and theological, was reluctant to attach too much weight to these obscure personages, preferring to remain centered on the person of Christ.

With Rupert of Deutz the thrust is more in the line of Leo the Great. There is no explicit censure of the blindness of the Jews, but the Magi are wise and learned men who of their own will sought to know Christ and to accept the faith he came to teach: they symbolize the assent of the pagan nations.[274] Rainald of Dassel, in his letter to the people of Cologne dated 12 June 1164, says that the emperor had made him a gift "of the bodies of the three Wise Men-Kings, symbolic first fruits of the nations and presage of the Church to come from among the nations, who brought their precious gifts to Christ lying in the stable."[275] The text is important, since the author uses the words *in typum* for the first time, these words being the key to typological exegesis. Note, too, that Rainald wrote his letter seventeen years before Nicolas of Verdun executed the Klosterneuburg ambo. Moreover, Rainald's successor in Cologne commissioned Nicolas to make a reliquary in which the remains of the Kings would be enshrined—a detail worth noting. We must not be too quick, as H. Rauh perhaps is,[276] to see a trace of violent hostility toward the Jews[277] in this newborn typology, but the 1164 letter deserves thoughtful consideration: it may well turn out to be a landmark of the first importance.[278] In it, for the first time, the typological significance of the Magi was unmistakably affirmed in the empire, at the very time the empire was seeking foundations, as we have seen, for the universalism evoked by Otto of Freising.

The operation conducted at Cologne some months after the translation of the relics was unquestionably one of wide-ranging import: planned by Frederick I[279] and Rainald in concert, its purpose was to make the Rhineland metropolis a focus from which the light of Christianity should radiate. Rainald was enthroned on 2 October 1165. On 25 December the remains of Charlemagne were raised at Aachen. On 28 January 1166 (after a *pro forma* consultation with antipope Paschal III), the archbishop of Cologne, by imperial command and upon his own authority as metropolitan, proclaimed the sanctity of the founder of the Empire of the West. The vicissitudes of the struggle with Rome after Rainald's death in 1167, and the failure of Frederick I's projects, assured this ceremony a less than glorious future: all that was left was a student celebration on the feast day of St. Charlemagne, observed until World War II. But at no other time in the Middle Ages was a similar ideological effort made to give the Germanic Empire a prestige at once religious and temporal. The Magi were closely connected with this effort, which aimed at widening the Christian empire to the ends of the earth, thus embracing the pagan nations whose precursors they had been at the feet of Christ. Is it surprising, therefore, that a whole body of traditions, in the form of liturgies and plays, was put together at Cologne around the Magi-Kings?[280] As early as 1164, and of course at Cologne, definitive names were attributed to the Three Kings.[281] It was only later that Peter Comestor's *Historia scholastica*, written between 1170 and 1178, popularized their names.[282]

A twelfth-century apocryphal writing,[283] long attributed to Bede, describes the Three Kings in precise detail. Melchior is an old man with white hair and beard, clothed in a blue tunic and an orange cloak: he carries the gold. Gaspar is a beardless young man dressed in an orange tunic and red cloak; he brings the frankincense. Balthasar is dark-skinned—*fuscus*—bearded, wearing a red tunic; he offers the myrrh. Surely an invitation to portray such remarkable personages in order to assure their renown!

The vision of Elizabeth of Schönau[284] is more troublesome. On the feast of the Epiphany in 1154 she had a vision of three crowned kings who adored Christ, laid their crowns at his feet, and received them again from him.[285] One year later on the same feast day a second vision evoked the coming of the Three Magi: one of them offered coins to the Infant[286]—an important detail originating in a Pseudo-Matthew.[287] The dates of these visions are disconcerting: they are earlier than the finding of the bodies in Milan and their transfer to Cologne (Elizabeth died before they arrived there), and antedate most of the works we know of, with the possible exception of the one that Rupert of Deutz dedicated to the archbishop of Cologne, in which such details do not appear. As for the ancient apocrypha, it seems fairly certain that Elizabeth could not have had knowledge of them. The critical examination of the second vision, therefore, poses problems of erudition that we were not in a position to investigate. The first is no less interesting: does it not constitute a veritable manifesto in favor of the imperial and antipapal theories, according to which the king—in this context the emperor—owes his crown to God alone? In 1154 this theme was still put forth very discreetly, but this was not so a year or two later, and *a fortiori* after the translation in 1164. Thus we are drawn toward the hypothesis of a late interpolation of the content of these apparitions.

And who was this Elizabeth of Schönau, whom the Church canonized[288] and considered a great mystic? In 1141, at the age of twelve, she entered the Monastery of Schönau, near Bonn, and was professed there in 1147. She began to have revelations when she was twenty-three years old. She made the content of these known (her contemporaries scorned them) to her brother Eckbert, a fellow-student of Rainald of Dassel, a canon of Bonn, and a future abbot of Schönau. Eckbert provided his sister, whose education was limited, with edifying reading matter, including the story of St. Ursula—again a reminiscence of Cologne. Elizabeth died at Schönau, probably on 18 June 1164.[289] The account of her visions was not put in final form by Elizabeth but by her brother, who, as F.W.E. Roth himself admits, reshaped them considerably.[290] The manuscript tradition of this material is so confused that recently K. Köster[291] made a remarkable effort at critical classification which reveals Eckbert's modifications, but the study of the text itself is still to be done. The rather ambiguous personality of Eckbert would merit attention.[292] He became a priest at his sister's instigation, urged on by her visions. He seems to have been destined for higher things by the archbishops of Trier and Cologne, but to have been modest enough to be satisfied with the abbacy of Schönau. After having prosecuted heretics he was writing a satire directed against the Jews when death overtook him in 1184.[293] One is tempted to wonder whether Eckbert might be responsible for the twice-repeated allusions to the Magi, and might have deemed it important to divulge them after the event, for the glory of his sister, of Schönau, and of Cologne. A final "disconcerting" text: in the thirteenth century[294] a prayer attributed to the nuns of Schönau completed the twelfth-century Pseudo-Bede mentioned above[295] without really adding anything new; it changed Balthasar *fuscus* to Balthasar *niger*.

If we consider these details in relation to the black queen at Klosterneuburg, dated 1181, we see that in different cases the dark color has a significance that must be examined. Are these blacks in the ethnic sense, meaning Africans? Are we faced with a black Queen of Sheba and a Wise Man already representing the black continent, or is this a new phase in the development of Occidental symbolism? We note first that in general we are concerned only with *dark* color; the sources speak indiscriminately of *fuscus* and of *niger*, although the authors knew full well the nuance that distinguished the two words.[296] The iconography of the Queen of Sheba confirms the symbolic significance, not the ethnic implication, of the color, which varies from dark brown to bluish gray depending on the support chosen. Moreover there is not yet any effort at realistic portraiture of blacks: the Queen of Sheba is fair-haired. So, at the end of the twelfth century, there is no "ethnicism" in the area of the empire. Dark color roughly symbolizes the pagan peoples, but the earlier pejorative intention is absent, since the Gentiles are called to the faith and to salvation; however, they are not yet explicitly connected with Africa. It seems to us that the question does not arise with regard to the empire until the thirteenth century, when real portraits of blacks made their appearance; but even then they were exceptional, and until the end of the fifteenth century the representation of the black was based on symbolic rather than ethnological considerations.

That difference was to have increasing weight in the area around the Mediterranean. There the imperial point of view was not readily adopted, and the thorny question of the positive figuration of blacks in the light of their association with the world of believers and with salvation was framed in entirely different terms. The theme also underwent a very distinct development in that region. The debate about the signification of black color will have to be freshly studied in depth so far as the fourteenth and fifteenth centuries are concerned.[297]

In the empire the cult of the relics of the Magi was maintained and developed methodically in the thirteenth century.[298] The interests of the imperial authority, which used the cult to reinforce the ideology of the autonomy of kingly power, coincided with those of the people of Cologne, both clerical and lay. Surprisingly, despite the clear leads furnished by the Pseudo-Bede and the Schönau prayer, artists did not exploit the theme. Neither the manuscript painters, nor Nicolas of Verdun on the reliquary he made for Cologne, represented one of the Wise Men as a black. This fact contrasts with the remarkable appearance of the Queen of Sheba in 1181.

We might note, merely as an aside, a painting in a manuscript executed in Catalonia in the late twelfth century and, unfortunately, destroyed during the last war:[299] in it the Adoration of the Magi included one King fig. 104
with a black face. A careful examination of the photograph shows that the black color was added later, and that whoever retouched the painting forgot to do the neck and the hands. This fact is rather intriguing, since we know that the manuscript was taken to Germany at a date which, regrettably, we have not been able to determine, so that the example is not of much use to us. But imagine what hypotheses could be built on such an

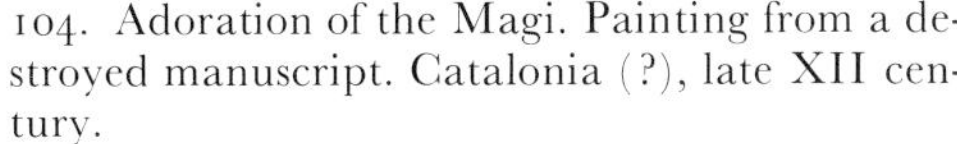
104. Adoration of the Magi. Painting from a destroyed manuscript. Catalonia (?), late XII century.

104

example if the history of this manuscript were known in detail and if we still had the manuscript itself: it may be that we would have in hand the first instance of the deliberate portrayal in Germany of a black Wise Man. On the contrary, what we have is one more indication of how slow the artists were in adopting the proposed program. Could this have resulted from a conscious, ideological refusal? One would be hard pressed to think so, particularly with regard to Nicolas of Verdun, given the example of the Queen of Sheba.

Inevitably, therefore, we must lean toward other interpretations, purely hypothetical as they are for the time being. The allusions to a "dark" King are, in fact, very rare in the texts, and might have emanated from a strictly limited milieu "around Cologne." Eckbert we can leave aside: if he had wanted to make much of the idea that one of the Magi was a black, he would not have hesitated, given the opportunity, to add a third vision to his account of his sister's mystical experiences. The Rhine region, however, is still the most likely place of origin of the Pseudo-Bede and the Schönau prayer. The date might well be put at the very end of the twelfth century or in the early thirteenth, after the Klosterneuburg representation became popular. But the "Magi record" looks very weak to us in comparison with the image of the Queen of Sheba: there was no profound ideological justification for making one of the Kings an African. Typologically and in the overall perspective the Magi were signs of the Gentiles: only later did they come to represent different regions of the pagan world. We have seen that imperial circles, with Otto of Freising and after him, turned their attention to Asia, not to Africa. In the late twelfth century there was no logical connection in the minds of the artists between *fuscus* or *niger* and the African continent: at the most, they might think of the Indian blacks who surrounded St. Thomas. For a long time the Three Kings symbolized the three ages of humanity, not the three regions of Gentility.[300] No one of the Magi could have been represented as a personage of color and then as a black man, until a chain of reasoning based on "proofs" had enabled the painters to acquire the "certitude" that one King was, historically, a black. What we must find out, then, is when the ideological link with Africa came to light. In our opinion, as in M. Elissagaray's, it was John of Hildesheim who first made the connection and created the historical conditions for the blackening of one of the Magi in the fourteenth century. John of Hildesheim will be treated further on in this volume.

Coming back to the empire of Frederick Barbarossa: it is clear that during the second half of the twelfth century, but in different historical circumstances, Prester John, introduced by Otto of Freising, the Queen of Sheba, the first product of Rupert of Deutz's typological exegesis, and the Magi, placed at the center of a remarkable politico-religious machinery, rejoined the older heritage connected with Edessa. This whole ensemble was linked with the Orient, not with Africa.[301] Alexander, also an "Oriental," was not present; he does not seem to have attracted much interest during the twelfth century, but the literature of the time is still to be studied in this regard. This entire corpus of legends, new interpretations, and promising personages had to undergo a long ripening and eventual synthesis. But the elements of a logical and coherent dream were in place and would be able to open out during the centuries to come, as the possibly variable fortunes of the empire allowed. In any case the thought currents in this realm differed sharply from those in the Mediterranean sector, and would continue to do so.

NEW MEDITERRANEAN VIEWS OF THE BLACKS IN THE THIRTEENTH CENTURY

Ambiguous and diverse as it was, the thirteenth century, as we have seen, shows here and there that it maintained the older unfavorable traditions with regard to blacks, particularly in the representation of executioners and in the testimony of the Crusaders.[302] But already evidences of a change of cf. figs. 27-37
heart were coming to the fore. In the field of iconography there is not much evidence of this kind. Italy gave the established theme of the Adoration of the Magi a historical dimension in which the cortège received increased prominence. On one of the panels of the Siena pulpit Nicola Pisano[303] carved an entourage in which, amidst the mounted retainers and in front of the three white Kings, two black camel drivers, clearly typed and with fig. 105
expressive faces, stand out. Does this indicate the infiltration of a typological image closely resembling the one in the Canterbury window, or perhaps the starting point of a tendency to admit Africans as personages of History? We do not have enough evidence to enable us to decide. On the other

105

105. Nicola Pisano. Black camel drivers in the cortège of the Magi. Relief on a pulpit (detail). 1266-68. Siena, Cathedral of Sta. Maria Assunta.

hand, certain themes which were revived in the late twelfth century are illustrated in the vast Gothic area. At Semur-en-Auxois, for instance, a tympanum in which the life of St. Thomas is represented was placed in the north portal of the Church of Notre-Dame. In it we see the saint distributing to the poor the money he had received from King Gundaphorus to build a palace (he was reputed to be a first-rate architect); in that way he built a spiritual palace.[304] The capping of the right-hand jamb may represent two persons involved in the preceding scene: one of them is a peasant carrying a purse, the other a figure with the conventional features of a black, the body covered with thick hair.[305] In order to grasp the meaning of this tympanum, we must probably keep in mind the fact that since the late twelfth century a debate, decisive for the evolution of Christianity, had been opened in the Mediterranean area. The debate concerned the morality of acquiring personal wealth—a prime objective in a society in which commerce was thriving. With St. Francis of Assisi the thirteenth century devoted much deep thought to this question, stressing the connection between the growth of riches and the outbreak of violent disputes among men and seeking, by the exaltation of "poverty"—meaning an attitude of serenity with regard to earthly goods—to modify the way people treated each other in the Christian world at that time.

fig. 106

fig. 107

By that very fact, and however bizarre the lines of effort on the part of Dominicans and Franciscans, a new state of mind appeared concerning "the other." This was particularly true regarding Islam and, by way of consequence, Africa and Africans. Moreover, a certain number of Franciscans went to Africa to preach and suffer martyrdom. Thus was born a mode of thought of far-reaching import: it belonged to a minority within a Church seduced by the institutional embodiment of wealth and held in thrall by its mechanisms, but it lent new vigor to the old current of optimism which we have discerned in the origins of Christianity and to which Origen gave form. Nor were the Mendicants the only ones to ask new questions and to adopt more favorable attitudes. Cluny, which had been so violently hostile to the Muslims, in the twelfth century undertook, under Peter the Venerable, a serious study of "the adversary." In England in the same years, William of Malmesbury, whose attitude toward blacks,[306] as we see from a passage in the *Gesta regum Anglorum*, was anything but friendly, gave evidence of an open mind regarding Islam,[307] not forgetting that for a Western European the Muslims were pretty much identified with the hated race of the Turks.

A further step was taken with and by the Mendicants, especially in Africa, which was considered to be more liable to come to terms with the Christians, and might in time return to Christianity. North Africa from Egypt to Morocco became a mission territory and an object of study. Blacks formed part of the population in this area, and were to become concrete partners for the Mediterraneans. We have seen the results of this in Spain, where the theme of the baptism of the black Moor developed in the second half of the thirteenth century and where twelfth-century French exegetical writings, particularly those of Peter Comestor,[308] were widely circulated. Generally speaking, the thirteenth century, after the nervous tics of the twelfth and the intellectual and religious crisis of the early decades, displayed a healthy optimism that belied the somber predictions of

106. Legend of St. Thomas. Carved tympanum. XIII century. Semur-en-Auxois, north portal of the Church of Notre-Dame.

107. Detail of figure 106: two crouching figures, one a wild man. Capping of the right-hand jamb.

107

106

Otto of Freising. M.-D. Chenu has called attention to the fact that the discovery of vast sections of the world-to-be-converted was a stimulus to theologians and philosophers; moreover, the victory of the papacy over the empire gave the ecumenical vision an abstract, spiritual perspective which it had been in danger of losing in the preceding century,[309] and opened for Christianity a future without foreseeable limits. The reasonable, optimistic character of Mediterranean Christendom, especially in the latter half of the thirteenth century, has been brought out by F. de Medeiros:[310] the aggressive attitude toward "the other" progressively gave way to a willingness on the part of a culture sure of its own values to enter into dialogue with the alien cultures now to be faced.

One might ask whether all Europe shared this state of mind. We have seen that the empire apparently had other views, at least until Frederick II's defeat. A web of quite original themes was woven around St. Maurice:

108

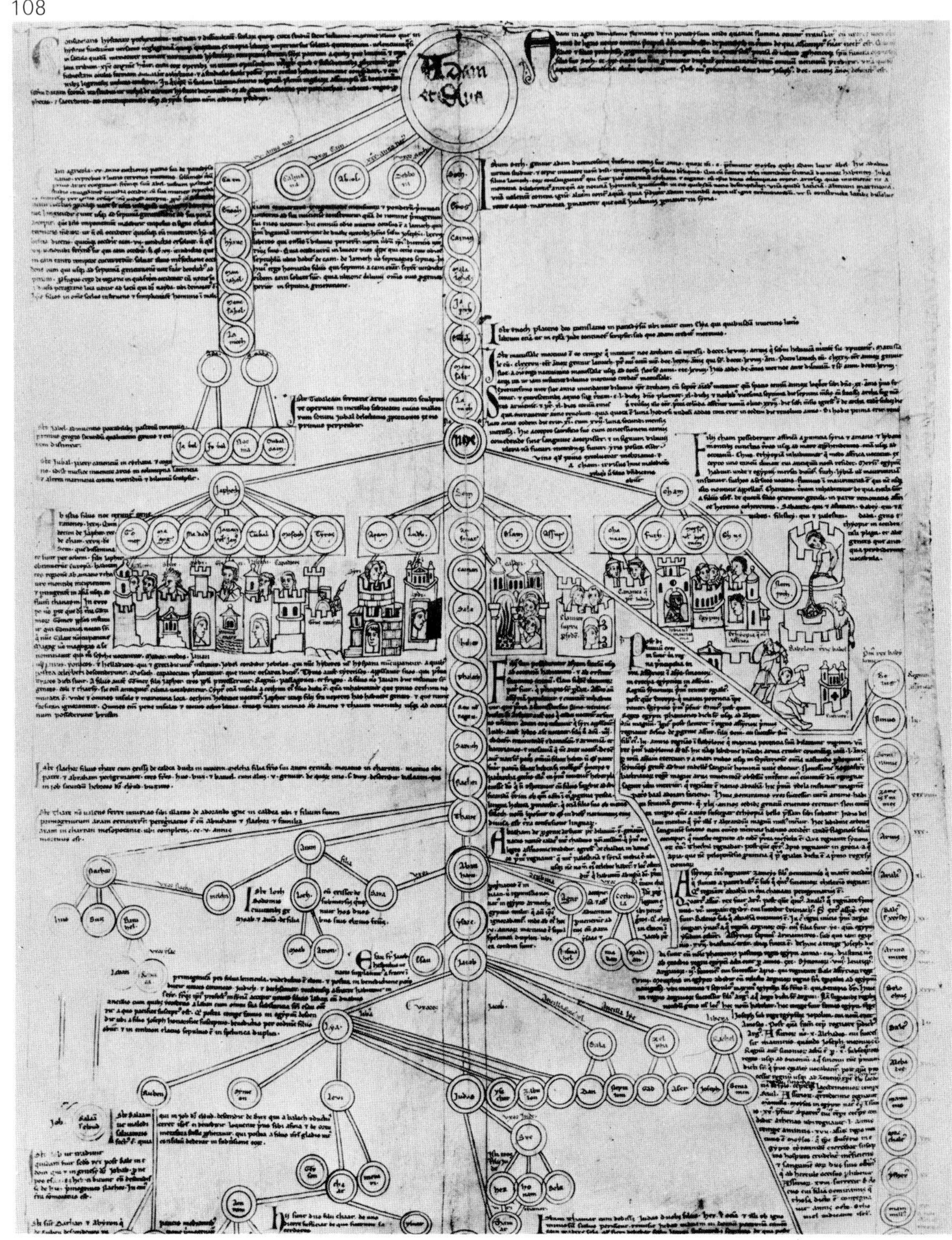

108. Beginning of a genealogy of Christ. Rotulus. From Soest, Cathedral of St. Patroklus. About 1230. Berlin (GFR), Staatsbibliothek Preussischer Kulturbesitz.

109. Detail of figure 108: descendants of Ham.

this we shall study later on. Furthermore, we must take note of an interest in biblical genealogy which was to develop extensively in subsequent centuries, taking the form of an effort to put some order into the flood of data made available in the Jewish and Arabic texts then being translated, and in the Oriental apocrypha gradually becoming known in Western Europe.[311] The dominant concern turned to the classification of human groups. The rudimentary definitions provided by the old commentaries on the diaspora after the destruction of the Tower of Babel were no longer enough.

In a roll of parchment dating from about 1230 and coming from Soest[312] we find an attempt to regularize the genealogical ideas then in circulation: the genealogical tree is worth some consideration. In fact this genealogy is almost entirely male; the immediate descendants of Adam (Abel dead, Cain cursed) are regarded as negligible and receive little attention. Emphasis is rather placed on Seth, last of Adam's sons and true figs. 108, 109

109

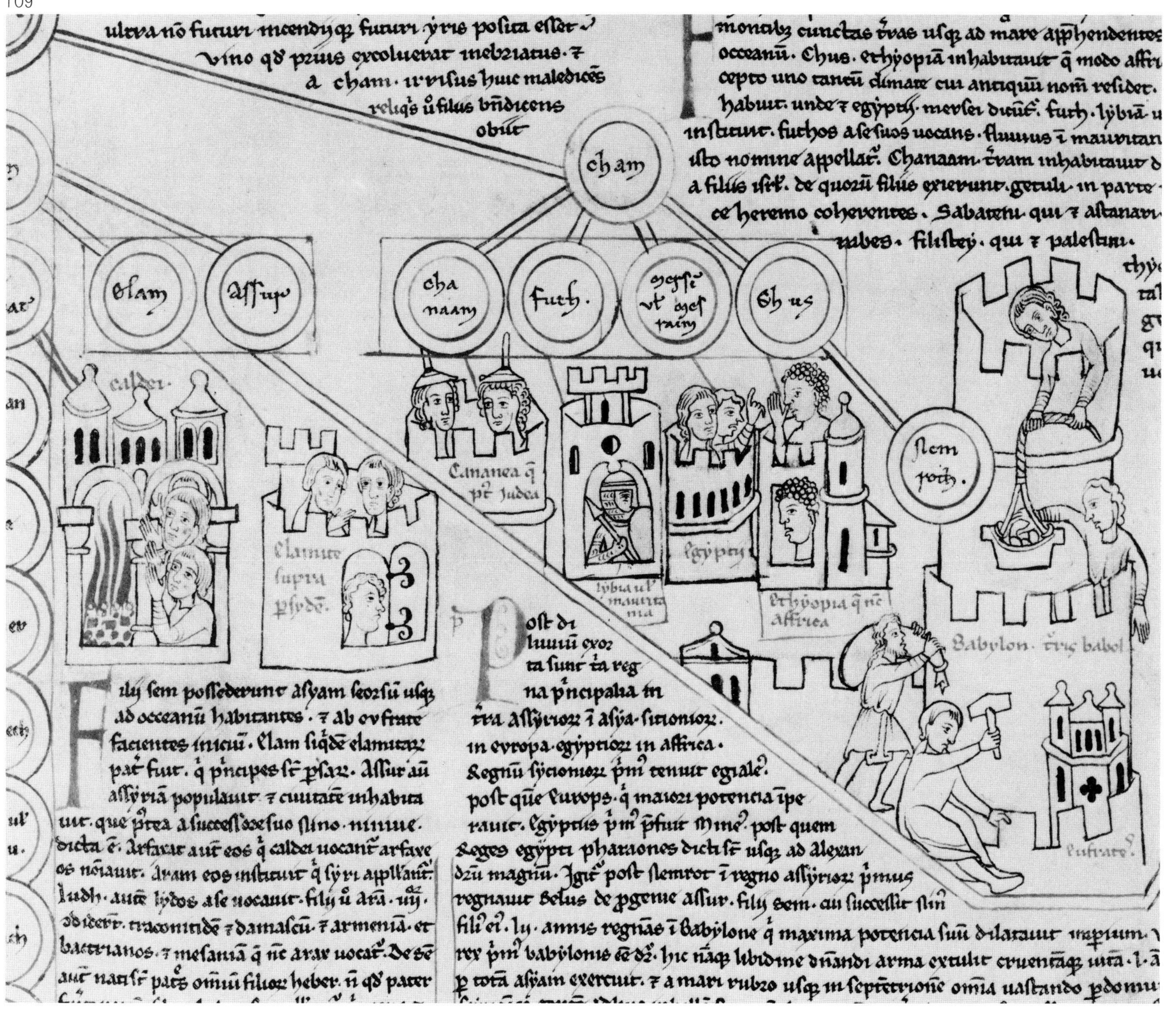

ancestor of Christ.[313] "Patrilinear" succession is assured down to Noah, and then the human race is redeployed. In the line under Noah, Shem and his descendants find their place. To the left of the central line Japheth's posterity is listed, but goes no further than the generation of his sons once they are settled in their respective areas. To the right we find Ham, whose unseemly conduct toward his father, briefly noted in the text, draws a curse upon his children, the curse being passed over quickly. Once again, the enumeration of Ham's descendants stops with his sons, Chus excepted. This image, as both text and probability indicate, should be read from right to left: on the right, Chus, who, according to the text, "lives in Ethiopia, called Africa, except for a climate[314] to which its ancient name remains attached." No further detail is given. Chus has a son, Nimrod, whose name is associated with the Tower of Babel, symbol of the pride of the descendants of Ham. The picture shows the family of Chus as blacks, recognizable by their profile and the conventional details of the hair, and, like the text, locates them in Ethiopia, "which today is called Africa."[315] Mersius, or Mizraim,[316] says the image, lives in Egypt; the text adds nothing. Futh lives in Libya, "which is now called Mauritania," says the text, "and where the name of a river is derived from his name"; the image simply confirms this detail. Chanaam lives in the land from which the children of Israel were driven out; among his descendants are numbered the Gaetuli, who settled in Africa close to the deserts. Lastly the text mentions Dathan, a personage we shall come across much later on—his posterity settled in western Ethiopia—and other peoples descended from Ham, their names not having survived, but here the image does not follow the text, and Dathan did not get a tower to live in, as his four brothers did. The author is discernibly uncertain, like his sources: Dathan turns up several times in the biblical story, but his identity is not clearly established, since he is connected with different genealogies.

It has been noted in passing that Jewish biblical commentaries certainly influenced the construction of this genealogy. It is possible to go much further: the whole construction was directly inspired by the Jewish exegesis of the Old Testament.[317] From Adam to Noah the human race evolved undivided, and guilty of more or less serious defections from God. After the Deluge and the episode of the Tower of Babel, nations and languages separated. Japheth and Ham were of little interest; the central branch, issuing from Shem, is the important one, since it leads to Abraham. With Abraham the age of the Just—the Hebrews—opens, as they return to monotheism and renew the alliance with God. Thus was determined, intentionally or not, a "montage" concerning the origin of mankind which, some centuries later, gave rise to theories of racial inequality.[318] By dint of insisting on—and giving pointed graphic representation to—the idea that the sons of Shem were the real descendants of Adam, this line of exegesis was in danger of promoting the idea that the origin of mankind was not unique.[319] An instructive comparison can be made between this Jewish influence and one that worked in the opposite direction, for we can observe the infiltration of Otto of Freising's Christian conceptions in a Frankfort midrash also dating from the thirteenth century. Here, then, is a rich field of investigation bearing on the two interpretations of the Bible current in the empire.

But there we are dealing with abstractions, while Africa was increasingly becoming a concrete reality to the eyes of people along the Mediterranean. One proof of this was the creation of a new religious order, the Trinitarians.[320] There had been tentative but unsuccessful efforts in twelfth-century Spain to create an order specifically devoted to the ransoming of captives.[321] John of Matha, according to tradition a Provençal and now a canonized saint, decided at the close of the twelfth century to bring this project to fruition and to ransom captives held in North Africa by the Muslims, using funds collected in the churches. He would also have to combat the shameful sale of Christians to Muslims by certain European traders.[322] Pope Innocent III approved the Rule of the new order 17 December 1198.[323] Drawing upon texts of St. Ambrose, St. Caesarius, archbishop of Arles, and St. Gregory the Great,[324] the Rule provided that the essential purpose of the Trinitarians would be to free captives from slavery. One third of the order's revenues was to be devoted to this work.[325] Success came quickly, and the order had houses, mostly in France,[326] but, as time went on, also in Flanders, Spain, England, and even in Ireland. Shortly after the turn of the century the pope gave John of Matha the convent of San Tommaso in Formis, located on the Caelian.[327] The building still stands: one enters through an arched opening, the sides of which

110

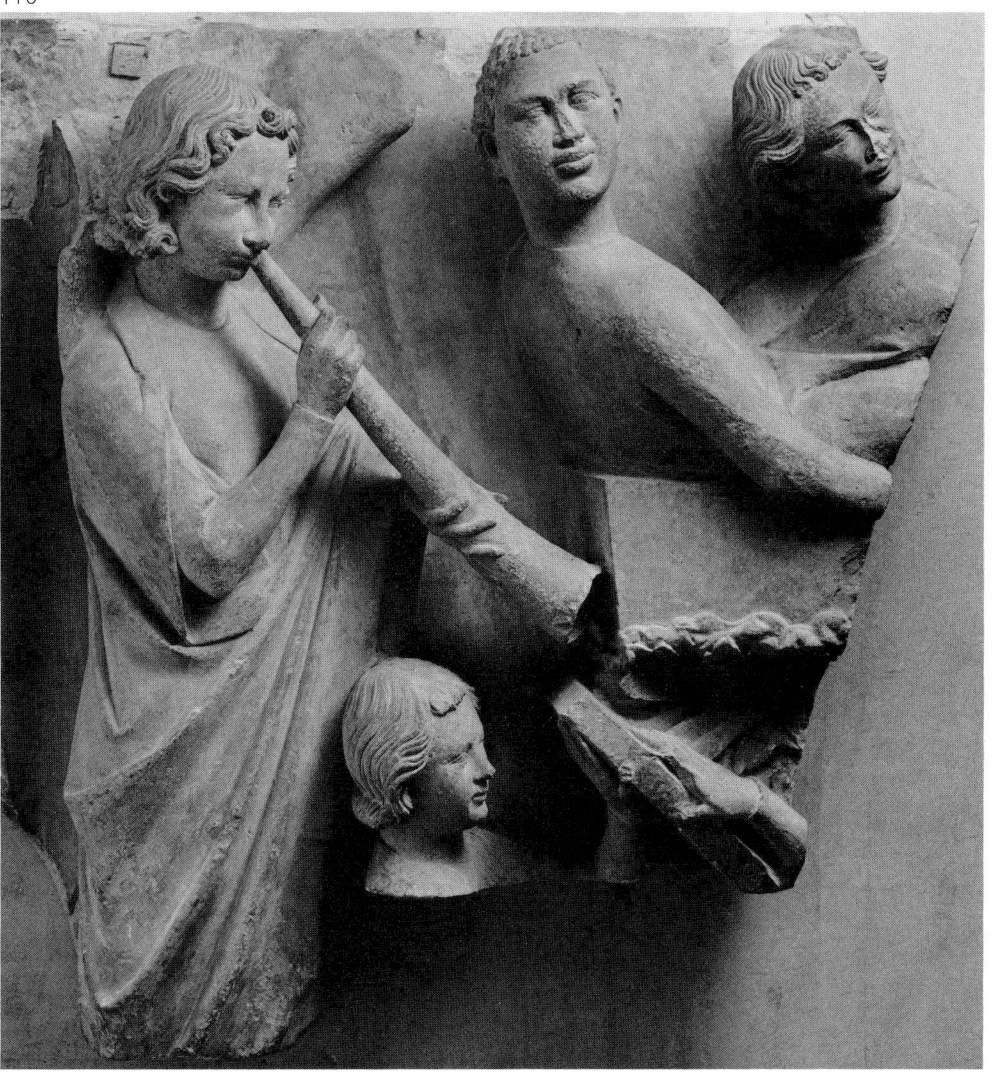

110. Resurrection of the Dead. Fragment of a carved tympanum. From the central portal of the west façade of the Cathedral of Notre-Dame in Paris. About 1220-30. Paris, Musée de Cluny.

111. Resurrection of the Dead (detail). Fragment of a carved tympanum. From the central portal of the west façade of the Cathedral of Notre-Dame in Paris. About 1220-30. Paris, Musée de Cluny.

112. Workshop of the Cosmati. Christ between two captives. Mosaic. About 1212. Rome, former Trinitarian convent of S. Tommaso in Formis.

are faced with marble. Above the opening is a blind arcature which shelters a large medallion in mosaic.[328] This medallion is of special interest to us. fig. 112 Against a gold field it shows a large Christ Pantocrator enthroned, his hands extended to hold two slaves by the arms, the one on his right a white man holding a long staff topped with a blue and red cross,[329] the one on his left a black: both have their feet shackled. A circular inscription leaves no doubt that the choice of this motif was deliberate, since it defines the emblem of "the Order of the Holy Trinity and of the Captives."[330]

The seals preserved in Paris[331] for documents drawn up by the Mathurins establish the fact that at least in the thirteenth century[332] the official seal of the Trinitarians represented Christ liberating two captives. This theme, however, disappeared in the fifteenth century.[333] Texts related to the history of the order throw light on this change. A poem dated 1444 puts the matter clearly: the order was then negotiating with the pagans to obtain the release of Christian prisoners. The generous goals conceived in the thirteenth century had become a marketplace procedure.[334] On the other hand, a prose account written in the fifteenth century[335] faithfully echoes a text, probably composed earlier, and describes the vision of John of Matha: the saint had seen God in a dream (more likely it was only an angel in the beginning) holding the chains of two slaves, one white and the

111

112

SIGNVM • ORDINIS • SANCTA • TRINITATIS • ET • CAPTIVORVM

other black. This, of course, is the theme of the San Tommaso mosaic. It must therefore be admitted that if the merchant mentality of the fifteenth century saw the "Saracen" as an object to be bought and sold, the Trinitarians of the thirteenth had regarded the black man as the equal of the white, to be ransomed and saved. It is both enlightening and painful to perceive that at least in the terms of a popular poem the high purposes of the thirteenth century had, in two hundred years, been completely shuffled under, and that the vision of the enemy Saracen had won out over the ecumenical message of Christ.

A more convincing proof of the change of attitude that was taking place in Europe is, as we see it, a figure on the portal of Notre-Dame de Paris, dating from about 1220-30. There among the dead rising from the grave at the sound of the trumpet of the Last Judgment, we find a young black man.[336] He is not yet explicitly included among the elect, but those who viewed the scene had to recognize him as a member of the human race—a lesson which the works of the twelfth century, beginning with Gilbert de la Porrée, had been teaching.

figs. 110, 111, 113

113

113. Head of the black in the Resurrection of the Dead. Detail of figure 110.

III

A SANCTIFIED BLACK: MAURICE

SAINT MAURICE: LEGEND AND HISTORY

Saint Maurice is a baffling personage. His historical existence is so doubtful that more than once the legitimacy of his cult has been vigorously contested.[1] On the other hand, as we shall see, rarely has a saint been accorded such manifestations of respect in different periods and in widely varying circumstances.[2]

The story of the martyrdom of Maurice and his companions of the Theban Legion has given rise to markedly divergent interpretations, some of them very critical, like D. van Berchem's,[3] others, like L. Dupraz's,[4] directed rather to determining what is historical and what is not. L. Dupraz, reexamining the difficult documentation as a whole, has attempted to refute D. van Berchem's hypercritical arguments. The texts, few in number, have probably been largely altered over the years. The basic document is the *Passion of the Martyrs of Agaunum*, written in the fifth century by Eucherius, bishop of Lyons;[5] a contemporary letter guarantees its authenticity.[6] In the eleventh century Marbod of Rennes made a versified version of the *Passion*.[7] In the twelfth it was Sigebert of Gembloux's turn to comment on the old text.[8] Anonymous authors at different times wrote poems of varying length in honor of Maurice and his companions. More worthy of note is an anonymous *Passion*, apparently composed in two stages, which supplements Eucherius's account at length.[9] On the whole, for what concerns the Life of St. Maurice, the manuscript tradition previous to the thirteenth century essentially concerns the political area of the empire.

L. Dupraz has sifted through all these stories. He establishes the fact that the Maurice of Eucherius's account is not to be confused with the Eastern saint of the same name, Maurice of Apamea.[10] He carefully matches up the stages of development of the Maurice cult with the archeological discoveries made at Saint-Maurice (Agaunum). He concludes that the martyrdom is entirely historical[11] and rejects the idea that Maurice may have been black.[12] He holds that the relics of the martyrs were brought to Agaunum between 386 and 392 through the good offices of a bishop named Theodore;[13] from Agaunum the cult spread to Tours, where St. Martin gave Maurice's name to his church,[14] and to Auxerre.[15] The major difficulty with the time sequence proposed by L. Dupraz lies in the hundred-year gap between the appearance of the relics at Agaunum and the foundation of the abbey.

At any rate the stories, whether or not the "facts" are historical, relate that Maurice, Candidus, Victor, Innocent, and their companions suffered martyrdom for refusing to renounce Christianity and to worship the gods of Rome. The incident is supposed to have taken place at a site not clearly defined, somewhere between the Danube and the Rhine.[16] The *Passion* containing the account of the martyrdom emphasizes the reason these officers and soldiers gave for their resistance: they were not refusing obedience to the emperor nor respect for military orders, but their conscience required them to accept death rather than renounce their faith. Marvelous themes for meditation in later centuries!

The foundation of the Abbey of Agaunum in 515 opens the history of the cult of St. Maurice.[17] A letter of St. Avitus, bishop of Vienne, dated 22 September 515, praises the Burgundian king Sigismund who had just inaugurated the perpetual chanting of psalms in honor of St. Maurice and his companions.[18] From then on the name of Sigismund is closely associated with that of Maurice.[19] Between 400 and 800 the cult of St. Maurice did not develop as did that of St. Martin, for instance. In addition to such centers of the Maurician cult as Angers and Tours there were some few others, of which we probably still have a very incomplete inventory.[20]

Hagiographical literature gave some attention to Maurice and his companions. Venantius Fortunatus devoted a poem to them,[21] making no reference to their "Theban" origin. Gregory of Tours celebrates them, likewise without connecting them with the East. During the early centuries of the Middle Ages it was another group of martyrs, then venerated at Cologne, who were honored under the name of "Thebans." A sixth-century Hieronymian Martyrology, coming from Auxerre, mentions Maurice and his companions at 22 September,[22] and the date became traditional. In the ancient sources the anonymous fellow martyrs of Maurice are always counted in very large (and obviously symbolic) numbers; most often the figure varies from three thousand to more than six thousand.[23]

It seems, however, that the successive masters of the region fostered the cult of the martyrs of Agaunum for motives that were essentially political. D. van Berchem[24] shows how after Sigismund's death Agaunum became the center for the defense and diffusion of the orthodox faith against all the trends that still threatened the propagation of Roman Christianity in Gaul. To further their own interests, the Merovingians continued the favorable treatment the Burgundian dynasty had granted the abbey.[25]

Liturgical sources provide far more precise information relative to the geography and chronology of the cult of St. Maurice. B. Opfermann's recent study,[26] which shows remarkable erudition, gives us a partial but significant view of the transformations this devotion underwent; yet it would seem that the author did not intend to draw out all the historical information that we think his essay brings to light. The prayers relating to Maurice fall into two chronologically distinct groups: one belongs to the period from the seventh to the twelfth century, the other essentially concerns the fifteenth and sixteenth centuries. For the time being it is the first group that will hold our attention; it furnishes some interesting pointers on the locations where the Maurice cult took root and from which it spread outward. The seventh- or eighth-century Gothic Missal probably came from Autun;[27] with the ninth- or tenth-century Gelasian Sacramentary from Verona (?)[28] and the Gregorian Sacramentary from Liège (823-55),[29] the Missal constitutes a self-contained whole, and its texts do not at first sight seem to have been copied or circulated to any great extent. At most we should note that (as B. Opfermann points out) the prayers dedicated in the Gregorian Sacramentary to Maurice and his companions use to a large degree the formulas found in those reserved in earlier versions for St. Lucy and St. Geminianus, at 16 September. Rome showed no great interest in St. Maurice, whereas the "Gaulish" texts gave him a place of honor from the beginning. The detail is worth noting, since it bears upon the propagation of the Maurice cult.[30]

The important liturgical text of this first period, the Sacramentary of Angoulême, dates from the ninth century:[31] it is of major historical significance since some of its prayers were reproduced several times until the twelfth century.[32] Hence Angoulême and the Carolingian world furnished a solid focal point for the Maurician liturgy, as Fulda did in the tenth and eleventh centuries.[33]

Thus the historic area of diffusion of the Maurice cult is clearly defined. Until the Carolingian period it was situated between the Massif Central and the Meuse: the expansion eastward, as we shall see again later on, took place beginning in the tenth century.[34] Italy is scarcely involved except through the copying of northern texts, with one exception. This is the Ambrosian Missal of Milan,[35] which constitutes an entirely independent tradition; there the emphasis is on the military aspect of Maurice's career and especially on his martyrdom for the faith.

We must give particular attention to the Carolingian period and area, if we are to understand how this cult was transformed from within. We learn much about this from the sacramentaries and martyrologies.[36] Until the middle of the ninth century the mention of Maurice, with the obligatory accompaniment of his companions, is routine. His martyrdom is celebrated on 22 September;[37] his name figures in the litanies.[38] Maurice is only one martyr among many whose merits are invoked for the remission of sins, as appears from the texts unearthed by B. Opfermann. Soon, however, new forms appear in the liturgy, while mention of the martyrs becomes more common. Whereas the Carolingian Martyrology of Usuard cited them at the time it was compiled,[39] their presence in the ninth-century Martyrologies of Bede and Florus[40] is often due to later interpolations. From then on the masses composed in honor of the martyrs of Agaunum[41] specifically request their protection.[42] And it seems reasonable, in view of the generalization of the formulas, to think that it was a very concrete military protection that was sought in the period when the raids from Scandinavia were developing. It would be interesting to determine whether these invocations were particularly frequent in the most threatened areas, from Flanders to the Loire.[43]

The poets of the Carolingian period paid their tribute to St. Maurice and his companions, as they did to St. Thomas, with the same rhetorical flourishes.[44] But the novelties—except for a form of folk piety that was fairly popular in northwestern France—appeared at another level: in the ninth century St. Maurice came to be cultivated by the ruling powers.[45] Charlemagne seems to have attributed to the saint the virtues of the perfect Christian warrior,[46] and this was a decisive change of direction in the Maurice cult. Like the populace, which relied on his intercession for protection, the Carolingian dynasty prayed to this military saint for the strength to resist and overcome attacks by enemy forces.[47]

Between 800 and 860 approximately, the cult of St. Maurice developed in two diametrically opposite directions, especially in France. One of them, popular with the common people and the clergy, led to the establishment of confraternities,[48] at least at Tours and in the Paris region; the other one, prevalent in official circles, connected the saint with the king and the army of the Franks. The first trend lost its point when the Capetians abandoned St. Maurice[49] in favor of St. Denis, and faded away after the eleventh century. On the contrary the second trend, deriving from the military, aristocratic, and royal tradition and passing through a series of transformations over a wide area, enjoyed constant success and underwent some unforeseen developments. Thus far St. Maurice is seldom Theban and always white. Of course the cult continued at Agaunum[50] and at Vienne,[51] where it took on new features at the end of the ninth century. About this same time, due to the importing of a sacramentary that probably was compiled on the Continent, the Maurice cult came into England.[52] It was not, however, destined to have any significant development there.[53]

The most important change was the eastward expansion of the cult during the tenth and eleventh centuries. The liturgical texts directly reflect what many other sources confirm. By the twelfth century, all the liturgical transformations being then complete, we see that St. Maurice was really celebrated only in the political sphere controlled by the empire, and in a vestigial way between the Seine and the Loire.[54] In the areas where the cult was in vogue, significant adjustments were made upon the old manuscripts.[55] In the Germanic lands, moreover, and especially in Bavaria, the name of St. Emmeram was associated, beginning in the eleventh century, with those of St. Maurice and his companions.[56]

Vienne had built its devotion to St. Maurice on a secondary legend,[57] according to which some of the saint's remains had been thrown into the Rhone by the executioners and were recovered in the town. At the beginning of the eighth century the bishop of Vienne had an oratory constructed to shelter the relics, and the cathedral later built on the same site was dedicated to St. Maurice. At the end of the ninth century a split within the Carolingian family (Boso, brother-in-law of the deceased emperor Charles the Bald, had himself proclaimed king in Provence), while confirming the royal character of the cult, moved its principal center toward southeastern France. Boso showed great devotion to the Theban saint, making him the protector of his newly acquired kingship. At the same time Maurice's name was detached in the liturgy from those of his companions: he came first, but only his companion Victor and St. Sigismund were left with him.[58] Thereafter, the dynasty ruling the "kingdom of Burgundy," which was separated from France before being united to the empire in the eleventh century, displayed a spectacular reverence for its patron saint, both at Agaunum[59] and at Vienne.[60]

In the late ninth and early tenth centuries the cult of St. Maurice had started to make its way across the Rhine, and it went through a considerable development there from the tenth to the twelfth century.[61] A.J. Herzberg's study shows that Maurice figured more and more as a knight, one of the military saints to whom those close to the emperor and those engaged in the profession of arms addressed their prayers. Here Niederaltaich, moreover, certainly played a leading role: the Abbey of Altaha, created following the victories over the Avars,[62] was to help spread Christianity in the annexed territories. The dual vocation—religious and military—is implied in the foundation of the abbey, and St. Maurice was chosen as its patron saint. Anno, archbishop of Cologne, made a pilgrimage to Agaunum in 1064 and brought back relics that made possible the development of the Maurician cult at Cologne, where it was entirely autonomous but not of primary importance. In fact it was simply added to other devotions already current in Cologne, all of them gradually making the city a center for the diffusion of cults and legends coming from or related to the East.[63]

On the other hand, it is beyond dispute that one factor stimulated the diffusion of the cult and completely changed the boundaries of the area of "fidelity" to St. Maurice. Otto I of Saxony borrowed the patronage of the saint from the kings of Provence and assigned it to the royal (later imperial) crown.[64] The alliance between the ducal family of Saxony and the reigning family in Provence began under Henry I, father of Otto the Great. In 926 Rudolf II of Burgundy had sent to Henry I the lance believed to be the one that pierced the side of Christ.[65] It seems that for at least a century the lance had been an emblem of royal authority among the Saxons.[66] The transfer of the "Holy Lance" therefore not only strengthened the bonds between Saxons and Burgundians but also supported a symbolism of Germanic Christian imperial power. When Otto I became king he quickly put his plan of action for converting the Slavs and fighting the Hungarians under the aegis of St. Maurice.[67]

Magdeburg thereupon became a key point for the advancement of imperial policy.[68] In 937, when he was twenty-four years old, King Otto, surrounded by eight bishops, founded there a Benedictine abbey dedicated to the martyrs Maurice and Innocent and their companions.[69] The monks were to pray for the welfare of Otto and his wife and of Rudolf of Burgundy. The first building was erected on the site of the present Gothic cathedral, and in time became the pantheon of the Saxon dynasty.[70] Otto I himself was buried in the east crypt. It seems to have been Otto's thought regarding the role of Magdeburg that the city should have the same significance for his dynasty that Aachen had for Charlemagne's.

As an archdiocese with special privileges conferred by Rome in 968,[71] Magdeburg was charged with evangelizing the Slavic lands and began to propagate the cult of St. Maurice and his companions, now entirely official, throughout its suffragan dioceses. Thus the eastward aims and policies of the empire were placed under the aegis of the knightly saint and so remained, despite checks and eclipses, until the sixteenth century. At the same time its bonds with Agaunum and Burgundy-Provence secured the restored empire's relations with Italy; thus St. Maurice was no stranger to Italian politics. The Saxon king took special care to provide Magdeburg with the foundation, indispensable in the Middle Ages, for a permanent pilgrimage—namely, Maurice's relics. Having been widowed, His Majesty married Adelaide of Burgundy in 951. Ten years later, at the Abbey of Agaunum, he received the saint's remains, which were transported with great pomp to Ratisbon and then on to Magdeburg.[72] Throughout his life Otto the Great manifested the deepest reverence for St. Maurice and the sanctuary he had had dedicated to him.

Otto II and Otto III, being more preoccupied with European and Italian affairs, paid less attention to the city on the Elbe. We note here that Otto III sent a replica of the Holy Lance, already christened "Lance of St. Maurice,"[73] to the Polish king Boleslaw I the Great.[74] On the other hand, Henry II's attitude was of great importance. W. Schlesinger[75] shows that the emperor frequently visited the town—before expeditions into Italy[76] and into Poland,[77] but also in 1012, 1013, 1017, 1021—and that he endowed the bishopric generously.

Another development, however, is of much greater importance. In the tenth century it was the policy of the Ottoman rulers to establish St. Maurice as a common bond of veneration between the German and the Slavic peoples.[78] The great revolt of the Slavs east of the Elbe against Germanization and evangelization, which marked the second quarter of the century, disrupted this policy. Under Henry II, Maurice, as patron saint of the empire, became the protector of the imperial army against the enemy Slavs. The Germanic clergy violently criticized the tactical entente between Henry II and the Lusatians, pagans and therefore possessed of the Devil but also Slavs.[79] The "Holy Lance" was confiscated for the benefit of Christian Germanism against the Slavs. A further step quickly ensued. In 1007 Magdeburg was protected from an attack by the Poles—Christian Slavs coming out against the saint, no less!—by Maurice's clear and evident intercession.[80] Whereas a common crusade might have been mounted against the pagans across the Elbe by the Christians from west of the Elbe and east of the Vistula, with the banner of St. Maurice leading them, the saint became the symbol of the Germanic offensive against the Slavs. Hence it is not surprising that his cult again grew stronger in Germanic areas and on the contrary was abandoned in Slavic regions, even those converted to Christianity. It is quite certain that this development, though practically indiscernible to the people of the time, did much to transform radically and lastingly the significance of the Maurician cult. Already an "imperial" saint, Maurice in the twelfth century became a "Germanic" saint.[81] This sly appropriation comes out clearly at the level of vocabulary and symbol. Early in the eleventh century the men-at-arms, vassals of Magdeburg, were called *milites mauriciani*:[82] a little later, in the thirteenth century—and probably a lot sooner—the banner of St. Maurice was carried at the head of the troops when they marched against the Slavs.[83] From then on, it seems to us, every attempt to pillage Slavic lands or to convert the people themselves was put under the authority and protection of St. Maurice. Obviously it would be of great interest to know how the Poles and the Slavs in general reacted to all this. For the moment we can only point to their evident disaffection from the cult of the saint, practiced for some time in the tenth century.

That matter is still to be studied. As of now we can make one general observation that can open the way to further insights: Honorius of Autun, in the twelfth century, took over the descriptions of the world that were dear to the Greeks and the Arabs, putting them in a Christian, Occidental perspective. Like the Arabs, who themselves had inherited the ideas of the ancients, he felt that the "normal" world was the world that surrounded him geographically and ideologically. Just as the Greeks considered the Hyperboreans quite as dangerous as the peoples of Africa, so Honorius thought that the Christian West lay under the menace of the pagan peoples of the North. Moreover, allegorical interpretations relative to the North multiplied at that time: the North was the country of evil and sin. Honorius of Autun, and some time after him Rupert of Deutz,[84] thought that in the North, Aquilo, a chilling, torpor-producing wind,[85] had its effect on the heathens.[86] So in the twelfth century the North, with which the pagan Slavs could be associated, could be seen as a land of menacing darkness, the haunt of sin, as the Mediterranean exegetes of past times had seen Ethiopia. This developing allegory could therefore free the color black from some part of its ancient connotations, thus making it available for new applications. St. Maurice, as we shall see, profited by this release.

The spread of the Maurician cult went along at least two lines. The archbishops of Magdeburg slowly promoted its expansion around their city and through their province. E. Neuss[87] has shown how the cult progressed: almost nonexistent in the tenth century, it spread considerably in southern Saxony in the eleventh and especially in the twelfth and thirteenth centuries but was never of outstanding importance.[88] Its development was more spectacular in the cities of Magdeburg's dependency: Halberstadt adopted it as early as 1015; Halle dedicated a church to the saint not later than 1184; at times the devotion overran the boundaries of the ecclesiastical province.[89] Throughout the region, Maurice, already the protector of the towns against military dangers, also became an arbiter of local conflicts.[90]

The other line of development—the diffusion of the cult due to the emperors' official veneration—was much more influential. Even though they rarely went to Magdeburg, Conrad II and Henry III[91] maintained traditions, fictions, and political choices as their immediate predecessors had established them.[92] Thereafter Maurice, along with St. Sebastian and St. George, had his place in the life and social rites of the military aristocracy. He was one of the saints invoked at the investiture of a knight[93] and became his model. One might therefore wonder whether Maurice had any influence on the religious orders, particularly on the military orders. The first elements contributing to an answer to this question have struck us as very disappointing.[94] Utilization of Maurice as a persuasive figure by the imperial court and the legal theorists who sided with the empire probably reached its peak, on the level of ideology, at the time of the great confrontations between emperors and popes in the late eleventh and during the twelfth century. Benzo of Alba put him in the vanguard of the fight for antipope Cadalus of Parma[95] and enlisted his support against Gregory VII.[96] Honorius of Autun also made the point that Maurice could teach some sound lessons to the papacy: he had refused, at the cost of his life, to take up arms against Christians and the Christian religion.[97] This line of argument was just about unanimous among the partisans of the empire.[98] In this situation the knightly saint of Magdeburg stood little chance of being promoted to the status of universal veneration. Rome had tolerated him, but in the twelfth century, according to A.J. Herzberg,[99] seems to have suddenly turned a cold shoulder, suppressing the mass in honor of St. Maurice in the course of revising the liturgy. B. Opfermann indirectly confirms this Roman coolness, which is not hard to understand. In 1570 Rome admitted Maurice to the missal prescribed for the universal church, but granted him a feast of only minor rank.[100] Then the emperors' appropriation of the saint had its full effect, and he belonged solely to the empire.[101]

We have already shown the role of Frederick Barbarossa and the joint effort of Otto of Freising and Rainald of Dassel, to exalt all the saints and all the ideological resources that might help to bolster the imperial idea. Otto of Freising, moreover, devoted an important passage to Maurice. The saint stands out in still greater relief in connection with the new Mediterranean concerns of the Hohenstaufen dynasty. No document, perhaps, throws more light on the transformation that was under way than the spurious letter of Frederick Barbarossa to Saladin, composed probably in England[102] in the thirteenth century.[103] In it the emperor reproaches Saladin for having seized the Holy Land and, putting it more broadly, lands that belong to the empire—Judea, Samaria, the territory of the Palestinians. By the will of God, Frederick says, he governs "the two Ethiopias, the country of the black Moors, the country of the Parthians, Syria, Persia..., Arabia, Chaldea, and Egypt itself...."[104] Do we not have here "positive evidence" upon which to base the utilization of a "black Moor" native to these lands? The "imperialist" doctrine formulated here is all the more interesting in that Henry VI and Frederick II, Barbarossa's son and grandson, did everything they could to enforce it.

The will and action of the emperors came into play at Magdeburg. In 1152 Frederick I forced the election of Wichmann, already bishop of Zeitz, to the archepiscopal see.[105] Wichmann vigorously pushed the territorial, religious, and economic expansion of his city. This archbishop's extraordinary activity in the second half of the twelfth century contributed largely to the rise of the Maurician cult, or at least to the growth of the area in which his name became known. Before 1184 Wichmann founded a collegiate church of Augustinian canons in Halle and dedicated it to the Theban saint;[106] he cemented relations with the Abbey of Niederaltaich, which was closely bound to its patron saint Maurice,[107] as we have already noted. But our main interest is in what he did to colonize the Slavic lands across the Elbe and to extend the law of Magdeburg more widely. It was probably in 1174 that he installed German settlers in an *oppidum* taken by force from the Slavs on the left bank of the Nuthe, a small tributary of the Havel, granting them burgher rights. Jüterbog, known by various names in the Germanic sources since the early eleventh century as a nucleus of Slavic resistance and a center of pagan worship, became the easternmost point of Germanic presence beyond the Elbe for a long period of time.[108] Germanic agricultural colonization of the areas round about was immediately undertaken.[109] Jüterbog, destroyed by the Slavs as early as 1180,[110] was retaken and fortified, and placed under Maurice's protection—toward the end of the twelfth century, in all likelihood—since the city received relics of the saint and his companions.[111] In 1184 Wichmann made it an archdeaconry.[112]

The policy of the archbishop of Magdeburg obviously fits into the broader context of the resumption, after more than a century and a half of calm, of the crushing of the Slavs across the Elbe by their Germanic neighbors.[113] Following the same pattern of conquest, conversion, and creation of posts of economic contact with the Baltic coast,[114] Margrave Albert I the Bear established a small settlement called Stendal in 1160-70, granting it the law of Magdeburg. The construction of a cathedral dedicated to St. Nicholas was begun there in 1188.[115] Lastly, in 1171, Wichmann founded an abbey at Kloster Zinna, another stronghold taken from the Slavs[116] located north of Jüterbog, and installed Cistercians who came from Altenberg in the province of Cologne. It is probable that the Slavs very soon destroyed this monastery, but it rose again later and became a center for Germanic Christian colonization. This effort was part of an overall policy that went on developing in the thirteenth century.[117] Maurice took his place as leader of the fighting men and, still more directly than in the eleventh century, as the adversary of the Slavs. All the names just mentioned will turn up again shortly.

For Magdeburg, conquest and forced conversion were not the only forms of "Maurician imperialism."[118] By the end of the twelfth century its urban law was adopted by several hundred towns and cities and was considered the "German law" *par excellence*.[119] The city found another way to make Maurice known—the coining of money and tokens in his honor.[120] The archbishops early made use of the right to coin money, granted them by Otto the Great in 968. By the end of the tenth century a second factory for this purpose was established; in the twelfth there were at least five of them. The coins struck in the eleventh century were silver pfennigs,[121] very often bearing the image of a fortification or a sword.[122] In the late eleventh and early twelfth centuries the quantity of minted coins increased. Some were so badly made that the images came through from one side to the other. These pieces were called "bracteates."[123] In the twelfth century the quality of the coins improved, and the effigy of St. Maurice appeared on one side.[124] The type of representation varies widely. Sometimes Maurice is unarmed and surrounded by the instruments with which he was tortured, sometimes he has a halo. Most often, as the protector designate of the town and its region,[125] he is shown as a warrior with two or three towers behind him; sometimes he is armed with a sword, more frequently he carries the standard which became the symbol of his presence beside the people of Magdeburg in any critical situation,[126] or again he holds a shield. A large number of these coins have been published; they raise problems which none of the authors consulted has dealt with. We hear that the pieces are abundant, but what were the defective ones used for? Everything leads us to think that in the twelfth century these faulty pieces were deliberately struck less thick; the quality of the images shows this. But were these bracteates used as money, or were they medals? How widely and in what quantity were they circulated?[127] In any event, this would seem to have been a very effective way to make the protector of Magdeburg known. Yet this coinage disappeared in the thirteenth century, precisely when St. Maurice was achieving still greater glory; moreover, his image did not appear on all the coins. The whole problem will have to be researched before firm conclusions can be reached.

The first half of the thirteenth century shows us no important innovations related to the veneration of St. Maurice; it even seems that representations of the saint were not spread abroad in such abundance as in the preceding period. The observation is worth making, since the middle of the thirteenth century was to witness a sensational mutation in the field of iconography—the appearance of a black Maurice. Until then his image had been that of a white man, and it would seem that no question had ever been raised on this point. One might wonder whether the emperors themselves had not looked now and then for protectors and symbols other than the Theban martyr for their policy of expansion eastward. Its anti-Roman aspects aside, was not the effort to canonize Charlemagne, in Frederick Barbarossa's reign, expressive of a wish to choose a patron saint closer in time and with more prestige than Maurice?[128] Was not the rivalry of Roland, a Frankish knight and a slayer of Muslims, prejudicial to the Theban?[129] But these suppositions hardly bear close scrutiny. On the contrary, all the evidence indicates the persistence of the association of the Magdeburg saint with the politics of the archbishops of that city, of the emperors, and of the great aristocrats responsible for the expansion toward the east.

Wichmann's successors pursued the work so energetically begun.[130] Albert II of Küfernberg, archbishop from 1205 to 1232, was named papal legate in 1213, in which year Rome also put him in charge of the Order of the Teutonic Knights.[131] Thus he was directly associated with the moves that were in preparation for execution beyond the Elbe—a final assault upon the pagan enclaves still holding out between the empire and Christian Poland, aimed both at getting rid of the enemies of Christianity and at facilitating relations with the Baltic coast between the Elbe and the Vistula, where traffic was then increasing remarkably. The revolt of the Prussians in 1222 led, after the agreement of 1230, to the organization of expeditions of conquest and occupation carried on by the Teutonic Knights. These expeditions went on for more than fifty years and reached as far as Estonia. The conquered places, which remained under the control of the order, often followed the law of Magdeburg;[132] this was also the case, in another context, for the port of Stettin (Szczecin) in 1243.[133] One may well ask, then, whether the Teutonic Order was not one of the most effective agents for the propagation of the Maurician cult, and whether the Theban saint played the same role in the Teutonics' battles as he had in those of the empire in preceding centuries. Neither the Acts relating to the order[134] nor a letter from the conservator of its archives[135] furnished proof that the Teutonics paid any attention to St. Maurice. However, a recent work does give us one definite clue: in 1431 the banner of the master of Livonia bore the image of a black St. Maurice in armor and was placed with the banner of the Virgin and Child.[136] The expansion of the order, decided upon and defined by Frederick II in accordance with an imperial program and without any interference from Rome,[137] and directed by Hermann of Salza until 1239, seems to have coincided with the introduction of St. Maurice's image in Livonia. The Teutonics were strong in Saxony[138] and had a monastery at Magdeburg[139] and another at Halle.[140] Furthermore, the Templars, who were in Magdeburg and, after 1211, in central and eastern Europe, do not seem to have had any part in spreading the name of Maurice.

Returning to Magdeburg itself, we find that Albert II was very active.[141] In 1207 a disastrous fire had destroyed the cathedral begun under Otto I and completed in the eleventh century. Albert II decided to construct an entirely new building, discarding the former plan: he turned the axis of the cathedral seven degrees farther to the north.[142] His decision raised large problems, the sculpture to be used in decorating the choir being one of them. Otto's porphyry columns were to be used again, and this led to the placement in the choir, contrary to all aesthetic principles, of statues originally intended for a porch. These included a white St. Maurice with characteristics close to the contemporary German iconography of the princely class.[143] On 28 September 1220, Albert placed the most important relic of St. Maurice—the head, obtained from Frederick II[144]—in Magdeburg. Thereafter, the relics were brought out once a year for public veneration.[145] When the Collegiate Church of St. Maurice at Halle was dedicated, the papacy showed how important it considered the newly established pilgrimage: Honorius III granted an indulgence of thirty days to those who visited the church.[146]

At Albert's death Gregory IX honored the departed prelate with high praise:[147] Thanks to him, the pope wrote, Magdeburg had become one of the pillars of Christianity. This latter manifestation by the pope occurred at a time when Rome and Frederick II were at loggerheads, but this did not involve Maurice. The earlier one, on the other hand, belongs to the period when papacy and empire were still on friendly terms. It is not very likely, therefore, that the papacy had much to do with the new departures, or that it was trying at that time to reclaim for its own advantage the tradition of veneration for St. Maurice which the archbishops of Magdeburg were promoting. On the other hand, it seems that the decisive initiatives came from the emperor and from Magdeburg itself. The success of the archbishops' ventures was rapid and widespread: Paderborn, Trier, and Freising introduced Maurice into their diocesan devotional patterns.[148]

In Magdeburg, after the brief episcopate of Burchard (1233-35), Albert's brother Wilbrand governed the province from 1235 to 1254: it was he, by the way, who finished the work on the main body of the new cathedral. Wilbrand, who was influential at the court of Henry VII, wanted to foster popular devotion to St. Maurice: was he perhaps responsible for the abrupt transformation of the saint's iconography, which we are about to take up? Yet ordinary good sense would not induce the prelates of Magdeburg to make so spectacular a change as the blackening of Maurice at the very time when an effort was afoot to enlarge the patron saint's following in the province and to build up a pilgrimage[149] that involved numbers of images connected with the relics. Public sensibility, as well as the cost of the necessary changes to be made in the familiar representation of the Magdeburg Maurice, argue against the idea that an archbishop of

114-116. Statue of St. Maurice. About 1240-50. Magdeburg, cathedral.

that city might have commissioned the splendid statue of a black that we shall soon discuss.

Maurice, as we have seen, was not a people's saint but a companion of those in power. The aristocracy had nothing to gain by changing his image; the archbishops had to count the risks and the cost. As for the emperor, his hands were free. What reasons may he have had to make him consider so complete a change in the representation of the Theban martyr, until then always seen with white features? There is no direct evidence indicating that Frederick II manifested the slightest interest in the patron saint of Magdeburg.[150] Yet three categories of observations lead to different conclusions.

First, the emperor did not let the marks and signs of imperial devotion to the holy protector of the empire and its army fall into disuse. Frederick II was anointed in Rome at the altar of St. Maurice in St. Peter's Basilica.[151] The insignia of power and the place where the king of Germany was crowned refer to the saint.[152] Frederick's reign marked the apogee of knighthood in Germany and witnessed a spirited production of literary works devoted to chivalry.[153] Frederick II himself laid emphasis upon the sanctity of lay persons and the importance of the nobility,[154] and tended to "divinize" the reigning dynasty in order to withdraw it from papal control.[155] Note, too, that the devotion of the secular powers to Maurice was not the prerogative of the emperors alone. For reasons which are to be sought in the secret imperial ambitions of the Capetian house, Louis IX himself gave proof of a profound veneration for the saint[156]—and this after the Maurician cult had been missing for centuries in French territory. This royal French devotion finally led to the translation of Maurice's relics to Senlis in 1261, at a time when the empire was beset with the difficulties of the Great Interregnum;[157] but the Capetians never adopted the new iconography that was making its appearance in Germany.

A second possible reason for interest in Maurice on Frederick II's part might in future be looked for in his Mediterranean policy. Far more than Frederick Barbarossa or Henry VI, he took care to uphold the theory of his sovereign rights over the distant lands around the eastern Mediterranean.[158] Having seen something of life in the East,[159] he was no doubt aware of the prestige that the protection of an Eastern saint could bring. St. George was too compromised with Rome and the crusading armies; Maurice was a Theban, and in the long run the theme might be fruitfully exploited. Egypt, since the time when Saladin's counteroffensive started from there to wipe out the Christian holdings, exerted a fascination on the European mind that was probably stronger and more conscious than has hitherto been recognized. From every point of view—economic, military, political, and cultural—Egypt was the land that drew the attention of Western Christians, Crusaders and merchants alike, in the thirteenth century. If he could not conquer the country, Frederick could at least demand that it furnish him the geographic, and then the ethnic, origin of St. Maurice.[160] We admit that at the moment all this is no more than a hypothesis, but the inferences are thought-provoking even if we have not yet discovered any sure evidence.

The final set of assumptions completes the creation of a climate favor-

115 116

117. Master Theodorik. St. Maurice. Painted panel. Before 1367. Karlštejn, castle, Chapel of the Holy Cross.

able, as we see it, to the "Orientalization" of St. Maurice. We base these assumptions on the literature of the period. The Crusades inspired successive waves of literary texts, as abundant as they are full of surprises, which have not yet been satisfactorily studied. The initial triumphalism was followed, after the defeat at the Horns of Hattin, by a certain despondency, but also by the awakening of a growing curiosity about this mysterious East. Germany, as we have already pointed out more than once, was caught up in this widespread movement.[161] The research done by F. de Medeiros[162] enables us to go a little further. Whereas hostility to the "black Moors" was intense in the twelfth century, early in the thirteenth Wolfram von Eschenbach in his *Parzival*, gives a distinguished role to Belakane, the black queen of an Eastern country. Gahmuret, Parzival's father, unhesitatingly defends this queen against her enemies and lives with her. Of this union is born a child whose skin is mottled black and white.[163] Medeiros goes on to show that while there was still a deep distrust of pagans in general, critical studies on the texts of Wolfram von Eschenbach prove that Belakane's son, "ideal type of the pagan knight," was the only one able to rival his half-brother Parzival.

To conclude: whatever may have been its exact causes, it is certain that a resurgence of favorable attention to St. Maurice occurred between 1220 and 1250, and the abrupt change in the saint's iconography brought about the creation of works startling in their novelty.

A MUTATION IN THE OFFICIAL ICONOGRAPHY: SAINT MAURICE BECOMES A BLACK MAN

The program for the decoration of the Cathedral of Magdeburg, undertaken about 1240-50, included a surprising departure in St. Maurice's iconography: until then represented as white, he became a black man. Nor was this an ephemeral phenomenon. With few exceptions, the saint was portrayed as black until the sixteenth century in Magdeburg, Halle, and Halberstadt. At least we are led to this conclusion by the information now available to us.[164] The working hypothesis which emerges is that a command from the emperor caused St. Maurice to be depicted as a black in Magdeburg, the city where his relics were enshrined. In this first period the iconography of the black saint was influenced by the fluctuations of imperial power, which waned during the Great Interregnum and rose again, enhanced in strength and prestige, only with Charles IV. Behind the politics of the emperors the strategy of Magdeburg and its archbishops was active, both city and prelates turning the new iconographic theme to their own advantage, especially in the fifteenth century. Finally, in the sixteenth, Cardinal Albert of Brandenburg took it over. The fact is, however, that before clear, definitive conclusions can be reached in this field, a lengthy, comparative chronological and geographical investigation of all types of representation of St. Maurice, black or white, from the thirteenth to the sixteenth century, will have to be made.

When, after the deposition of Louis IV the Bavarian, Charles of Bohemia[165] became emperor in 1346, he set about gathering to his side the saints recognized as protectors of the imperial power and symbols of the unity of the empire. Maurice was one of them, and Charles had him represented,

118

118. Reliquary bust of St. Maurice. Bohemia, about 1440. Kroměříž, Umĕleckohistorické Muzeum.

and distributed his image, as a black: as we see it, this is a proof, albeit a late one, of the imperial choice made a century earlier. If, therefore, in a little more than a hundred years, Maurice, Gregory the Moor at Cologne, and one of the Magi were represented as blacks without any scandal or noticeable disavowal, we conclude that besides the decisions that were made, there must have been a profound sense of acceptance at various levels of the imperial society.

Yet we must point out immediately that at no time did the portrayal of St. Maurice as a black become universal. It belonged to Magdeburg and the regions influenced by that city. This iconography was not welcomed in Trier or Aachen, nor, in its early phase, in Bavaria,[166] nor in France nor Italy, although the cult of the saint was at times strong in these areas. Such selective reactions also marked the career of the black Wise Man. But, by way of contrast to the latter case, at present we know of no text that explains the extraordinary innovation that came to light in Magdeburg.

The marvelous sandstone statue in Magdeburg, although fairly often illustrated and described,[167] is dated rather hazily between 1240 and 1250, figs. 114-1 and art historians throw no light on its origins. So far the studies have concentrated mainly on details, particularly on the description of the military costume. Attention has rightly been called to the importance of the sword and to the presence of a banner once held in the right hand (it has now disappeared).[168] But nothing is known about who ordered the statue or who carved it, nor about the circumstances of its execution, perhaps with a black man as model. Yet close attention should be paid to its characteristics, and efforts made to go a little further in identifying it historically. E. Schubert[169] notes similarities between this St. Maurice and a whole group of thirteenth-century statues that are chronologically and stylistically comparable. He sees in the style of the Magdeburg Virgins a northern French influence, perhaps passed on to Magdeburg through Bamberg. He also sees a close relationship between, on one hand, the St. Maurice and the Wise Virgins at Magdeburg, and on the other, the famous statues in the west choir of Naumburg Cathedral; he leans toward dating the Magdeburg works just before or just after those at Naumburg. It is not easy to agree that the initiative that endowed Magdeburg with a black St. Maurice came from Naumburg itself: his cult was very modest in that little city.[170] As E. Schubert judiciously remarks, this inquiry ends at an impasse, at least for the time being. There is good reason to try to push it further given the importance, at all possible levels of analysis, of the advent of the black Maurice.[171]

The theme was to enjoy an almost uninterrupted success for at least three centuries, and for this the archbishops of Magdeburg were largely responsible. (The maps at the end of this volume illustrate the wide diffusion of this theme.[172]) But after the Great Interregnum it was another emperor, Charles IV, who revitalized the Maurician cult. His plan was to collect relics of all the saints of importance to the empire and keep them in Prague.[173] In 1354, with the full consent of Rome, he instituted the Feast of the Holy Lance.[174] He had received the famous lance as an insigne of imperial authority, and with it two swords, one attributed to St. Maurice, the other to Charlemagne;[175] and in 1365 an arm of the saint was granted him.[176] At Karlštejn, near Prague, he built a castle,[177] the raison d'être of

119. St. Maurice and a Benedictine pope. Painted panel from an altarpiece. Bohemia (?), about 1420-30. Quittelsdorf, evangelical church.

119

which was the sumptuous Chapel of the Holy Cross constructed to house the imperial insignia.[178] The walls were covered with panels on which were painted bust-length images of saints, male and female: Maurice was among them.[179] Although in many things Charles of Bohemia followed the example of his uncle, Charles V of France, in this instance he broke with the French tradition, which always represented Maurice as white;[180] at Karlštejn the Magdeburg model was adopted. To decorate the chapel

fig. 117

Charles IV called upon a painter named Theodorik, who may have come from Western Europe but was steeped in local tradition, while for the embellishment of Prague he engaged artists from the court at Avignon. Theodorik organized his studio as a corporation, and it is very hard to distinguish the paintings done by his own hand from those produced by his collaborators and pupils.[181] Each panel is separated from the others by a wide damasked border. There has been disagreement about the attribution of Maurice's panel to Theodorik,[182] but the painting blends in with the whole group in which the stylistic characteristics are easily recognizable: the massive treatment of bodies and faces, the absence of depth and landscape (here an embossed gold background is used instead), the gorgeous fabrics, all differ sharply from any contemporaneous work, even in Prague. Probably painted before 1367,[183] Maurice is a black man characterized not only by color but by the hair and facial traits: he carries the sword, the banner, and the shield with heraldic bearings. So far as we know, this was the first picture of the martyr of Agaunum painted on a panel, and, like the Magdeburg statue, it was a brilliant stroke.

The emperors' favor created an environment in Bohemia that proved lastingly receptive to the representation of Maurice with the features of a black man. A Bohemian martyrology dating from the early years of the

120

120. Coronation of the Virgin (detail): martyrs and confessors. Central panel of a painted altarpiece. Dated 1465. Brandenburg, cathedral.

121

122

121. St. Maurice. Detail of a painted panel from the outer right-hand wing of a polyptych. From the Abbey of Wiener Neustadt. 1447. Vienna, Stefansdom.

122. St. Maurice. Detail of the painted reverse of the right wing of an altarpiece. About 1370-80. Brandenburg, cathedral.

fifteenth century[184] shows him, with his companions, as a black, as does an unusual reliquary bust, executed about 1440 and now in Kroměříž, on which the Theban saint wears a ducal headdress.[185] Among the mural paintings in the chapel of the castle at Zvíkov, dating from the end of the fifteenth century, we find a black Maurice in armor:[186] this work is approximately contemporaneous with that at Kloster Zinna (about which more later) and their style is very similar. Once again those in power drew attention to Maurice: thereafter he was black. Yet signs of popular acclaim or spontaneous imitation remain rare, and Bohemia[187] does not seem to have made much room for such representations during the fifteenth century. We note the St. Maurice painted about 1420-30 on the wing of an altarpiece, now separated and kept in Quittelsdorf: the somewhat affected posture, the small, delicate head, and the elegantly draped garments suggest fairly close kinship with the Bohemian painting of the early fifteenth

fig. 118

fig. 119

123

124

125

123. Statue of St. Maurice. About 1360-70. Magdeburg, cathedral, gable over the west portal.

124. St. Maurice. Side of a stall (detail). About 1470-80. Halberstadt, Church of St. Maurice.

125. St. Maurice. Stained-glass window (detail). About 1430-40. Stendal, cathedral.

century. Considering the modest dimensions of this panel, it might very well have been brought into Thuringia from Bohemia at an unknown date.

Bavaria, once a seat of the Maurician cult, not only failed to adopt this new iconographic type in the fourteenth and fifteenth centuries (as far as our research has shown), but also saw the almost complete disappearance of the saint's name from the calendars and martyrologies of that period.[188]

In Austria, in these same years, a black Maurice, wearing the ducal crown as at Kroměříž, appears among numerous saints on an altarpiece executed in 1447 for the abbey church at Wiener Neustadt.[189] Here we fig. 121
observe the effacement of the religious character from the iconography typical of the thirteenth century in favor of more worldly images; Maurice has left knighthood behind and has been adopted by courtly art.

In Brandenburg we again see the will and influence of Charles IV at work. Twelve saints, one being Maurice, are painted on the back of a wing fig. 122
belonging to the altarpiece formerly on the high altar of the cathedral: the altarpiece portrays the crowning of the Virgin.[190] For the first time, so far as we know, Maurice's shield and gonfalon bear the eagle of the House of Brandenburg. Almost a century later another altarpiece in the cathedral repeats the same theme,[191] but the place assigned to Maurice is strikingly fig. 120
more modest. Still seen among other saints, popes, bishops, and abbots, he is placed in the background; only his black head and his gonfalon being visible, and the gonfalon bears the cross that was generally attributed to him in Magdeburg. These variations merit attention. Charles IV attached great importance to the old March of Brandenburg, which made contact with the Baltic Sea possible through the Slavic territories then in process of

126 

127

126. Statue of St. Maurice. Before 1411. Halle, Church of St. Maurice.

127. Statue of St. Maurice. 1513. Halberstadt, cathedral.

colonization. In 1373 he spent some time in Brandenburg itself: his thought was to remove the bishopric from the province of Magdeburg and to attach it to Prague. At the same time he was taking care to create in Berlin the arrangements that would allow the growth of a center of commercial exchange with the Baltic.[192] The acquisition of the March of Brandenburg followed that of Lusatia and took place simultaneously with the annexation of a section of Mecklenburg; in this way Charles IV extended his territories

128. Silver statuette of St. Maurice. From Magdeburg (?). About 1470-80. Medingen, abbey.

129. Virgin and Child between St. Maurice and St. Sebastian. Central panel of a carved altarpiece. About 1500. Frankenhain, church.

toward the north. Charles IV ordered a complete description of the lands newly accrued to his crown.[193] He intervened frequently in the affairs of the March and of the bishopric, the bishop of Brandenburg being on bad terms with Charles at the time. The gift, after 1377, of a triptych on which there was an image of St. Maurice with the eagle of Brandenburg, tallied perfectly with the policy of getting the March under the emperor's control. Probably this pressure also explains Maurice's "exile" in the 1465 altarpiece. If these interpretations turn out to be correct, the likelihood is that the first altarpiece was executed before 1378, the year of Charles IV's death. This event was followed in the March by a period of serious disorders, which finally came to an end with the installation of Frederick I of Hohenzollern as margrave in 1411.

Magdeburg did not give up the representation of Maurice with the features of a black.[194] Work on the west façade, begun at the end of the thirteenth century, continued until 1360-70 with the construction of the towers and the architectural part framed in by them. The main portal, and notably the statue of Maurice in the gable under a very high canopy,[195] fig. 123

130

131

132

133

130. St. Maurice (detail). Right wing of a carved triptych dated 1517. Braunsdorf, church.

131. Studio of Valentin Lendenstreich. St. Maurice and St. Catherine. Detail of the central panel of a carved triptych dated 1498. Rottenbach, church.

132. St. Maurice. Detail of the left wing of a carved altarpiece. About 1450-1500. Wienhausen, abbey.

133. St. Maurice. Detail of the left wing of a carved altarpiece dated 1492. Delitzsch, Church of SS. Peter and Paul.

134

134. Bust of St. Maurice. Lower compartment of the left wing of an altarpiece. About 1430-40. Teterow, church.

135. St. Maurice. Detail of the central panel of a carved altarpiece. About 1430-40. Wismar, Church of St. Nicholas.

136. St. Maurice. Mural painting (detail). About 1464. Roskilde, Domkirke.

date from this period. In 1520, the two towers being finished, the central porch was enclosed and transformed into a funerary chapel to house the monumental tomb of Archbishop Ernest of Saxony, to whom we shall return later.

However, before turning to this new phase of the Magdeburg iconography of the black Maurice, we must try to measure the reception the iconography met with. Taken over and used both by the imperial authorities and by the archbishops of Magdeburg, Maurice was so marked a hero that to accept or to reject his representation as a black saint could not possibly be a matter of indifference. The variations in the heraldic bearings accompanying him take on a real significance (we are beginning to suspect) in connection with any effort to estimate the rivalries and the attempts to usurp Maurice's prestige to the detriment of the empire but also to the detriment of Magdeburg. It is therefore rewarding to survey a "geography of acceptances, adaptations, and rejections" starting from the province of Magdeburg, before applying our special attention to what happened in that city at the end of the fifteenth and during the sixteenth century.

The ecclesiastical province of Magdeburg welcomed the black saint in its episcopal sees, monasteries, and humble rural churches. For the moment we shall take note of some few examples.[196] Halle presents us with two stone statues of Maurice in the church dedicated to him.[197] One of them, signed by Conrad von Einbeck and dated 1411, is not very characteristic: the intention to make the saint black is expressed only in the dark color of the face. The other, a little earlier, shows both in posture and in costume some [fig. 126] close similarities to the statue in Jüterbog, about which we shall speak [cf. fig. 13] further, and to the stained-glass window in Stendal,[198] in which the saint is [fig. 125] standing under a canopy: the pose, the armor, and the shield blazoned with a cross are the same. At Halberstadt, in the church named for him, Maurice is figured on the side of a stall made at the end of the fifteenth [fig. 124] century,[199] and a later statue in the cathedral, standing against a pillar,[200] [fig. 127] shows him holding a shield on which the two-headed eagle stands out; but it is hard to be sure that this statue has not been more or less restored or transformed several times.

In Lower Saxony, three abbeys still today possess representations of the black Maurice. Medingen—Maurice was its patron saint—has two silver statuettes,[201] the older of which, dated approximately 1470-80, shows the [fig. 128] saint in armor, wearing a sort of bandeau around his head and carrying a banner with a cross pattée. Ebstorf has some interesting and diverse fifteenth-century reminders of Maurice.[202] Lastly, at Wienhausen, among other images there is a triptych carved in the second half of the fifteenth century,[203] which has on its left-hand wing three saints in high relief, of [fig. 132] which one is Maurice with cape and armor.

In a number of places in Saxony and Thuringia there is an abundance of representations of the black St. Maurice, dating from the end of the fifteenth and the beginning of the sixteenth century.[204] Here we present only a few that have points in common: they are carved polychromed altarpieces with the central panel reserved for a Virgin and Child. At Delitzsch the polyptych dated 1492[205] shows Maurice in the left wing, [fig. 133] wearing an ample cape over his armor and without a shield. On the other hand, at Frankenhain,[206] about 1500, he is pictured just to the Virgin's [fig. 129]

135

136

right in the central panel, his head circled with a kind of bandeau as in Medingen. Rottenbach[207] in 1498 and Braunsdorf in 1517[208] offer us a bare-headed, haloed Maurice holding a lance added more recently. figs. 131, 130

The Magdeburg bracteates, the economic bond between that city and the Baltic merchants, and the efforts made under Charles IV to develop commerce between the empire and the north provide sufficient explanation for the possible expansion of the black Maurice in that direction. However, the thing is not so simple. The "imperial" image of Brandenburg met with resistances, choices, and contradictory interpretations that must be clarified. Yet as early as 1430-40 the church at Teterow housed a black Maurice carrying the gonfalon blazoned with the lance.[209] Teterow, sold by its Slavic owner to a monastery of Premonstratensians, a dependent of Lund, is located on the trade route to the north.[210] During this same period Wismar, on the Baltic, adopted Magdeburg's saint with the cross pattée. The image presented by the "Krämeraltar"[211] in Wismar has little in common with the Teterow image except for the costume: here Maurice's hair hangs in long curls and he wears a kind of turban—which shows how free the artists were, being far removed from the center of Saxony. Still farther north, our search has found black Maurices in Denmark, notably at Roskilde,[212] where the painter's fantasy is expressed both in the pointed shield and in the headdress, in which the feather attached to the bandeau

fig. 134 · fig. 135 · fig. 136

137. Statue of St. Maurice. Early XV century. Formerly in Riga, House of the Black Heads.

138. Virgin and St. Maurice beneath the heraldic bearings of the city and the Black Heads. 1522. Reliefs on the door jambs of the House of the Black Heads in Riga.

137

lends an exotic touch to the black-skinned figure. But an overall problem emerges: the relative abundance of representations of the black saint contrasts with the spread of the cult of St. George along the Baltic.[213] A fine statuette of St. Maurice in polychromed wood,[214] dating from the early fifteenth century, once belonged to the treasure of the House of the Black Heads in Riga: the name of this organization probably marks the semantic limits of the "blackness" of Maurice. The latest study to appear on the subject[215] leaves open the possibility that the name was chosen by the participants without any connection with Maurice, to point up the youth of the members of the brotherhood compared to the old Hansards. If that be the case, in the beginning there would have been no reference to Africans and very little to Maurice, although the Black Heads counted him among their protectors from the time of their foundation in the fifteenth century; but they directed their veneration to St. George. Likely enough the "image of the black"—the real black was so far away!—was freed of all deeply significant correction and used by way of allusion. The seal of the Black Heads in Riga bore the image of a "black Moor's head" with a frontal ribbon.[216] When the city's cathedral was done over, four heads of "black Moors" were put in the stained-glass window given by the Black Heads.[217] In Lübeck the Morum family played on the meaning of their name: their epitaph shows a white Maurice, but the shields with the family's arms have three heads of blacks.[218] The heads figured in the heraldic bearings on the main door of the House of the Black Heads in Riga, the home of the brotherhood, wear the "Moorish bandeau." Below them Maurice is represented following the convention then in use (the sculpted door dates from 1522) at Magdeburg and Halle, as we shall see further on. The saint's banner and shield bear the cross pattée;[219] according to E. Thomson the cross was red on a white ground on the banner, the colors being reversed on the shield.[220] This conventional black Maurice is only a copy of the official iconography widely propagated at the time by authority of Cardinal Albert of Brandenburg. Thus the Baltic area appears, it would seem, as a zone where the models coming from Magdeburg were feebly reproduced, but still more as a place where the image no longer followed the precise conventions to which it was subject in Saxony.

fig. 137

fig. 138

In the Cologne region we come up against another resistance and another limit: the whole area set itself against the pressure from Magdeburg. Cologne, proud of the cult of the Magi, did not share Magdeburg's need to exalt the exotic knight. The city was not hostile to St. Maurice,[221] almost always represented him as white, and, if a historic black hero had to be venerated, preferred Gregory the Moor to the Theban.[222] Gregory made his appearance in Cologne's iconography in the early fourteenth century, notably in the Church of St. Gereon, where his relics were kept, but neither he nor the Holy Moors, whose leader he was, were prominent in the city's devotions. Probably nothing more clearly shows Cologne's independence from Magdeburg than the representation of a white St. Maurice and a black St. Gregory on two wings of the same altarpiece, dated 1520, the work of Anton Woensam.[223]

The Münster area was a zone of contact between separated regions and opposing influences. A "missal" from the priory of Bilzen, produced at the

end of the fifteenth century,[224] brings together a remarkable collection of liturgical texts, lessons, and sermons devoted to St. Maurice, some of them by celebrated authors.[225] But in the miniature of his martyrdom,[226] he is represented as white. Black is reserved for the Holy Moors, a group of martyrs connected with Cologne, whom we find in the same manuscript.[227]

Other representations of Maurice convey the same impression of marginality and instability of the theme that we met in the Baltic area: in Fröndenberg a statue[228] recently repainted in accord with the old polychromy gives the saint a dark skin but no other characteristic traits. Thus a veritable cartography takes shape, at least for the fourteenth and fifteenth centuries, showing where the representation of Maurice as a black was accepted and where it was refused, after having been launched in Magdeburg in mid-thirteenth century, probably upon imperial initiative.

From this point of view it is interesting to explore the reactions in the Alpine and Rhone regions, where the cult of St. Maurice had taken hold before it was annexed by the Ottonians. In general the area west of the Rhine—Flanders, France, Italy—showed total resistance to the adoption of the black Maurice. King René of Anjou's effort to revive the saint's cult in Provence occasioned new representations of Maurice in the south of present-day France during the fifteenth century: he is always white. In a rather unexpected way the House of Savoy adopted the Maurician cult. The origins of the ducal family of Savoy before the year 1000 are still not clear,[229] but by the middle of the eleventh century its power was well established. The center of its possessions was the region called the Bugey in southern Burgundy, but by that time one of its members was abbot of Saint-Maurice at Agaunum and another was bishop of Sion in the Swiss Valais.[230] The cult of St. Maurice, diligently spread abroad by the Savoyards, slowly gained ground in the new duchy,[231] emerging again after being eclipsed as a result of the appropriation of the cult by the empire. Agaunum and Susa minted coins for the dukes of Savoy in the thirteenth century,[232] and in the fourteenth struck the large *mauriziani* which bore the image of the saint:[233] no sample of these seems to have survived. In the fifteenth century St. Maurice was depicted in a Book of Hours made for Louis of Savoy.[234] The saint, who carries a shield with a red cross, is designated as patron and protector of Savoy. He is white, as are his companions.

139

The foundation in 1434 of the chivalric Order of St. Maurice,[235] the creation of which was granted by Rome to the Duke Amadeus VIII of Savoy, might have advanced the popularity of St. Maurice, but no such thing ensued. The order did not spread beyond Savoy (in 1572 it was decided that the grand master would invariably be chosen from the ducal family[236]), and there is no trace of a black Maurice either in the insignia of the order or in the statues that adorned its basilica in Turin.

A remote area of the Magdeburg province—the area of Jüterbog and Kloster Zinna—furnishes important examples of the transition from the ecclesiastical and imperial iconography, which we have been analyzing, to the pronounced transformations that made their appearance at the end of the fifteenth and during the sixteenth century, mostly due to the initiatives of Cardinal Albert of Brandenburg. We have already noted the interest

139, 140. Fragments of the altarpiece of the old high altar: statue of St. Maurice and scenes from his legend. About 1425. Jüterbog, Church of St. Nicholas.

141. St. Maurice. Mural painting (detail). Second half XV century. Kloster Zinna, former abbatial guesthouse.

141

taken by the archbishops of Magdeburg in Jüterbog and Kloster Zinna in the twelfth and thirteenth centuries; now, in the fourteenth, it was the turn of the Hohenzollerns, the new titularies of the March of Brandenburg,[237] to direct their attention to this far-eastern sector of the March. These margraves freed Brandenburg from the heavy pressure exerted by Charles IV and his successors of the House of Bohemia and developed their policies in full accord with the bishops and with Rome. These "anti-imperial" decisions quickly secured the local predominance of the Hohenzollern family, both on the political level and in church matters—the latter by having its members installed in the episcopal sees.[238] All these facts are fraught with consequences.

In the fourteenth and fifteenth centuries Jüterbog received a certain number of new monuments,[239] among them the Church of St. Nicholas, in which St. Maurice was particularly favored if we judge by the fragments of the altarpiece executed around 1425 for the former high altar. The statue figs. 139, 140
in polychromed wood shows us an already familiar type of Maurice with woolly hair and thick lips; the painted panels now set up as an enclosure for the choir[240] give us more significant information. Here, for the first time, we have a pictorial sequence that places the exotic Theban among the numerous saints whose lives have been the subject of narrative cycles in art. It was logical to suppose that the baptism of a personage so firm in his faith must itself have been extraordinary, and it was tempting to paint that event although no text related it. This is the old theme of the *Aethiops*, resurgent after a long progress that lies outside the scope of the present inquiry.[241] The refusal to renounce the faith and sacrifice to the gods of pagan Rome is another frequent topic. As they are in many similar fifteenth-century works, the pagan gods are symbolized here by a grotesque devil with bat's wings. The hero's refusal leads to his beheading in the presence of the emperor. It is important for us to emphasize that Maurice is brought before the emperor three times, and that the emperor is a negative personage, treated here in an obviously unfriendly way; moreover, the saint carries the gonfalon marked with the Brandenburg eagle, not with the cross we find most often. As we see them, these details are of great historical interest: the work manifests attachment to the March—to the margraves?—with no more fear of offending Magdeburg than at the time when Charles IV, in our opinion, forced upon the Cathedral of Brandenburg an image of Maurice bearing the eagle. But here there is no question of an imperial command. The personage of the emperor, an iconographic type familiar to the people of the time, is discreetly but firmly brought to trial by repeatedly presenting him as a symbol of evil, whereas the clergy figures only in the scene of the baptism. These clues seem to imply rather strongly the autonomy of the new margraves, an autonomy resting upon the local clergy and upon Rome; and this series of scenes appears to us to be a cautious but effective political manifesto coming from the new masters of the territory.[242] Was it by chance that the "reigning" family of Brandenburg thereafter took possession of the black Maurice to such a degree that the most brilliant period in the saint's iconography coincided with the elevation of a Hohenzollern, Albert, to the archepiscopal throne of Magdeburg?

As was the case in the twelfth century, Kloster Zinna now found its lot closely linked to that of Jüterbog. The guesthouse of the abbey was decorat-

142

143

142. Detail of figure 143: figures of St. Maurice and St. Stephen on the bishop's mitre.

143. Peter Vischer. Funerary monument of Archbishop Ernest of Saxony. 1495. Magdeburg, cathedral.

144. Detail of figure 143: statue of St. Maurice on the base of the tomb.

ed in the fifteenth century with an important painting in which SS. Andrew, Sebastian, and Maurice are grouped between the Virgin and St. Bernard.[243] When the painting was cleaned in 1958,[244] the image of St. Maurice was uncovered:[245] a knight helmeted and with a halo, his face a fig. 141 reddish brown, he is a more imposing figure than we find in many contemporary works. His heraldic bearings give us food for thought: the gonfalon is marked with the cross pattée (which recalls Magdeburg), but the cross is black on a white ground, following the usage of the Teutonic Knights; the eagle on the shield proclaims that the House of Brandenburg is in charge.

SAINT MAURICE AS CARDINAL ALBERT OF BRANDENBURG PICTURED HIM

Before talking about this great patron of artists and the arts, we shall deal briefly with the important role played by Ernest of Saxony,[246] his immediate predecessor. Ernest, archbishop of Magdeburg from 1476 to 1513, prefigured the renowned humanist Albert of Brandenburg, and in many ways his episcopate prepared Albert's and helps us to understand it. His installation in 1476 was the occasion for a gala performance in which over four thousand horsemen took part. Ernest and his successor already were powerful Renaissance princes; their taste for art and letters inclined them toward theatricality and ostentation, and this in turn transformed everything around them. The day after his grand "entry" at Magdeburg, Archbishop Ernest presided at a solemn mass in honor of St. Maurice and the Theban Legion, during which the saint's relics were exposed for veneration:[247] so began the new turn the archbishop planned for the Maurician cult. In 1467 his predecessor, pressed for funds needed for the completion, decoration, and maintenance of the cathedral, had set up tighter regulations controlling the veneration of the relics possessed by Magdeburg.[248] It must have been at this time that a new statue of St. Maurice, in alabaster,

145

146

was executed: the "Negroid" characteristics are barely discernible.[249] All the parish clergy and all priests in charge of chapels were to levy a tax on their people for the purpose of organizing the pilgrimage to Magdeburg, now obligatory. The idea of bringing a whole province together for a great religious demonstration was no doubt a good one, but the methods chosen seem more than questionable. In fact, the travel expenses ate up the best part of the funds collected. In 1491 Archbishop Ernest decided to change the 1467 rules.[250] Thereafter it was the relics that would be brought to where the people were—with the same indulgences as those granted in 1467. The pastors and chaplains would collect the money contributed "spontaneously" by the faithful and send it to Magdeburg in closed sacks bearing their name and the name of the parish.[251] The new procedure must have proved more profitable than the old because Albert of Brandenburg was to make it still more rigorous. This new policy quite certainly explains the proliferation of images of the black Maurice which we shall observe shortly in the parish churches. The liturgy also reflects this renewal of the Maurician cult. B. Opfermann has brought together an impressive sheaf of texts[252] whose root dates from this very time.[253] The Magdeburg Missal, which in part carries over the texts of the ninth and the tenth and eleventh centuries, is the common trunk of a ceremonial which proceeded to spread widely and rapidly.[254]

Ernest of Saxony took further steps to strengthen the prestige of his city's patron saint. In 1511 a "Book of Relics" boldly ranked the city banner, which bore the name of St. Maurice, with the banner of Charlemagne.[255] The archbishop's predilection for Maurice was expressed in concrete form on the tomb which he, while still very much alive, commissioned Peter Vischer the Elder to build for him, and which was completed in its essentials in 1495.[256] Maurice, armed, wearing a halo, and carrying figs. 142-144 the banner with the cross pattée, figures with St. Stephen on the mitre of the recumbent statue of the deceased and appears again, as a black, in a carving of extraordinary liveliness, on the base of the tomb on the head side, the place of honor.

Magdeburg, however, did not prove entirely amenable to the archbishop's leadership. The taxes imposed in order to implement resistance to the Turks caused friction,[257] and this foreshadowed the troubles later encountered by Albert.

The activities of Ernest of Saxony in the little city of Halle are worthy of still closer attention. Halle was in the salt trade and provided sizable revenues to the archdiocese of Magdeburg. Probably the town had a chapel of St. Maurice as far back as the year 1000. A monastery dedicated to him was founded there, with a school attached, in 1184. In 1200 Albert II built a hospital named for the saint.[258] In 1411 Conrad von Einbeck's statue, already mentioned,[259] was placed in the Church of St. Maurice, and a statue of Maurice was erected on the south side of the town hall.[260] In 1479 Ernest autocratically cut down the rights of the citizens of Halle[261] and, the better to keep the town under surveillance, built a fortress above it. This was only one of the castles built by his order, and this one he named for St. Maurice: the Moritzburg.[262] There he began to gather together the relics he had bought at high prices; they were to become a miraculous source of revenue for his successor.

145. Altarpiece of the high altar, wings closed. Late XV-early XVI century. Halle, Church of St. Maurice.

146. St. Maurice. Statue from a niche in the central panel of the altarpiece in figure 145.

147. Hans Baldung Grien. St. Maurice and St. George. Altarpiece wings. From the collegiate church at Halle. 1507. Berlin (GFR), Staatliche Museen, Gemäldegalerie.

Once the monuments were built, Archbishop Ernest's next thought was to decorate them, and for that purpose he commissioned works of art. It is in the Church of St. Maurice that Ernest's taste for magnificence was most sumptuously displayed. In 1507 Hans Baldung Grien painted a triptych for the church, which is now in Berlin (GFR).[263] On one of its wings Maurice appears without any conventional characteristic: the type of the black is strongly marked; the beard and moustache accentuate the individuality of the personage, the treatment of the figure being as precise as that of the black King in the Adoration of the Magi, which occupies the central panel; the large, flowing banner bears the eagle, the cross being left to St. George, who appears on the other wing. A huge altarpiece, with an unusually large, delicately carved cornice, today adorns the high altar; its three pairs of painted wings, dated 1511, are the work of Jehner von Orlamünde.[264] Maurice is represented three times. As the church's patron saint he dominates the whole composition in a niche in the cornice with its complex arcatures: there he wears a helmet with chinstrap and carries a shield decorated with an eagle. A second statue of the saint, dated at the end of the fifteenth century,[265] at once vigorous and sensitive in execution, is placed in the central panel: the artist took care to give him a particularly expressive and realistic head, and he holds a shield bearing the cross. We find him again painted on the stationary wing to the right, with the banner bearing the eagle: here the type is much less emphasized. Curiously enough, the first wing on the right shows three companions of St. Maurice, a bit stiff and awkward and treated with a touch of exoticism.

fig. 147
fig. 145
fig. 146
fig. 153

It is very important to reflect upon the heraldic bearings that appear on the banner and shield. In fact, it was not until 1501 that the "historic" standard of St. Maurice, mentioned in the thirteenth century, was described for the first time.[266] It was said, as Sebastian Weynmann informs us, that Charlemagne long ago, and more recently the archbishops of Magdeburg, used the banner in every war, offensive or defensive, against their adversaries: it was of white silk and bore the image of Christ, and it was taken out of safekeeping only on the rarest occasions in order to save it from destruction, so that only a few privileged persons who had seen it could describe it.[267] It would seem that only by a deliberate choice could painters and sculptors have adopted entirely different blazons for St. Maurice.

With Albert of Brandenburg,[268] who succeeded Ernest as archbishop of Magdeburg in 1513, the seminal ideas of the latter were brought to fruition. Historians of art have so admired Albert's role as Maecenas that they have too often overlooked the innocently scandalous side of his way of living. A prince, rich, humanist from his youth, Albert displayed in every field of action a vigor and a taste for life that mark him as a true Renaissance man.

Albert's attention was drawn to Halle more than to Magdeburg, because of the possibilities the smaller city offered to so remarkable an "architect." In 1514 he had some hundred relics transferred from Magdeburg to the Moritzburg to be placed alongside those which Ernest had begun to accumulate there.[269] In 1515 he conceived the idea of a Pan-German pilgrimage to Halle; apparently the pope then granted the authorization to collect fees from the pilgrims. Albert's grand design was to make

148

149

148. St. Maurice. Left wing of an altarpiece dated 1529. Halle, "Marktkirche."

149. Nikolaus Glockendon. St. Maurice and his companions. *Missal* of Cardinal Albert of Brandenburg, fol. 437ᵛ. 1524. Aschaffenburg, Hofbibliothek.

150. Reliquary statue of St. Maurice. *Heiltumsbuch*, fol. 227ᵛ. 1525-27. Aschaffenburg, Hofbibliothek.

151. Matthias Grünewald. St. Erasmus and St. Maurice. From Halle, collegiate church. About 1520-24. Munich, Bayerische Staatsgemäldesammlungen, Alte Pinakothek.

152. Detail of figure 151.

151 152 ▷

154

155

153. Jehner von Orlamünde. Three companions of St. Maurice. Interior of the first wing on the right of the altarpiece of the high altar, dated 1511. Halle, Church of St. Maurice.

154. Peter Schro. Statue of St. Maurice. 1525. Halle, collegiate church.

155. Peter Schro. Plaque commemorating the dedication of the collegiate church at Halle. 1523. Halle, collegiate church.

Halle the leading center of resistance to the Reformation, and he transformed the city to achieve it.

In order to accomplish his purpose he would have to do three things: to show an openness toward humanism, to spread a body of teaching opposed to that of the University of Wittenberg, and to reestablish the cohesion of the Germanic Christian community. To the first objective corresponded the prelate's display of reverent respect for Erasmus of Rotterdam;[270] to the second, his efforts to launch in Halle a university which could rival Wittenberg;[271] to the third, his intention to "remodel" Halle. The remodeling would begin with the building of a great church, which would be *the* monument to the cardinal's memory and a suitable setting for large-scale exposition of the sacred relics.

The grand idea began to take flesh in 1519. In that year Albert set about putting the canons out of the Collegiate Church of St. Maurice in order to install his own foundation there. Then, having obtained the necessary authorization from Rome,[272] and by agreement with the Dominicans, he ceded the Convent of St. Maurice to them in exchange for theirs, which could more easily be adapted to his uses.[273] Thereupon the Dominican church became a collegiate church dedicated to St. Maurice and St. Mary Magdalene, to whom St. Erasmus was added.[274] Furthermore, the church was entirely renovated in accordance with an exact decorative program.

At that moment, if we follow E. Wind's very appealing hypothesis, the commissions looking toward the ornamentation of the buildings in Halle had already been awarded, and some were partly executed. Wind proposes, on the strength of what seem to be solid arguments, to set the date of the completion of Grünewald's picture, inspired by the Maurice theme, in 1517,[275] and not in 1521, the traditionally accepted date.[276] The painter found himself constrained by a very exact program when the young archbishop commissioned him to work on a subject unheard of until then, viz., the meeting of St. Maurice and St. Erasmus. Erasmus, bishop of Antioch at the close of the third century, could never, of course, have met Maurice; in Germany he was honored in the fourteenth century as one of the Fourteen Auxiliary Saints.[277] Indeed, it was the fact that he had the same name as the Renaissance Erasmus that won him the honor of figuring opposite St. Maurice. E. Wind sees the scene as allegorical: Maurice, patron saint of Magdeburg and Halle, *is welcoming* St. Erasmus,[278] whose features are those of Albert himself.

Grünewald's painting,[279] now in Munich, has been studied time and again from the standpoints of history and art.[280] We are concerned here only with the figure of Maurice. He appears as an Oriental prince; he wears an astounding head covering[281] and traditional armor richly embellished by the painter; lance and banner are left off. In any case, the purpose was not to represent the Maurice of tradition but to show him playing his part in the event itself—the meeting with St. Erasmus—whether this was intended as an allegory signifying acceptance of the latter saint as co-patron of Halle or whether it was meant to commemorate a legendary baptism of Maurice[282] by Erasmus, as L. Grote suggests.[283] Whatever the date of its execution, Albert of Brandenburg thought of this painting as a manifesto. It is interesting to note that in it he had the painter respect the tradition of the black Maurice—probably for purely aesthetic reasons, as we shall see. The realism of the painting would suggest, as it has in other cases, that Grünewald may have sought out a living person as a model. figs. 151, 152

The silver statue of Maurice cast about 1520 by order of the cardinal did not long survive; it disappeared as early as 1540, since Albert needed the metal for coinage.[284] This statue was probably the one copied in the painting at folio 227^v of the *Liber Ostensionis*, also called the *Hallesche Heiltumsbuch*,[285] an inventory of the reliquaries and precious objects in Halle, drawn up in 1525-27: we shall see more of this. Only minute details distinguish this picture from the painting on the wing of an altarpiece, dated 1529, in the "Marktkirche" at Halle, the work of an anonymous associate of Cranach:[286] we see the same sumptuously engraved armor and the same huge, plumed hat, while the elegant warrior-prince holds a long, precious sword in his left hand and a huge banner, bearing the Brandenburg eagle, in his right. fig. 150 fig. 148

From then on this was the usual image, whether used on painted panels, in illumination, or in sculpture. That is how Nikolaus Glockendon pictured Maurice, surrounded by his companions in martyrdom with their fig. 149

helmets gorgeously decorated with white plumes, in a rich missal executed in 1524 for the cardinal, whose taste for luxury and display was rarely indulged so freely.[287] Maurice also appears in two ornamented initials in the same missal,[288] bareheaded or with the plumed hat, as well as in a full-page painting in which, together with Mary Magdalene, he presents the prelate's coat of arms.[289] His image is engraved above Albert's portrait on the silver plaque that adorns the binding. In the Collegiate Church of St. Maurice and St. Mary Magdalene in Halle—now called the "Dom"—there is a statue, recently attributed to Peter Schro[290] and dated 1525, which represents Maurice with the same attributes. We find him again, wearing armor and the broad hat, on two plaques commemorating Albert's dedication of the church in 1523; their purpose was to give future generations visual evidence of the cardinal's generosity and love of display. The larger plaque was carved in Eifel tufa by Peter Schro;[291] it has suffered some damage—notably its upper cornice is gone[292]—but Maurice is intact. Mary Magdalene rests one arm, as does Maurice, on the coat of arms of the House of Brandenburg. The second of these plaques is usually attributed to Loy Hering,[293] author of a carved epitaph in a similar style.[294] Hering gives a simpler version of St. Maurice, presenting him as a young soldier, bareheaded, with definitely kinky hair, holding a large banner.

fig. 154

fig. 155

The map charting the representations of the black St. Maurice in the sixteenth century[295] brings out the importance of the changes that took place by comparison with earlier centuries. The Saxon nucleus was still at the base.[296] In Jüterbog the importance accorded to the Theban saint was such that in 1508 he was represented life-size on the façade of the town hall:[297] the monumental character of the image forced the abandonment of superfluous detail and gave the helmeted warrior (this helmet we have seen only at Kloster Zinna) an undeniably fine bearing. Small churches and monasteries in Saxony welcomed the black Maurice as they had in the preceding period; his representations became more numerous especially between Halle and the Elbe, northwest[298] and south of the city. Probably the influence of the Pan-Germanic pilgrimage also accounts for the presence of many examples of the black Maurice in Lower Saxony (the Lüneburg triptych[299] is a case in point), in Schleswig,[300] and even in the Danish islands. And again, once one gets away from the principal center of the province of Magdeburg, the details of local iconography show vacillations and adaptations; in the castle of Marienburg, for instance,[301] the altarpiece called the "Calenberger Altar" has, on the left wing, a white Maurice whose turban gives him an exotic air, surrounded by his companions, who alone are clearly black.

fig. 156

fig. 157

fig. 159

South Germany, where, as we have seen, the veneration of the Theban had lost ground and the black iconography had made little penetration in the fifteenth century, shows a certain number of examples in the sixteenth.[302] On the wing of an altarpiece executed about 1520 and coming from Schwaigern,[303] Maurice, wearing a hat of more modest proportions than those at Halle, holds a curious shield decorated with three heads of blacks. From Swabia come two painted altarpiece wings, dating from about 1525 and now in Nuremberg,[304] on which Maurice, bareheaded, holding the shield with the eagle and the banner with the red cross, faces

fig. 158

St. George. The church at Limbach, near Pommersfelden, possesses a work of high quality, Hans von Kulmbach's so-called Altarpiece of the Holy Knights ("Ritteraltar"), from the early sixteenth century.[305] Maurice is figured on the stationary wing to the left; his woolly hair and earring accentuate the ethnic type. By the sober style of the armor, the absence of any headgear, and the meditative cast of the face, the painter succeeded in giving his subject an intensity we have seldom found before. figs. 160, 161

As usual, the liturgy confirms what we learn from works of art. Passau in 1494, Ratisbon in 1510, Constance in about 1485, and Basel about 1486, all revive the cult of St. Maurice. The Ratisbon Missal borrowed directly from the Magdeburg liturgy.[306]

Albert of Brandenburg's policies bore fruit. The plan to initiate a kind of great Pan-German pilgrimage to Halle did in fact awaken a favorable echo among the empire's Catholics;[307] a sumptuous display of riches was centered around it.[308] The cardinal's theatrical exposition of the relics that he and his predecessor had assembled[309] was intended, of course, to stir up the mystical sentiment of a Germany united in the veneration of its saintly protectors, but, paradoxically, it also turned out to be a profitable business enterprise. Luther's violent criticism of the project[310] may have been Albert's reason for waiting to put it into action, which he finally did in 1523.

A breviary dated 1532[311] gives us a clear idea of the theatricality that distinguished the annual pilgrimage, and lets us see how the entire liturgy

156. Statue of St. Maurice. From the façade of the town hall in Jüterbog. 1508. Jüterbog, Kreis-Heimatmuseum.

157. St. Maurice and his companions. Upper half of the right wing of a triptych. From the chapel at Gross-Wittfeitzen. About 1520. Lüneburg, Museum für das Fürstentum Lüneburg.

at Halle was organized around the exposition of the relics.[312] One element stands out immediately in these ceremonies, and that is the marked preference for black vestments, with silver also dominating. Here we see some reason to wonder whether the continued representation of Maurice as a black was not prompted by aesthetic considerations rather than by an ethnic significance inherited from the thirteenth century.

158. St. Maurice. Altarpiece fragment. From Schwaigern. About 1520. Formerly in Stuttgart, Württembergisches Landesmuseum.

159. St. Maurice and his companions. Left wing of the so-called Calenberger Altar. About 1515. Marienburg, castle, Collection of H. R. H. the Prince of Hannover.

159

158

160

161

The breviary goes into minute detail on the way the relics were set out for each feast. It is evident that they played a major role in the liturgical ceremonies, which were designed to appeal to the emotions more than to reason. It seems that large tables were erected with an arrangement of steps on top, one table in the center and two others at the sides, each covered with a profusion of rugs and tapestries. Thus every spatial dimension was exploited, with the spoken word to heighten the effect. The relics exposed in the center varied with the saint being venerated and the rank of the feast; the number of relics on display also varied. The pilgrims were also allowed to venerate precious objects called *Plenaria*, which were used in the liturgy: there were twelve of them at Halle. They were not reliquaries but objects in gold and silver plate on which were images of Christ, the Virgin, and the foremost saints.[313] Depending on the solemnity of the feast day, seven, eight, ten, or twelve *Plenaria* were exposed following a strictly determined hierarchical order, table by table and step by step on each table:[314] the twelve were shown only on exceptional occasions.[315] Maurice, we should emphasize, was given very special treatment; indeed, he was the only saint whose feast days, twice every year, brought out the whole group of *Plenaria*. The anniversary of the translation of his head to Halle was more solemnly commemorated than his relics' transfer in the tenth century.[316]

The same breviary describes in detail the ceremonies of the pilgrimage.[317] In September a place close to the church was made ready, decorated with tapestries and lighted with candles and lanterns. At the tenth hour on the first day the bells summoned the pilgrims three times. A sermon preparing the faithful to venerate the relics was followed by a general confession. Then came the procession, strictly programmed, with alternate singing and playing of trumpets and flutes. The procession first passed[318] before the relics of the saints, the second time before those of Christ, the third before those of the Virgin Mary. The fourth *Gang*, or "passing," involved the veneration of particular saints and the prophets, the fifth, the Apostles and Evangelists, the sixth, martyrs, the seventh, confessors and doctors of the Church, the eighth, virgins, and the ninth and last, the relics of venerable widows and women in religion. After these nine *Gänge* the preacher led the pilgrims in prayers for the Church, the empire, the province of Magdeburg, and the diocese of Halle. Then the list of indulgences was read, and the ceremony ended to the pealing of the bells.

All that precedes has to do with the "noble" aspects of the pilgrimage. What went on on the side is not so rosy. There had been a certain degree of freedom about the event as originally organized, but it quickly became a matter of obligation for the people of the province. The clergy had to herd their flocks together, collect the "alms" that were a requirement of the pilgrimage, and deliver the receipts, in bags sealed with their name before witnesses, to the treasury of the Collegiate Church of Halle. The sale of indulgences was now a custom. The cardinal's need of money never stopped growing, especially after the death of his brother Joachim in 1535. His demands gave rise to coolness, then to hostility, in the citizens of Halle, who in 1534 made their own claim for a tax on the pilgrims!

Conquered by the progress of the Reformation, Albert, in 1540, put an end to the exposition of the precious relics at Halle and ordered most of them transferred to Mainz.[319] This gave Luther the chance for a savage

160, 161. Hans von Kulmbach. St. Maurice. Stationary left wing of the so-called Ritteraltar. About 1518. Limbach, church.

162. Covered ciborium topped with a bust of St. Maurice. *Heiltumsbuch*, fol. 335v. 1525-27. Aschaffenburg, Hofbibliothek.

162

triumph over his adversary. A brochure falsely attributed to Albert of Brandenburg was circulated in Wittenberg in the summer of 1542. The German public was thereby invited to a new pilgrimage center to adore some particularly spectacular relics—including a nice piece of Moses' left horn, three flames from the Burning Bush, three tongues of fire and one egg from the Holy Spirit, one tip from the banner brought back from Hell by Christ, a big curl from the beard of Beelzebub, a feather from the archangel Gabriel's wing, a full pound of the wind that blew past Elijah on Mount Horeb, two long notes sounded by the trumpets at Mount Sinai, thirty clangs of the timbrel played by Moses' sister Miriam, a large, heavy chunk of the shout raised by the children of Israel to bring down the walls of Jericho, five fine strings from David's harp, three of the hairs by which Absalom hung from the oak tree. And the pilgrims were promised the remission of great numbers of sins.[320] The cardinal made no response to this tirade—savage, it is true, but brought on by his own excesses.

It is within this tragicomic framework that we must place the last images of St. Maurice that enter into this study. In order to advance the success of the Halle pilgrimage, the cardinal had ordered the compilation

163. Drinking horn decorated with a statuette of St. Maurice. *Heiltumsbuch*, fol. 291v. 1525-27. Aschaffenburg, Hofbibliothek.

163

of a catalogue of the reliquaries and the most valuable liturgical objects. This work in printed form appeared in 1520, illustrated with 237 woodcuts by Wolf Traut.[321] A more elaborate manuscript catalogue—the number of reliquaries and sacred objects increased steadily—was compiled between 1525 and 1527. This manuscript, which we cited earlier, is generally known as the *Heiltumsbuch*;[322] originally it included 364 paintings. After the relics were transferred to Mainz, a new handwritten inventory was drawn up in 1540;[323] it did not list all the objects and contained no illustrations.[324]

The Aschaffenburg manuscript alone presents some twenty objects in or on which a black Maurice makes his appearance:[325] his statuette stands on one side of three reliquary monstrances, with St. Mary Magdalene or St. Ursula on the other side;[326] wearing a bandeau, he is sculpted in high relief on a reliquary;[327] he is seen on the wing of a triptych[328] and in scenes from the life of the Virgin;[329] he adorns the scabbard of a sword, his image, curiously, being repeated six times;[330] more often, a small erect statuette, in armor and carrying the gonfalon and the sword or shield, he stands atop some reliquaries,[331] a fifteenth-century ciborium,[332] and an unusual drinking horn resting on three bird's feet.[333] fig. 162 fig. 163

164

165

164, 165. Wolf Traut. Reliquary busts of Fidis and Maurice. Woodcuts from the *Heiltumsbuch* printed in 1520. Nuremberg, Germanisches Nationalmuseum.

166. Reliquary bust of Fidis. *Heiltumsbuch*, fol. 376^{v}. 1525-27. Aschaffenburg, Hofbibliothek.

167. Reliquary bust of St. Maurice. *Heiltumsbuch*, fol. 228^{v}. 1525-27. Aschaffenburg, Hofbibliothek.

It should be said that in all the above examples Maurice is represented
as a more or less "typed" black, with no originality whatever. With the
exception of the fine silver reliquary statue already referred to,[334] what we
find are mostly objects of rich gold or silver plate, some of them bizarre,
intended to stir the imagination; the images of Maurice hold our interest
only by the frequency of their occurrence. Two reliquary busts, however,
deserve closer attention. One of them represents "Fidis," an imaginary fig. 166
sister of Maurice, with black skin and kinky hair. Her turban and rings
contrast with the rich apparel of the period:[335] the 1520 catalogue already
presents her in the same turban and clothing rendered more sketchily, but fig. 164
there the wood engraving did not allow the blackening of the face—a banal
one at best—whereas the facial traits of the Fidis in the Aschaffenburg
manuscript are delicate and regular. This cannot be said of the features of
Maurice on the other reliquary bust, which are deliberately "typed."[336] fig. 167
Once again our saint carries the shield with the eagle, and his headdress is
not unlike the one Grünewald gave him; oddly enough, this headdress is
absent in the 1520 catalogue, where Maurice, with strongly marked black fig. 165
features, is bareheaded. It may be that the crown in the Aschaffenburg
manuscript was added later, but it is not possible to establish the exact
relationship between that picture and Grünewald's painting. At any rate,
in these two reliquary busts we have works that, for all their ostentatiousness, are powerful and tell us much about the personality of Albert of Brandenburg.

After the cardinal's demise, the theme that he had caused to be represented more often than at any other time lost some of its significance, and
although its popularity fell off sharply, it did not completely disappear. In
the late sixteenth century the members of the cathedral chapter of Magdeburg commissioned some large enameled glass goblets, which form a fairly
uniform series: the armorial bearings of aristocratic families figure in the
lower register, and a black St. Maurice in armor, wearing the plumed hat fig. 168
and carrying the banner with the cross and the shield with the eagle, is
represented in the upper band.[337] Could the goblets have been intended as presents? Were they a new kind of Magdeburg "propaganda," like the coins circulated some centuries earlier? St. Maurice appears on them only by allusion to his role as a protector of the city. Inside the city he survived in another way, surprising in view of the Reformation. The new pulpit, erected in the late sixteenth century in the cathedral, by now a Protestant church, still presents the alabaster images of the saints so long venerated there, and among them Maurice, identified by a cartouche; his hair is kinky, and he faithfully carries the banner that protects his city, and a shield decorated with the two-headed eagle.[338]

Lastly, in the classical period, the black Maurice survived in some few localities situated, oddly enough, in a horizontal zone going from Münster to Magdeburg:[339] we find a painted statue, sometimes standing alone,[340] sometimes inserted in a large sculptured group (baroque altarpiece at Hildesheim[341] and at Langenweddingen,[342] monumental tomb in Münster Cathedral[343]); Maurice is a black man-at-arms, usually wearing the helmet and cuirass and carrying either the lance or the gonfalon with the cross.

166

167

In Magdeburg, from the thirteenth century onward, Maurice was a black saint. Did this amount to an explicit proclamation of the equality of black Africans as men destined to salvation? One might think that this was so in the twelfth and thirteenth centuries, in the midst of the universalist movement in which Otto of Freising took the initiative, when, too, there were manifestations of sympathy that reached the black queen Belakane, mother of a perfect knight.[344] But this perspective did not last. After 1250 the empire abandoned the Hohenstaufens's Mediterranean dreams and became more German than European. Its contacts with the black world remained extremely tenuous at the very time when things were changing in the Mediterranean area. The image of the black Maurice was saved in the empire, but at the cost of concessions to liturgical or aesthetic fashion; as a result, in the sixteenth century the Theban saint was no more than an exotic figure whose black color was in style. Moreover, whether on account of hostility to the empire or because other intellectual trends were developing, the rest of Western Europe showed little or no disposition to adopt the imperial iconographic program. This combination of trends singularly diminishes the historical significance of the beautiful iconography of the black Maurice.

So it is that the empire, which blackened the Queen of Sheba in 1181, St. Maurice around 1250, and one of the Magi-Kings (at least in the texts) in the early thirteenth century, drew no ethnographic or historical conclu-

168

168. Enameled glass goblet decorated with a figure of St. Maurice and the armorial bearings of the canons of Magdeburg. 1568. Cleveland, Cleveland Museum of Art.

sions from all this. These images and forms of devotion never became popular or deeply rooted, except perhaps in the case of the Magi, and we note again that one of them was not represented as black before the fourteenth century. The diffusion of the black Maurice, its extent and relatively long continuation notwithstanding, is marked, beginning with the earliest examples, by a progressive withdrawal from the ideas and biblical interpretations that gave rise to his first appearance.

The most cogent reason for this situation is certainly that the entire debate on the theoretical vocation of blacks to salvation and sainthood went on in closed circles. It was first argued in the thirteenth century among high-ranking and highly educated clerks who were concerned only with theological and philosophical speculation; later, the debate was simply transferred to the imperial circle, where the new images appear to have been utilized to the full in order to reinforce the emperor's prestige, to carry on the struggle against pagans, and to loosen the empire's bonds with Rome.

There remains the masterpiece in Magdeburg. The object, admittedly, is an example of the flourishing of thirteenth-century statuary. Its iconographic audacity obviously sprang from a trend of thought devoted not to Africa, but, more fundamentally, to man and the Christian as conceived by the society in which this creation saw the light of day. Yet one would search in vain in medieval art and probably in Western art as a whole for a representation of the African as faithfully and powerfully rendered as this one. Beyond its realism and its historicity this statue, in the plenitude of its expressiveness, embodies the ultimate vocation to offer a blackness through which the light of sanctity might shine. In later times Western Christendom, despite efforts at rapprochement, would betray its inability to convey the personality of the African through a vision as lofty and as true as the one offered by this image of a man transfigured.

ABBREVIATIONS

AdE	*Annales d'Ethiopie*
AnalBoll	*Analecta Bollandiana*
Annales E.S.C.	*Annales. Economies, Sociétés, Civilisations*
ArtB	*The Art Bulletin*
AthMitt	*Mitteilungen des deutschen Archäologischen Instituts. Athenische Abteilung*
BiblEcChartes	*Bibliothèque de l'Ecole des Chartes: Revue d'érudition*
BMMA	*Bulletin of the Metropolitan Museum of Art, New York*
CahArch	*Cahiers archéologiques*
CCL	*Corpus Christianorum, Series Latina* (Turnhout, 1954-)
CSEL	*Corpus Scriptorum Ecclesiasticorum Latinorum* (Vienna, 1866-)
GBA	*Gazette des Beaux-Arts*
GCS	*Die Griechischen christlichen Schriftsteller der ersten drei Jahrhunderte* (Leipzig, 1897-1941; Berlin and Leipzig, 1953; Berlin, 1954-)
JPKS	*Jahrbuch der Preuszischen Kunstsammlungen*
MZ	*Mainzer Zeitschrift*
PG	*Patrologiae Cursus Completus, Series Graeca*, ed. J.-P. MIGNE (Paris, 1857-66)
PL	*Patrologiae Cursus Completus, Series Latina*, ed. J.-P. MIGNE (Paris, 1844-64)
PO	*Patrologia Orientalis*, ed. R. GRAFFIN and F. NAU (Paris, 1903-)
Rendiconti Sc. Mor.	*Atti della Accademia nazionale dei Lincei: Classe di Scienze morali, storiche e filologiche, Rendiconti*
RHES	*Revue d'histoire économique et sociale*
S.C.	Sources chrétiennes (Paris, 1940-)
ZfK	*Zeitschrift für Kunstgeschichte*

THE THEME OF "ETHIOPIA" AND "ETHIOPIANS" IN PATRISTIC LITERATURE

1 ORIGEN *Contra haereses* 5.9, 10.34 (*PG* 16.3158, 3454).

2 CAESARIUS *Dialogi* 3.145-47 (*PG* 38.1096-97).

3 AUGUSTINE *De Genesi ad litteram* 8.7 (*CSEL* 28.1.240).

4 AUGUSTINE *De Gen. ad litt.* 8.7 (*CSEL* 28.1.242).

5 CLEMENT OF ALEXANDRIA *Stromata* 7.4 (*PG* 9.427-28). Cf. ARNOBIUS *Adversus nationes* 3.14-16 (*CSEL* 4.121-22), where he discusses the differentiation of the gods and the possibility of their recognizing each other. Among the *proprietates signorum differentium* are: flat nose, prognathism, woolly hair, etc. Arnobius, however, alludes to the theory that these images did not pretend to represent the gods but fulfilled a cultic requirement. Moreover, he mentions Isis blackened *(furua)* by the glare of the Ethiopian sun (idem *Adv. nat.* 1.36 [*CSEL* 4.24]).

6 ORIGEN *Contra haer.* 4.6 (*PG* 16.3068).

7 MELETIOS *De natura hominis* (*PG* 64.1279-82).

8 ATHANASIUS *Liber de definitionibus* 3 (*PG* 28.541).

9 ATHANASIUS *Quaestiones ad Antiochum ducem* 24 (*PG* 28.611). The authenticity of this text and the preceding one is doubtful, but they certainly belong to the Alexandrian *Gedankenkreis.*

10 ARNOBIUS *Adv. nat.* 7.19-20 (*CSEL* 4.253-54).

11 ARNOBIUS *Adv. nat.* 2.36-37 (*CSEL* 4.77). This is an extension of Plato's idea in the *Timaeus*—souls thought of as being the work of the demiurge.

12 ORIGEN *Peri Archon* 2.10.8 (*PG* 11.240).

13 ORIGEN *Peri Archon* 3.6 (*PG* 11.333-42).

14 ORIGEN *Contra Celsum* 6.64 (*PG* 11.1395). Concerning the "body" of God walking in the Garden, see idem *In Genesim homelia* 1.13 (*PG* 12.155-60).

15 This is one of the dominant notes in Origen's approach to the subject; cf. ORIGEN *Commentaria in Ioannem* 13.22 (*PG* 14.435).

16 Cf. ORIGEN *Commentaria in Matthaeum* 10.11 (*PG* 13.857 ff.).

17 AUGUSTINE *De civitate Dei* 16.8 (*CSEL* 40.2.139-41); see also idem *De civ. Dei* 21.8 (*CSEL* 40.2.532).

18 On this teleological theme (man's upright stance as related to his being destined for gnosis), see A. WLOSOK, *Laktanz und die philosophische Gnosis: Untersuchungen zu Geschichte und Terminologie der gnostischen Erlösungsvorstellung*, Abhandlungen der Heidelberger Akademie der Wissenschaften, Philosophisch-historische Klasse, 1960, 2 (Heidelberg, 1960).

19 AUGUSTINE *De Gen. ad litt.* 3.12 (*CSEL* 28.1.78).

20 This is the objective of Augustine's treatise *De anima et ejus origine* and of numerous developments in his *De Trinitate.*

21 AUGUSTINE *De Gen. ad litt.* 10.25, 24 (*CSEL* 28.1.329, 327). Our inability to conceive incorporeal beings leads us to imagine souls with "colors."

22 AUGUSTINE *De Trinit.* 2.9.4-5.

23 AUGUSTINE *De civ. Dei* 22.19 (*CSEL* 40.2.630).

24 See, for example, AUGUSTINE *De baptismo* 3.19.25 (*CSEL* 51.216), and idem *Epistula ad catholicos de secta Donatistarum* 8.21-22, 21.28 (*CSEL* 52.254-56, 306).

25 AUGUSTINE *Quaestionum in Heptateuchum libri VII* 4.20 (*CSEL* 28.2.331).

26 BOETHIUS *In categorias Aristotelis* 3 (*PL* 64.248).

27 DIDYMUS THE BLIND *De Trinitate* 1.16 (*PG* 39.332-37).

28 The Latin text reads: "Dicitur etiam rationale nigrum et irrationale nigrum, quippe si equus et homo Aethiops nigri sunt. Dicitur etiam risibile nigrum cum hominum quis niger fuerit. Dicitur etiam individuum nigrum, cum sic quis unus homo ex Aethiopia nominatur" (BOETHIUS *In Porphyrium dialogus* 1 [*PL* 64.30]).

29 BOETHIUS *In Porphyr. dial.* 2 (De accidenti) (*PL* 64.56-70). "At vero hominis, id est Aethiopis, amisso nigro colore, erit ejus species candida, sicut etiam aliorum hominum" (*PL* 64.56). However, black color does not distinguish a man from ebony or crows, whereas being capable of laughter *(risibile)* is an absolutely distinctive human trait (*PL* 64.70).

30 BOETHIUS *In Porphyrium commentaria* 4 (De accidenti) (*PL* 64.132-33). It is quite possible to *imagine* a white Ethiopian.

31 There is a trace of nominalism here, which is due to the etymology of the ancient name; cf. BOETHIUS *In Porphyr. comm.* 5 (*PL* 64.145-46): ". . . nam si interrogemur qualis est Aethiops, respondebimus accidens, id est niger."

32 BOETHIUS *In Porphyr. comm.* 5 (*PL* 64.156-58).

33 BOETHIUS *In categ. Arist.* 2 (*PL* 64.209).

34 BOETHIUS *In categ. Arist.* 3 (*PL* 64.247-48).

35 ORIGEN *Commentarium in Canticum Canticorum* 2 (*PG* 13.101 ff.). The entire passage should be read for the full development of the theme.

36 G. D. MANSI, ed., *Sacrorum conciliorum nova et amplissima collectio*, vol. IX (1763; reprint ed., Berlin and Leipzig, 1902), col. 226; THEODORE OF MOPSUESTIA *In Canticum Canticorum* (*PG* 66.699). See also ANASTASIUS *In Hexaemeron* 8 (*PG* 89.977) (against allegorical interpretation of the Song of Songs).

37 Cf. the reconstruction of the "staging" of this mystery play in the introduction of O. ROUSSEAU's edition of ORIGEN's *Homélies sur le Cantique des Cantiques*, 2d ed., S.C., no. 37bis (Paris, 1966).

38 Scriptural references: Num. 12:1-2, 10 (Miriam's punishment); 1 Kings 10:1-12; 2 Chron. 9:1-12 (cf. Matt. 12:42); Ps. 67 (68):32; Zeph. 2:12, 3:10; Jer. 38:7-13.

39 Origen recalls the traditional explanation of the characteristic color of the black race: "Ita denique et apud illam omnem gentem Aethiopum ferunt, cui naturalis quaedam inest ex seminis carnalis successione nigredo, quod in illis locis sol radiis acrioribus ferveat, et adusta jam semel atque infuscata corpora genuini vitii successione permaneant" (ORIGEN *Comm. in Cant. Cant.* 2.6 [*PG* 13.110]).

40 "Nam neque aspectu, sed despectu solis inuritur, neque nascendo, sed negligendo . . ." (ORIGEN *Comm. in Cant. Cant.* 2.6 [*PG* 13.111]).

41 DIDYMUS THE BLIND *Sur Zacharie* 3.83 (ed. and trans. L. DOUTRELEAU, S.C., no. 84 [Paris, 1962]), vol. II, pp. 658-61.

42 DIDYMUS THE BLIND *Sur Zacharie* 3.195-96, vol. II, pp. 712-15. *The Shepherd* differs from the *Epistle of Barnabas* in that it does not directly characterize the demon in terms of color. The blacks come from the first mountain, which also is black. Blasphemers and apostates, they are doomed to death; they are black because they are a lawless race (γένος ἄνομον). Cf. HERMAS *Le Pasteur* 96.1 (ed. and trans. R. JOLY, 2d ed., rev. and enl., S.C., no. 53bis [Paris, 1968]), pp. 332-33. We find this theme turned upside down, as it were, in the exegesis of the marriage of Moses to an Ethiopian. *Le Pasteur* (83.4, pp. 302-3; 92.1, pp. 324-25) again reverts to the symbolic value of blackness with reference to the choice of stones for the tower (i.e., souls classified according to their color and so accepted or rejected), and again to the guilty unions of certain believers with beautiful women dressed in black—allegorical personifications of unbelief, intemperance, disobedience, and deceitfulness, all of these being demoniacal manifestations in the soul. Cf.

idem *Le Pasteur* 22.10, pp. 134-35; 24.2, pp. 138-39.

43 Didymus the Blind *Sur Zacharie* 4.312 (S.C., no. 85), vol. III, pp. 964-65.

44 Jerome *In Zachariam* 2.9 (*PL* 25.1480-87). Jerome also includes Hippolytus among his sources.

45 Jerome *In Hieremiam* 3.22 (*CSEL* 59.170).

46 Ambrose *Expositio Psalmi CXVIII* 2.8 (*CSEL* 62.23-24).

47 Ambrose *Exp. Ps. 118* 2.9 (*CSEL* 62.24-25).

48 Ambrose *Exp. Ps. 118* 12.25 (*CSEL* 62.265-66).

49 Ambrose *Exp. Ps. 118* 14.34 (*CSEL* 62.321).

50 Ambrose *Exp. Ps. 118* 15.36 (*CSEL* 62.349).

51 Ambrose *Exp. Ps. 118* 16.21, 15.13, 22.33 (*CSEL* 62.364, 337, 505).

52 Ambrose *Exp. Ps. 118* 19.26-27 (*CSEL* 62.435). There is an interesting remark on the meaning of the copulative *et* in *nigra et formosa* in idem *Exp. Ps. 118* 18.33 (*CSEL* 62.414-15).

53 Ambrose *De Paradiso* 3.16 (*CSEL* 32.1.275-76).

54 Ambrose *Exp. Ps. 118* 14.7 (*CSEL* 62.302).

55 Ambrose *De Noe* 34.128 (*CSEL* 32.1.496).

56 Gregory the Great *Moralium libri, sive Expositio in librum B. Job* 18.52 (*PL* 76.88-89).

57 Gregory the Great *Moralia* 32.22 (*PL* 76.663).

58 *Epître de Barnabé* 4.10, 20.1 (ed. and trans. P. Prigent and R.A. Kraft, S.C., no. 172 [Paris, 1971]), pp. 100-101, 210-11.

59 *Historia Lausiaca* 22 (*PL* 73.1119-22). The hermit's name is Moses, a detail that casts doubt on his very existence.

60 It should be noted that these anecdotes cover a limited area, mostly close to Ethiopia. There is absolutely no question here of a general topic. In North Africa, where Tertullian, Cyprian, and Augustine give ample play to the devils, these are never presented as being black.

61 Palladius *Lausiaca* 2 (*PL* 74.347).

62 John Moschus *Pratum spirituale* 105, 160 (*PL* 74.171, 200).

63 John Moschus *Prat. spirit.* 66 (*PL* 74.150).

64 *Vie de sainte Mélanie* 54 (ed. and trans. D. Gorce, S.C., no. 90 [Paris, 1962]), pp. 234-35. This mode of disguise is inspired by 2 Cor. 11:14—"Satan himself transformeth himself into an angel of light"—with the colors reversed. On the role of demons in illnesses, often cyclical, see Tertullian *Apologeticum* 22.4-12 (*CSEL* 69.61-62), and numerous later testimonies.

65 Rufinus *Historia monachorum* 30 (*PL* 21.456). It may be that we have here a kind of inverted allusion to martyrdom (the palm is won by braving fire).

66 Rufinus *Hist. monach.* 29 (*PL* 21.454). The text is worth quoting in its entirety: "Et ecce vidit per totam Ecclesiam, quasi parvulos quosdam puerulos Aethiopes tetros discurrere huc atque illuc, et velut volitando deferri. Moris est autem inibi, sedentibus cunctis, ab uno dici Psalmum, ceteris, vel audientibus, vel respondentibus. Discurrentes ergo illi Aethiopes pueruli, singulis quibusque sedentibus alludebant, et si cui duobus digitulis oculos compressissent, statim dormitabat; si cui vero in os immersissent digitum, oscitare eum faciebant."

67 *Hist. Laus.* 27 (*PL* 73.1126).

68 Anastasius *Oratio in sextum Psalmum* (*PG* 89.1142).

69 *Passio Perpetuae* 3.2 (*PL* 3.40).

70 Victor of Vita *Historia persecutionis Africanae provinciae* 2.18 (*CSEL* 7.30-31).

71 Athanasius *Vita beati Antonii abbatis* 4 (*PL* 73.130).

72 *Hist. Laus.* 52 (*PL* 73.1155).

73 *Vitae Patrum* 5.5 (*PL* 73.879).

74 John Moschus *Prat. spirit.* 160 (*PL* 74.200).

75 *Vit. Pat.* 3.38 (*PL* 73.763).

76 Rufinus *Hist. monach.* 7 (*PL* 21.415).

77 *Vit. Pat.* 9.26 (*PL* 74.99-102).

78 Augustine *De civ. Dei* 22.8 (*CSEL* 40.2.601).

79 John Chrysostom *In acta Apostolorum homiliae* 19 (*PG* 60.149); cf. Epiphanius *Liber de mensuris et ponderibus* 9 (*PG* 43.252). Isidore of Pelusium, writing to Zosimus (*Epistolae* 1.61 [*PG* 78.221-24]), says: "Are you not Ethiopian in spirit? Do you understand what you are reading?" Epiphanius, in the text referred to, mentions the library of Alexandria and says that it could have been filled out, notably in the area of the Scriptures, with the many books that were in Ethiopia.

80 Gregory of Nyssa *De vita Moysis* (*PG* 44.385). There Philip is described as the "bather" of the eunuch.

81 Epiphanius (*Adversus haereses* 1-4.6 [*PG* 41.185]) reinstates Nimrod as the father of the *malae artes* (astrology, magic) attributed to Zoroaster. Cf. Origen *Comm. in Matth.* 12.28 (*PG* 13.1047), and Athanasius *De titulis Psalmorum* Ps. 7 (*PG* 27.667).

82 Athanasius *Oratio de Incarnatione Verbi* 51 (*PG* 25.188).

83 Athanasius *Quaest. ad Antioch.* 123 (*PG* 28.676). The heat of the fire restrains the Ethiopians from drinking too much wine and makes them irritable and libidinous. On the "road," cf. idem *Sermo in sanctum Pascha* 8 (*PG* 28.1092); idem *Synopsis Scripturae Sacrae* 51, 34 (*PG* 28.405, 361).

84 Athanasius *Expositio in Psalmos* 67.32 (*PG* 27.303).

85 Epiphanius *Adv. haer.* 31.31 (*PG* 41.533).

86 Origen *Comm. in Matth.* 24.9-14 (*PG* 13.1655).

87 Theodoret *Thérapeutique des maladies helléniques* 8.6 (ed. and trans. P. Canivet, S.C., no. 57 [Paris, 1958]), vol. II, pp. 311-12.

88 Theodoret *In Habacuc* 3.7 (*PG* 81.1828).

89 Epiphanius *Adv. haer.* 64.2. The story runs that Origen agreed to burn a few grains of incense, figuring that he had better choose the lesser of two evils. Cf. Nemesius of Emesa *De natura hominis* 30 (*PG* 40.722). The story is doubtful, and recalls the rhetorical theme of the priestess-prostitute or the apologetical theme of the Christian woman condemned to the lupanar.

90 Cf. *supra*, n. 61.

91 Ennodius *Epistulae* 7.21 in *Monumenta Germaniae historica: Auctores Antiquissimi*, vol. VII, ed. F. Vogel (Berlin, 1885), p. 246.

92 Cf. Gregory of Nazianzus *Oratio XL: In sanctum Baptisma* (*PG* 36.397). Theodoret *Interpretatio in Psalmos* In Psal. LXXIX (*PG* 80.1514), In Psal. LXXI (*PG* 80.1435).

93 The expression is Jerome's, translating Origen; cf. Jerome *Interpretatio homiliarum Origenis in Canticum Canticorum* Homilia 1 (*PL* 23.1125-26). On the Bride's 'metanoia', cf. Cyril of Alexandria *Explanatio in Psalmos* 67.32 (*PG* 69.1160).

94 Arator *De actibus Apostolorum* 1.673-707 (*CSEL* 72.52-54); cf. 1 Cor. 6:9.

95 Arator *De act. Apost.* 1.690-99 (*CSEL* 72.53-54).

Non parva figurae
Causa sub obscurae regionis imagine lucet:
Comprobat Omnipotens taedarum foedere Moysen
Aethiopam sociasse sibi, quem dogmata produnt
Postea cum Domino vicinius ore locutum.
Quid mirum si legis amor tunc crescere coepit

Ecclesiae cum iuncta fuit? Quod sponsa perennis
Hac veniat de gente magis, nec Cantica celant,
Quae fuscam pulchramque vocant; haec pergit ab austro
Aethiopum qui torret humum . . .

96 Cf. *supra*, pp. 21-22.

97 JEROME *In Sophoniam* 1.1 (*CCL* 76 A.656 ff.).

98 The usual references to Pss. 67 (68):32, 71 (72):9-11.

99 JEROME *In Soph.* 2.12-13 (*CCL* 76 A.690).

100 JEROME *In Soph.* 3.10-13 (*CCL* 76 A.703-4).

101 HERACLIDES *Paradisus* 7 (*PL* 74.277 ff.). More novella than historical document, this text is similar to an anecdote in the *Lausiac History* (*Hist. Laus.* 22 [*PL* 73.1119 ff.]).

102 TERTULLIAN *De spectaculis* 3.

103 PETER OF ALEXANDRIA *Epistola canonica* 4 (*PG* 18.473).

104 THEODORET *Quaestiones in Numeros* 12.22 (*PG* 80.376); idem *In Canticum Canticorum* 1 (*PG* 81.68).

105 JUSTUS OF URGEL *In Cantica Canticorum Salomonis explicatio mystica* 1.8 (*PL* 67.965).

106 ISIDORE OF SEVILLE *Allegoriae quaedam Scripturae Sacrae* 62 (*PL* 83.109).

107 LEO ALLATIUS *In Eustathii Antiocheni Hexameron notae* (*PG* 18.1052).

108 JOHN CHRYSOSTOM *In Ioannem homiliae* 2 (*PG* 59.32).

109 That is why his symbol is the eagle.

110 JOHN CHRYSOSTOM *In Matthaeum homiliae* 26 (*PG* 57.339 ff.).

111 JOHN CHRYSOSTOM *In act. Ap. hom.* 19 (*PG* 60.149 ff.).

112 GREGORY OF NAZIANZUS *Carmina moralia* 10.824 ff. (*PG* 37.739).

113 GREGORY OF NAZIANZUS *Orat. XL* (*PG* 36.396-97).

114 JEROME *Tractatus in Psalmos* 67.32 (*CCL* 78.47).

115 JEROME *Tract. in Psal.* 86.4 (*CCL* 78.114).

116 PAULINUS OF NOLA *Carmina* 28.249-54 (*CSEL* 30.302).

117 AUGUSTINE *Quaest. in Hept.* 4.20 (*CCL* 33.247).

118 PAULINUS OF NOLA *Epistulae* 23.29-30 (*CSEL* 29.185-86). Here he gives some notes on the tropological ambiguity of the crow and its black color.

119 SIMEON THE NEW THEOLOGIAN *Hymnes* 50.315 ff. (ed. and trans. J. KODER, J. PARAMELLE, and L. NEYRAND, S.C., no. 196 [Paris, 1973]), vol. III, pp. 180-81.

120 Cf. AUGUSTINE *De natura et gratia* 22.24-25, referring to Paul in Rom. 1:21, "obscuratum est insipiens cor eorum."

121 PROSPER OF AQUITAINE *Carmen de ingratis* vv. 856 ff. (ed. and trans. C.T. HUEGELMEYER, The Catholic University of America, Patristic Studies, vol. 95 [Washington, D.C., 1962]). For the error still abroad in part of the world, note the formulas: "Consilio legit tetrae nigrescere noctis" (v. 858) and "et dira innumeri demersi nocte peribant" (v. 285).

122 AUGUSTINE *De nat. et grat.* 40.46.

123 CASSIODORUS *Expositio Psalmorum* 73.14. On the theology of grace underlying this text, cf. R. SCHLIEBEN, *Christliche Theologie und Philologie in der Spätantike: Die schulwissenschaftlichen Methoden der Psalmenexegese Cassiodors*, Arbeiten zur Kirchengeschichte, no. 46 (Berlin and New York, 1974), pp. 73-74.

124 EPHRAEM SYRUS *The Pearl, or Seven Rhythms on the Faith* 3.2-3 (ed. and trans. J.B. MORRIS, Library of the Fathers, no. 41 [Oxford, 1847]), pp. 92-93.

125 PETER CHRYSOLOGUS *Sermones* 61 (*PL* 52.369).

126 PETER CHRYSOLOGUS *Sermones* 60 (*PL* 52.365).

127 ORIGEN *In Numeros homiliae* 6.4 (*GCS* 30.35-36).

128 ORIGEN *In Num. hom.* 7.2 (*GCS* 30.39-40).

129 In JEROME's Latin translation of the *In Hiezechielem* 9.29, 30 (*CCL* 75.412, 424-25).

130 JEROME *In Hiezech.* 8.27 (*CCL* 75.379).

131 AUGUSTINE *Enarrationes in Psalmos* 67.40-41 (*CCL* 39.897-99).

132 JEROME *Commentariorum in Esaiam* 7.18.1-3 (*CCL* 73.274-75).

133 JEROME *In Osee* prologus (*CCL* 76.3).

134 GREGORY OF ELVIRA *In Canticum Canticorum* 1.23-30 (*CCL* 69.176-79).

135 JEROME *In Amos* 3.9.7-8 (*CCL* 76.343). The blackening of the body is also the result of the sin of Adam and Eve; the flesh recovers its beauty in the Incarnation. Cf. the texts cited in the preceding notes.

136 QUODVULTDEUS *Livre des promesses et des prédictions de Dieu* 2.9.15 (ed. and trans. R. BRAUN, S.C., no. 101 [Paris, 1964]), vol. I, pp. 328-29.

137 QUODVULTDEUS *Livre des promesses* 3.36.38 (S.C., no. 102), vol. II, pp. 562-63.

138 QUODVULTDEUS *Livre des promesses* 3.6.7, vol. II, pp. 510-11.

139 On the historical value of the work, cf. R. BRAUN's introduction in QUODVULTDEUS *Livre des promesses*, vol. I, pp. 65-74.

140 QUODVULTDEUS *Livre des promesses* 4.5, vol. II, pp. 596-97.

141 A recent bibliography on the subject can be found in the large documentation brought together by A. HERMANN for the article "Farbe" in T. KLAUSER, ed., *Reallexikon für Antike und Christentum*, vol. VII (Stuttgart, 1969), cols. 358-447. See also G. LANCZKOWSKI, "Aethiopia," *Nachträge zum Reallexikon für Antike und Christentum* published in *Jahrbuch für Antike und Christentum* 1 (1958): 134-53.

142 E.g., Augustine, refuting the Donatists' claim to privileged treatment by God for North Africa, reminds them that the South, place of mystical repose (Song of Songs 1:7), should be understood as "the land south of scorched Egypt" (*Sermones* 46.15). For ANASTASIUS *In Hexaem.* 8 (*PG* 89.977 ff.), the Gihon, a river whose source is unknown, is a figure of Christ.

143 Cf. CYRIL OF ALEXANDRIA *Glaphyrorum in Numeros liber* 2 (*PG* 69.593).

144 Cf. RUFINUS *Historia ecclesiastica* 1.9; SOCRATES *Historia ecclesiastica* 1.15; THEODORET *Historia ecclesiastica* 1.22; SOZOMEN *Historia ecclesiastica* 2.23.

I

CHRISTIANS AND BLACK

1 It seems to us that on this point Hellenistic iconography is of great interest. We shall mention immediately a recent, remarkable book to which we shall often refer, even though we are not always in agreement with the unilateral optimism of its conclusions, and which we regard as indispensable reading for an understanding of the present study. This is F. M. SNOWDEN, JR., *Blacks in Antiquity: Ethiopians in the Greco-Roman Experience* (Cambridge, Mass., 1970); see also idem, "Iconographical Evidence on the Black Populations in Greco-Roman Antiquity," in *The Image of the Black in Western Art*, vol. I, *From the Pharaohs to the Fall of the Roman Empire* ([Fribourg], 1976), pp. 133-245.

2 We use this expression, traditional but more and more devoid of content, since we cannot undertake the discussion which would be needed in order to arrive at a different definition of periods. So far as Egypt is concerned, the real transformation that moved it from one way of life to another took place roughly between the end of the Byzantine era (mid-seventh century) and the coming of the Fatimids (end of the tenth century).

3 Competition from the Sassanids in the Persian Gulf and later on the seas, beginning in the sixth century, considerably hampered Byzantine relations with the East.

4 Professor Michalowski's remarkable excavations at Faras have shown that the influence of Christianity had penetrated to the northern part of Nubia well before the date traditionally assigned, which connected the conversion of the Nubians with the activity of Justinian. See K. MICHALOWSKI, "Open Problems of Nubian Art and Culture in the Light of the Discoveries at Faras," in E. DINKLER, ed., *Kunst und Geschichte Nubiens in christlicher Zeit: Ergebnisse und Probleme auf Grund der jüngsten Ausgrabungen* (Recklinghausen, 1970), pp. 11-28.

5 In this connection it is worthwhile to reread the curious account of the pilgrimage of Etheria. This woman, probably from Galicia in Spain, traveled in the East toward the end of the fourth century. Cf. ETHERIA *Journal de voyage* (ed. and trans. H. PÉTRÉ, S.C., no. 21 [Paris, 1957]).

6 It would be extremely interesting to study *as a whole* the relations in the northeast quarter of Africa between Egyptians, Nubians, Ethiopians, and blacks of the various peripheral regions on the one hand and the Red Sea, the Indian Ocean, the Arabian peninsula, and the Near East on the other. See, for instance, G. VANTINI, "Le roi Kirki de Nubie à Baghdad: Un ou deux voyages?," in DINKLER, *Kunst und Geschichte Nubiens*, pp. 41-48.

7 Large-scale excavations were carried on there early in the twentieth century. See C. M. KAUFMANN, *Die heilige Stadt der Wüste: Unsere Entdeckungen, Grabungen und Funde in der altchristlichen Menasstadt weiteren Kreisen in Wort und Bildgeschildert*, 2d and 3d eds. (Kempten, 1921); idem, *La découverte des sanctuaires de Ménas dans le désert de Maréotis* (Alexandria, 1908); idem, *Die Menasstadt und das Nationalheiligtum der altchristlichen Aegypter in der westalexandrinischen Wüste* (Leipzig, 1910).

8 On this saint, more or less legendary like so many others of the period, see L. RÉAU, *Iconographie de l'art chrétien*, vol. III, *Iconographie des saints*, pt. 2 (Paris, 1958), pp. 948-50. Probably he was an officer, beheaded in 296 at Alexandria. See also R. MIEDEMA, *De heilige Menas* (Rotterdam, 1913).

While not much is known about the saint himself, a quick personal visit to Alexandria in 1971 allowed us to estimate both the importance and the interest that would attach to a broad study of his cult and of the influence of the monastery on the Copts. We expect to undertake this inquiry in the future.

9 IBN ḤAWQAL, *Configuration de la terre (Kitab Surat al-ard)*, ed. and trans. J. H. KRAMERS and G. WIET, Collection Unesco d'œuvres représentatives: Série arabe (Beirut and Paris, 1964), vol. I, p. 58: "Between [the Maghreb] . . . and the region of the Zanj, there are vast, sandy wildernesses which were traveled over in the past: it was the route from Egypt to Ghana. But ceaseless winds harassed caravans and travelers without baggage: more than one caravan and more than one lone traveler perished—not to mention the bandits who often were the cause of their loss. . . ."

10 R. M. BLOMFIELD, "Saint Ménas d'Alexandrie," *Bulletin de la Société archéologique d'Alexandrie* 6, n.s. 1, fasc. 1 (1904): 4. The author stressed the fact that the patron saint of the Egyptian city must not be confused with a St. Menas whose feast day is celebrated in Constantinople on 10 December. The Greek Church commemorates the Alexandrian saint on 11 November, while the Jacobites and the Ethiopians honor him on 4 October. On the contrary, other authors are convinced that Menas was the object of a widespread but constantly changing cult: in Florence San Miniato would be Menas; in Rome there is competition between two saints, Menas and Martin, both soldiers, whose feasts are celebrated on 11 November. After the eighth century the West definitely gave preference to St. Martin. Cf. *Vies des Saints et des Bienheureux, selon l'ordre du calendrier, avec l'historique des fêtes*, vol. XI, *Novembre* (Paris, 1954), pp. 328-37.

11 H. LAMMENS (*L'Arabie occidentale avant l'hégire* [Beirut, 1928]), in the chapter entitled "Les Chrétiens à la Mecque à la veille de l'hégire," p. 19, mentions the meeting between Muhammad and a Christian named Mina or Menas. On the other hand, the name *Menas* is not widely used in the Occident. We have, however, come across the instance of a hermit called Menas, who lived in Italy; see GREGORY THE GREAT *Dialogi libri IV* 3.26 (ed. U. MORICCA, Istituto storico Italiano, Fonti per la Storia d'Italia, Scrittori-Secolo VI, no. 57 [Rome, 1924]), p. 195.

12 *Vies des Saints et des Bienheureux*, vol. XI, *Novembre*, p. 331, emphasizes the "business angle" of the formation of the collection of miracles attributed to the saint: "The moral with which almost every episode closes is as clear as it is distasteful: repentant sinners and grateful believers are at one in making generous gifts to the basilica."

13 For example, C. CLERMONT-GANNEAU, "Horus et saint Georges d'après un bas-relief inédit du Louvre (Notes d'archéologie orientale et de mythologie sémitique)," *Revue archéologique*, n.s. 32 (1876): 196-204, 372-99. The ancient Horus may have gone through a whole series of mutations, appearing not only in the guise of St. George but of other knightly saints as well; cf. P. P. V. VAN MOORSEL, "Die Wandmalereien der zentralen Kirche von Abdallah Nirqi," in DINKLER, *Kunst und Geschichte Nubiens*, pp. 103-7, which gives some particularly interesting examples in iconography. It is generally agreed that the "legionary" Horus, represented on horseback and clothed as a Roman warrior, thrusting his lance through a crocodile (the incarnation of Seth), served as a prototype for the iconography of St. Sisinnius and later for that of St. George. See *Encyclopédie photographique de l'art*, vol. I (Paris, 1935-36), p. 159.

14 Kaufmann found two potters' shops in which a part of the stock still lay about: this included various models of ampullae and some molds, as well as other terracotta objects handled in the town's commerce. Unfortunately the digs were not conducted systematically, and we have no idea of the ratio between the different types of ampullae and the total stock, nor of the places in which these stocks were stored.

15 We have long known how popular these ampullae, of uniform shape but variable size, were with the pilgrims. They were intended to contain water which was always miraculous, no matter what saint it was connected with: see A. GRABAR, *Ampoules de Terre Sainte (Monza-Bobbio)* (Paris, 1958). At the Monastery of St. Menas an inscription advised the traveler to make a cautionary purchase: "Take some St. Menas water if you wish to cure whatever is wrong with you."

From the sixth century on, a vast pool, uncovered by Kaufmann, awaited those seeking a miraculous cure. Menas was reputed to cure leprosy, among other diseases; cf. C. M. KAUFMANN, *Zur Ikonographie der Menas-Ampullen mit besonderer Berücksichtigung der Funde in der Menasstadt nebst einem einführenden Kapitel über die neuentdeckten nubischen und aethiopischen Menastexte*, Veröffentlichungen der Frankfurter Menasexpedition, pt. 5 (Cairo, 1910), p. 12. The first miracle attributed to Menas by the monks (the date is indecipherable) was the healing of a young shepherd. A tent-shaped building was promptly erected over the saint's tomb; a lamp, fed by a sweet oil, was hung in the interior and burned night and day. Pilgrims drew oil from this lamp and took it home with them (a theme we shall come upon several times); the oil was used to anoint the sick, and cured every kind of malady (idem, *Ikonographie der Menas-Ampullen*, p. 43).

16 Quoted by BLOMFIELD, "Saint Ménas d'Alexandrie," p. 38.

17 KAUFMANN, *Ikonographie der Menas-Ampullen*, pp. 79 ff. The conventional inscription ran: "May [name of the god invoked] open a good year for [name of recipient]." Kaufmann says that there are many specimens of this kind of ampulla in western European museums.

18 SNOWDEN, *Blacks in Antiquity*, pp. 124-25. See also H. WINNEFELD, "Alabastra mit Negerdarstellungen," *AthMitt* 14 (1889): 41-50, and E. BETHE, "Zu den Alabastra mit Negerdarstellungen," ibid. 15 (1890): 243-45.

19 These decorated flasks measured from 15 to 20 cm. in height and may have been used to contain or to indicate products coming from Africa. On the *kulla* which, according to Kaufmann, derives from the largest flasks (250-500 cm.^{3}) found in the St. Menas Monastery, cf. KAUFMANN, *Ikonographie der Menas-Ampullen*, pp. 62 ff.

20 Ibid., p. 12.

21 Ibid., pp. 110-11: several ampullae represent Menas overcoming crocodiles. One of the miracles attributed to the saint shows him riding up to the bank of a river and snatching a peasant from the jaws of a crocodile. The theme of the hero-protector, killer of crocodiles (and, by extension, of other more or less fantastic monsters), of course runs through every mythology and every iconography. It is not yet clear, however, how this Horus theme passed from the Egyptian god to his Christian successors. The representations of George, Mercurius, and Sisinnius may to a large extent overlap each other and also that of St. Menas, who, in exceptional cases, plays the same role. The whole matter is still to be studied: here we can only stress its interest.

A text recently published by the Institut français d'Archéologie orientale in Cairo throws a wonderful light on the realism of the Egyptian myth: "To defend yourself against them you must be armed with a lance or a pike, and must drive these weapons into their maw. Only when they are wounded will they stop barring your path." Cf. *Voyages en Egypte des années 1589, 1590, et 1591 : Le Vénitien anonyme, Le Seigneur de Villamont, Le Hollandais Jan Sommer*, ed. and trans. C. BURRI, N. and S. SAUNERON, and P. BLESER, Collection des voyageurs occidentaux en Egypte, no. 3 (Cairo, 1971), p. 284.

22 J. DORESSE, *Des hiéroglyphes à la Croix : Ce que le passé pharaonique a légué au christianisme*, Uitgaven van het Nederlands Historisch-Archaeologisch Instituut te Istanbul, no. 7 (Istanbul, 1960), p. 20.

23 Of course the correspondence between the legends of the two saints is neither automatic nor complete. The legends probably reflect the expression, varying from one time and place to another, of identical obsessions. It must be said, however, that there is a striking similarity of posture between Horus the crocodile killer and St. George. Without being influenced by superficial and misleading comparisons, research should also follow this line: we cannot at present claim to have sure knowledge of the origin of the St. George cult; did it not exist in Nubia in the ninth century? In any event, we need a study of the relationship between Horus, Menas, and George: St. Maurice, of whom more later, could in some respects be added.

24 See H. DELEHAYE, *Les légendes grecques des saints militaires* (Paris, 1909); RÉAU, *Iconographie de l'art chrétien*, vol. III, *Iconographie des saints*, pt. 2, pp. 571-79. L. Réau's hesitations, which are well founded, show that this legendary life deserves a painstaking study.

25 See fig. 4, in which Menas is seen mounted. In Cairo, Coptic Museum, 3429, we noted an eighteenth-century icon which purports to represent St. Menas fighting a dragon.

26 KAUFMANN, *Ikonographie der Menas-Ampullen*, p. 13.

27 Ibid., pp. 13-14.

28 Ibid., p. 14.

29 Ibid., pp. 16 ff. The Ethiopian texts are not earlier than the sixteenth century. They frequently reproduce the older Greek and Coptic sources, with interesting variants. But they have no relation with the theme we are treating here, and for that reason, we leave them aside. Kaufmann, however, points out (p. 18) that Menas was venerated in Ethiopia as far back as the Axumite era.

30 This posture is seen in Egyptian statues of pharaonic times. The person represented holds in one hand, and at times in both, an object about which there is discussion, but which seems clearly to be connected with the person's desire for survival.

31 E. QUATREMÈRE, *Mémoires géographiques et historiques sur l'Egypte, et sur quelques contrées voisines, recueillis et extraits des manuscrits coptes, arabes, etc., de la Bibliothèque Impériale* (Paris, 1811), vol. I, p. 489.

32 For example, in Alexandria, Greco-Roman Museum, 13850, the marble relief, undated (fourth to sixth century?), from the Ennaton Monastery.

33 Let us point out, among others, the fresco in Alexandria, Greco-Roman Museum, 20210, from the Kom Abu Gingeh.

34 We present here, as an example, a frequently reproduced ampulla in the Musée Borély in Marseilles, inv. 1214. For an inventory of these ampullae, cf. KAUFMANN, *Ikonographie der Menas-Ampullen*, pp. 68-78. See also the following exhibition catalogues: *Frühchristliche Kunst aus Rom*, Exhibition catalogue, Essen, Villa Hügel, 3 September-15 November 1962 (Essen-Bredeney, 1962), pp. 110-16 and three illustrations; *Frühchristliche und Koptische Kunst*, Exhibition catalogue, Vienna, Akademie der bildenden Künste, 11 March-3 May 1964 (Vienna, 1964), pp. 153-55, nos. 471, 478-79.

35 Such protection was no doubt often invoked at the edge of the Libyan Desert by caravaners setting out on their long journey westward. That route, which passes through the Fezzan and may, in the last years of antiquity and in the early stages of the Muslim establishment in Egypt, have reached the bend of the Niger, is in any event long and dangerous. In the future it would be important to give attention to the possible discovery of St. Menas ampullae along this route.

The Menas legend retains traces of the question, current as late as the seventh century, as to whether Menas had not been a simple camel driver in his lifetime. A late interpretation, dating from the fifteenth century (KAUFMANN, *Ikonographie der Menas-Ampullen*, p. 43), asserts that the Roman prefect, unable to have the relics of St. Menas transported by dromedaries, was said to have ordered the sculptured image of the saint standing between two kneeling camels. Here we have *at least* the proof that the image in question was still known in the fifteenth century—a detail which has its importance.

36 Ibid., pp. 98-99; Kaufmann indicates the interest of a comparison with the iconography of the Buddha flanked by two elephants.

37 E. SALIN, *La civilisation mérovingienne d'après les sépultures, les textes et le laboratoire*, pt. 4, *Les croyances* (Paris, 1959), p. 312, emphasizes the fact that a great many of the ampullae found in the West bear this representation. In the author's opinion St. Menas in this figuration is shown rather as dominating two monsters, the identity of which is hard to

discern. E. Salin is inclined to connect this iconography with the Ethiopian legend about the *naval* episode in which the saint's relics were involved—an episode we shall come back to later. He forgets, as we see it, that the episode in question appears later than the others in the accumulation of texts relative to the saint. We maintain that what we see here are probably two squatting dromedaries, but we do not reject the idea of a domination over "wild beasts," reassuring to the possessor of the saint's ampullae, on which E. Salin insists (idem, *La civilisation mérovingienne*, pt. 4, *Les croyances*, pp. 310-11).

38 The inventory in KAUFMANN, *Ikonographie der Menas-Ampullen*, pp. 68-78, gives only eighty-nine numbers, although the author himself talks about mass production from the fourth to the ninth century (p. 7) and about the discovery of ampullae by the thousands (pp. 59 ff.). For examples of ampullae without decoration, see idem, *Ikonographie der Menas-Ampullen*, p. 87, figs. 27-30. It was out of the question to research here *all* the types of representation which might be inventoried, our purpose being to retain only the examples in which Menas is shown as a black.

39 There are five certain examples in the Kaufmann inventory (ibid., p. 70). The ampullae in the Greco-Roman Museum in Alexandria, photographs of which were kindly furnished by the Director of the museum, belong to the series described by Kaufmann, although the museum's inventory numbers do not for the moment enable us to identify them more exactly among Kaufmann's numbers 22 to 26.

40 We publish here one of them, inv. MNC 140 (from Alexandria). Five others of the same type are known; two of them are partially illegible. Let us here express our thanks to Mademoiselle Catherine Metzger for the valuable information she has been kind enough to furnish us.

41 KAUFMANN, *Ikonographie der Menas-Ampullen*, pp. 16 ff., examines the dossier of the Greek, Coptic, Syriac, and Ethiopian traditions. No text, whatever its provenance, casts doubt on the saint's white, Egyptian origin, nor does any text connect a single episode of his life or miracles with Nubia.

42 Ibid., p. 16.

43 E.A.W. BUDGE, ed., *Texts Relating to Saint Mêna of Egypt and Canons of Nicaea in a Nubian Dialect, with Facsimile* (London, 1909). The author dates this manuscript between the ninth and tenth centuries.

44 Ibid., pp. 14-15.

45 London, British Library, MS. Oriental 6805, fol. 10[r]; from Edfu. The first part of this manuscript relates a miracle worked by St. Menas; the second deals with the Canons of Nicaea.

46 KAUFMANN, *Ikonographie der Menas-Ampullen*, pp. 18 ff. The Coptic Synaxarion narrates that Menas had a vision in the desert of a martyr wearing a crown. The Ethiopian Synaxarion in turn relates that Menas was visited by an angel wearing three crowns of light, who told him of his approaching martyrdom. The first of the three crowns signified recognition of his holiness and chastity as a youth, the second his perseverance in sanctity, and the third his martyrdom. A Life of St. Menas, of Ethiopian origin and dating from the fourteenth or fifteenth century, recalls the theme: "After the manner of the Blessed Trinity, in whose love thou hast grown, thou shalt receive imperishable crowns—one for thy virginity, one for thy self-denial, and one for thy martyrdom" (idem, *Ikonographie der Menas-Ampullen*, p. 36). A future study will have to compare the crowns shown here with those seen, for instance, in the frescoes uncovered by recent excavations in Nubia. There is certainly much to think about in relation to the origins and symbolism of crown insignia throughout the Nile Valley. See DINKLER, *Kunst und Geschichte Nubiens*, and K. MICHALOWSKI, *Faras: Die Kathedrale aus dem Wüstensand* (Einsiedeln, Zurich, and Cologne, 1967), pls. 12-13, 58-95a and line drawings on pp. 35, 44, 95.

47 KAUFMANN, *Ikonographie der Menas-Ampullen*, pp. 123 ff.

48 Ibid., p. 97 and p. 117, fig. 61.

49 Ibid., p. 74, no. 49c.

50 *Vies des Saints et des Bienheureux*, vol. XI, *Novembre*, p. 334. The body of St. Menas is being transported by ship, and on a very rough day the ship is surrounded by monstrous sea beasts, with "long, high necks" and heads like camels'. These beasts try to snatch the passengers off the ship, but the saint's body miraculously drives them away.

51 This might explain why our polymorphous saint was never thought of as black in the West, although his cult spread there very early, and soon died out to make room for others.

52 A letter from Mr. Z. Kiss of the Research Academy of Warsaw, dated 12 August 1971, affirms that the cult of St. Menas was widespread in Nubia in the eighth century.

53 This was a tribute established in 651 and maintained without interruption into the thirteenth century; it called for the delivery, at least symbolically, of 360 slaves per year.

54 We know the importance of St. George in the iconography of Faras from the ninth century on; see DINKLER, *Kunst und Geschichte Nubiens*, and MICHALOWSKI, *Faras: Die Kathedrale*.

55 The learned study by CLERMONT-GANNEAU, "Horus et saint Georges," should be consulted on this point.

56 Georgios (Kirki) I was king between 856 and 920; he is represented as dark-skinned in a painting at Faras. Cf. MICHALOWSKI, "Open Problems of Nubian Art," in DINKLER, *Kunst und Geschichte Nubiens*, p. 13. Another king bore the same name in the eleventh century, as did a bishop of Qasr Ibrim who died in 1125. *Mīnā*, as a patronym, probably occurred less frequently: we have not come across a single instance in the works so far published.

57 The fact that these saints are said to have been put to death for refusing to sacrifice to idols should, we think, be examined closely. But it is the only point in common—a tenuous one, it is true—between the two legends.

58 This hypothesis seems to us all the more important in that a very considerable amount of exchange with the South, in matters both economic and religious, via the Nile Valley and the Red Sea, was certainly characteristic of the Byzantine era; whereas, after the eighth century the cataracts shut off the Nubians in the land they occupied, where they resisted any Muslim penetration.

59 We shall return to this question apropos of Byzantine iconography.

60 Paris, Bibliothèque nationale, MS. nouv. acq. lat. 2334. See A. GRABAR and C. NORDENFALK, *Le Haut Moyen-âge: Du quatrième au onzième siècle*, Les grands siècles de la peinture (Geneva, 1957), pp. 101-5; J. PORCHER, *Les manuscrits à peintures en France du VIIe au XIIe siècle*, Exhibition catalogue, Paris, Bibliothèque nationale, 1954 (Paris, 1954), p. 12, no. 22; and more recently B. NARKISS, "Towards a further Study of the Ashburnham Pentateuch (Pentateuque de Tours)," *CahArch* 19 (1969): 45-60 and 6 pls.; idem, "Reconstruction of some of the Original Quires of the Ashburnham Pentateuch," ibid. 22 (1972): 19-38. The origin of this manuscript remains as much a subject of controversy as its exact date. Africa, Spain, and Italy, three areas often held to be its place of origin, would connect it with the Mediterranean, and, in the first case, to the African church which is so important in our present context. But it is often suggested that this manuscript may be of a later date—the sixth or seventh century—and may have been executed much farther to the north. We have closely examined the paintings which interested us. Granted that in several places there has obviously been retouching, this occurs only very rarely in the case of the representations of blacks to which we shall be giving attention. Thus we are forced to conclude that these paintings go back to the origin of the manuscript.

61 Paris, Bibliothèque nationale, MS. nouv. acq. lat. 2334, fol. 10[v]: dromedary, lions, fennec, scorpion, serpents; fol. 21[r]: dromedaries; fol. 30[r]: dromedaries with particularly interesting packsaddles, etc.

62 Ibid., fol. 21r (marriage of Isaac: Genesis 24): black and white camel drivers in the upper right of the folio; other individuals, hard to identify, in the lower register. Isaac, according to Genesis, is not in Egypt; therefore, the black drivers must be visitors. The dark color used for the blacks' faces is the same as that of the packsaddles on the dromedaries. The faces are painted with the eyes left in reserve. The hair, generally lighter, seems to have been added after the faces were painted.

63 Ibid., fol. 44r: Joseph receives his brothers in Egypt (Gen. 43:16-44:2). The picture follows the biblical text very closely: "And when it [bread] was set on, for Joseph apart, and for his brethren apart, for the Egyptians also that ate with him, apart, (for it is unlawful for the Egyptians to eat with the Hebrews, and they think such a feast profane:)" (Gen. 43:32). Faces and hair, in at least three instances, are painted as in the preceding example (cf. *supra*, n. 62). Two blacks appear even in Jacob's funeral cortège (fol. 50r).

64 Ibid., fol. 65v (Exod. 12:29-30): the first-born stricken by the tenth plague are represented with characteristics very close to those seen in the preceding folios. The Egyptian blacks are markedly fewer in number than the whites.

65 Ibid., fol. 68r (Exod. 14:26-29): only five black horsemen. Their coloration seems original.

66 The essential work in this field is the *Christian Topography* of Cosmas Indicopleustes. See W. Wolska, *La topographie chrétienne de Cosmas Indicopleustès: Théologie et Science au VIe siècle*, Bibliothèque byzantine, Etudes, 3 (Paris, 1962). J. Doresse, *L'empire du Prêtre-Jean* (Paris, 1957), vol. I, *L'Ethiopie antique*, p. 161, notes that Cosmas saw at Axum a palace with four towers, each topped with a statue of a unicorn; this is the probable starting point for a host of later legends. The same author (pp. 161-62) reports Procopius of Caesarea's story: the Ethiopians lent strong support to the Christians of Arabia persecuted by the Himyarites who were of the Jewish religion. The Ethiopian effort met with little success. The massacre of the Christians at Najrān brought on the expedition of the Ethiopian king Caleb, who thus won for himself a mention in the Roman Martyrology (27 October), so the West knew of this incident. Here again are the seeds of many future developments.

67 Wolska, *La topographie chrétienne de Cosmas Indicopleustès*, pp. 211-12, stresses Cosmas's total opposition to the idea that the antipodes exist. The entire Christian tradition followed him on this point: in the eighth century Pope Zacharias forbade any allusion to such a possibility as being heretical. On this matter see W. G. L. Randles, *L'image du Sud-Est africain dans la littérature européenne au XVIe siècle* (Lisbon, 1959), pp. 4 ff.

68 We present here a map taken from E. H. Bunbury, *A History of Ancient Geography* (London, 1879), vol. II, p. 238, pl. III: the *oikoumenē* of Strabo. This map is reproduced in Wolska, *La topographie chrétienne de Cosmas Indicopleustès*, p. 263, fig. 21.

69 From the point of view which here concerns us, we have at present no really good study on the African churches from the fifth to the twelfth century. In this field all the work is still to be done.

70 We may see here a sort of automatic reaction which is very familiar in our time. To be "less black" entails both the satisfaction of belonging to the "superior" world of the whites and the acceptance, as a consequence of this "promotion," of the white ideology, as well as an increased anxiety to stay clear of those who are still "entirely black." The events of history indicate that this is how Egyptians and Ethiopians reacted, even if there may have been very good reasons, as yet undiscovered, for their attitudes.

71 About all that Byzantium retained was a set of canon laws (not looked upon favorably by Rome, by the way) relating to this Christian group, and the names of a few saints who were quickly "absorbed" by Western theology.

72 From this point of view it is impossible to overstress the bad effect of the "encapsulation" of ancient culture by the encyclopedists of every breed in the fifth and sixth centuries. Equally to be kept in mind is the dangerous conformism introduced into Western Europe by what is called the Carolingian Renaissance.

73 Madame Sylvie Laquement has successfully completed a research project begun under my direction a few years ago at the Université de Lille III. She has authorized me to use some of her reference cards. As occasion arises, I shall call attention to her most important conclusions.

74 This is the reasoning of all the medieval compilers, without exception, from Isidore of Seville *Etymologiarum sive Originum libri XX* 14.2 (ed. W. M. Lindsay, Scriptorum classicorum bibliotheca oxoniensis [Oxford, 1911]) to Honorius of Autun *De imagine mundi libri tres* 1.7 (*PL* 172.122-23), including Rabanus Maurus, Hincmar, Remigius of Auxerre, and a good many others. On the "maps" which decorate the manuscripts, Africa is always shown as a fairly small continent opposite Europe. There is a great lack of precision with regard to its western, southern, and eastern boundaries.

75 On this point some of Isidore of Seville's statements are both preposterous and amusing; cf. Isidore of Seville *Etymologiae* 9.2.115-27, 14.5. Yet he is only essaying a logical explanation of the inconsistencies handed down by ancient tradition. From Herodotus (4.42) to St. Augustine the ambiguity of the two names was recognized, but no clear choice was made between them. Martianus Capella bequeathed the fundamental ambiguity to the commentators, who, to a man, copied him: "Africa vero ac Libya dicta ab Afro, Lib*yis* Herculis filio . . ." ! Cf. Martianus Capella *De nuptiis philologiae et Mercurii* 6 (ed. A. Dick and J. Préaux, 2d ed., Bibliotheca scriptorum Graecorum et Romanorum Teubneriana [Stuttgart, 1969]), p. 331. After Isidore of Seville all the writers perpetuated this confusion. Remigius of Auxerre says: "Libya vel Africa" and "Libyae id est Africae"; cf. Remigius of Auxerre *Commentum in Martianum Capellam* 4.153.10, 6.333.9 (ed. C. E. Lutz, vol. II [Leiden, 1965]), pp. 17, 153-54. A manuscript of Isidore of Seville (Oxford, Bodleian Library, MS. Can. Misc. 560, fol. 3r) has a note on a mappemonde: "Africa quae et libia . . . ." A *Divisio orbis terrarum* dating from the end of antiquity says: "Orbis dividitur tribus nominibus: Europa, Asia, Libya vel Africa"; cf. *Geographi latini minores*, ed. A. Riese (Heilbronn, 1878), p. 15 (hereafter cited as *G.l.m.*).

76 Pomponius Mela *De chorographia libri tres* 1.4-5 (ed. C. Frick, Bibliotheca scriptorum Graecorum et Romanorum Teubneriana [Leipzig, 1880]), pp. 6-8. The region was held by Numidians and Mauri. The *Divisio orbis terrarum* in *G.l.m.*, p. 19, reflects the double meaning of the name *Africa*. Some lines after having applied the word to the continent, the text defines *Africa* as the Romans did, i.e., as embracing the Carthaginiensis and Numidia, bound on the east by the Syrtes (this is the classical administrative division under the late Roman Empire, long retained by the Muslims), on the west by the Ampsaga (Wadi el Kebir); farther to the west are Gaetulia and Mauretania, of which more later. Important examples are found in *Annales de Saint-Bertin*, ed. F. Grat, J. Vielliard, and S. Clémencet, Société de l'Histoire de France, Série antérieure à 1789, no. 470 (Paris, 1964), pp. 43, 80.

77 Pomponius Mela *De chorogr.* 1.4, p. 5; Richer *Histoire de France (888-995)* 1.1 (ed. and trans. R. Latouche, Les classiques de l'histoire de France au Moyen âge, 12 [Paris, 1930]), vol. I, pp. 6-7: Africa is separated from Asia by the Nile. These ideas, Christianized, reappeared in the biblical geography which Byzantine and Occidental writers fashioned out of the ancient data.

78 Until the fifteenth century, when Ptolemy's geography became known, the West was more influenced by Macrobius than by any other author; cf. Randles, *L'image du Sud-Est africain*, pp. 1-3. But the Muslim world put Ptolemy first and foremost.

79 The most striking example is the planisphere of al-Idrisi, of which we here present a reproduction of the facsimile located in Paris, Bibliothèque nationale, Département des Cartes et Plans, Ge AA 2004; this facsimile, made in 1844, is based on 68 maps in a

thirteenth-century Arabic manuscript, also in the Bibliothèque nationale (MS. arabe 2221), which is a copy of a lost original dating from 1140-50.

80 We cannot pursue the point here, but we note that in the matter of *adab* literature the Muslims give quite as much rein to the imagination as do the Occidentals. Cf. A. Miquel, *La géographie humaine du monde musulman jusqu'au milieu du 11e siècle*, vol. I, *Géographie et géographie humaine dans la littérature arabe des origines à 1050*, 2d ed., Ecole pratique des Hautes Etudes, Sorbonne. Sixième section: Sciences économiques et sociales. Centre de recherches historiques. Civilisations et Sociétés, no. 7 (Paris and The Hague, 1973).

81 Isidore of Seville *Etymologiae* 14.5.15, locates marvelous resources of hyacinths and chrysoprases in this mysterious region. The Muslim authors, at least from al-Ya'kūbī on, knew that the area between the Nile and the Red Sea was a source of emeralds.

82 Sylvie Laquement stresses the idea that only the Spaniard Beatus of Liébana, a ninth-century commentator of the Apocalypse, manifested any interest in the events which took place in North Africa after the Muslim occupation. For all the other authors Africa became an abstract concept, both geographically and theologically. This was true at least until the eleventh century.

83 Doresse, *L'empire du Prêtre-Jean*, vol. II, *L'Ethiopie médiévale*, pp. 227-28, notes that Joinville sought information from the Egyptians about the mysteries of the Nile. He was told that the people who lived on its banks stretched nets across the river every night and gathered ginger, rhubarb, aloes, and cinnamon!

84 Remigius of Auxerre is one of the most affirmative among the medieval authors: "Duae sunt Libiae, una quae tantum Libia, altera quae Xerolibia, id est sicca Libia, appellatur" (Remigius of Auxerre *Comm. in Mart. Cap.* 6.333.9, vol. II, pp. 153-54). The African interior is peopled with Leucoaethiopes, i.e., whites; idem *Comm. in Mart. Cap.* 6.335.3, vol. II, p. 155.

85 Pliny the Elder *Naturalis historiae libri XXXVII* 5 (ed. C. Mayhoff, Bibliotheca scriptorum Graecorum et Romanorum Teubneriana [Leipzig, 1906]), vol. I, pp. 360 ff.

86 "Est autem Meroe maxima insula Nili ab una parte habens Aethiopiam, ab alia, Aegyptum" (Remigius of Auxerre *Comm. in Mart. Cap.* 8.452.1, vol. II, p. 276).

87 Isidore of Seville *Etymologiae* 14.5.16-17: Ethiopia extends in an arc from the south of Egypt to the Strait of Gades. The name of the country, says Isidore of Seville, who establishes a connection between this name and the dark color of the inhabitants, comes from this color, which is due to the nearness of the sun. Rabanus Maurus *De universo libri XXII* 12.4 (*PL* 111.352), repeats this idea and quotes Isidore of Seville at length.

88 Isidore of Seville *Etymologiae* 14.5, 13.21.6-8. William of Conches *De philosophia mundi libri quatuor* 4.4 (*PL* 172.86-87), gives the same information.

89 Honorius of Autun *De imag. mundi* 1.33 (*PL* 172.131).

90 "Aethiopum regio (Acts 8:27) ab Indo flumine consurgens, juxta Aegyptum inter Nilum et Oceanum, et in meridie, sub ipsa solis vicinitate jacet: quorum tres sunt populi Aegypti, Hesperiae, et Occidentis" (Jerome *Liber nominum locorum, ex Actis* [*PL* 23.1298]). On this point as on many another relating to Africa and the Africans, Jerome contributed generously to the confusion of the men of the Middle Ages.

91 ". . . Oceanus, qui solis calore dicitur fervere ut cacabus" (Honorius of Autun *De imag. mundi* 1.33 [*PL* 172.131]).

92 Isidore of Seville *Etymologiae* 14.5.8. The author mixes vague geographical knowledge with the administrative traditions of the late Roman Empire, drawing on accumulated experience, not on intellectual speculation. He details at length and correctly the limits of the various provinces: this is an Africa well known to the men of his century, before Islam got established. Isidore of Seville seizes upon the occasion to give further refinement to the details, obscuring in the process the exact content of the words. He says, for instance: "Ipsa est et vera Africa inter Byzacium et Numidiam sita, a septentrione mari Siculo juncta, et a meridie usque ad Gaetulorum regionem porrecta . . . ."

93 "India ulterior. Finitur ab oriente flumine Gange et oceano Persico, ab occidente flumine Indo, a septentrione monte Tauro, a meridie oceano Indico" (*Divisio orbis terrarum* in *G.l.m.*, p. 19).

94 It would seem possible that old linguistic and ethnic traditions mingle with this more or less legendary information. F. Altheim and R. Stiehl, *Die Araber in der Alten Welt*, vol. V, pt. 2, *Nachträge—Das Christliche Aksūm* (Berlin, 1969), pp. 177-78, point out that the Ethiopian vocalic writing is related to the Indian.

95 "Indiae tres esse ab historiographis asseruntur, in quibus traduntur fuisse oppidorum quinque millia, populorum vero novem millia. Prima India ad Aethiopiam mittit, secunda ad Medos, tertia finem facit" (Ordericus Vitalis *Historia ecclesiastica* 2.15 [*PL* 188.165]).

96 Sylvie Laquement is right in affirming that the medieval commentators had no means of really reconciling the diverse inherited data relative to Africa. Her remark applies to the Roman heritage, administrative and cartographic on the one hand, literary on the other, to the Hellenistic legacy, mainly cosmographic in content, and to the Jewish and Christian traditions.

97 For William of Conches *De philos. mundi* 4.3 (*PL* 172.86), Libya and Ethiopia are uniformly hot and dry. Remigius of Auxerre *Comm. in Mart. Cap.* 2.74.13, vol. I (1962), p. 200, had also emphasized the dryness of Africa from end to end.

98 "—quippe cum omnia paene animantia vel germinantia patientius et tolerabilius ad summum frigoris quam ad summum caloris accedant—ea scilicet causa est, Africam per omnia situ et populis minorem videri: quia et natura sui minus habeat spatii et caeli inclementia plus deserti cuius descriptio per provincias et gentes haec est . . ." (Orosius *Historiarum adversum paganos libri VII* 1.2.86 [*CSEL* 5.31]).

99 Isidore of Seville furnishes this information. According to him, elephants were no longer found anywhere except in India. Here is another element of resemblance between *India* and *Africa*, just as saurians connected the Indus to the Nile, according to the Muslim authors.

100 Isidore of Seville *Etymologiae* 14.5.15.

101 Solinus *Collectanea rerum memorabilium* (ed. Th. Mommsen [Berlin, 1895]), p. 133, lines 14 ff., notes its rarity in Rome and the astonishment aroused by its appearence there. The *camelopardalis* of antiquity became the medieval *cameleopardus*. The animal kept its ancient prestige at the Mediterranean Muslim courts: it was the favorite gift offered by black rulers to their friends in North Africa.

102 "En . . . cogitis me, in Aethyopia figere tentorium, ut habitem in medio scorpionum et frater fiam draconum et socius strucionum . . ." (Honorius of Autun *De offendiculo* [ed. I. Dieterich] in *Monumenta Germaniae historica: Libelli de lite Imperatorum et Pontificum. Saeculis XI. et XII. Conscripti*, vol. III [Hannover, 1897], p. 38 [hereafter cited as *MGH*]).

103 The information comes from Solinus, and is repeated, of course, by Isidore of Seville *Etymologiae* 14.5.15, and in the ninth century by Rabanus Maurus *De univ.* 12.4 (*PL* 111.352).

104 Solinus *Collectanea*, p. 134, lines 10 ff. In the patristic period these giant ants were associated with the gold lodes supposedly buried in Africa. The fable was equally welcomed by writers in Arabic.

105 Isidore of Seville *Etymologiae* 14.5.15.

106 Isidore of Seville *Etymologiae* 14.5.15. See also a poem by an anonymous writer of the eighth century, "Versus de Asia et de universi mundi rota" v. 37 (*CCL* 175.451-52).

107 It is impossible to sum up in a few lines the accumulation of myths relating to this river. Further on we shall look at several of them. Islam and Western Europe paid the Nile the same reverential awe and the same respect: was the river not in flood in the hottest season, when its waters should have been at their lowest ebb?

108 PLINY THE ELDER *Nat. hist.* 5.1, vol. I, p. 362. At night the Atlas glows with innumerable fires—still another theme which passed into medieval literature, where the phenomenon was attributed to the islands of the Atlantic—and "Aegipanum Satyrorumque lascivia inpleri, tibiarum ac fistulae cantu tympanorumque et cymbalorum sonitu strepere. . . ." MARTIANUS CAPELLA *De nuptiis* 6, p. 331, set forth the same themes. Isidore of Seville, who transmitted the legacy to the Middle Ages, did not change it much. "In ipso vero Oceano est mons Atlas altissimus, unde Atlanticum mare appellatur. Atlas autem erat rex Africae, frater Promethei, a quo mons nomen accepit, quia in eo residens, Astrologiam descripsit, unde et coelum sustinere dicitur" (HONORIUS OF AUTUN *De imag. mundi* 1.33 [*PL* 172.131]). This northwestern section of Africa kept its bad reputation for a long time, to judge by a *Hadith* attributed to Muhammad and reported by al-Bakrī in the eleventh century: "There is in the Maghreb a mountain called DRN [it is situated in the Atlas]; on the day of the Resurrection it will go into Hell with all its inhabitants, like a young bride being brought to her husband"; cf. V. MONTEIL, "Al-Bakrî (Cordoue 1068), Routier de l'Afrique blanche et noire du Nord-Ouest," *Bulletin de l'Institut fondamental d'Afrique noire: Série B, Sciences humaines* 30 (1968): 55. Is this a reminiscence of ancient traditions, or of military reverses in northwest Africa transformed into a "curse" upon the scene of the reverses and put under Muhammad's authority? We will never know more about it.

109 ". . . quidam et in eo tractu modicos colles amoena opacitate vestitos Aegipanum Satyrorumque produnt" (PLINY THE ELDER *Nat. hist.* 6.30, vol. I, p. 513). This description of the landscape fits the Rif better than the Moroccan Atlas. The passage is quoted by Solinus and Martianus Capella.

110 SNOWDEN, *Blacks in Antiquity*. See also the very important review by J. DESANGES in *Revue des études latines* 48 (1970): 87-95 and esp. p. 93 for the author's reservations regarding Snowden's optimism.

111 The word and the thing are the sad property of today's world, even if the *roots* are often very old, as this whole study leads one to think.

112 Although even on this point J. Desanges's reservations seem unusually important to us.

113 London, British Library, MS. Cotton Tib.B.V. Compilation of various texts among which (fols. 78v-87v): *De rebus ex Oriente mirabilibus*, from Winchester, second quarter of the eleventh century (?), fol. 86r; cf. E. TEMPLE, *Anglo-Saxon Manuscripts 900-1066*, Survey of Manuscripts Illuminated in the British Isles, vol. 2 (London, 1976), pp. 104-5, no. 87.

114 Not to mention here that reducing blacks to slavery was justified as a way of leading them to Christianity, as we read in some few writings of the fifteenth and sixteenth centuries. RANDLES, *L'image du Sud-Est africain*, pp. 124-25, gives some noteworthy texts on this point.

115 In our examination of the Muslim attitude we have drawn largely upon the monograph by B. LEWIS, *Race and Color in Islam* (New York, Evanston, San Francisco, and London, Harper Torchbooks, 1971).

116 The Muslim shared this point of view with the Mediterranean Christian. B. Lewis's book (cf. *supra*, n. 115) shows this, as do the research studies of Sylvie Laquement and François de Medeiros on the Occidentals. But our recent research carried out in seminars shows that the Muslim position was not at all unanimous and that on this point Lewis was mistaken.

117 Here we must quote Ibn Khaldūn, who in the fourteenth century provided an authoritative summary of Muslim culture. Cf. IBN KHALDŪN *Muḳaddima* 1.3 in J. M. CUOQ, ed. and trans., *Recueil des sources arabes concernant l'Afrique occidentale du VIIIe au XVIe siècle (Bilād al-Sūdān)*, Sources d'histoire médiévale (Paris, 1975), pp. 357-58:

> We have explained how the inhabited zone of the emergent lands is situated in the Center, between the burning South and the glacial North. . . . [Ibn Khaldūn retains the division into seven climates from south to north which was inherited from antiquity: the first touches the Equator, the seventh is that of the North.] Thus the fourth climate is the most *balanced* [italics ours] one of the inhabited earth, and the third and fifth, which border on it, are closest to this balance. . . .
>
> That is why the sciences, technics, buildings, clothing, food, fruits, and even animals and everything produced in the three middle climates are distinguished by balance. . . . [Ibn Khaldūn classes the whites living around the Mediterranean among the *balanced* people, and his description goes from France and present-day Spain to China.]
>
> As to the climates far removed from the temperate zone . . . the inhabitants are just as far from being balanced in their mode of life. Their dwellings are built of mud or reeds; they feed on millet and herbs; their clothing is made of leaves sewn together or of animal skins; furthermore, most of them go naked. The fruits grown in their lands and their condiments are strange and tend to be excessive. For business transactions, instead of the two precious metals, they use copper, iron, or pelts to which they assign an exchange value. Moreover, their mores are like those of animals.
>
> Most of the Sūdān in the first climate live, we hear, in caves or in the bush. They live on grass. They are savages without any civilization. They eat each other. . . .
>
> The reason for all this lies in their being at a distance from the temperate zone. This situation puts them close to the beasts' way of living, and by that much sets them apart from humanity.

If, as is evident, Ibn Khaldūn foreshadowed Montesquieu in more than one way, he was, as we have said before, faithfully repeating what the legacy of the past made available to him; and it is not hard to trace the path that led from antiquity to him, passing through the Arab tradition.

118 So Ibn Khaldūn, who refuses to regard the blacks as the accursed sons of Ham, attributes to them peculiarities due to the climate.

119 See MAS 'ŪDĪ *Les Prairies d'or* (ed. and trans. C. BARBIER DE MEYNARD and J.-B. PAVET DE COURTEILLE, rev. and corr. C. PELLAT, Société asiatique, Collection d'ouvrages orientaux [Paris, 1965]), vol. II, pp. 321 ff.

120 See R. MAUNY, V. MONTEIL, A. DJENIDI, S. ROBERT, and J. DEVISSE, eds. and trans., *Textes et documents relatifs à l'histoire de l'Afrique: Extraits tirés des Voyages d'Ibn Baṭṭūṭa*, Université de Dakar, Faculté des Lettres et Sciences humaines, Publications de la Section d'Histoire, no. 9 (Dakar, 1966), esp. pp. 49-55.

121 Without going into the details of a study which will have to be conducted very carefully, Lewis (*Race and Color in Islam*) notes the change of attitude with regard to Africa and Africans which took place in Muslim milieus from the end of the seventh century onward.

122 MAS 'ŪDĪ *Les Prairies d'or*, vol. I (1962), p. 69, par. 171, concerning the Zanj: ". . . al-Kindī . . . declares: '. . . His country being very hot, the heavenly bodies exert their influence and draw the humors to the upper part (of his body). Hence his bulging eyes, his drooping lips, his big, flat nose, the flaccidity of his head resulting from the abundance of humors drawn to the top of his body. Thus the mixture (of humors) in his brain is no longer in balance, and the soul cannot exert its full influence upon him; his discernment is altered, and the acts of the intelligence desert him'." Idem *Les Prairies d'or*, vol. I, p. 69, par. 170: "Galen . . . explains the irritability characteristic of the Zanj by the imperfect organization of his brain, whence results the weakness of his intellect."

123 Ibid., par. 172; Mas 'ūdī says, "Such is . . . the opinion of a modern Muslim poet and astronomer:

The dean (of these stars) is sublime Saturn, a majestic ancient, a powerful monarch.
His temperament is black and cold—black as a soul in the throes of despair.
His influence is exerted on the Zanj and on (black) slaves, and also on lead and iron."

124 AVICENNA *al-Qānūn* 4.7, quoted in L.-M. DEVIC, *Le pays des Zendjs ou la côte orientale d'Afrique au Moyen-âge (Géographie, Mœurs, Productions, Animaux légendaires) d'après les écrivains arabes* (Paris, 1883), p. 131.

125 IBN KHALDŪN *Prolégomènes*, quoted in DEVIC, *Le pays des Zendjs*, pp. 130-31: "Mas 'ūdī had undertaken to seek out the cause that produced in the blacks their lightheadedness, their absentmindedness, and this tendency to extreme gaiety; but for his solution he adduces only one statement of Galen and al-Kindī, according to which these characteristics come from a weakness of the brain that results in a weakness of the intellect. This explanation has no value and proves nothing."

126 Of course, exception must be made for the areas that were really known—North Africa, at least in the eastern part, the Nile Valley up as far as the cataracts, Nubia and Ethiopia to a lesser degree. Mysteries, monsters, and dangers begin where direct knowledge stops, even if certain of the known areas were exotic enough compared with the civilizations north of the Mediterranean: to see this it suffices to study the mosaics which portray the unusual character of the Nile fauna. The perilous "elsewhere" begins at the Maghreb "Far West" (which was not well known south of the Bou Regreg), at the Sahara, at the cataracts, and, for the east coast, at the latitude of Mogadiscio. The exact localization of the *fables* in each of these regions is, in our opinion, so sure a guide to the advances and retreats of *real* knowledge of Africa in the Middle Ages that it would seem useful to undertake a systematic study of this theme. We shall mention here only one example. POMPONIUS MELA *De chorogr.* 3.9, pp. 74-75, situates "in Ethiopia" a place where food is plentiful. The food is of divine origin and never in short supply. Close by this place live sphinxes, strange horned birds, and winged horses; south of it stretches the desert. The Letter of Prester John is in the offing. . . . In order to arrive at a valid estimate of the importance of texts like these, their dispersion in manuscript should, of course, be studied in each case. In this connection the Institut de Recherche et d'Histoire des Textes in Paris kindly informed me that it has in hand a register of over seventy medieval manuscripts of Pomponius Mela's work, also known as *De situ orbis*.

127 ISIDORE OF SEVILLE *Etymologiae* 9.2.130.

128 MARTIANUS CAPELLA *De nuptiis* 6, pp. 347, 349, informs his medieval commentators of their existence. Remigius of Auxerre, in the ninth century, keeps only the name of this people.

129 REMIGIUS OF AUXERRE *Comm. in Mart. Cap.* 6.344.11, vol. II, p. 159.

130 POMPONIUS MELA *De chorogr.* 1.8, p. 11: they scream more than they talk, live in caverns, and feed on the flesh of snakes, which abound in their country. FILASTER *Diversarum hereseon liber* 14 (*CCL* 9.222): they are pagans, and their blind adoration leads them to live in caverns. ISIDORE OF SEVILLE *Etymologiae* 9.2.129: swift runners, they hunt wild beasts on foot. REMIGIUS OF AUXERRE *Comm. in Mart. Cap.* 6.293.22, vol. II, p. 135, locates them on the shore of the Red Sea; they eat snakes.

131 REMIGIUS OF AUXERRE *Comm. in Mart. Cap.* 4.153.10, vol. II, pp. 16-17, taken from MARTIANUS CAPELLA *De nuptiis* 6, pp. 333-34.

132 POMPONIUS MELA *De chorogr.* 1.8, p. 11: they have no such thing as legitimate marriage; women and children belong to all the men in common. TERTULLIAN *De virginibus velandis* 10.2 (*CCL* 2.1219), mentions them only by name. ISIDORE OF SEVILLE *Etymologiae* 9.2.125, derives their origin from an eponymous hero, Garamans, who, of course, founded their capital, Garama. They are on the fringe of mankind, due to their cruelty. Remigius of Auxerre simply mentions their name.

133 TERTULLIAN *Apologeticus adversus gentes pro Christianis* 8 (*PL* 1.312), raises problems about their conversion. ISIDORE OF SEVILLE *Etymologiae* 11.3.23, speaks of them only from hearsay and furnishes the description which inspired Vézelay. HONORIUS OF AUTUN *De imag. mundi* 1.12 (*PL* 172.124), repeats all the fantastic legends. On all these "monsters," cf. ISIDORE OF SEVILLE *Etymologiae* 11.3.7-39.

134 It is true that here we touch on a subject a little different from our main topic—namely, the study of myths related to the limits of the known world. Man has always pushed back his fears and phantasms to the zones of his universe which were not yet sufficiently known. On this see *De Monstris et Belluis liber* in J. BERGER DE XIVREY, ed., *Traditions tératologiques ou Récits de l'Antiquité et du Moyen âge en Occident* . . . (Paris, 1836), pp. 156 ff.

135 POMPONIUS MELA *De chorogr.* 1.8, p. 11: they are so beaten down by the heat that they curse the sun at its rising and setting. Their food is unknown to the rest of mankind. MARTIANUS CAPELLA *De nuptiis* 6, p. 335, says the same thing.

136 POMPONIUS MELA *De chorogr.* 1.8, p. 11: they wear no clothes and have not learned the use of iron.

137 SOLINUS *Collectanea*, p. 128, lines 13 ff.: they live between the Troglodytes and the Nasamones, in houses with roofs built of salt. They sell carbuncles to the Troglodytes.

138 MARTIANUS CAPELLA *De nuptiis* 6, p. 345, locates them in *India*; they live in the mountains and have no kings. Remigius of Auxerre merely mentions them. ISIDORE OF SEVILLE *Etymologiae*: ". . . alia parvitate totius corporis, ut nani, vel quos Graeci Pygmaeos vocant, eo quod sint statura cubitales" (11.3.7); "Est et gens ibi statura cubitalis, quos Graeci a cubito Pygmaeos vocant. . . . Hi montana Indiae tenent, quibus est vicinus oceanus" (11.3.26).

139 THEODULF *Carmina* in *MGH: Poetae Latini aevi Carolini*, vol. I, ed. E. DUEMMLER (Berlin, 1881), p. 493:

Pygmaei tantum cupientes quarere pacem,
Propter bella gruum.

140 *De Monstris* in BERGER DE XIVREY, *Traditions tératologiques*, p. 101. HONORIUS OF AUTUN *De imag. mundi* 1.11 (*PL* 172.123-24), places them in India which gets its name from the Indus. "In montanis Pygmaeos duorum cubitorum homines, quibus bellum est contra grues. . . ."

141 ISIDORE OF SEVILLE *Etymologiae* 9.2.124-25: there are no serpents in their island; they live as nomads. Orosius mentions their existence: "Tingitana Mauretania ultima est Africae . . . a meridie gentes Autololum, quas nunc Galaules vocant, usque ad oceanum Hesperium contingentes" (OROSIUS *Adv. pag.* 1.2.94 [*CSEL* 5.34-35]). On the Autololes and the Galaules, cf. J. DESANGES, *Catalogue des tribus africaines de l'Antiquité classique à l'ouest du Nil*, Université de Dakar, Faculté des Lettres et Sciences humaines, Publications de la Section d'Histoire, no. 4 (Dakar, 1962), pp. 208-11, 215-16.

142 THEODULF *Carmina* in *MGH: Poetae*, vol. I, p. 461.

143 Following Martianus Capella, REMIGIUS OF AUXERRE *Comm. in Mart. Cap.* 6.331.7, vol. II, p. 152, picks up the theme of the golden apples of Hesperides. After Pomponius Mela a theme we shall see more of is associated with the Autololes: among them abundance prevails, their table is always well supplied.

144 We may, however, point to the representations of the *Aethiopes*, alongside Sciapodes, Satyrs, and Pygmies, in the rose window of the south transept in the Lausanne Cathedral, executed between 1231 and 1235 and restored at the end of the nineteenth century. See E.J. BEER, *Die Rose der Kathedrale von Lausanne und der kosmologische Bilderkreis des Mittelalters*, pt. 2 (Berne, 1952).

145 Antiquity handed on a very positive image of the Ethiopians. Herodotus and Pausanias describe them as a just people. Pliny the Elder, however, already considers them exceptional beings. The first Christians to encounter *Aethiopes* were struck by their unusual characteristics. ANTONINUS MARTYR *De locis transmarinis sacris* in T. TOBLER and

A. Molinier, eds., *Itinera hierosolymitana et descriptiones Terrae Sanctae*, Publications de la Société de l'Orient latin, Série géographique, vols. 1-2 (Geneva, 1879), vol. I, p. 131: the pilgrims met "homines ex Ethiopia, habentes fissas nares et aures, Calliculas calciatos, et per digitos in pedes anulos missos." On the use of the word *Aethiops* in antiquity, cf. F.M. Snowden, Jr., "The Negro in Classical Italy," *American Journal of Philology* 68 (1947): 266-92. It is important to keep in mind that *Aethiops* is first of all a synonym for "burnt face"—burnt, i.e., by the sun—and that various synonyms, to which we shall return—*Afer, Indus, Maurus*—were already in use in antiquity. Snowden's article is, of course, indispensable for the understanding of several of the points of view that are now to be considered.

146 Boethius *In Isagogen Porphyrii commenta* 2.9 (*CSEL* 48.101), is particularly explicit on this point. One Ethiopian, he says, may be more or less black than another, but he is fundamentally black. This color is also inseparably attached to the crow, coal, and ebony: "It is a matter of truth that the Ethiopian and the crow are never abandoned by the color black." This essential characteristic of the *Aethiopes* is so fundamental that it constitutes a commonplace for rhetors and grammarians.

147 For the Middle Ages, see particularly Remigius of Auxerre *Comm. in Mart. Cap.* 6.335.3, vol. II, p. 155.

148 Souvigny, abbatial church: a sculpted, octagonal column, on one face of which are represented the strangest peoples on earth, among whom is an "Ethiopian," the figure illustrating the *Polyhistor* of Solinus. Cf. E. Mâle, *L'art religieux du XIIe siècle en France*, 7th ed. (Paris, 1966), pp. 323-24.

149 Nevers, Musée Archéologique du Nivernais: capital from the priory of Saint-Sauveur on which a personage astride a dragon is designated as "Ethiop." Cf. ibid., p. 325.

150 Isidore of Seville *Etymologiae* 9.2.121-22: the Medes mingled with the Libyans, who corrupted the Medes' name while at the same time darkening their skin. From the Greek came the name "Mauri" (Moors), which designates the dark shade given by the African sun to the ancient Medes. More or less widely distributed in Africa and the Occident, the Moors are therefore dark in color.

151 "Interea, Beneventanis inter se dissidentibus, Saraceni ab Africa ab eis invitati . . ." (*Annales de Saint-Bertin*, p. 43). In the beginning the word designated a people in the Arabian peninsula; cf. Jerome *Commentariorum in Esaiam* 12.42.10-17 (*CCL* 73 A.484). Isidore of Seville *Etymologiae* 9.2.6, still connects the Saracens with an Oriental group; thus the word underwent a rapid and profound mutation.

152 The Middle Ages localized some Moors—the name had now become synonymous with Muslims—who were manifestly white, in Africa, and later had them scattered here, there, and everywhere. So the term *white Moors* was needed, just as the ancient authors had needed the term *white Ethiopians.* But there were also blacks or dark-skinned men among the Muslim troops. For them the expression *black Moors* was used until the West had occasion to see that all blacks were not Muslims. The upshot was that in Western Europe after the eleventh century black Moors and white Moors often replaced the old Ethiopians of the very early Middle Ages in the haphazard geography of Africa.

153 Isidore of Seville *Etymologiae* 9.2.122. M. Roblin, in a communication on the sense of the term *Mauritania*, *Bulletin de la Société nationale des antiquaires de France* (1948-49): 171, n. 6, assigns a Punic origin to this word, which he links with the Arabic *Maghreb* and the Hebrew *Maarev*. According to the author (p. 172), the Greek μαύρος, meaning 'dark', and the Latin *morus*, meaning 'blackberry', led to the use of the word *Maurus* to designate a person of color. Roblin cites (p. 172, n. 1) Plautus who speaks of a Negro as *morulus*; the writer holds that in medieval Latin *maurus* is a synonym for *niger*.

154 A study of the history of prejudice would be of great interest and importance.

155 On this point an important recent work has added some notable complements to our conclusions; see F. de Medeiros, "Recherches sur l'image des Noirs dans l'Occident médiéval (XIIIe-XIVe siècles)" (Ph.D. diss., 3e cycle, Université de Paris VIII, 1973). This work will be published soon.

156 Rabanus Maurus *De univ.* 7.7 (*PL* 111.195). Here Rabanus Maurus exactly follows St. Augustine's lead.

157 Thus "Christianized," the anomalies presented by antiquity could properly be carried over. They were not dangerous, since in the final analysis God was their author.

158 This is expressed clearly in Tertullian *Liber de anima* 49 (*PL* 2.733): the Atlantes, people of Libya, are reputed to sleep without dreaming. This can only be a manifestation of the divine will, "no race anywhere on earth being a stranger to God, since the Gospel radiates to the ends of the world." Conversely, the opinion that before the Deluge extraordinary beings could have been born of the union of angels and women was rejected as *heretical*. The women would have given birth to giants, Nimrod being the type of these. In fact, says a fourth-century source (Filaster *Diver. heres.* 108.1 [*CCL* 9.272]), Nimrod is none other than Chus, son of Ham; he was called a giant because of his tall stature . . . ! By two different roads the Christian tradition annihilates the dangers of dispersion and contradiction inherent in the ancient traditions.

159 In fact this is the principal argument offered by the theologians against the idea that men might be living in a temperate zone south of the Equator. Since it is impossible to pass from one temperate zone to the other—this being the accepted view—it would be necessary to posit the creation of two Adams.

160 Filaster *Diver. heres.* 121.3 (*CCL* 9.285).

161 See *Chronica minora*, ed. Th. Mommsen, vol. I in *MGH: Auctores Antiquissimi*, vol. IX (Berlin, 1892), pp. 78 ff. (*Liber generationis:* fourth century); pp. 154-96 (*Liber genealogus:* MSS of the seventh to eleventh centuries). See also *Divisio orbis terrarum* in *G.l.m.*, p. 19. Here again there is need of a systematic study of these texts, including a comparison with Hebraic, Byzantine, and Muslim traditions. This work is in progress in a research seminar at the Université de Paris I.

162 *Chronica minora*, vol. I in *MGH: Auctores Antiquissimi*, vol. IX, p. 89 *(Liber generationis)*: "terrae divisio tribus filiis Noae."

163 We find no clear definition of the geography of this territory.

164 Nimrod became in time the symbol of human pride: he sought to lift himself above his brothers and refused to acknowledge God's omnipotence; cf. Walafrid Strabo *Glossa ordinaria: Liber I Paralipomenon* 1.10 (*PL* 113.631). Ambrose *De Noe* (*CSEL* 32.1.411-97), developed the theme with an added element to which we shall have to return: Nimrod is identified with Aethiops. See also Lucas of Tuy *Chronicon mundi* in *Hispania illustrata* . . ., ed. A. Schott, vol. IV (Frankfort, 1608), p. 8.

By chance we have come across a text from the end of the eighteenth century which shows the persistence of myths relating to Nimrod:

> The author of Genesis tells us that Nimrod, great-grandson of Noah, was a mighty hunter before the Lord; or, following the Hebrew [Philo], the mightiest under heaven. He is considered to be the first who, weapons in hand, having mustered a troop of young men trained to use the bow in hunting, set himself up as a tyrant after subjugating numerous peoples whom he ruled from Babylon, where, beginning with the reign of his son Ninus, he was adored under the name of Belus, Bel, or Baal. . . .

Cf. J.B.L. Carré, *Panoplie ou Réunion de tout ce qui a trait à la Guerre, depuis l'origine de la Nation française jusqu'à nos jours* (Châlons-sur-Marne and Paris, 1795), vol. I, p. 13.

The theme of giants, "oversized" in comparison with normal men, appears in the Bible with Goliath (Muslim authors sometimes make Nimrod an ancestor of Goliath, who was said to have taken refuge in North Africa after he was defeated), as well as in the story of Alexander, so often repeated and embellished between the seventh and the seventeenth centuries, and in the Scandinavian *Edda* in which the giants symbolize proud, witless excess.

165 *Chronica minora*, vol. I in *MGH: Auctores Antiquissimi*, vol. IX, p. 101 *(Liber generationis)*.

166 Ibid., pp. 101 ff. *(Liber generationis)*: Ethiopia is opposite India, but another Ethiopia borders on the Red Sea; quite possibly Ptolemy's influence is responsible for this eastward extension of Ethiopia. Libya extends toward Cyrene, but another Libya goes from Lepcis to Syrtis Minor. A Mauritania—no longer Mauretania—occupies northwest Africa.

167 Isidore of Seville *Etymologiae* 9.2.

168 On this theme, Augustine *De civitate Dei* 16.11-12 (*CCL* 48.513-15).

169 Bede *Hexaemeron* 3 (*PL* 91.116-17); Rabanus Maurus *Commentariorum in Genesim libri quatuor* 2.9-10 (*PL* 107.525-27). Arnobius Junior *Commentarii in Psalmos* Ps. 104 (*PL* 53.481), with more care for exactness, had counted 394 languages in the lands of Ham.

170 Augustine *De civ. Dei* 16.8 (*CCL* 48.508).

171 Ambrose *De Noe* (*CSEL* 32.1.485 ff., esp. 490-92).

172 Claudius Marius Victor *Alethia* 3.76-95 (*CCL* 128.169-70).

173 "Sed Cham, quod sopitum vino patrem riserat, maledictum a patre meruit. Huius filius, Chus nomine, Nebroth gigantem genuit, a quo Babylon civitas constructa traditur" (Sulpicius Severus *Chronica* 1.4 [*CSEL* 1.6]).

174 "Primogenitus vero Cham, Chus. Hic fuit totius artis magicae, imbuente diabolo, et primus idololatriae adinventor. Hic primus statuunculam adorandam diaboli instigatione constituit: qui et stellas, et ignem de coelo cadere, falsa virtute, hominibus ostendebat" (Gregory of Tours *Historiae ecclesiasticae Francorum libri decem* 1 [*PL* 71.164]). So Chus, by the action of the Devil, is the inventor of magic—a new addition to the results of the curse.

175 Tertullian and Isidore of Seville furnished the texts that ensured the necessary alterations. Tertullian *De spectaculis* (cf. *infra*, n. 177); Isidore of Seville *Etymologiae* 7.6.19-22: "Canaan filius Cham interpretatur motus eorum. Quod quid est aliud nisi opus eorum? Pro motu enim patris, id est pro opere ejus, maledictus est. . . . Chus Hebraice Aethiops interpretatur; a posteritate sui generis nomen sortitus. Ab ipso enim sunt progeniti Aethiopes." In the Carolingian era, Rabanus Maurus *Comm. in Gen.* 2.9 (*PL* 107. 525-26): "Cham porro qui interpretatur *callidus*, . . . nec in primitiis Israelitarum, nec in plenitudine gentium permanens. Significat non solum Judaeorum, sed haereticorum genus callidum. . . ." Still another step forward: Ham and his posterity are the ancestors of those who do not believe in Christ, and whom the men of the Carolingian era obviously considered as damned *ipso facto*.

176 "Cibus autem impiorum omnium exsecrabilis ipse diabolus, prophetae vaticinio concrepante: 'Dedisti eum escam populis Aethiopibus' (Psal. LXXI, 14). Ex quibus omnibus approbatur, Christum pro daemonibus non posse crucifigi, ne daemones corporis et sanguinis ejus participes fiant" (Hincmar *De praedestinatione Dei et libero arbitrio dissertatio posterior* [*PL* 125.278]).

177 "Sic omnis gens peccatrix vocatur Aegyptus et Aethiopia (Is. 14 et alibi.), a specie ad genus" (Tertullian *De spect.* 3 [*PL* 1.635]).

178 Bede *Hexaemeron* 2 (*PL* 91.112-14): Noah knew that the posterity of Ham's son would be a sinful one; does it not include the inhabitants of Sodom? Here appears a myth of the culpability of blacks which refused to die out: immoral, given to all the vices, accustomed to marriages without sanction or morality, they attracted both the envy and the fear of unthinking medievals. We shall return to this point apropos of the traces the *Aethiops* left in the medieval mind.

179 Muslim authors carried over the legends relating to the origin of blacks. Mas'ūdī (tenth century) is one of the first to develop at length the theme of the descendants of the sons of Ham. See Mas'ūdī *Les Prairies d'or*, vol. II, pp. 321 ff.; vol. I, pp. 32 ff. A little later than Mas'ūdī the *Abrégé des Merveilles* sets forth the traditions concerning the descendants of Noah: "The traditionalists say that Noah cursed Ham, praying God that Ham's descendants might become horrible and black and that they be subjected as slaves to those of Shem. He had a son, after Kanā'ān, Kush, who was black. . . . Kanā'ān had a son Sūdān, who was black"; cf. *L'Abrégé des Merveilles*, trans. B. Carra de Vaux from the Arabic after manuscripts in Paris, Bibliothèque nationale (Paris, 1898) in *Actes de la Société philologique* 26 (1897): 99-101.

There was some questioning of this interpretation before the fourteenth century. At that time Ibn Khaldūn (*Kitab al-'Ibar*, vol. VI [Beirut, 1959], p. 410), quotes the texts of his predecessors, including Mas'ūdī, in summary form. But in the *Muḳaddima* 1.3 in Cuoq, *Recueil des sources arabes*, p. 359, Ibn Khaldūn wrote as follows:

> Certain genealogists, ignorant of the nature of things, imagined that the Sūdān, who are the descendants of Ḥām b. Nūh (Ham, son of Noah), are set apart (from other men) by their black color as a result of the curse (which Noah) laid upon their father (Ḥām). . . .
>
> To connect the black color of the Sūdān with (the curse laid upon) Ḥām is to fail to understand the nature of heat and cold, and of their influence on climate and on the condition of animal life.

This position is not so new nor so favorable as it may at first seem. True, Ibn Khaldūn, here repeating ideas taken from Galen, did attribute the blackness of the Sūdān to the action of the sun, and therefore, adopting a "naturalistic" explanation of the phenomenon, denounced the false and dangerous character of the earlier moral-theological explanation. Thus he introduced a sort of "climate theory" which became increasingly popular. But this theory itself was turned against the Sūdān! A few lines further on, Ibn Khaldūn very seriously explains that, due to the very nature of climate, only the men of the "temperate" zone can be characterized by *balance*. Thus we are brought back to the Mediterraneocentrism we have already talked about. Beyond the "temperate" zone, whether to the north or to the south (cf. *supra*, n. 117), climatic excesses engender dangerous excesses of character.

Nevertheless, the general conclusion is optimistic (Ibn Khaldūn *Muḳaddima* 1.4 in Cuoq, *Recueil des sources arabes*, p. 363):

> Al-Mas'ūdī undertook to explain the lightheadedness of the Sūdān, their inconstancy, their exuberance. His explanation goes no further than that given by Galen and Ya'ḳub b. Iṣḥāḳ al-Kindī, to wit, that (their behavior) is said to be due to the weakness of their brain, which causes a weakening of the intellect. That is an unverified and purely gratuitous assertion. 'God guides whom he will' (Koran).

180 Cf. Agapius *Kitab al-'Unvan (Histoire universelle)*, ed. and trans. A. Vasiliev (*PO* 5, 7, 8, 11; esp. 5.631), which gives some not unfavorable attention to Nimrod.

181 *Le Livre des mystères du ciel et de la terre*, ed. and trans. of Ethiopian text J. Perruchon and I. Guidi (*PO* 1.25-26). This is a text dating from the fifteenth or sixteenth century, which locates the "descendants of Ham" in the Near East. Here again there is no unfavorable interpretation.

182 Mas'ūdī makes this theme his own. The blacks divided into about seventy peoples: some had no other clothing than animal skins, others live on grass, others wear bone horns on their heads and eat . . . white mice. . . . Among them a man marries ten women. Here some of the ancient themes reappear transfigured. The Zanj made their way as far as Sofala, the limit of navigation of the ships from Oman and Siraf in the sea of the Zanj.

183 Remigius of Auxerre *Comm. in Mart. Cap.* 2.42.1, vol. I, p. 143: in the evening the sun plunges into the ocean, according to the poets, and there renews its powers, rising regenerated in the morning. We recognize the old Egyptian myth; but there would be no difficulty in finding similar themes regarding the world-girdling ocean in the Scandinavian and other mythologies. Remigius of Auxerre goes on: It is true, if we believe the fictions of poets, that the ocean

waters nourish the heavenly bodies. The Ethiopians live near the ocean in which the seven planets renew their fires.

184 A. GRAF, *Miti, leggende e superstizioni del medio evo*, vol. I, *Il mito del paradiso terrestre . . .* (Turin, 1892), gives a large number of texts.

185 Islam again adopts the same point of view: since Alexander's time these monsters are kept in check north of the Caucasus. We should not forget that Joinville still speaks of them in his History of St. Louis.

186 Gen. 2:10-15.

187 Obviously we cannot here pass in review even briefly the thousands of texts which concern the Nile from this point of view. The legendary history of the river would merit an international, interdisciplinary monograph, which would constitute an imposing example of the slow progress of human reason and knowledge. But on the whole, all our authors stressed the fact that the river was in flood at the period of greatest heat. All, even the Muslim masters of Egypt, believed, or pretended to believe, that the Negus held the key to the prosperity of the Lower Valley by controlling the dams on the river.

188 OROSIUS *Discriptio terrarum (e codice Albigensi 29)* (*CCL* 175.475-76), still speaks of the ancient version regarding the sources of the Nile: the river rises in the mysterious Mountains of the Moon. In CLAUDIUS MARIUS VICTOR *Alethia* 1.274-92 (*CCL* 128.139), Eden replaces these mountains.

189 "Geon fluvius Aethiopiae de paradiso emergens quem Nilum usitato nomine appellant. Phison fluvius Indiae idem quoque a paradiso fluens, hunc alii Gangen vocant" (EUCHERIUS *Instructionum libri duo* 2 [*CSEL* 31.152]). This idea is repeated by REMIGIUS OF AUXERRE *Comm. in Mart. Cap.* 6.302.8, vol. II, p. 146.

190 ISIDORE OF SEVILLE *Etymologiae* 13.21.7.

191 "Quatuor autem flumina paradisi ex uno fonte procedentia . . ." (BEDE *In Pentateuchum commentarii: Expositio in primum librum Mosis* 2 [*PL* 91.207]). Another sample of Bede's imagination in this area: idem *Hexaemeron* 1 (*PL* 91.45).

192 Thus an opening is made for a new transformation of these themes (we shall see more of this later): to consider the descendants of Chus a segment of humanity vowed to damnation came as a shock to a large number of exegetes. The role of Gihon, a river rising in Paradise, brought in a useful corrective: this river flowed around an entire region of Africa. The allegorical interpretation of this biblical geography is that the land of Kush is encircled by grace, and that therefore its inhabitants can hope for redemption. Matthew the Evangelist is reputed to have been the apostle of this part of Africa and of Ethiopia. This was clearly expressed by Rabanus Maurus in the ninth century (*De univ.* 11.10 [*PL* 111.320]).

193 WALAFRID STRABO *Glossa ordinaria: Liber Genesis* 2.10-14 (*PL* 113.87), proffers texts from Augustine and Gregory the Great on this subject. RABANUS MAURUS *De univ.* 11.10 (*PL* 111.319).

194 HONORIUS OF AUTUN *De imag. mundi* 1.10 (PL 172.123). The western source of one branch of the Nile is a constant medieval topic among the Muslims as well as among Occidental Christians. On this subject see the work dating from approximately 750 and attributed to ANSILEUB *Liber glossarum* in Y. KAMAL, ed., *Monumenta cartographica Africae et Aegypti*, vol. III, *Epoque arabe*, fasc. 1 ([Cairo], 1930), p. 505[v].

195 In the Western exegetical tradition it is the Ganges which is "rolling in gold," and Asia which provides precious stones.

196 Pomponius Mela's descriptions (*De chorogr.* 3.9, p. 75), which have the Ethiopians making well chains out of gold to save the less abundant copper, were not, in our opinion, perpetuated in Western Europe.

197 A further question to be considered is whether the feeling of hostility toward the color black had pre-Christian antecedents. G. Dumézil's studies have shown the importance of color symbolism in social matters, and black is one of the colors discussed.

198 SNOWDEN, *Blacks in Antiquity*, esp. p. 189. The author emphasizes the presence of numbers of blacks in the ceremonies of the Isiac and Osirian cults; hence Christian hostility was perhaps not totally "disembodied."

199 Ibid., pp. 196 ff.

200 We here express our thanks to the Benedictines of Beuron Abbey, who granted us the use of their excellent card indexes, thus enabling us to complete this inquiry.

201 Gen. 30:35, 40; Lev. 13:31, 37; Song of Songs 1:4, 5:11; Bar. 6:20; Zech. 6:2, 6; Matt. 5:36; Apoc. 6:5, 12.

202 Apoc. 6:5.

203 We have not found any favorable interpretation.

204 "His head is as the finest gold: his locks as branches of palm trees, black as a raven" (Song of Songs 5:11).

205 "Nigra sum sed formosa" (Song of Songs 1:4). Note that the Latin authors very soon tried to avoid the difficulty by substituting *fusca* for *nigra*. Ambrose and Arator are good examples of this. Origen, so often liberal, authored the commentary which thereafter was accepted as authoritative in the majority of cases; cf. ORIGEN *Homiliae in Canticum Canticorum* 1.6 (*GCS* 33.36). All men are destined to salvation, even the Ethiopians, provided they get rid of their blackness by doing penance; blackness is not in itself a fault (idem *Commentarium in Canticum Canticorum* 2 [*GCS* 33.125]). GREGORY THE GREAT *Expositiones in Canticum Canticorum* 32 (*CCL* 144.32-33), probably represents the clearest legacy from Origen on this point: "Black by her own deserts but beautiful by grace; black by her former life, beautiful by her coming conversion"—so the bride is described. Jerome and Bede take similar positions, but with less open minds. The exegesis of this verse seems to have taken another turn after the year 1000, and the blackness Ordericus Vitalis and Baudry of Bourgueil talk about may well be closer to repentance than to sin. Ordericus writes: ". . . ut anima mea in monachili possit computari collegio, sumptoque religionis schemate, renovata, in praesenti jam cantare saeculo: 'Nigra sum, sed formosa . . .'" (ORDERICUS VITALIS *Hist. eccles.* 5.21 [*PL* 188.443]). BAUDRY OF BOURGUEIL *Œuvres poétiques* 204 (ed. P. ABRAHAMS [Paris, 1926]), p. 262, says:

"Fusca quod existo mirare desinitote,
  Ardor enim solis me facit esse nigram.
Me facit esse nigram cor contritum, caro trita,
  Veri solis amor me facit esse nigram.
Fusca quidem mundo, caelestibus albico rebus,
  Turpis et atra solo, pulcra nitensque polo."

206 The same research was done with regard to the words *nigredo* (Nah. 2:10) and *nigresco* (Ezek. 30:18, 32:7); the results were insignificant.

207 "*Denigrata est super carbones facies eorum.* Nigri enim post candorem fiunt, quia, amissa Dei justitia, cum de se praesumunt, in ea etiam quae non intelligunt, peccata dilabuntur . . ." (GREGORY THE GREAT *Moralium libri, sive Expositio in librum B. Job* 32.22 [*PL* 76.663]).

208 Num. 12:1-2.

209 AUGUSTINE *Quaestionum in Heptateuchum libri VII* 4.20 (*CCL* 33.247).

210 For *Africa*: Isa. 66:19; Nah. 3:9. For *Africum*: Josh. 18:14; Ps. 77 (78):26; Isa. 21:1; Ezek. 20:46; Acts 27:12.

211 Isa. 6:6: a live coal purges Isaiah's lips of their sin; Isa. 33:11-12: Yahweh will purify Israel by fire; Isa. 66:15-16: Yahweh will punish "all mankind" by fire. See also Isa. 1:18:

Though your sins are like scarlet,
they shall be as white as snow;
though they are red as crimson,
they shall be like wool.

[Biblical references in nn. 211-15 are from the *Jerusalem Bible* (Garden City, N.Y., 1966).]

212 On the relations between Egypt and the Hebrews in earlier times, see *Ramsès le Grand*, Exhibition catalogue, Galeries nationales du Grand Palais, Paris, 1976 (Paris, 1976), pp. XLIII-XLVI. On the events of Isaiah's time, see W. REICHHOLD, "Les Noirs dans le Livre du Prophète Isaïe," in *Afrique noire et monde méditerranéen dans l'antiquité*, Colloquium held in Dakar, 19-24 January 1976 (Dakar and Abidjan, 1978), esp. pp. 277-78: King Hezekiah sought the support of the pharaohs of the Twenty-fifth ("Ethiopian") Dynasty against Assyria. Isaiah opposed this alliance, but his text shows that he was familiar with the Nile Valley, where he makes a distinction between the Egytians and the Kushites, "a people tall and bronzed" (Isa. 18:2, 7).

213 Isa. 7:18: the Hebrews are threatened with intervention by "mosquitoes from the Delta of the Egyptian Niles" and by "bees from the land of Assyria."

214 Isaiah first explains that the peoples who were to break down the pride of Israel would be punished by God—so regarding Egypt and Assyria (Isa. 10, 11). But the prophet goes much further; in their turn these peoples will be converted:

> Thus says Yahweh:
> The peasants of Egypt and the traders of Kush,
>
> . . . .
>
> They will bow down before you,
> they will pray to you:
> 'With you alone is God, and he has no rival;
> there is no other god'. [Isa. 45:14]

And in another passage: "At that time, offerings will be brought to Yahweh Sabaoth on behalf of the tall and bronzed nation, on behalf of the nation always feared, on behalf of the mighty and masterful people in the country criss-crossed with rivers, to the place where the name of Yahweh Sabaoth dwells, on Mount Zion" (Isa. 18:7).

215 Cf. Isa. 56: Yahweh promises to welcome foreigners as proselytes; see also Isa. 66:19: "I will give them a sign and send some of their survivors to the nations: to Tarshish, Put, Lud. . . ." There can be no doubt about Jerome's identification of Put; cf. JEROME *Comm. in Esaiam* 18.66.18-19 (*CCL* 73 A.786): ". . . *ad gentes, in mare, in Africam, in Lydiam*. . . ."

216 Jerome's exegesis of the verses we have just cited is decidedly weak. He gets out of the difficulty by means of the sort of geographical or genealogical developments we have already seen: "Phud autem, sive Phul, Libyes omnisque Africa usque ad mare Mauritaniae, in qua fluvius hodie qui Phud dicitur; et cuncta circa eum regio Phutensis appellatur" (JEROME *Comm. in Esaiam* 18.66.18-19 [*CCL* 73 A.786]). Jerome pays no attention to this Africa, and not much more to the Ethiopia that "shall soon stretch out her hands to God"; yet Jerome's text was part of the "basic intellectual equipment" of the educated medieval clerk. See, for instance, J. DEVISSE, *Hincmar Archevêque de Reims 845-882*, Travaux d'histoire éthico-politique, no. 29 (Geneva, 1976), vol. III, pp. 1381, 1498.

217 See the recent work of H.D. RAUH, *Das Bild des Antichrist im Mittelalter: Von Tyconius zum deutschen Symbolismus*, Beiträge zur Geschichte der Philosophie und Theologie des Mittelalters, n.s., vol. 9 (Münster, 1973), pp. 130-38.

218 H. WALTHER, ed., *Proverbia sententiaeque Latinitatis medii aevi*, Carmina medii aevi posterioris Latina, no. II/3 (Göttingen, 1965), pt. 3, gives some examples:

> Niger olor, nivea cornix, nigra nix, aqua sicca:
> Inveniuntur ea citius quam pulchra pudica. [P. 122, no. 16623]
> Nigra petit nigrum: petit et monachum monialis.
> [P. 123, no. 16624 (fourteenth century)]
> Nigri caldaris manus ex tactu maculatur:
> Per turpem socium vir cadit in vitium.
> [P. 123, no. 16626]

219 "Quid enim per Indiam quae nigrum populum mittit, nisi hic mundus accipitur, in quo vita hominum per culpam obscura generatur. Tincti autem colores Indiae, sunt hujus mundi sapientes. . ." (GREGORY THE GREAT *Moralia* 18.46 [*PL* 76.82]).

220 "Quid Aethiopiam, nisi praesentem mundum accipimus? quae coloris nigredine designat peccatorem populum, foeditate meritorum" (GREGORY THE GREAT *Moralia* 18.52 [*PL* 76.88]).

221 See A. CAQUOT, "Hébreu *ṣiyyim*, Grec *Aithiopes*," in *Mélanges Marcel Cohen*, ed. D. COHEN, Janua linguarum, Series maior, 27 (The Hague and Paris, 1970), pp. 219-23.

222 The Arabic term is less widely applied than the Latin *Aethiops*: numerous branches became known by their own distinctive names, such as Bujja, Nūba, Sūdān, Zanj, etc.

223 BEDE *Hexaemeron* 2 (*PL* 91.112-13). The Anglo-Saxon tradition is very unfavorable to the *Aethiopes*: cf. ALDHELM *De virginitate* 1 in *MGH: Auctores Antiquissimi*, vol. XV, ed. R. EHWALD, pt. 1 (1913), p. 306; Noah cursed the descendants of Ham (BEDE *Hexaemeron* 2 [*PL* 91.112-13]).

224 Solinus illustrates the point: the morals of the inhabitants of Africa are far from commendable. Thus a double current of prejudice develops: the blacks are erratic, inconstant, lazy; they are also addicted to the most revolting vices.

225 FLODOARD *De triumphis Christi sanctorumque Palestinae libri tres* 1.13 (*PL* 135.498):

> Aethiopium gentem, peccato et corpore nigram,
> Candorem nitidum docuisti sumere Christi.

Ambrose had already written: "Color Aethiopis tenebras animae squaloremque significat, qui adversus lumini est, claritatis exsors, tenebris involutus, nocti similior quam diei" (AMBROSE *De Noe* 34.128 [*CSEL* 32.1.496]). See also GREGORY THE GREAT *Moralia* 30.38, 32.22 (*PL* 76.542, 663).

226 The size and significance of the Jewish colonies in pre-Islamic Arabia and in Ethiopia have not yet been determined. The little we know about the dramatic events at Najrān, and about the Hebrew communities in Ethiopia, is evidence enough of the interest which would attach to such an inquiry.

227 For commentary on this passage and on the text concerning Moses, about which more later, see the essay by J. Courtès, *supra*, pp. 21-22 and p. 25.

228 This text was not the subject of significant literary or exegetical development in the following centuries. A Pseudo-Cyprian, probably of the third century (*De rebaptismate* 5 [*CSEL* 3.3.74]), reproduces it word for word. FLODOARD *De triumphis Christi sanctorumque Palestinae* 2.10 (*PL* 135.521), does the same. See another trace in idem *De triumphis Christi sanctorumque Palestinae* 2.10 (*PL* 135.522).

In the Orient the theme of the struggle between Judaism and Christianity, woven around the eunuch's conversion, has left more vestiges. A Nestorian synod held in 585 upholds this doctrine:

> The minister of Qandaq, queen of the Ethiopians, . . . following an ancient custom, went to Jerusalem to worship the God of the Hebrews, the true God, Creator and Ruler of the universe: he had come up from his country not as a heathen suffocated by error but as a Jew suckling the milk of infancy; he returned and went down to his country no longer the Jew wrapped in the obscurity of the Law, teacher and pedagogue of babes, but the virile Christian who had found the Master of perfection, end of the Law and the expectation of the nations, thanks to the herald of perfection, the apostle Philip.

Cf. *Synodicon orientale ou Recueil de synodes nestoriens*, ed. and trans. J.B. CHABOT (Paris, 1902), p. 443.

229 There are traces of these Western fears in the twelfth century in GERHOH OF REICHERSBERG *Liber de simoniacis* (ed. E. SACKUR) in *MGH: Libelli*, vol. III, pp. 265-66: "Ex quo manifestum est, quod Judei et heretici et omnia conventicula dogmatum perversorum, quia in ecclesia non comedunt, non eos agni carnes, sed draconis comedere, qui datus est in escam populis Ethiopum." See also HINCMAR *De praedest. Dei* (*PL* 125.278). Cassiodorus probably provided the starting point: "*Tu confregisti caput draconis; dedisti eum in escam populo Aethiopum. . . . capita draconum*, significare volens nequitias spiritales. . . . *Aethiopes* bene peccatores advertimus, qui ante fuerant tenebrosa mente teterrimi; sed

ad Dominum conversi, escam coeperunt habere diabolum, cum de ejus detractione satiantur" (CASSIODORUS *Expositio Psalmorum* Ps. 73:14 [*CCL* 98.679-80]).

230 Quite certainly a study should be made of the fascination exerted by Alexander on Western minds. The pupil of a stern philosopher, morally corrupt, explorer of the ends of the earth, dead in the flower of life, the Greek emperor both charms and repels the Christian moralists. What a *dilator mundi christiani* he would have been if God had called him to the faith! This nostalgia is ever present in Western reflections on Alexander.

231 Like Alexander, Nimrod represents an excessive attachment to earthly things, a noble but ill-directed ambition, since its objective was not God but human goods. No text has impressed us as illustrating this view so much as a thirteenth-century chronicle by LUCAS OF TUY *Chronicon mundi* in *Hispania illustrata*, vol. IV, p. 8: "Fuit autem Nembrot potens in terra, et robustus venator hominum coram domino, id est, extinctor et oppressor amore dominandi." This was an exegetical commonplace; see, e.g., AMBROSE *De Noe* 34.127-28 (*CSEL* 32.1.496), who combines Nimrod's inordinate physical size and his excessive human ambition. The hunter who pursues earthly glory—the Promethean hero—is contrasted with the type of the fisher of men for God's glory, represented by Peter and the Apostles. According to AMBROSE *De Noe* 34.128 (*CSEL* 32.1.496): "Nembroth autem per interpretationem Aethiops dicitur." Sulpicius Severus makes him a giant descended from Ham.

232 This theme is not developed until the twelfth century. It is studied in this essay (cf. *infra*, pp. 129-131) and in part 2, pp. 17-22.

233 We refer once more to the importance of the Nubian regions, which still await thorough study.

234 Matthew's Ethiopian apostolate received very significant treatment in medieval poetry. See VENANTIUS FORTUNATUS *Carmina* 5.2.9-10 in *MGH: Auctores Antiquissimi*, vol. IV, pt. 1, ed. F. LEO (1881), p. 104:

> Mattheus Aethiopos adtemperat ore vapores
> vivaque in exusto flumina fundit agro.

See also *Dialogus Agii* 320 in *MGH: Poetae*, vol. III, ed. L. TRAUBE, pt. 2, fasc. 1 (1892), p. 379: "Et sunt Mathaeo Aethiopes nitidi" (written by an anonymous Carolingian); and *Annalium de gestis Caroli Magni Imperatoris libri quinque* 5.685 ff. in *MGH: Poetae*, vol. IV, pt. 1, ed. P.K.R. VON WINTERFELD (1899), p. 71: "Matheus Aethiopes niveos baptismate factos . . ." (written by an anonymous, ninth-century Saxon). What clearer expression could be given to the identification of blackness with sin and of whiteness with redemption? We shall return to this topic. In the twelfth century Otto of Freising considers the tradition so solidly established that he refers to it only by allusion; cf. OTTO OF FREISING *Chronica sive Historia de duabus civitatibus* 3.14 (ed. and trans. A. HOFMEISTER and W. LAMMERS, Ausgewählte Quellen zur deutschen Geschichte des Mittelalters, vol. 16 [Berlin, (1960)]), pp. 238-39. See DORESSE, *L'empire du Prêtre-Jean*, vol. I, *L'Ethiopie antique*, pp. 249 ff.

235 "Ambassadors shall come out of Egypt: Ethiopia shall soon stretch out her hands to God" (Ps. 67 [68]:32).

236 JEROME *Excerpta de psalterio* Prologus, cited by H. DE LUBAC, *Exégèse médiévale: les quatre sens de l'Ecriture*, Théologie, no. 41 (Paris, 1959), pt. 1, vol. I, p. 258, n. 2.

237 JEROME *In Amos* 3.9.7-8 (*PL* 25.1091-92).

238 "If they agreed to do penance, the Ethiopians would become the children of God; the children of God who plunge into sin become Ethiopians" (JEROME *In Amos* 3.9.7-8 [*PL* 25.1092]).

239 JEROME *Comm. in Esaiam* 5.20.1, 5.22.1, 7.18.1 ff., 7.19.1 ff. (*PL* 24.188, 195, 246-47, 251). Even the well-known verses—"I am black but beautiful. . . . Do not consider me that I am brown, because the sun hath altered my colour" (Song of Songs 1:4-5)—win no favor for Ethiopia. Origen's interpretation is taken over with emphasis; cf. ORIGEN *Comm. in Cant. Cant.* 2 (*PG* 13.101 ff.).

240 Cassiodorus repeats the theme in his commentary on the Song of Songs: ". . . conversatus sum inter persecutores et peccatores *infidelitate* nigros" (CASSIODORUS *Expositio in Cantica Canticorum* 1 [*PL* 70.1058]). Later in a similar vein on the same passage, see HONORIUS OF AUTUN *Expositio in Cantica Canticorum* 1.4 (*PL* 172.367 ff.).

241 India is sometimes included with Ethiopia. Alcuin stresses St. Bartholomew's apostolate: "Qui docuit nigros . . . Indos"; cf. ALCUIN *Carmina* in *MGH: Poetae*, vol. I, p. 335.

242 The *De vocatione gentium* has been attributed to St. Ambrose and to Pope Leo I. At present, historians are almost unanimous in recognizing Prosper of Aquitaine as its author. The work takes its origin and its power from the long quarrel over predestination which set Augustine against various opponents. Disagreeing on more than one point with Augustine, of whom he was often a faithful follower, Prosper of Aquitaine declares that all men without exception are called to salvation. Probably he had not thought of the geographical applications or of the ethnic developments which this theological generosity implied. But the idea had some success in the Middle Ages, as the Vézelay tympanum proves.

243 God's universal salvific will is affirmed in the *City of God* and treated more at length in the *Enarrationes in Psalmos*. The Ethiopians, who are not within the Roman Empire, will be in God's kingdom; AUGUSTINE *De civ. Dei* 18.32 (*CCL* 48.624). Even Jerome, in one instance, shows sympathy with this view (JEROME *Comm. in Esaiam* 4.11.6 ff. [*PL* 24.150]).

244 CASSIODORUS *Exp. Psal.* Ps. 86:4 (*PL* 70.619); FAUSTUS OF RIEZ *Sermones* 8 (*CSEL* 21.253); JOHN OF SALISBURY *Policraticus* 7.10, cited in LUBAC, *Exégèse médiévale*, pt. 1, vol. I, p. 258, n. 2. St. Bruno later paved the way for a broadening of the twelfth-century theme. In the ninth century Walafrid Strabo is the only one to echo Prosper of Aquitaine: "Tradunt enim historiae quod apostoli toto orbe diffusi praedicaverunt Evangelium: et quidem Persas, Indosque penetraverunt, ut Aethiopia manum daret Deo" (WALAFRID STRABO *Glossa ordinaria: Prophetia Isaiae* 11.11 [*PL* 113.1251]).

245 The Ethiopian's "change of skin," a frequent literary theme, is still another proof of medieval Christianity's ethnocentrism. See, for instance: "Ibi enim quod Jeremias admirando proloquitur, mutavit Aethiops pellem suam, id est, sorde de peccatorum abluta, de lavacro Jesu dealbatus ascendit" (BEDE *Super Acta Apostolorum expositio* 8 [*PL* 92.962]); FLODOARD *De triumphis Christi sanctorumque Palestinae* 1.13 (*PL* 135.498) (cf. *supra*, n. 225) and 2.10 (*PL* 135.522):

> Mutavitque atram, tinctus baptismate, pellem
> Hic niger eunuchus, gentilia corda figurans.

The theme of Queen Candace's eunuch fits nicely into this pattern of reasoning.

246 Augustine originated this allegorical exegesis; cf. AUGUSTINE *Enarrationes in Psalmos* Ps. 67 (*CCL* 39.898). "Aethiopia quoque, idest, anima peccatis denigrata *praeveniet manus ejus*, idest, antecedet vindictam ejus, credens Deo, ut peccata dimittantur" (RUFINUS *In Psalmos LXXV commentarius* Ps. 67 [*PL* 21.920]). "Aliquando vero Aethiopiae nomine specialiter gentilitas designari solet, infidelitatis prius nigra peccatis. . . . Priusquam Judaea credat, salvandam se offert omnipotenti Deo peccatis nigra gentilitas" (GREGORY THE GREAT *Moralia* 18.52 [*PL* 76.88-89]). "Quid Aethiopia? nisi praesentem mundum accipiemus, quae coloris nigredine designat peccatorem populum foeditate meritorum" (ETHERIUS OF OSMA *Ad Elipandum epistola* 1.56 [*PL* 96.927]). "Aethiopia Gentilitas nigra peccatis, festinat manus dare Deo. . . . Id est, vindictam ejus, per confessionem, ne manentes in peccatis puniantur" (WALAFRID STRABO *Glossa ordinaria: Liber Psalmorum* Ps. 67:32 [*PL* 113.945]). Bruno establishes the distinction between the Jews, who are hardened in their attachment to the appearances of earthly things and refuse to adhere to Christ, and the Ethiopians who forestall the divine justice by accepting the faith; cf. BRUNO *Expositio Psalmorum* Pss. 67, 71 (*PL* 142.255, 271).

247 GREGORY THE GREAT *Epistolae* 3.67 (*PL* 77.668).

248 VICTOR OF VITA *Historia persecutionis Africanae provinciae* 2.18 (*CSEL* 7.30).

249 AUDRADUS MODICUS *Carmina* in *MGH: Poetae*, vol. III, pt. 1 (1886), p. 94:

Ad umbras
Inferni plebs Aethiopum ducebat iniqua
Me, . . .

250 HINCMAR *De visione Bernoldi presbyteri* (*PL* 125.1115): ". . . pannosos et denigratos, . . ."

251 HINCMAR *De vis. Bern.* (*PL* 125.1117).

252 See C. M. JONES, "The Conventional Saracen of the Songs of Geste," *Speculum* 17, no. 2 (1942): 201, n. 1; 204, n. 2.

253 GREGORY THE GREAT *Dialogi* 2.2, p. 78.

254 ZACHARIAS SCHOLASTICUS *Vie de Sévère*, ed. and trans. M.-A. KUGENER (*PO* 2.1.38).

255 *Histoire Nestorienne (Chronique de Séert)*, ed. and trans. A. SCHER and R. GRIVEAU, pt. 2, fasc. 2 (*PO* 13.478-79).

256 I thank B. Hisard Martin, Maître Assistant, Université de Paris I, for providing me with the details needed to write the passage on Abba Moses. There are several accounts relative to this personage, all drawing more or less upon an initial text which is found in PALLADIUS *Historia Lausiaca* (*PG* 34.1065-68 and in *Acta Sanctorum*, Augusti, vol. VI [Antwerp, 1743], pp. 208-11); this text is completed by the *Apophthegmata Patrum* (*PG* 65.281-90), and SOZOMEN *Historia ecclesiastica* 6.29 (*PG* 67.1373-78).

Abba Moses is recorded in various traditions. In the Greek world most of the texts seem to go back to the tenth century. They include: a *Life* (V. LATYŠEV, ed., *Menologii anonymi Byzantini saeculi X quae supersunt*, vol. II [St. Petersburg, 1912], pp. 330-34; *Acta Sanctorum*, Augusti, vol. VI, pp. 209-11), an unpublished *Laudatio*, and a passage of the *Synaxarium ecclesiae Constantinopolitanae* 28 August (*Propylaeum ad Acta Sanctorum: Novembris* [Brussels, 1902], cols. 929-32). All these have a considerable similarity with the *Lausiac History*. A Syriac tradition has been translated into Italian; cf. I. PIZZI, trans., "Storia di San Mosè ladrone," *Bessarione* fasc. 63 (November-December 1901): 387-89. Ethiopia, too, at a date difficult to determine (probably toward the end of the Middle Ages), made room for a version of Abba Moses' life; cf. *Le Synaxaire éthiopien: Les mois de Sanê, Hamlê et Nahasê*, ed. and trans. I. GUIDI, fasc. 1, *Mois de Sanê* (*PO* 1.665 ff.). The Coptic tradition is not easy to use, being very fragmentary; cf. H. G. E. WHITE, *The Monasteries of the Wâdi 'n Natrûn*, Publications of the Metropolitan Museum of Art Egyptian Expedition, no. 7 (New York, 1932), pt. 2, *The History of the Monasteries of Nitria and of Scetis*, ed. W. HAUSER, among the texts relating to St. Macarius. The Arabic-speaking world also made mention of Abba Moses; cf. *Synaxarium Alexandrinum*, ed. and trans. J. FORGET, Corpus scriptorum Christianorum Orientalium, vol. 90, Scriptores Arabici, tome 13 (Louvain, 1953), plus some allusions in the eleventh-century version of the *History of the Patriarchs of Alexandria*. In Western Europe, Moses appears in the Roman Martyrology, in Cassian's *Conferences*, and in *The Golden Legend* by Jacob of Voragine. The Western references, however, are cursory and of little interest to our inquiry. The West did not see Abba Moses as a black.

257 The later Greek texts repeat this detail. The Constantinople Synaxarion indicates that the saint "was of Ethiopian origin and his body was completely black." A Syriac text in Palladius's *Book of Paradise* reiterates this theme: Moses is described as "by race an Indian, i.e., an Ethiopian"; cf. E. A. W. BUDGE, ed. and trans., *The Book of Paradise . . . by Palladius...*, Lady Meux Manuscript, no. 6 (London, 1904), vol. I, *English Translation*, p. 328. The value of this information will be apparent when, further on in this study, we take up the question of St. Thomas and his "mission to India."

258 An Alexandrian and Ethiopian tradition. On this point the study could be pushed much further. Insofar as the Ethiopian tradition is of later date and emphasizes the idea that it was Moses' *blackness* that frightened the monk, it falls in with the "colonial" syndrome already mentioned.

259 Here again we have a topic relating to the Negro to which we shall have to return more than once.

260 Cf. *supra*, n. 256.

261 *Apoph. Pat.* (*PG* 65.283). The text emphasizes that what is meant is a *trial* to which Moses is subjected: the *Aethiops*, more than anyone else, needs humility in order to draw near to God. Very logically, the Ethiopian Synaxarion puts this trial *before* the ordination and completes the consecrator's statement as follows: "You are whitened wholly, within and without" (*Le Synaxaire éthiopien*, fasc. 1, *Mois de Sanê* [*PO* 1.667]). Cassian is not misled. He retained neither Moses' ethnic origin nor the color of his skin, but he stressed the exceptional spiritual road which the allegory sums up: "It was fear of the death penalty, to which he was liable for killing a man, that drove him to seek refuge in a monastery. But he profited by this forced conversion so well that his own ardor made it a free and voluntary sacrifice, and so he rose to the highest summits of perfection"; cf. CASSIAN *Conférences* 3.5 (ed. and trans. E. PICHERY, S.C., no. 42 [Paris, 1955]), vol. I, p. 144. The *Aethiops*-sinner has become a saint. The proof is rounded out by the Ethiopian Synaxarion: "The power of penance . . . transformed a servingman, *a black slave*, impious, murderous, lecherous, a thief, and made him a father superior, a doctor, a consoler, a priest . . ." (*Le Synaxaire éthiopien*, fasc. 1, *Mois de Sanê* [*PO* 1.669]).

262 Vercelli, Museo Camillo Leone: fragment of a mosaic from the Collegiate Church of Sta. Maria Maggiore, eleventh century.

263 C. SIEGFRIED and H. GELZER, eds., *Eusebii canonum epitome ex Dionysii Telmaharensis chronico petita* (Leipzig, 1884), p. 32.

264 E. SACKUR, *Sibyllinische Texte und Forschungen: Pseudomethodius, Adso und die tiburtinische Sibylle* (Halle, 1898).

265 F. VIGOUROUX, ed., *Dictionnaire de la Bible*, 3d ed., vol. I, pt. 1 (Paris, 1926), cols. 256-58.

266 *Thesaurus linguae latinae*, vol. VI, pt. 1 (Leipzig, 1912-26), cols. 422-23, s.v. "fel." Prudentius, Sulpicius Severus, and Gregory of Tours associate the word *fel*, as well as some others, with anger and blackness; see also ISIDORE OF SEVILLE *Etymologiae* 11.1.127-28, 17.9.33.

267 Troia, cathedral, Archivio capitolare. Cf. *Mostra dell'Arte in Puglia dal tardo antico al Rococo*, Exhibition catalogue, Bari, Pinacoteca Provinciale, 1964 (Bari, 1964), p. 25, no. 26. These rolls are numerous in central and particularly in southern Italy from the twelfth to the fourteenth century; see A. M. LATIL, *Documenti per la storia della miniatura in Italia*, vol. III, *Le miniature nei rotoli dell'Exultet* (Montecassino, 1899). Their iconography is very stereotyped in several scenes, but in the details shows a freedom which would merit study.

268 Here we must mention the article by I. SACHS, "L'image du Noir dans l'art européen," *Annales E.S.C.* 24, no. 4 (1969): 883-93.

269 The remarkable study by F. J. DÖLGER, *Die Sonne der Gerechtigkeit und der Schwarze: Eine religionsgeschichtliche Studie zum Taufgelöbnis*, Liturgiegeschichtliche Forschungen, no. 2 (Münster, 1918), analyzes a large number of texts and formulates some very appealing hypotheses. Osiris and Pluto, gods of the dead, partially explain the origin of the anti-Christian demon. Once again Egypt is involved, and it would certainly be fruitful to study in detail the relation of the cults of Isis and Osiris to Christianity. See also idem, "'Der Schwarze' als Benennung des Teufels," *Antike und Christentum* 3 (1932): 282. This subject has also received the attention of P. DU BOURGUET, "La couleur noire de la peau du démon dans l'iconographie chrétienne a-t-elle une origine précise?," in *Actas del VIII Congresso internacional de arqueología cristiana*, Barcelona, 5-11 October 1969, Studi di antichità cristiana, no. 30 (Rome and Barcelona, 1972), vol. I, *Texto*, pp. 271-72. See also O. A. ERICH, *Die Darstellung des Teufels in der christlichen Kunst*, Kunstwissenschaftliche Studien, no. 8 (Berlin, 1931), and A. RECHEIS, *Engel, Tod und Seelenreise*, Temi e testi, no. 4 (Rome, 1958).

270 Most often dark ochres, sometimes with violet tints, also dark greens—these choices be-

ing determined, of course, by the available coloring materials.

271 See, for instance, G. RADKE, *Die Bedeutung der weissen und der schwarzen Farbe in Kult und Brauch der Griechen und Römer* (Jena, 1936), and DÖLGER, "'Der Schwarze' als Benennung des Teufels," p. 282.

272 See J. BALTRUŠAITIS, *Le Moyen Age fantastique: Antiquités et exotismes dans l'art gothique*, Collection Henri Focillon, no. 3 (Paris, 1955).

273 Rome, Sta. Maria Antiqua: a fresco which is nearly obliterated on one of the pilasters. This fresco was included in a survey done by J. WILPERT, *Die römischen Mosaiken und Malereien der Kirchlichen Bauten vom IV. bis XIII. Jahrhundert*, 2d ed. (Freiburg im Breisgau, 1917), vol. IV, *Tafeln: Malereien*, pl. 168, 2.

274 Patmos, Haghios Yoannis Theologos Monastery, MS. Patmiacus Graecus 171. *Book of Job* (with a series of the Fathers), p. 50: three angels and a black demon, all about the same size.

275 Valenciennes, Bibliothèque municipale, MS. 99. *Apocalypse*, ninth century, fol. 37ʳ; see H. OMONT, "Manuscrits illustrés de l'Apocalypse aux IXᵉ et Xᵉ siècles," *Bulletin de la Société française de reproductions de manuscrits à peintures* 6 (1922): 73 ff. and pl. XXVIII. This folio illustrates passages of the Apocalypse pertaining to the second death (Apoc. 20:9, 11, 14-15, 21:8): the shining whiteness of Christ's throne (upper register of the miniature bearing the caption: *Et vidi thronum magnum candidum*) is contrasted with the darkness of Hell (lower register with caption: *Hic est stagnus ignis et sulforis . . . et infernus*).

C. Nordenfalk thinks that the themes illustrating this manuscript are of English origin (Northumberland, about 700); cf. GRABAR and NORDENFALK, *Le Haut Moyen-âge*, p. 122. J. Porcher differs: for him the manuscript is a work from the Salzburg ateliers, illustrated in the Italo-Alpine manner; cf. J. HUBERT, J. PORCHER, and W.F. VOLBACH, *L'empire carolingien*, L'univers des formes ([Paris], 1968), pp. 181, 352.

276 Burgo de Osma, Cathedral Museum, Cod. 1, manuscript dated 1086, fol. 155ᵛ: the inscription labels the figure *Sathanas solutus* ("Satan unbound"); cf. A.M. MUNDO and M.S. MARIANA, *El Comentario de Beato al Apocalipsis: Catálogo de los Códices* (Madrid, 1976), pp. 22-23, no.3. We have examined a series of photographs apparently relating to the same manuscript and found black devil-figures in four places, with the radiating hair arrangement having from six to eleven points, most often seven or eight. The numerous painted manuscripts that contain Beatus of Liébana's *Commentary on the Apocalypse* ought to be studied systematically.

In his text Beatus betrays strong hostility toward Africa, where the Muslim menace came from. See especially H.A. SANDERS, ed., *Beati In Apocalipsin libri duodecim*, Papers and Monographs of the American Academy in Rome, vol. 7 ([Rome], 1930), pp. 338 ff.

277 Paris, Bibliothèque nationale, MS. lat. 8878. Beatus of Liébana, *Commentary on the Apocalypse*, from the Abbey of Saint-Sever, dated 1028-72, fol. 4ᵛ: Christ delivers the Gospel to St. John. See PORCHER, *Les manuscrits à peintures en France*, p. 104, no. 304; MUNDO and MARIANA, *El Comentario de Beato al Apocalipsis*, pp. 42-43, no. 20.

278 Escorial, Real Monasterio, Biblioteca, Cod. Vitr. 17. *Evangelistary* of Emperor Henry III *(Codex Aureus)*, Echternach, between 1043 and 1046, fol. 117ᵛ: Parable of the Rich Man and Lazarus.

279 Gerona, Museo de la Catedral de Gerona, MS. 7. Beatus of Liébana, *Commentary on the Apocalypse*, dated 975, fol. 17ʳ: Hell. Cf. GRABAR and NORDENFALK, *Le Haut Moyen-âge*, pp. 168, 170; MUNDO and MARIANA, *El Comentario de Beato al Apocalipsis*, pp. 25-26, no. 6.

280 Boulogne-sur-Mer, Bibliothèque municipale, MS. 20. *Otbert Psalter*, from the Saint-Bertin Abbey in Saint-Omer, about 1000, fol. 101ʳ, historiated initial: Temptation of Christ; cf. L. GRODECKI, F. MÜTHERICH, J. TARALON, and F. WORMALD, *Le siècle de l'an mil*, L'univers des formes ([Paris], 1973), p. 197.

281 ERICH, *Die Darstellung des Teufels*, p. 12, fig. 1; p. 18, fig. 7; p. 29, figs. 18 and 19; p. 37, figs. 25 and 26; p. 60, fig. 49; p. 61, fig. 50.

282 Ibid., p. 56.

283 Ibid., p. 58.

284 See P. PALOL DE SALELLAS, *Arte hispánico de la época visigoda*, Biblioteca de arte hispánico (Barcelona, 1968), p. 125, fig. 85; idem, "Esencia del arte hispánico de época visigoda: Romanismo y germanismo," in *I Goti in Occidente: Problemi*, Spoleto, 29 March-5 April 1955, Settimane di studio del Centro Italiano di studi sull'alto medioevo, no. 3 (Spoleto, 1956), pp. 65-126 and pl. XXIX, fig. 34.

285 I. OLAGÜE, *Les Arabes n'ont jamais envahi l'Espagne* ([Paris], 1969), pp. 133 ff.

286 Laon, Bibliothèque municipale, MS. 422. Isidore of Seville, *De natura rerum*, from North France, ninth century, fol. 53ʳ. Cf. PORCHER, *Les manuscrits à peintures en France*, p. 41, no. 95. It is doubtful that the painter intended to represent the sun as *black*, although he used brown, whereas ordinarily a very dark blue was used to render black color. Madame S. Martinet, Conservateur of the Bibliothèque municipale in Laon, was kind enough to inform us, for which we thank her, that the sun, like other painted elements in this codex, is done in a tone halfway between vermilion and orange, tinted with a touch of maroon.

287 Besides the two examples illustrated further on, we mention first a very marginal case, then two other representations: Laon, Bibliothèque municipale, MS. 108. *Sancti Pauli Epistolae*, from Vauclair Abbey, early twelfth century, fol. 46ʳ: a centaur with reddish bust and head figures in the loop of the *P* in *Paulus*; Boulogne-sur-Mer, Bibliothèque municipale, MS. 2. *Bible*, from Saint-André-au-Bois Monastery, second half of the twelfth century, vol. II, fols. 247ᵛ and 271ᵛ: two decorated initial *P*'s, one introducing the First Epistle to the Corinthians, the other the Second Epistle to Timothy; both present a nude man, colored blue, his arms raised.

288 Regarding this text, often erroneously attributed to St. Augustine, see A. WILMART, "Sommaire de l'Exposition de Florus sur les Epîtres," *Revue bénédictine* 38 (1926): 205-16.

289 Paris, Bibliothèque nationale, MS. lat. 11576. *Expositio in epistolas Pauli*, from Corbie Abbey, 1164, vol. II, fol. 67ᵛ: the nude man, painted blue, is partially covered by a shield; he forms the stem of the initial *P* which introduces the Epistle to the Colossians. Cf. PORCHER, *Les manuscrits à peintures en France*, p. 60, no. 140.

290 Bourg-en-Bresse, Bibliothèque municipale, MS. 1. *New Testament and Psalter*, second half of the twelfth century, fol. 91ᵛ: the stem of the *P* at the head of the Epistle to the Colossians is formed by a tall blue man.

291 Let it be understood that some of these "blue" figures do not have clear "black" characteristics. Moreover, our present list is not definitive; other comparable representations may come into this series once its real significance is discovered.

292 J. PORCHER, *L'enluminure française* (Paris, 1959), p. 27.

293 C. DE MÉRINDOL, "La production des livres peints à l'abbaye de Corbie au XIIᵉ siècle: Etude historique et archéologique" (Ph.D. diss., Université de Paris I, 1975).

294 Paris, Bibliothèque nationale, MS. lat. 11576. *Expositio in epistolas Pauli*, vol. II.

295 MÉRINDOL, "La production des livres peints à l'abbaye de Corbie," pp. 254, 476, 568 ff.

296 We add here and *infra*, nn. 297-300, the references given in the footnotes to C. de Mérindol's thesis. Paris, Bibliothèque nationale, MS. lat. 11576, fol. 104ʳ.

297 Paris, Bibliothèque nationale, MS. lat. 11576, fol. 39ʳ.

298 Ibid., fol. 115ᵛ.

299 Ibid., fols. 67ᵛ, 75ᵛ. MÉRINDOL, "La production des livres peints à l'abbaye de Corbie," pp. 468-69.

300 Mérindol, "La production des livres peints à l'abbaye de Corbie," pp. 464 ff., makes comparisons with several English manuscripts. The body, he says, is "violet, modeled with a darker, slightly yellowish purple and with white" (p. 647). For other illustrations in MS. lat. 11576 in Paris, Bibliothèque nationale, fol. 67v: "dark slate-colored blue body modeled with white and black"; fol. 82v: "purplish-blue body modeled with a vivid blue and with white" (p. 647). C. de Mérindol defines the colors used following the codes established in the two-volume work by H. Roosen-Runge, *Farbgebung und Technik frühmittelalterlicher Buchmalerei: Studien zu den Traktaten "Mappae Clavicula" und "Heraclius"*, Kunstwissenschaftliche Studien, vol. 38 (Munich and Berlin, 1967).

301 A well-known, ninth-century (824) vision does indeed show the Devil appearing in the guise of a priest to the person he is trying to tempt; cf. *Libellus de visione et obitu Wetini* (*PL* 105.771).

302 León, San Isidoro, crypt, mural painting. This probably goes back to one of the episodes of the life of St. Martin reported by Sulpicius Severus *Vie de saint Martin* 3.2 or 7.5 (ed. and trans. J. Fontaine, S.C., no. 133, Série des textes monastiques d'Occident, no. 22 [Paris, 1967]), vol. I, pp. 264-65, 306-9.

303 Gregory the Great *Dialogi* 2.4, pp. 87-88.

304 *Le Synaxaire éthiopien*, fasc. 1, *Mois de Sanê* (*PO* 1.580).

305 L. Oeconomos, *La vie religieuse dans l'Empire byzantin au temps des Comnènes et des Anges* (Paris, 1918), p. 83.

306 Paris, Bibliothèque nationale, MS. lat. 8846. *Psalter*, from Canterbury, about 1200, fol. 3v: miracles and parables of Christ (second register, first panel on left).

307 Matt. 8:28-34; Mark 5:1-20; Luke 8:26-39.

308 See H. Skrobucha, *Kosmas und Damian*, Iconographia ecclesiae orientalis (Recklinghausen, 1965), pp. 57, 69. The author gives two interesting but very late examples: a Polish icon of the fifteenth or sixteenth century shows Cosmas driving a dark demon out of a camel's body; another icon, this one from the seventeenth century, shows two dark demons beating a woman.

309 "Et exivit quidam contra me Aegyptius, foedus specie . . ." (Tertullian *Passio sanctarum martyrum Perpetuae et Felicitatis* [*PL* 3.40]).

310 Barcelona, Museo de Bellas Artes de Cataluña, 15833, painted panel, late twelfth century: seven scenes from the Passion, including the Scourging, the Carrying of the Cross, Christ on the Cross.

311 *L'art roman*, Exhibition catalogue, Barcelona and Santiago de Compostela, 1961 (Barcelona, 1963), p. 93, MAB 15833: the panel may have been "part of the decoration of a baldachin." M. Olivar, *Das Museum Katalanischer Kunst in Barcelona*, trans. I. Schauber, Galerien und Kunstdenkmäler Europas (Munich, 1964), p. 58, thinks the panel belonged to the top of an altarpiece.

312 We were unable to find a trace of this in, for example, C. Bernis Madrazo, *Indumentaria medieval española*, Artes y artistas (Madrid, 1956).

313 Without going into the studies already done by Spanish historians and by E. Lévi-Provençal, which tend to prove that importing blacks from western Africa was nothing unusual until the eleventh century, we must point out the increased movement of black labor northward and into Spain, at least under the Almoravids and perhaps a little earlier. Ibn 'Abdūn indicates clearly the distrust in which the Almoravids, and more especially the blacks, were held in Andalusia: "Ferrymen who provide passage across the river at various landing stages must be ordered not to take aboard Negroes or Berbers, who are known to be thieves and to enter private properties in the hot hours and eat fruit"; cf. E. Lévi-Provençal, *Séville musulmane au début du XIIe siècle: Le traité d'Ibn 'Abdun sur la vie urbaine et les corps de métiers*, Islam d'hier et d'aujourd'hui, vol. II (Paris, 1947), p. 127, par. 204; on the Almoravids, pp. 61-63, par. 56.

314 A text dated 1068, quoted by C. Verlinden, "L'esclavage dans le monde ibérique médiéval," *Anuario de historia del derecho español* 11 (1934): 397, n. 73, shows that blacks were not absent from the Christian North either: "Sciatur a cunctis quia pro defensione ecclesiae Agerensis feci ego offerenda a domino apostolico Nicholao quinque millia solidos aureos Valentiae: similiter a domino apostolico Alexandro tria millia solidos aureos Valentiae et decem captivos nigros." The church of Ager is situated 66 km. north of Lérida.

315 Laon, Bibliothèque municipale, MS. 550. *Evangelistary*, from Marbach-Schwarzenthann, late twelfth century, fol. 6r, historiated initial: the Scourging.

316 *Guibert de Nogent: Histoire de sa vie (1053-1124)* (ed. G. Bourgin, Collection de textes pour servir à l'étude et à l'enseignement de l'histoire, no. 40 [Paris, 1907]).

317 Ibid., p. 160. His owner calls the laborer a *Maurus* (p. 164).

318 Paris, Bibliothèque nationale, MS. lat. 8846. *Psalter*, Canterbury School, about 1200, fol. 2v: twelve scenes from the Old Testament; lower right: Beheading of John the Baptist.

319 Rouen, Cathedral of Notre-Dame, west façade, tympanum of the north portal, lowest register on the right: Beheading of John the Baptist.

320 Chartres, Cathedral of Notre-Dame, north portal, lower register of the tympanum over the right doorway, about 1220.

321 Auxerre, Cathedral of St-Etienne, west façade, high relief to the right of the archivolts of the south portal, late thirteenth-early fourteenth century.

322 Paris, Cathedral of Notre-Dame, portal of the south transept, lowest register of the tympanum, after 1257.

323 Paris, Bibliothèque nationale, MS. nouv. acq. fr. 16251. *Images de la vie du Christ et des saints*, from Hainaut (?), about 1280-90, fol. 37v. The same headsman appears, this time as a soldier with "Negroid" features at fols. 24v (Massacre of the Innocents), 86v (Martyrdom of St. Maurice and his Companions), and 101v (Martyrdom of St. Ursula and her Companions).

324 Ibid., fol. 76r. Again we find the headsman, blackened and wearing a tunic, at fols. 63v (Torture of St. John the Evangelist) and 99r (Martyrdom of St. Lucy).

325 This head comes from the outer cordon of archivolts of the north door of the west façade; it is now conserved in Rheims, Palais du Tau. We borrow these details from Madame A. Paillard, who describes the head in "Têtes sculptées du XIIIe siècle provenant de la cathédrale de Reims," *Bulletin monumental* 116 (1958): 36.

326 Troyes, Cathedral of SS. Peter and Paul, absidal chapel, stained-glass window illustrating the legend of St. Peter, about 1215: in the first lower medallion, Simon Magus tries to revive a dead man; in the second, St. Peter raises the dead man to life.

327 Manchester, John Rylands Library, MS. Lat. 24. *Sarum Missal*, Salisbury, thirteenth century, fol. 150v.

328 Angers, Cathedral of St-Maurice, stained-glass window in the north side of the nave, twelfth century: Life of St. Catherine; second lower medallion: executioner near Emperor Maxentius. Here we show photographs of the window before and after restoration.

329 It is thought-provoking (to say the least!) to find in Madame de Sévigné's correspondence further evidence of the lasting impression these stereotypes made on the European mind. Writing to her daughter, Madame de Grignan, she tells an intriguing story: "The Comte d'Estrées told us that on his travels in Guinea he found himself among Christians, and, going into a church, saw twenty Negro canons, entirely nude except for their square bonnets and amices on the left arm, singing the praises of God. He begs you to give thought to this sight, and to believe that they wore no surplice whatsoever, but were as one comes from one's mother's womb, and *black as devils*" (Madame de Sévigné, *Lettres de Madame de Sévigné avec les notes de tous les commentateurs* [Paris, 1843], vol. I, p. 204, no. 120).

II

THE BLACK AND HIS COLOR: FROM SYMBOLS TO REALITIES

1 Byzantium's attitude toward Islam varied over time and in different geographical areas. A hostile interpretation of Islamic thought throve at times side by side with close political and economic relations with Muslims; see A.-T. Khoury, *Les théologiens byzantins et l'Islam: Textes et auteurs (VIIIe-XIIIe s.)* (Louvain and Paris, 1969); A. Ducellier, *Le Miroir de l'Islam: Musulmans et Chrétiens d'Orient au Moyen Age (VIIe-XIe siècles)*, Collection Archives, no. 46 ([Paris], 1971). With Fatimid Egypt, at least, the Byzantines maintained important connections; cf. M. Hamidullah, "Nouveaux documents sur les rapports de l'Europe avec l'Orient musulman au moyen âge," *Arabica* 7, fasc. 3 (1960): 281-300; M. Canard, "Les sources arabes et l'histoire byzantine aux confins des Xe et XIe siècles," in *Byzance et les musulmans du Proche-Orient*, Variorum Reprints, no. CS18 (London, 1973), pp. 284-314. Further on we will see a trace of these connections in iconography. Yet, as a general rule, the hostile trend developed in Byzantium during the eleventh century, particularly within religious circles that were both very conservative and abysmally ignorant about the real nature of Islam. Erroneous translations from Arabic to Greek led the Byzantines to believe that the God of the Koran was an "eminently spherical God," or again a "God hammered out of metal." This latter translation gave rise to the legend adopted in Western Europe, according to which Muslims adored an idol, Tervagan, made of metal cleverly fabricated so that a human voice seemed to issue from it! The translators did just as badly with the origin of mankind: thus they claimed to have discovered that, according to the Muslims, man was "born of the leech," a view which understandably aroused considerable indignation. A direct reflection of these mistakes is found in the rite of abjuration imposed on Muslim converts by Nicetas Choniates *Ordo qui observatur super iis qui a Saracens ad nostram Christianorum puram veramque fidem se convertunt* (*PG* 140.131): "Anathematizo Moamedis doctrinam de fictura hominis, in qua dicit hominem ex humo, stilla, sanguisugis et materia manducata fictum esse. . . ." The Muslims concerned must have felt some surprise at being conjured to pronounce anathema on Muhammad's teaching that man was partially formed out of a leech.

2 On the place of blacks in twelfth-century Egypt, see a little known but interesting text: Usāmah ibn Munqidh, *Souvenirs historiques et récits de chasse par un émir syrien du douzième siècle: Autobiographie d'Ousâma ibn Mounkidh...*, trans. H. Derenbourg (Paris, 1895). Egypt, to which we have already devoted a good deal of attention, and which Byzantines knew much better than did Western Europeans, deserves to be carefully studied with respect to the history of its population and the clashes of influence which set Turks and blacks against each other. Many historians generally see these themes as merely anecdotal, but we think they ought to be reexamined with great care.

3 On this topic see U. Monneret de Villard, *Lo studio dell'Islām in Europa nel XII e nel XIII secolo*, Studi e testi, no. 110 (Vatican, 1944).

4 One must read the incredibly stupid things repeated over and over again by the authors of the songs of the Crusades in order to sound the depth of the anti-Muslim feeling that stirred European aristocratic circles, especially after the fall of Edessa. See particularly Richard the Pilgrim *La Chanson d'Antioche composée au XIIe siècle par Richard le Pèlerin renouvelée par Graindor de Douai au XIIIe siècle* (ed. P. Paris and trans. the Marquise of Sainte-Aulaire, Chronique des Croisades [Paris, 1862]), and A. Hatem, *Les poèmes épiques des Croisades: Genèse, historicité, localisation: Essai sur l'activité littéraire des Colonies franques de Syrie au Moyen Age* (Paris, 1932). The theologians got involved on the theoretical side, constructing a justification of the "just war" against the Muslims of which the songs are a direct reflection; cf. Richard the Pilgrim *La Chanson d'Antioche*, p. 6:

> Notre-Seigneur nous demande d'aller à Jérusalem
> Pour occire les païens et détruire ce peuple sans foi
> Qui ne veut pas croire en Dieu ni honorer ses actions,
> Ni suivre ses commandements. Mahomet, Tervagan
> Doivent être écrasés par nous. Nous devons fondre leurs images
> Et en offrir à Dieu la matière;

On the theology of war, cf. C. Erdmann, *Die Entstehung des Kreuzzugsgedankens*, Forschungen zur Kirchen- und Geistesgeschichte, vol. 6 (Stuttgart, 1935), and A. Noth, *Heiliger Krieg und heiliger Kampf in Islam und Christentum: Beiträge zur Vorgeschichte und Geschichte der Kreuzzüge*, Bonner historische Forschungen, vol. 28 (Bonn, 1966).

5 In the twelfth century, the Ethiopians at Vézelay and Souvigny are abstract. The way of looking at blacks changed in the thirteenth century.

6 Paris, Bibliothèque nationale, MS. arabe 5847. Al-Harīrī, *Makāmāt*, paintings by Yaḥyā al-Wāsīti, year 634 of the Hegira (1236/37), fol. 105r: slave market.

7 Paris, Bibliothèque nationale, MS. arabe 6094. Al-Harīrī, *Makāmāt*, dated 619 of the Hegira (1222/23), fol. 16r: Abū Sa'id a guest at supper with a group of savants.

8 Paris, Bibliothèque nationale, MS. arabe 5847, fol. 119v: ship crossing the Persian Gulf.

9 On these questions, see B. Lewis, *Race and Color in Islam* (New York, Evanston, San Francisco, London, Harper Torchbooks, 1971).

10 All historians note the presence of blacks in the Almoravid armies in Spain. A. Huici-Miranda, "Contribución al estudio de la dinastia almorávide: El gobierno de Tašfin Ben 'Alī Ben Yūsuf en el-Andalus," in *Etudes d'orientalisme dédiées à la mémoire de Lévi-Provençal* (Paris, 1962), vol. II, p. 608, speaks of a levy at Fez, in 1125-26, of three hundred young blacks to reinforce the Almoravid army in Spain. See also J. Devisse, "Routes de commerce et échanges en Afrique occidentale en relation avec la Méditerranée: Un essai sur le commerce africain médiéval du XIe au XVIe siècle," *RHES* 50, no. 3 (1972): 396-97.

11 Barcelona, Museo de Bellas Artes de Cataluña, 71447: mural painting, thirteenth century, from Barcelona, Palacio Aguilar.

12 We have already seen (*supra*, pp. 75-76) that Christian Spain, especially in the northern sector which was strongly influenced by the Carolingian world, had probably adopted iconographic themes and treatments from the Carolingian and post-Carolingian Christian Occident.

13 Escorial, Real Monasterio, Biblioteca, Cod. T. I, 6. *Chessbook* of Alfonso the Wise, dated 1283; cf. A. Steiger, *Alfonso el Sabio, Libros de Acedrex, dados e tablas: Das Schachzabelbuch König Alfons des Weisen*, Romanica Helvetica, vol. 10 (Geneva and Zurich, 1941), and C. Nordenfalk, "En medeltida schackbok," in P. Grate, ed., *Spanska Mästare: En konstbok från Nationalmuseum*, Årsbok för Svenska statens konstsamlingar, no. 8 (Stockholm, 1960), pp. 21-36.

14 The publication of this group of illustrations in A. Steiger's book and the republication of the essential ones, accompanied by color transparencies, in C. Nordenfalk's article, make it possible to gauge the realistic accuracy of detail brought to the work by the painter or painters in the décor, the chess games, the male and female costume, and the personages, whether Moor or Christian, prince or pauper. We may note especially the use in several places of the flowered *kaffiyeh* of the thirteenth century. At fol. 64r a Christian knight and a Muslim play chess in a tent: on the tent is a large inscription in Arabic characters which, translated, reads approximately, "Praise and thanks to God." At fol. 22r two noble Moors—dark-complexioned, however—are at their game; one of them rests his elbow on a cushion inscribed "Fas" (*Fez* in Arabic). A black servingwom-

an brings food and drink; a musician, also black, in a yellow burnous, is seated on a taboret and plucks a fourteen-stringed harp. There are other examples at fols. 10^{r}, 14^{r}, 17^{v}, 41^{v}, and 45^{v}. It would be extremely interesting to compare the paintings in this manuscript both with those in *Las Cántigas de Santa Maria* which we shall presently discuss, and with those in the *Makāmāt* of al-Harīrī, these latter being of Muslim execution. At fol. 2^{v} of the Escorial manuscript (Cod. T. I, 6) the picture of an Indian prince receiving three sages is very close to comparable scenes in the illustrated versions of the *Makāmāt.*

15 Escorial, Real Monasterio, Biblioteca, Cod. T. I, 6, fol. 22^{r}.

16 Ibid., fol. 55^{r}.

17 This cloth headband, which eventually became the *tortil*, seems to us to have been a simple sweatband to keep perspiration out of the eyes in moments of heavy physical exertion. Yet from the fourteenth century on it was frequently inseparable from the image of the black, becoming, as it were, one of his heraldic attributes. It would be interesting to make an inventory of the blacks so represented by painters before the heraldic stereotypes became fixed, and particularly to see whether or not royal personages like the Wise Man-King were portrayed wearing the *tortil.*

18 *Las Cántigas de Santa Maria.* Much has been published about this text and the paintings which decorate some of the manuscripts. Concerning the text, see L.A. de Cueto, *Estudio histórico, crítico y filológico sobre las Cantigas del Rey Don Alfonso el Sabio*, 2d ed. (Madrid, 1897). It is very interesting to compare the contents of the *Cántigas* of Alfonso X the Wise with the contents of Gautier de Coincy *Les Miracles de la Sainte Vierge* (ed. A.-E. Poquet [Paris, 1857]). Of course the allusions to black Moors, which are so important in the *Cántigas*, are completely absent in the *Miracles*; yet Gautier de Coincy's text would seem to be of the same period as Alfonso's, or a little later.

There are four manuscripts of *Las Cántigas de Santa Maria*: two in Escorial, Real Monasterio, Biblioteca; one in Madrid, Biblioteca nacional, and one in Florence, Biblioteca Nazionale Centrale. The earliest in date is the one in Madrid, which was executed in Toledo about 1255; cf. L.A. de Cueto, ed., *Cantigas de Santa María de Don Alfonso el Sabio*, 2 vols. (Madrid, 1889). The manuscript in Florence, Biblioteca Nazionale Centrale, MS. BR 20, II.I. 213, dates from the second half of the thirteenth century. It has been studied by N. Aita, *O Codice Florentino das "Cantigas" do Rey Alfonso o Sabio* (Rio de Janeiro, 1922); see also *Mostra storica nazionale della miniatura*, Exhibition catalogue, Rome, Palazzo di Venezia, 1953 (Florence, 1953), pp. 293-94, no. 468. One of the manuscripts in Escorial, Real Monasterio, Biblioteca (Cod. B. I, 2) has musical notations. The other (Cod. T. I, 1), which we shall examine here, has been the object of a meticulous study by J. Guerrero Lovillo, *Las Cántigas: Estudio arqueológico de sus miniaturas* (Madrid, 1949). We shall use this edition for reference.

19 Guerrero Lovillo, *Las Cántigas*, pp. 33 ff.

20 Ibid., pp. 47-265.

21 Ibid., pls. 13, 14, 31, 39, 44, 46, 51, 53, 82, 84, 127, 132, and 139. In some instances the demons are completely white.

22 Ibid., *Cantiga* LXXXII, pl. 91, image 2: a black devil is disturbing a monk, who is already surprised by pigs coming into the place where he is praying; image 3: the devil speaks to the pigs while the monk prays to the Virgin. The texts for these two images read:

Como viu entrar pela porta un diaboo grande negro . . . .

Como aquele demo negro disse a aqueles porcos . . . .

23 Ibid., *Cantiga* XCIX, pl. 110, image 4: two blacks appear among the Muslims who occupy a Christian town; image 6: the Muslims leave the town, and the blacks follow on foot at the rear of the column on either side of a pack animal; however, one black man is shown on horseback and wearing a turban, and there is no discrimination between him and the white Moors with him.

24 Ibid., *Cantiga* XLVI, pl. 52, image 1; perhaps *Cantiga* LXIII, pl. 70, image 4; *Cantiga* CLXV, pl. 180, image 1. An exception to this rule (scarcely discernible in the photographs) is *Cantiga* CLXIX, pl. 185, image 6: blacks taking part with Muslims in the siege of a church; one black seems to be wearing a white cloth veil closely resembling the one we found in the Barcelona paintings.

25 They are present in the big crowd scenes, often in the first images of a series, but are out of the picture when "the action begins."

26 Guerrero Lovillo, *Las Cántigas*, *Cantiga* XCV, pl. 105, image 4.

27 Here again both profile and hair are characteristic.

28 Guerrero Lovillo, *Las Cántigas*, *Cantiga* XCV, pl. 105, images 5 and 6, and pl. 106, image 4.

29 Ibid., p. 417 and pl. 202.

30 On sexual problems and mixed marriages in Spain, see Lewis, *Race and Color in Islam*, pp. 92-93.

31 G. López de Tovar, *Las siete partidas del Rey Don Alfonso el Sabio, cotejadas con varios códices antiguos por la Real Academia de la Historia*, new ed. (Paris, 1846), vol. II, p. 394 (Part 7, Title 25, Law 10).

32 Ibid., p. 391 (Part 7, Title 25, Law 1): "*Sarracenus* en latin tanto quiere decir en romance como moro . . . ."

33 Guerrero Lovillo, *Las Cántigas*, *Cantiga* CXCII, pl. 210, images 1-6.

34 To have done with the theme of conversion, we note that in other instances this collection shows scenes of the conversion of white Moors whose social status is clearly well above that of our black.

35 F. de Medeiros, "Judaïsme, Islam et Gentilité dans l'œuvre de Raymond Lulle" (Ph. D. diss., University of Munich, 1976).

36 The laws of Alfonso the Wise, to which we have referred (*supra*, nn. 31-32), provided that such conversions could be obtained only by persuasion, not by force or by purchase.

37 Aachen, Dr. Peter and Irene Ludwig Collection. *Fueros del Reino de Aragon*. . ., after a manuscript called *Vidal Mayor*, about 1260-80, from Barcelona (?), fol. 242^{v}: *De Judeis et Sarracenis baptizandis*; fol. 244^{r}: *De los moros fuidiços*. Cf. *Weltkunst aus Privatbesitz*, Exhibition catalogue, Cologne, Kunsthalle, 18 May-4 August 1968 (Cologne, 1968), D 62.

38 The theme of the baptism of the black Moor traveled through Western Europe along paths which we have not been able to study, but which ought to be clarified.

39 Escorial, Real Monasterio, Biblioteca, Cod. H. I. 15. *Lapidario* of King Alfonso X the Wise, thirteenth century. This manuscript has been published only once: *Lapidario del Rey D. Alfonso X*, ed. J. Fernandez Montaña (Madrid, 1881). This edition includes excellent photographic reproductions, and the text is given in its entirety.

40 Alfonso the Wise *Setenario* Laws 32, 54 (ed. K.H. Vanderford, Facultad de filosofía y letras de la Universidad de Buenos Aires [Buenos Aires, 1945]), pp. 63, 90.

41 This correlation is not surprising. When Alfonso X was doing his best to learn all he could in the areas of knowledge that interested him, the explicit linking of the color black to heathenism had been a commonplace in imperial circles for a century, as we shall soon see. We must also remember that in ancient mythology Saturn, father of Jupiter, was one of the oldest gods, being born of the marriage of Heaven and Earth.

42 The manuscript (Escorial, Real Monasterio, Biblioteca, Cod. H. I. 15) contains many original images that are worthy of attention: fols. 22^{v}, 32^{r}, and 43^{r} (boats); fol. 94^{r} (astronomical gauge with an astrolabe); fol. 17^{r} (Arab wearing a turban). We note that at fol. 68^{r} there is a superbly decorated initial showing a man in profile wearing a very elaborate headdress: this theme must have influenced the heraldists.

43 Ibid., fol. 91^{v} and especially fol. 95^{v}, where an elephant whose head is that of a black man is depicted in a circle. The stone in question is called *Zebech.*

44 Ibid., fols. 94^{v}, 97^{v}.

45 Ibid., fol. 63^{r}: two white men present a black stone.

46 See the recent publication by D. METLITZKI, *The Matter of Araby in Medieval England* (New Haven and London, 1977).

47 We here express our gratitude to Père Julien Leroy, whose authority in this field is unquestionable, and who has furnished us precious information on the manuscripts we have studied and has called our attention to others.

48 This is the opinion of Père J. Leroy who to date in the course of his research has examined 3,500 Greek manuscripts, most of them dating from before the thirteenth century.

49 Vatican, Biblioteca Apostolica Vaticana, MS. Vat. gr. 1613: called the *Menologion of Basil II*, from Constantinople, between 976 and 1025.

50 It is interesting to compare this iconography of the Blemmyes, here represented as blacks, with the opinion stated by J. Desanges in his review of the book by F. M. SNOWDEN, JR., *Blacks in Antiquity: Ethiopians in the Greco-Roman Experience* (Cambridge, Mass., 1970), to the effect that the ancient iconography of the Blemmyes, which has now been identified, made them out as "non-black"; see J. DESANGES, "L'antiquité gréco-romaine et l'homme noir," *Revue des études latines* 48 (1970):89.

51 Vatican, Biblioteca Apostolica Vaticana, MS. Vat. gr. 1613, p. 315 (painting by Michael of Blachernae): two black-skinned executioners, wearing turbans, are putting eight Fathers to death; p. 316 (painting by Pantoleon): three of the headsmen are black; p. 317: the thirty Fathers of Raïthu in the Sinai killed by Blemmyes; among the latter are three blacks. See *Menologium Basilianum* 2.99-104 (*PG* 117.253-56).

52 Vatican, Biblioteca Apostolica Vaticana, MS. Vat. gr. 1613, p. 107 (painting by Nestor): St. Philip converting the eunuch of Queen Candace.

53 Paris, Bibliothèque nationale, MS. grec 64. *Tetraevangelion*, early eleventh century, from Greece, fol. 4^{v}: a black, holding a whip, drives a dromedary toward a fountain at which an elephant is drinking; the man's body is very realistically treated, and the prognathism is pronounced; at fol. 5^{r}, another black waters a saddled horse and two oxen; see A. GRABAR, *La peinture byzantine*, Les grands siècles de la peinture (Geneva, 1953), p. 176. A. Grabar gives a list of comparable examples (idem, "L'art profane de la Russie pré-mongole et le 'Dit d'Igor'," in *L'art de la fin de l'Antiquité et du Moyen Age* [Paris, 1968], vol. I, p. 314); he also points out (idem, "Une pyxide en ivoire à Dumbarton Oaks," ibid., pp. 246-47) the presence of both black and white acrobats in the decorated initials found in twelfth-century manuscripts of Gregory of Nazianzus's sermons. In another twelfth-century Greek manuscript (Paris, Bibliothèque nationale, MS. grec 550), at fol. 94^{v}, a black, indifferent to the solemn last moments of St. Basil, wards off the attacks of a bear in the shade of a stylized palm tree; at fol. 251^{r} another black sits on a swing propelled by two playmates; the top of the folio is decorated with leopards. A similar theme is found at fol. 279^{r}. In this same manuscript a black boy, holding a gold ring, plays with a fennec (fol. 6^{r}), another holds a feather (fol. 9^{v}), a third carries on his head a cushion on which an animal is lying (fol. 99^{v}), and still another has a dog and a bird with him (fol. 100^{r}).

54 Venice, Biblioteca Nazionale Marciana, MS. Marc. gr. 479 (881), fols. 41^{r}, 53^{v}. Père J. Leroy brought this manuscript to our attention.

55 Cf. W. LAMEERE, "Apamée de Syrie et les Cynégétiques du Pseudo-Oppien dans la miniature byzantine," *Bulletin de l'Institut historique belge de Rome* 19 (1938):125-47. There are two copies after the Venice Oppian in Paris, Bibliothèque nationale: MS. grec 2736 (late fifteenth or early sixteenth century) and MS. grec 2737 (done in 1554); cf. *Byzance et la France médiévale: Manuscrits à peintures du IIe au XVIe siècle*, Exhibition catalogue, Paris, Bibliothèque nationale, 1958 (Paris, 1958), pp. 51-52, nos. 89, 95.

56 Vatican, Biblioteca Apostolica Vaticana, MS. Vat. gr. 747, *Octateuch*, eleventh century: very meticulously executed as a whole, but poorly preserved in some parts; MS. Vat. gr. 746: *Octateuch*, twelfth century: the style of the paintings is different from the preceding manuscript, and the parchment is of mediocre quality. We no longer have a Greek Octateuch from Smyrna of the late twelfth or early thirteenth century, which was destroyed by fire in 1922, and which would have allowed fruitful comparisons in an area of research where the representations are far from being easy to interpret. On the other hand, a twelfth-century Octateuch in Istanbul, Topkapi Saray Museum, MS. Topkapi 8, bears a sure resemblance to MS. Vat. gr. 746 in the type of ruling adopted and in the subjects illustrated—this is the opinion of Père J. Leroy, who unfortunately was able to consult only the first tome. Père Leroy proposes the hypothesis that these two manuscripts may have been produced in the same scriptorium.

57 MS. Vat. gr. 746, fol. 60^{v}: posterity of the sons of Noah—five groups of three men, one group composed of blacks. MS. Topkapi 8, fol. 64^{v}: same theme—a group of three blacks wearing turbans. MSS. Vat. gr. 746, fol. 61^{v}, Vat. gr. 747, fol. 33^{v}, Topkapi 8, fol. 65^{v}: destruction of the Tower of Babel and scattering of the nations. In the first manuscript, there is a black man among the "dispersed"; in the second, blacks figure in three groups; in MS. Topkapi 8, a black on the right and another on the left, both in the lower register.

58 To illustrate the same theme—Joseph distributing grain to the Egyptians—MS. Vat. gr. 746, fol. 134^{v}, represents the Egyptians as contemporary Muslims, copper-skinned and turbaned, while MS. Vat. gr. 747, fol. 62^{r}, shows them as blacks.

59 MS. Vat. gr. 746, fol. 186^{r}: departure from Egypt. Still more characteristically, in the illustration of the crossing of the Red Sea, this black is a giant in MS. Vat. gr. 747, fol. 89^{v}; he is of more normal size in the same scene in MS. Vat. gr. 746, fol. 192^{v}.

60 MS. Vat. gr. 746, fol. 190^{r}: flight of the Egyptians in the desert; MS. Vat. gr. 747, fol. 88^{v}: translation of Joseph's body.

61 MS. Vat. gr. 747, fol. 3^{v}: Ptolemy watching the preparation of the gifts—one of the workmen is black; fol. 6^{v}: Ptolemy presides at a banquet—one of the servers is black; fol. 35^{r}, top of page: Sarah is brought to Pharaoh; bottom of page: Pharaoh gives Sarah back to Abraham—two black servants in each scene; fol. 41^{r}: a black man conducts Sarah to Abimelech; fol. 47^{v}: two scenes concerning Abimelech, Isaac, and Rebecca with two black servants; fols. 61^{r} and 61^{v}: Pharaoh accompanied by two black slaves. MS. Vat. gr. 746 represents two black servitors *only once* (fol. 65^{r}).

62 MS. Vat. gr. 747, fol. 88^{r}, upper part: Pharaoh and his army.

63 Ibid., fol. 82^{r}: the sixth plague on Egypt; an Egyptian, covered with sores, is accompanied by two black servingmen.

64 MS. Vat. gr. 747, fols. 80^{r} and 82^{v}: one of the Pharaoh's magicians, before whom Aaron and Moses are summoned, is black.

65 MSS. Vat. gr. 746, fol. 126^{r} and Vat. gr. 747, fol. 62^{r}: Joseph sells grain to the Egyptians; in the first case a few Egyptians, in the second all of them, are black. Black also, some of them at least, or one or two of them, are the Egyptians in the following scenes: MS. Vat. gr. 746, fol. 150^{r}: the burial of Jacob; fol. 179^{r}: "Concerning the gold and silver vessels taken from the Egyptians" (the text describing the scene); MS. Vat. gr. 747, fol. 65^{v}: Joseph giving audience to three black Egyptians; fol. 79^{v}: "The Egyptians beat the Israelites on account of the bricks."

66 MS. Vat. gr. 746, fol. 166^{v}: Moses and Aaron before Pharaoh, whose figure still shows some traces of black paint. MS. Vat. gr. 747, fol. 35^{r}: Pharaoh is black.

67 MS. Vat. gr. 747, fol. 58^{v}.

68 Ibid., fol. 59^{v}. The images themselves strongly suggest comparison with the *Ashburnham Pentateuch* (Paris, Bibliothèque nationale, MS. nouv. acq. lat. 2334). At least one scene in an unpublished cycle of illustrations should be considered in connection with this iconographic series: Chillicothe, Ohio, Collection of Col. David McC. McKell (Phillips Catalogue, MS. 7706), fol. 11^{v}; cf. J. and O. Pächt, "An Unknown Cycle of Illustrations of the Life of Joseph," *CahArch* 7 (1954): 35-49, esp. p. 39, no. 8 and pl. XIII, 1.

69 MS. Vat. gr. 747, fol. 6^{v}: Ptolemy presides at a banquet; MS. Vat. gr. 746, fol. 134^{v}: Joseph distributes the grain; fol. 149^{r}: "The Egyptians mourn Jacob." The Egyptians are not black but dark-skinned, and wear turbans.

70 This raises many important questions. Blacks certainly played a role in the entourage of the Fatimids in the eleventh and twelfth centuries, and contacts between Byzantines and Fatimids were frequent. One might therefore attribute the blacks' place in illustrations of these centuries to a combination of circumstances. But the *Ashburnham Pentateuch* does not support so easy a solution of the question. It is, therefore, clear that in this period some of the Egyptian population were black of color and distinguished by their mode of dress from the rest of the Egyptians. Were they Nilotics who had come north, a surviving remnant of an ancient black population, as the extreme theses of Sheikh Anta Diop would have it? Were they blacks coming from lands farther to the south? It would be unreasonable, on the basis of a handful of images, to give a cut-and-dried answer. At least the question is clearly defined: for the Byzantines of the eleventh century, as for the painters of the *Ashburnham Pentateuch* four to six centuries earlier, some Egyptians were black. However, it never happens that all of them, or anywhere near all, are represented with "Negroid" features or characteristic attire.

71 Benjamin of Tudela, *Voyages... en Europe, en Asie et en Afrique . . .*, trans. J.-P. Baratier (Amsterdam, 1734), vol. I, p. 47, says that in the Hippodrome at Constantinople, "Every year the birthday of Jisho [Jesus] the Nazarene is celebrated with public rejoicings. On these occasions you may there see representations of all the nations who inhabit the different parts of the world. . . . All this is carried on in the presence of the king and the queen." It would be important to study the ceremonial of this annual assembly; some of the explanations we are looking for regarding the Byzantines' attitude toward all foreigners, blacks among them, would probably be discovered.

72 Paris, Bibliothèque nationale, MS. grec 510. Gregory of Nazianzus, *Homilies*, ninth century, from Constantinople, fol. 426^{v}.

73 Paris, Bibliothèque nationale, MS. grec 74. *Tetraevangelion*, mid-eleventh century, from Constantinople, fols. 20^{r}, 20^{v}; cf. *Byzance et la France médiévale*, pp. 13-14, no. 21.

74 London, British Library, MS. Add. 19352. *Psalter*, 1066, from Constantinople, Studion Monastery, fols. 19^{v}-20^{r}: preaching of the Apostles.

75 M. Garidis, "La représentation des 'nations' dans la peinture post-Byzantine," *Byzantion* 39 (1969): 86-103. The author was struck, as we are, by the impartiality of the paintings he studied. He writes (p. 89): "All these representations of the people . . . reflect the Byzantines' knowledge about the other peoples of the world and imply no critical intention whatever. The peoples are presented as equals. What differentiates them is their ethnic characteristics, noted without partiality." This interesting article furnishes some very useful complements to our findings on Byzantium. See also A. Grabar, "L'art religieux et l'empire byzantin à l'époque des Macédoniens," in *L'art de la fin de l'Antiquité*, vol. I, pp. 151-68; idem, "Le schéma iconographique de la Pentecôte," in ibid., pp. 615-27.

76 Acts 2:1-13. Are we to think that the mention of the Egyptians led to the introduction of black figures?

77 Hosios Lucas in Phocis (eleventh century), mosaic of Pentecost in the dome: there is a black among the representatives of the nations; cf. E. Diez and O. Demus, *Byzantine Mosaics in Greece: Hosios Lucas and Daphni* (Cambridge, Mass., 1931), pp. 72-73 and pl. XV and fig. 7.

78 Kastoria, Mavriotissa Monastery, Church of the Virgin: in the illustration of Pentecost (thirteenth century), a black wearing a loincloth; cf. E. Stikas, "Works of Anastylosis: Monuments of the Middle Ages in Greece," (in Greek) in *Actes du IXe Congrès international des études byzantines*, Salonica, 12-19 April 1953, Editions de la Société d'études macédoniennes, no. 7 (Athens, 1955), vol. I, pp. 450-58 and pl. 129. Ohrid, Church of St. Clement (1295): group of African blacks; cf. G. Millet, *La peinture du moyen-âge en Yougoslavie (Serbie, Macédoine et Monténégro)*, fasc. 3, ed. A. Frolow (Paris, 1962), pl. 11, 1.

79 G. Subotić, *L'église Saint-Démétrios à la Patriarchie de Peć*, L'ancien art yougoslave (Belgrade, 1964), pl. 36.

80 Paris, Bibliothèque nationale, MS. grec 550, fol. 37^{r}: in the painting of Pentecost the central figures are whites sumptuously attired.

81 Paris, Bibliothèque nationale, MS. Coislin 239. Gregory of Nazianzus, *Homilies*, twelfth century, from Constantinople, fol. 28^{r}. There may also be blacks in the badly damaged painting of Pentecost in Paris, Bibliothèque nationale, MS. suppl. grec 27, *Evangelistary*, twelfth century, from Constantinople, fol. 38^{r}. Two blacks are represented, again in the Pentecost scene, in a manuscript in Mount Athos, Monastery of Dionysiou, Cod. 587(m), *Gospel Lectionary*, dated 1059, fol. 36^{v}; cf. S.M. Pelekanidis, P.C. Christou, C. Tsioumis, and S.N. Kadas, *The Treasures of Mount Athos: Illuminated Manuscripts*, vol. I, *The Protaton and the Monasteries of Dionysiou, Koutloumousiou, Xeropotamou and Gregoriou*, trans. P. Sherrard (Athens, 1974), p. 174, pl. 213 and p. 438.

82 Venice, Basilica of St. Mark, high altar, Pala d'Oro, twelfth century: second panel from the right of the upper register and fourth panel from the right of the lower register; see W.F. Volbach, A. Pertusi, B. Bischoff, et al., *La Pala d'Oro*, Il Tesoro di San Marco, no. 1 (Florence, 1965), p. 43, no. 84 and col. pl. XLVII; p. 31, no. 62 and col. pl. XXXIII.

83 J. Leroy, *Les manuscrits syriaques à peintures conservés dans les bibliothèques d'Europe et d'Orient: Contribution à l'étude de l'iconographie des églises de langue syriaque*, 2 vols., Institut français d'archéologie de Beyrouth: Bibliothèque archéologique et historique, vol. 77 (Paris, 1964), vol. I, p. 377, no. 17; vol. II, pl. 134, 2. The manuscript is housed in a Syrian monastery (Dayr al-Zaʿfarān).

84 Ps. 104 (105): 28-36, verses describing the plagues of Egypt. Paris, Bibliothèque nationale, MS. grec 20, *Psalter*, tenth century, fol. 18^{r}; cf. H. Omont, *Miniatures des plus anciens manuscrits grecs de la Bibliothèque nationale, du VIe au XIVe siècle*, 2d ed. (Paris, 1929), pl. LXXVI.

85 Paris, Bibliothèque nationale, MS. grec 74, fols. 7^{r}, 65^{r}; MS. grec 510, fol. 165^{r}; cf. Omont, *Miniatures des plus anciens manuscrits grecs*, pl. XXXV.

86 Paris, Bibliothèque nationale, MS. grec 923. John of Damascus, *Sacra Parallela*, fol. 123^{r}.

87 Paris, Bibliothèque nationale, MS. grec 54: *Tetraevangelion*, fols. 32^{v}, 125^{v}; MS. grec 74, fols. 16^{r}, 69^{v}, 89^{r}, 119^{r}, 125^{r}; MS. grec 923, fols. 211^{v}-212^{r}; MS. grec 1128: *Life of Barlaam and Joasaph*, fourteenth century, fol. 36^{v}; MS. suppl. grec 27, fol. 68^{r}.

88 Paris, Bibliothèque nationale, MS. grec 74, fols. 51^{v}, 93^{v}.

89 Ibid., fol. 131^{r}. We find these winged black forms in another Greek manuscript in Paris, Bibliothèque nationale, MS. grec 543: Gregory of Nazianzus, *Homilies*, twelfth century, fol. 87^{v}, where the painter has illustrated the temptation of St. Justina by Cyprian.

90 Paris, Bibliothèque nationale, MS. grec 1208. James of Kokkinobaphos, *Homily*, fourteenth century, fol. 123^{v}: winged black devils figure in the illustration of the preservation of the Virgin from all contact with evil; MS. grec 1128, fols. 151^{r}, 151^{v}, 154^{v}, 158^{r}, 176^{r}; MS. grec 510, fol. 374^{v}: apostasy of Julian the Apostate.

91 The importance of Bari from the eleventh century onward, and probably for a long time before that, cannot be overemphasized. See, e.g., M. LOMBARD, *Espaces et réseaux du haut moyen âge*, Ecole Pratique des Hautes Etudes, Sorbonne, Sixième section: Sciences économiques et sociales, Le savoir historique, no. 2 (Paris and The Hague, 1972), pp. 95-106 ("La marine adriatique dans le cadre du haut moyen âge, VIIe-XIe siècles"), esp. p. 102.

92 I owe the following information to the kindness of three young researchers at the Université de Paris VIII, Mlle A. Courtaut and MM. H. Bercher and J. Mouton. They have ascertained that there were a certain number of blacks in Sicily in the twelfth and thirteenth centuries. The presence of twenty-three black slaves at Catania in 1145 is noted; cf. S. CUSA, ed., *I diplomi greci ed arabi di Sicilia, pubblicati nel testo originale, tradotti ed illustrati*, vol. I (Palermo, 1868-82), pp. 563-85. At Palermo a black slave was converted to Christianity in 1243 (idem, *I diplomi greci ed arabi di Sicilia*, vol. I, p. 96, Act no. 91). In the same city there was a gate called *Bab es Soudan* ("Gate of the Blacks"); cf. V. DI GIOVANNI, *La topografia antica di Palermo dal secolo X al XV*, vol. I (Palermo, 1889), p. 46. The study of the Abbey of Monreale undertaken by these three young scholars brings out the presence, in the twelfth century, of some thirty proper names that could designate blacks (CUSA, *I diplomi greci ed arabi di Sicilia*, vol. I, pp. 563-85)—as is highly probable for at least three quarters of them. These still fragmentary findings clearly show that the black was not unknown in Sicily, nor probably in southern Italy. In *every* case the blacks were slaves.

93 Berne, Burgerbibliothek, Cod. 120. Peter of Eboli, *Liber ad honorem Augusti*, also called *De rebus siculis carmen*, twelfth century. This is the only manuscript of the work, the text of which has been published in the following edition: PETER OF EBOLI *De rebus siculis carmen* (ed. E. ROTA, Rerum italicarum scriptores: Raccolta degli storici italiani dal cinquecento al millecinquecento, vol. 31, pt. 1, rev., enl., and corr. ed. [Città di Castello, 1904]).

94 In every scene in which they appear, the adversaries are mean, caricatured types. Peter of Eboli, moreover, was a practiced hand at this sort of thing: in another text, dealing with the baths at Pozzuoli, he gives ironic medical advice to the popes—his and the empire's adversaries—who suffer from constipation! In the *De rebus siculis carmen* the images follow closely the author's intentions and the indications in the text. The paintings in this manuscript (Berne, Burgerbibliothek, Cod. 120), are certainly the work of several hands. Some very realistic ones give a true picture of life in Palermo; see, e.g., fols. 3^{r} and 7^{r} (where we see that at the Palermo chancellery the texts were written in three languages—Latin, Greek, and Arabic), and fol. 8^{r} (where Tancred, Henry VI's rival and Matthew's candidate, is crowned in the midst of a group of turbaned mountebanks). On the other hand, all the iconography related to Henry VI is majestic and favorable.

95 The manuscript (Berne, Burgerbibliothek, Cod. 120) constantly exalts the Hohenstaufens: on fol. 129^{r}, Richard the Lion-Hearted, prisoner of Henry VI, kneels at his captor's feet. Henry VI, son of Frederick Barbarossa, had a hard time carrying out the imperial seizure of Sicily, due to the strenuous opposition of people at the Norman court in Palermo.

96 Ibid., fols. 6^{r} and 7^{r}.

97 Ibid., fol. 33^{r}: under the title *Scelera bigami* ("crimes of the bigamist"), all sorts of accusations are enumerated, including sodomy and fidelity to Lucifer.

98 Ibid., fol. 127^{r}.

99 All the paintings in this manuscript would repay close study, teeming as they are with interesting details and symbols; cf. H. GEORGEN, *Studien zu den Bildquellen und zum Erzählstil eines illustrierten Lobgedicht des Peter von Eboli* (Vienna, 1975). At fol. 123^{r} of the manuscript (Berne, Burgerbibliothek, Cod. 120), the illustration proves that a version of the *Roman d'Alexandre* dating from the end of the Roman Empire existed in southern Italy. Later on we shall see the significance of this.

100 ORIBASIUS *Oribasius latinus*, ed. H. MØRLAND, Symbolae Osloenses, supp. fasc. 10 (Oslo, 1940), pt. I; ALEXANDER OF TRALLES *De arte medica libri XII* (ed. A. VON HALLER [Lausanne, 1772]); idem *Practica* (Lyons, 1504). These authors say nothing about such a treatment, although they discuss gout several times. H. E. SIGERIST, *Studien und Texte zur frühmittelalterlichen Rezeptliteratur*, Studien zur Geschichte der Medizin, no. 13 (Leipzig, 1923), gives no antidote for podagra similar to the treatment depicted in this picture, nor do the manuscripts catalogued by E. WICKERSHEIMER, *Les manuscrits latins de médecine du haut moyen âge dans les bibliothèques de France*, Documents, études et répertoires publiés par l'Institut de Recherche et d'Histoire des Textes, no. 11 (Paris, 1966).

101 The itinerary of the ninth-century Frankish monk Bernard mentions this passage through Bari, after the pilgrimage to Monte Gargano, but he embarked at Taranto and sailed in Muslim ships. See BERNARDUS MONACHUS *Itinerarium* 3 in T. TOBLER, ed., *Descriptiones Terrae Sanctae ex saeculo VIII. IX. XII. et XV.* (Leipzig, 1874), p. 86.

102 V. MASELLIS, *Storia di Bari dalle origini al giorni nostri* (Trani, 1960), p. 88, notes that mariners contracted to transport wheat destined for Antioch, where there were some sixty people from Bari and others from Trieste, Taranto, Monopoli, and other places.

103 L. RÉAU, *Iconographie de l'art chrétien*, vol. III, *Iconographie des saints*, pt. 2 (Paris, 1958), pp. 976 ff. Réau's comments show the rapid elaboration of the legends and the way the cult spread in Europe. Nicholas was supposed to have endured a long captivity, after which he participated in the Council of Nicaea, and died in 342. Most of the miracles attributed to him had to do with the sea, and the sailors of Bari wanted to assure for themselves the care of this powerful protector. On the Continent itself, and particulary in eastern France, there was more interest, based on the Eastern legends, in a saint's qualifications as healer of the body's ills. Nicholas was credited with bringing back to life three children who had been hacked to death by a bloody butcher. Ordericus Vitalis, a Norman, has left us an account of the theft of the relics, embellished with marvels: he followed the story as told by a deacon of Bari; cf. ORDERICUS VITALIS *Historia ecclesiastica* 7.9 (*PL* 188.534 ff.).

104 MASELLIS, *Storia di Bari*, pp. 88 ff. Guillaume Pantoul, a Norman, brought a tooth of St. Nicholas from Bari into France in 1102, thus introducing the cult; cf. E. BERTAUX, *L'art dans l'Italie méridionale* (Paris, 1904), vol. I, *De la fin de l'Empire Romain à la Conquête de Charles d'Anjou*, p. 336. Considering the close relations that held together the different parts of the widespread Norman "Empire," there was nothing unusual about such a transfer. The devotion to St. Nicholas also spread to Lorraine, and, probably earlier and by way of Byzantium, to the Holy Roman Germanic Empire. At least this is the traditional interpretation, but I note that shortly after the death of the emperor Lothair of Supplinburg, Bruno, bishop of Cologne, went to Bari, died there not long after his arrival, and was buried in the Church of St. Nicholas; cf. OTTO OF FREISING *Chronica sive Historia de duabus civitatibus* 7.21 (ed. and trans. A. HOFMEISTER and W. LAMMERS, Ausgewählte Quellen zur deutschen Geschichte des Mittelalters, vol. 16 [Berlin, (1960)]), pp. 534-35. Hugo, Bruno's successor, also died in Puglia and was buried near Melfi. This interest in Bari was probably not due to chance.

105 MASELLIS, *Storia di Bari*, p. 90: the bearers of the body of St. Nicholas in Bari enjoyed enormous popularity. They may have formed a "brotherhood" named for their holy patron.

106 R. KRAUTHEIMER, "San Nicola in Bari und die apulische Architektur des 12. Jahrhunderts," *Wiener Jahrbuch für Kunstgeschichte* 9 (1934): 5-42, with excellent plans and elevations. The conclusions reached by this and virtually all other writers on the subject are contradicted by the new findings of F. SCHETTINI, *La basilica di San Nicola di Bari* (Bari, 1967). F. Schettini holds that the structure of the edifice was entirely determined by that of earlier buildings—the Byzantine civil basilica and the palace of the catapan—which were used as foundations

for a Romanesque structure which was built around them. F. Schettini particulary disagrees with the alleged similarities, taken for granted since E. Bertaux (*L'art dans l'Italie méridionale*, vol. I, *De la fin de l'Empire Romain*, p. 336), between this monument and certain churches in Normandy.

107 Unfortunately this mosaic has been studied only in bits and pieces, so to speak, and not very satisfactorily. The one recent overall study is a work of Christian apologetics rather than of historical criticism. See G. GIANFREDA, *Il mosaico pavimentale della Basilica Cattedrale di Otranto*, 2d ed. (Casamari, 1965) (the author refers to some earlier works in the bibliography); A. PETRUCCI, *Cattedrali di Puglia* (Rome, 1960), pp. 97-98.

108 These mosaics were bathed in the blood of Christians who had taken refuge in the cathedral at the time of the Muslim massacre in 1480 (cf. PETRUCCI, *Cattedrali di Puglia*, p. 97), and were extensively damaged; in fact this author thinks that the ones in the south nave may have been totally destroyed.

109 The pavement in the semicircular part of the choir has more or less fantastic animals, Samson opening the jaws of a lion, a king of Nineveh, and sailors in a boat.

110 In the south nave the pavement has animals that show the influence of Arabo-Persian bestiaries, and giants (?), probably forming a coherent ensemble, but one we have difficulty in interpreting. Here the mosaic is partly covered with furniture, allowing only a very incomplete inspection.

111 One might go on at length about the meaning of this tree, and Msgr. Gianfreda takes full advantage of the opportunity. We find it more interesting to note that here for the first time we come across a treatment, on a monumental scale, of the theme of the "stem" out of which history unrolls and which symbolizes historical time. The Occident repeatedly used this means of symbolizing time, a fact that justifies the attention we have given the Otranto mosaics.

112 On this point it seems permissible to follow Msgr. Gianfreda's interpretations.

113 Gen. 8:6-7 says nothing of the sort: "And after that forty days were passed, Noah, opening the window of the ark which he had made, sent forth a raven: Which went forth and did not return, till the waters were dried up upon the earth." Since the raven took care of itself with no concern for others, Noah sent out a dove. The contrast between the two colors quickly impressed the commentators, who rang the changes on the theme crow-black-sinful selfishness—"diabolical." The raven might have angered Noah by bringing to the Ark a piece of carrion found on the earth from which the waters were receding. Obviously Pantaleone was referring to some such fable when he represented his raven carrying a human leg. It took Ambrose to see the raven as an explicit symbol of sin.

114 This accords with Jewish exegesis which traces the positive alliance between Yahweh and the Just back to Abraham.

115 We might note in passing one can "recognize" this or that personage, animal, or episode. One may comment on the Oriental influences which undoubtedly affected Pantaleone. The fantastic treatment of African fauna and flora is consistent with a long tradition which, in Western Europe, had its roots in Isidore of Seville's Latin *Physiologus*, as well as in absorbed enjoyment of the lovely silks imported from the Orient.

116 Two centaurs with two or three heads that look "Negroid" might reward some research. Fragments of bodies of superimposed animals, and creatures that are half-beast, half-man, foreshadow "fantastic" representations which we shall find again in other lands and times. We have mentioned examples of this in the *Lapidario* of Alfonso of Castile, and there will be others in fourteenth-century Bohemia.

117 A. GRABAR, "Images de l'Ascension d'Alexandre en Italie et en Russie," in *L'art de la fin de l'Antiquité*, vol. I, pp. 291-93.

118 Cf. *supra*, n. 99. The story of Alexander is involved in Greek as well as in Islamic culture, so what we discover here is an offshoot of Eastern *romans* and legends: we shall see more about it. This little-known mosaic evokes the "Oriental" cultural climate in which South Italy lived. We are far from the Spanish realism of the time.

119 On Otranto's relations with the East, see J.M. HOECK and R.J. LOENERTZ, *Nikolaos-Nektarios von Otranto abt von Casole: Beiträge zur Geschichte der ost-westlichen Beziehungen unter Innozenz III. und Friedrich II.*, Studia patristica et byzantina, no. 11 (Ettal, 1965).

120 We ourselves have noticed important remnants of a decorative pavement at Trani, in the choir of the Cathedral of St. Nicholas, in which African animals are represented. BERTAUX, *L'art dans l'Italie méridionale*, vol. I, *De la fin de l'Empire Romain*, p. 492, notes that a similar mosaic existed at Taranto.

121 J.-L.-A. HUILLARD-BRÉHOLLES, ed., *Historia diplomatica Friderici secundi sive Constitutiones, privilegia, mandata, instrumenta quae supersunt istius imperatoris et filiorum ejus...*, vol. VII, *Préface et introduction* (Paris, 1859), p. CXCIII. See also G.-A.-A. LOISEL, *Histoire des ménageries de l'Antiquité à nos jours* (Paris, 1912), vol. I, *Antiquité, Moyen âge, Renaissance*, p. 146.

122 These thrones were studied more than seventy years ago by BERTAUX, *L'art dans l'Italie méridionale*, vol. I, *De la fin de l'Empire Romain*, pp. 444 ff., and much more recently in the remarkable chapter by A. GRABAR, "Trônes épiscopaux du XIe et XIIe siècle en Italie méridionale," in *L'art de la fin de l'Antiquité*, vol. I, pp. 365-92. For illustrations, see PETRUCCI, *Cattedrali di Puglia*, pls. 110-11. According to A. Grabar, the dating of the five thrones in question is established as follows: Monte Gargano, between 1034 and 1066; Canosa di Puglia, between 1078 and 1089; Bari, late eleventh century; Calvi, near Capua, twelfth century; Monte Vergine, near Naples, twelfth century. In all these thrones, except the one in Bari, lions, elephants, and dragons are prominent in the supports (GRABAR, "Trônes épiscopaux," in *L'art de la fin de l'Antiquité*, vol. I, pp. 366-68). A. Grabar insists on the relationship between these themes and ancient Eastern (particularly Sassanid) sources. The comparative study of the five thrones (idem, "Trônes épiscopaux," ibid., pp. 372-92) furnishes information of the greatest interest concerning cultural contacts in the Mediterranean world; unfortunately this information is not directly relevant to our present study. A. Grabar concludes that the *form* of the thrones in question is very close to that of the thrones of Muslim *princes*. Hence we would have here a borrowed form adopted for episcopal usage. As for the sculpted ornamentation, although its origin cannot be determined with total certitude, its inspiration comes from the old common Mediterranean stock we have already discussed, and its symbolism is entirely non-religious. SCHETTINI, *La basilica di San Nicola di Bari*, offers another interpretation. He thinks that this is the throne of the former catapan of Bari, "salvaged" for Elias and secured, after 1087, by the inscription that celebrates him.

123 SCHETTINI, *La basilica di San Nicola di Bari*, holds that Elias's throne, the one here in question, was placed in the apse of the Byzantine basilica on an *omphalos*, a raised disc of pavement typical of the Byzantine ceremonial.

124 GRABAR, "Trônes épiscopaux," in *L'art de la fin de l'Antiquité*, vol. I, p. 380 and n. 3.

125 Vatican, Biblioteca Apostolica Vaticana, MS. Vat. lat. 375. *Vitae Patrum*, Italy, fourteenth century, Book V, fols. 54^v-129^r. H. BUCHTHAL, "Early Fourteenth-Century Illuminations from Palermo," *Dumbarton Oaks Papers* 20 (1966): 103-18, ascribes a Sicilian origin to this manuscript, but Père J. Leroy, not convinced of this, simply emphasizes the Byzantinizing inspiration of the paintings, which would lead one to think of southern Italy.

126 Vatican, Biblioteca Apostolica Vaticana, MS. Vat. lat. 375, fol. 55^r. These miniatures illustrate the text of *Historia Lausiaca* 22 (*PL* 73.1119-20).

127 Vatican, Biblioteca Apostolica Vaticana, MS. Vat. lat. 375, fol. 54^v. At fol. 112^v, in a historiated initial, a tall black man wearing a loincloth and cutting wood illustrates a vision of Abba Daniel; cf. *Vitae Patrum* 5.18 (*PL* 73.978). See fig. 88.

128 This capital, dating from about 1212-20, comes from the cathedral in Troia and is now in the bishop's palace. Carved of limestone, it has four human heads at the corners of the capital.

129 New York, Metropolitan Museum of Art, The Cloisters, 55.66: a capital of the same period and probably coming from the Troia area. On the history and stylistic study of these capitals, see H. WENTZEL, "Ein gotisches Kapitell in Troia," *ZfK* 17 (1954): 185-88; the author dates the Troia capital *before 1229* and hazards hypotheses about the origin of the sculptor which seem shaky to us. See also V. K. OSTOIA, "To Represent What Is as It Is," *BMMA*, n.s. 23, no. 10 (June 1965): 367-72.

130 F. BOLOGNA, *I pittori alla corte angioina di Napoli 1266-1414 e un riesame dell'arte nell'età fridericiana*, Saggi e studi di storia dell'arte, no. 2 (Rome, 1969), pp. 26-27 and pl. I-4.

131 L. LEFRANÇOIS-PILLION, "La sculpture monumentale de la cathédrale de Rouen," *Congrès archéologique de France* 89 (1927): 72-101.

132 Abbey of Saint-Wandrille, keystone in the south gallery of the cloister, early fourteenth century; cf. M. AUBERT, "Saint-Wandrille," *Congrès archéologique de France* 89 (1927): 550-72, esp. p. 565.

133 As we pursue this study we must continue to distinguish clearly the socio-cultural levels of the Crusaders, to keep in mind the length of their stay in the Holy Land, and above all to consider the levels of responsibility at which they operated in that area.

134 LEO VI SAPIENS *Tactica* (*PG* 107.978-79), says that in the Muslim army the infantry "is composed of Ethiopians armed with long bows. These troops march in front of the cavalry, which makes it very hard for those who try to attack them. . . . They must first be attacked with arrows, because their mounted bowmen, both Ethiopians and others, whom they put in the vanguard, being naked are easily wounded and at once take flight."

135 WILLIAM OF TYRE *Historia rerum in partibus transmarinis gestarum* 19.18 in *Recueil des historiens des Croisades: Historiens occidentaux*, vol. I (Paris, 1844), pt. 2, p. 910, describes Cairo as follows: ". . . ad singulos introitus armatorum Aethiopum cohortes crebrae salutationis officium certatim soldano exhibentes . . . ." William of Tyre knew perfectly well where Ethiopia was and the role it played in the life of Africa. He readily used the term *Sarraceni* for white Muslims.

136 The First Crusade was the subject of a large, historical stained-glass window, probably dating from the mid-twelfth century, in the Abbey of Saint-Denis. The window is known only from inventories done for B. de Montfaucon before 1721; see L. GRODECKI, *Les vitraux de Saint-Denis: Etude sur le vitrail au XIIe siècle*, Corpus vitrearum medii aevi: France, Série "Etudes," vol. 1 (Paris, 1976), vol. I, pp. 115-16 and figs. 164-73. It seems that as early as the twelfth century the popularity of the theme of Crusaders doing battle was encouraged by the military orders of the Templars and the Hospitallers; on this subject, see P. DESCHAMPS and M. THIBOUT, *La peinture murale en France au début de l'époque gothique: De Philippe-Auguste à la fin du règne de Charles V (1180-1380)* (Paris, 1963), p. 220.

137 Cf. part 2 of this volume, pp. 65, 69 and figs. 73-76.

138 Pernes, Tour Ferrande, mural painting, late thirteenth century; see DESCHAMPS and THIBOUT, *La peinture murale en France*, p. 222 and pls. CXL-3, CXLI, 1. Another cycle of paintings, devoted to Charles of Anjou and showing his investiture in the kingdom of Sicily and his victories over Manfred and Conradin of Hohenstaufen, clearly places this representation in an anti-Ghibelline context. The authors note the parallels between William of Orange's combat with Ysore and the combat between Bertrand of Les Baux (who would also bear the name of Bertrand of Orange) and Manfred; see idem, *La peinture murale en France*, p. 234.

139 Although we have barely started on a new line of investigation, we should note for the moment that in thirteenth-century English literature there appears an "Ethiopian" giant named Alagolafre, who fights beside the Muslims; cf. METLITZKI, *The Matter of Araby in Medieval England*, pp. 193-97. In part 2 of this volume, pp. 65, 69 and pp. 274-75, n. 21, we shall see the combats of Wigalois and of the knight Yvain (pt. 2, p. 73) falling into a similar pattern.

140 J. B. SEGAL, *Edessa 'The Blessed City'* (Oxford, 1970). This recent work brings together all the documentation at present available on Edessa.

141 E. SIVAN, *L'Islam et la Croisade: Idéologie et Propagande dans les Réactions Musulmanes aux Croisades* (Paris, 1968), pp. 50 ff. The beginning of the twelfth century witnessed the rise of a movement of protest, coming as yet from a small minority, against the inability of the Muslim princes to unite against the Christians.

142 "There was no pulpit . . . that did not rock with joy, no Koran whose ink did not glow . . ." when the conquest restored to Islam "a city which for fifty years had lived a lie . . . . If the conquest of Edessa is the open sea, Jerusalem and *al-Sāḥil* . . . are its coasts" (ibid., pp. 46-47). The texts that relate the fall of the city surround Zengi's success with a bright cloud of marvels; cf. J.-T. REINAUD, comp., *Extraits des historiens arabes relatifs aux guerres des Croisades . . .*, 2d ed., rev. and enl. (Paris, 1829). Zengi, writes one Arab author, at the moment of his death was welcomed most warmly by God. Asked about the reasons for such a welcome, Zengi replied, "I took Edessa" (idem, *Extraits des historiens arabes*, p. 77).

143 J. DORESSE, *L'empire du Prêtre-Jean* (Paris, 1957), vol. I, *L'Ethiopie antique*, p. 268, demonstrates that this incident caused Syro-Armenian traditions to be carried over into Ethiopia. Generally speaking, J. Doresse puts much emphasis on Edessa's religious importance in the Near East. See also P. DEVOS, "Le miracle posthume de saint Thomas l'Apôtre," *AnalBoll* 66 (1948): 249-54.

144 The bibliography on this outstanding personage is extensive, but, curiously enough, there is no really satisfactory biography available. Here we shall indicate some recent studies, often very interesting but not easily accessible: R. FOLZ, "Sur les traces de Saint Augustin: Otton de Freising, historien des deux cités," *Collectanea Ordinis Cisterciensium Reformatorum* 20 (1958): 327-45; idem, "Otton de Freising: Témoin de quelques controverses intellectuelles de son temps," *Bulletin de la Société historique et archéologique de Langres* 13 (1958): 70-89; J. A. FISCHER, ed., *Otto von Freising: Gedenkgabe zu seinem 800. Todesjahr*, Sammelblatt des Historischen Vereins Freising, no. 23 (Freising, 1958); M. MÜLLER, *Beiträge zur Theologie Ottos von Freising*, St. Gabrieler Studien, vol. 19 (Mödling bei Wien, 1965); M. PACAUT, *Frédéric Barberousse* ([Paris], 1967); H. D. RAUH, *Das Bild des Antichrist im Mittelalter: Von Tyconius zum deutschen Symbolismus*, Beiträge zur Geschichte der Philosophie und Theologie des Mittelalters, n.s., vol. 9 (Münster, 1973).

145 Otto never hid his admiration for his famous nephew, on the first years of whose reign he wrote an important work; see OTTO OF FREISING *Gesta Frederici seu rectius Cronica* (ed. and trans. A. SCHMIDT and F.-J. SCHMALE, Ausgewählte Quellen zur deutschen Geschichte des Mittelalters, vol. 17 [Berlin, (1965)]).

146 His brother, Henry II Jasomirgott, successor to Leopold IV as margrave of Austria in 1141, married the niece of Manuel I Comnenus in Constantinople. The new margrave struck coins on which allusion is made to the struggle against the Infidels.

147 "Anno dominicae incarnationis MCXLV incipiente, in ipsa sacrosanctae nativitatis Christi sollempnitate lugubre et miserabile ex peccato Christiani populi accidit in oriente piaculum. . . . Edyssam, quae nunc Rohas dicitur . . . cum infinita Sarracenorum multitudine circumdedit ac in ipsa . . . irrupit . . ." (OTTO OF FREISING *Chronica* 7.30, pp. 550-51).

148 OTTO OF FREISING *Chronica* 7.30, pp. 550-53; SEGAL, *Edessa*, p. 256: the building was turned into a granary.

149 R. Duval, *Histoire politique, religieuse et littéraire d'Edesse jusqu'à la première croisade* (Paris, 1892).

150 W. Wolska, *La topographie chrétienne de Cosmas Indicopleustès: Théologie et Science au VIe siècle*, Bibliothèque byzantine, Etudes, 3 (Paris, 1962), p. 68, shows that Cosmas drew largely upon the teachings of the Nestorian school in Nisibis.

151 F. Nau, "L'expansion nestorienne en Asie," in *Conférences faites au Musée Guimet en 1913*, Annales du Musée Guimet: Bibliothèque de vulgarisation, vol. 40 (Paris, [1914]), pp. 193-383.

152 Communication between the Nestorian Church and the Roman Church was not renewed until the thirteenth century. In 1288 a Nestorian monk, Rabban Ṣaumā, was sent to Western Europe by the catholicos, the head of the Nestorian Church, and while in Rome he was questioned by the cardinals. He stated that Thomas, Addai, and Mari had evangelized the region occupied by the Nestorians. The legends, however, spread more speedily: the earliest mentions of Prester John, which date from the late twelfth century, stress the point that he was a Nestorian.

153 The traditions vary in detail: some say that Addai and Mari were disciples of Thomas; see *Synodicon orientale ou Recueil de synodes nestoriens*, ed. and trans. J.B. Chabot (Paris, 1902), p. 514, n. 1. The council held in 612 by royal command made this relationship official: ". . . the truth of our faith, which we learned directly from the preaching of the Prophets, the Apostles, and our Savior himself, and which this land of the Orient, most glorious of all lands, received from the blessed apostle Addai, one of the disciples of our Lord Jesus Christ . . ." (*Synodicon orientale*, p. 581). Bar Hebraeus mentions in his *Chronicle* the same version as does the *Synodicon orientale*; cf. Bar Hebraeus *Chronicon ecclesiasticum* 2.2 (ed. and trans. J.B. Abbeloos and T.J. Lamy, vol. III [Paris and Louvain, 1877]), cols. 11-12 ff.

154 The Monophysites, dissidents since their doctrine was condemned by the Council of Chalcedon in the middle of the fifth century, created churches which are better known under other names: the Jacobite Church (after its founder, Jacobus Baradaeus), which lived a clandestine existence within the Byzantine Empire, the Ethiopian Church, the Nubian Church, and finally (after the Muslim occupation of Egypt) the Coptic Church. Thus we find a vast group of territories, in this instance including a zone in eastern Africa, all of which escape the hold of Byzantium, let alone that of Rome. These areas preserved many sturdy traditions, which gradually became known in Western Europe after the beginning of the twelfth century.

155 The feast days we have noted are scheduled on the following dates: 27 January, the Wednesday of the second week after Easter, 14 March, 21 and 26 May, 20, 21, and 26 June, 5 July especially (this seems to be the date most often adhered to), 9 and 15 September (on the latter date, curiously enough, the finding of the saint's relics at Alexandria was celebrated), 17 and 18 September, and 5 and 9 October.

156 St. Bartholomew's feast was celebrated on 2 April (with St. Philip), 1 September, 19 October, and 19 November.

157 Agapius *Kitab al-'Unvan (Histoire universelle)*, ed. and trans. A. Vasiliev, pt. 2, fasc. 1 (*PO* 7.474-77).

158 Gregory of Nazianzus *Oratio XXXIII: Adversus Arianos et de seipso* 11 (*PG* 36.227-28).

159 Matt. 10:3; Mark 3:18; Luke 6:15; John 11:16, 14:5, 20:24-29, 21:2; Acts 1:13.

160 F. Vigouroux, ed., *Dictionnaire de la Bible*, 2d ed., vol. V, pt. 2 (Paris, 1928), cols. 2197-99, s.v. "Thomas." The apocryphal Gospel of Thomas as such does not interest us here since it concerns neither the missions of the apostle, nor Edessa, nor blacks; see G. Quispel, *Makarius, das Thomasevangelium und das Lied von der Perle*, Supplements to Novum Testamentum, vol. 15 (Leiden, 1967); J. Doresse, *Les livres secrets des gnostiques d'Egypte*, vol. II, *L'Evangile selon Thomas ou les paroles secrètes de Jésus* (Paris, 1959).

161 Socrates *Historia ecclesiastica* 1.19 (*PG* 67.125-26).

162 Socrates *Hist. eccles.* 4.18 (*PG* 67.503-4): the saint's body reposes in a magnificent basilica in which the recitation of prayers never ceases.

163 "Edessa namque Mesopotamiae urbs fidelium populorum est, Thomae Apostoli Reliquiis decorata" (Rufinus *Historica ecclesiastica* 2.5 [*PL* 21.513]).

164 The theme seems to have its source in a development by Eusebius *Historia ecclesiastica* 1.6, 3.1 (*PG* 20.123-24, 213-16).

165 "Bartholomaeus apostolus, Indis iis qui dicuntur fortunati, praedicavit Evangelium Christi, et Evangelium quod est secundum Matthaeum eis tradidit. Dormivit autem Albanopoli oppido majoris Armeniae. Thomas apostolus, quemadmodum traditum est nobis, Parthis et Medis et Persis et Carmanis et Hyrcanis et Bactris et Magis praedicavit Evangelium Domini. Dormivit in civitate Calamina, quae est Indiae. . . . Matthias . . . in altera Aethiopia . . . praedicavit Evangelium . . ." (Jerome *De vitis apostolorum* 4-5, 7 [*PL* 23.721-22]). A slightly modified and embellished account of this version appears again in the Pseudo-Dorotheus of Tyre *De septuaginta Domini discipulis* (*PG* 92.1071-72).

166 Vatican, Biblioteca Apostolica Vaticana, MS. Vat. gr. 1613, p. 93 (painting by Nestor): martyrdom of St. Thomas. A ninth-century manuscript in Paris, Bibliothèque nationale, MS. grec 510, fol. 32[v], presents the martyrdom of each of the Twelve Apostles. The executioner who has just thrust his lance through St. Thomas is the only one painted in dark ochre. He wears a loincloth, red with gold decoration, knotted at the waist, and a blue scarf tricked out with gold and fastened with a buckle at the left shoulder.

167 The old versions (tenth century?) explicitly mention the execution of St. Thomas, celebrated on 6 October by the Byzantine Church. Later another version appeared, according to which two of the executioners became converts after Thomas's death.

168 See, e.g., *Le Synaxaire arménien de Ter Israël*, ed. and trans. G. Bayan, fasc. 1, *Mois de Navasard* (*PO* 5.345-556, esp. pp. 415-17, 420-26: commemoration of 22 August). Thomas's missionary activity is much more extensive here, and we see another fusion of the legends in the making: "He also journeyed through Ethiopia, which is called Abyssinia, and preached Jesus Christ. *He betook himself to the provinces of the Three Magi* [italics ours] who came to adore the newborn Christ, and he baptized them and made them his partners in the preaching of the Gospel." This synaxarion contains, for 6 October, the same account as in the text previously cited relative to Thomas's martyrdom: the king of India "gave orders to take [Thomas] up into a mountain and kill him there with spears" (*Le Synaxaire arménien de Ter Israël*, ed. and trans. G. Bayan, fasc. 2, *Mois de Hori* [*PO* 6.343]). His remains were carried back to Mesopotamia (*Le Synaxaire arménien*, fasc. 2, *Mois de Hori* [*PO* 6.339]). See also Bar Hebraeus *Chron. eccles.* 2.1, vol. III, cols. 4-10, who gives one of the most detailed accounts of the apostolic mission to India to be found in a Nestorian version. Some episodes closely resemble those in the version that was circulated in Western Europe during the ninth century.

169 Etheria *Journal de voyage* 19 (ed. and trans. H. Pétré, S.C., no. 21 [Paris, 1957]), pp. 162 ff. Etheria reports that there were several *martyria* at Batanis, not far from Edessa. As soon as she arrived in the latter city, where she spent three days, Etheria went to the *martyrium* of St. Thomas, near which a large, beautiful church had just been built. Then she visited the palace of King Abgar—the same who, according to popular belief, had received a letter from Christ. She observed vast fountains in which fish were swimming: the fountains gushed up miraculously near the palace at a time when the Persians were besieging Edessa and had diverted the river which until then had flowed by the city. Edessa—the detail is significant—was forever protected by Christ's letter: "Every time an enemy tried to attack our city the letter was brought out and read

at the gate, and at once . . . the foe fell back." We note that St. Thomas had little to do with all this. For the basilica where the relics of St. Thomas were preserved, see A. Grabar, "Le témoignage d'une hymne syriaque sur l'architecture de la cathédrale d'Edesse au VIe siècle et sur la symbolique de l'édifice chrétien," in *L'art de la fin de l'Antiquité*, vol. I, pp. 31-50, esp. p. 32.

170 William of Tyre, Ordericus Vitalis, and Vincent of Beauvais also made use of this *Passion*. See U. Monneret de Villard, "La fiera di Batnae e la traslazione di S. Tomaso a Edessa," *Rendiconti Sc. Mor.*, 8th ser. 6, fascs. 3-4 (1951): 91, 93; the author also studies other texts relating to this transferal.

171 This would seem to be the way to interpret: "Hoc Theodorus qui ad ipsum locum accessit nobis exposuit" (Gregory of Tours *Libri miraculorum* 1.32 [*PL* 71.733]).

172 Gregory of Tours *Lib. mirac.* 1.32 (*PL* 71.733-34).

173 As we see it, the passage commented on here can refer only to Edessa, despite the reservations of P. Devos ("Le miracle posthume de saint Thomas l'Apôtre," pp. 239-40). Gregory of Tours never speaks of a *city* with reference to India, but only of a monastery; he says explicitly: "... in supradicta igitur urbe in qua beatos artus diximus tumulatos..." (Gregory of Tours *Lib. mirac.* 1.32 [*PL* 71.733]), which could only mean Edessa.

174 Gregory of Tours here furnishes information that entirely confirms U. Monneret de Villard's thesis on the translation of St. Thomas's relics to Edessa.

175 Gregory of Tours explicitly attributes this material prosperity to the merits of the saint.

176 Gregory of Tours *Lib. mirac.* 1.33 (*PL* 71.734).

177 Isidore of Seville *Etymologiarum sive Originum libri XX* 7,9 (ed. W. M. Lindsay, Scriptorum classicorum bibliotheca oxoniensis [Oxford, 1911]); idem *De ortu et obitu Patrum* 81 and app. 20.44 (*PL* 83.154, 1289).

178 Hormisdas *Epistularum ad diversos libri tres* 2.41 in *Monumenta Germaniae historica: Auctores Antiquissimi*, vol. VI (Berlin, 1883), pt. 2, ed. R. Peiper, p. 71 (hereafter cited as *MGH*): letter from Hormisdas to Avitus, bishop of Vienne, mentioning the apostle's mission in Thrace and Dardania.

179 Ambrose *In Psalmum XLV enarratio* 21 (*PL* 14.1143): in so many words, Thomas is sent off to India and Matthew to Persia.

180 The Roman Martyrology celebrates Thomas's feast day on 21 December, whereas the Hieronymian Martyrology puts his feasts in January (transfer of the ashes to Edessa), February, April, May, June (nativity), July (another date for the transfer to Edessa), and on 21 December. The Martyrology of Usuard, dating from the ninth century, copies those of Florus, deacon of Lyons, and of Ado, archbishop of Vienne, in fixing the apostle's celebration on 3 July (translation to Edessa) and 21 December (nativity and mission among the Medes and the Parthians and in India); this work also mentions St. Bartholomew on 24 August, describing him as having been martyred in India and resting in the Lipari Islands; cf. Usuard *Le martyrologe d'Usuard: Texte et commentaire* (ed. J. Dubois, Subsidia hagiographica, no. 40 [Brussels, 1965]). The Calendar of Heiric of Auxerre, also dating from the ninth century, combining the English traditions of which we shall take note and the Hieronymian tradition, celebrates Thomas on 20 December (nativity) and 21 December; cf. B. de Gaiffier, "Le calendrier d'Héric d'Auxerre du manuscrit de Melk 412," *AnalBoll* 77 (1959): 392-425. The Martyrology of Florus adds for 21 December the note that Thomas "passus est in India lancea quippe transfixus occubuit."

181 Anonymous Saxon *Annalium de gestis Caroli Magni Imperatoris libri quinque* 5.683-86 in *MGH: Poetae Latini aevi Carolini*, vol. IV, pt. 1, ed. P. K. R. von Winterfeld (Berlin, 1899), p. 71:

> Andreas populos post se producet Achivos,
> Johannes Asiae proferet ecclesias,
> Matheus Aethiopes niveos baptismate factos,
> Indorum Thomas ducet ad astra greges: . . .

Sylloga codicis Sangallensis CCCLXXXI 4.13-16 in *MGH: Poetae*, vol. IV, pt. 1, p. 319:

> Petrus cum Paulo, Thomas cum Bartholomeo
> Et Jacobus sanctis nos relevent precibus,
> Andreas, Matheus, Barnabas atque Johannes,
> Mathias, Lucas, Marcus et altisonus.

Dialogus Agii 320-21 in *MGH: Poetae*, vol. III, ed. L. Traube, pt. 2, fasc. 1 (1892), p. 379:

> Et sunt Mathaeo Aethiopes nitidi.
> Thomam Edissa tenet, habet India Bartholomaeum: . . .

Alcuin stresses Thomas's unbelief and states that Bartholomew "docuit nigros . . . Indos"; see Alcuin *Carmina* in *MGH: Poetae*, vol. I, ed. E. Duemmler (1881), p. 335. Rabanus Maurus *Carmina* in *MGH: Poetae*, vol. II, ed. E. Duemmler (1884), p. 233, and Florus *Carmina* in *MGH: Poetae*, vol. II, p. 511 ("In Evangelium Mathei"), mention Thomas and Bartholomew in terms similar to those of Alcuin. Wandalbert of Prüm *Carmina* in *MGH: Poetae*, vol. II, p. 601 ("Martyrologium: December"), notes for 21 December:

> Translati Thomae celebrat duodenus honorem,
> Aurea quo structore dei cognoscere regnum
> India promeruit signis commota tremendis.

182 Council of Chieti, 12 May 840: mention of the gifts made: "Ad victum vero et vestitum dedimus illi ecclesiam sancti Justini, ubi et ipsam canonicam ad honorem sancti Thomae construximus. . . . Haec quoque firmiter studuimus perficere ad honorem et laudem ... Thomae. . . ." Hence St. Thomas was venerated locally, at least, in Italy, although his cult had neither the strength nor the prestige to prosper.

183 The "knowledge" we have already reviewed is summarized in the *Passio sancti Bartholomaei apostoli*: "Indiae tres esse ab historiographis adseruntur. Prima est India quae ad Aethiopiam mittit, secunda quae ad Medos, tertia quae finem facit: nam ex uno latere tenebrarum regionem gerit, ex alio latere mare oceanum. In hac ergo India ingressus est Bartholomaeus apostolus" (the king of India, who was black, had Bartholomew beheaded); cf. M. Bonnet, ed., *Passio Andreae* . . . , Acta Apostolorum apocrypha, vol. I, pt. 2 (Leipzig, 1898), pp. 128 ff. See also the *Passio sancti Thomae apostoli* in M. Bonnet, ed., *Acta Thomae*, Supplementum codicis apocryphi, vol. I (Leipzig, 1883), pp. 133-60. No doubt the text repeats in large part the fifth-century *Passion*. This work was very popular, to judge from the number of surviving manuscripts from the ninth, tenth, eleventh, and, especially, the twelfth centuries. Thomas's adventures after he left Edessa are recounted in minute detail, and of course the apostle performs many miracles and edifying feats: he destroyed a metal idol which he was being forced to worship; he prayed to God, and the idol melted before the eyes of the pagans (*Passio sancti Thomae apostoli* in Bonnet, *Acta Thomae*, pp. 158-59). But the miracle cost him his life: the pagan priest ran him through with his sword. Alexander also gets involved in this story. It is at his insistence (in the text he becomes a Roman emperor!) that the apostle's body is surrendered to the Christians and transported to Edessa. The web of intermingled legends, the more tenacious for being so inextricably confused, was taking shape.

184 A. E. Medlycott, *India and the Apostle Thomas: An Inquiry with a Critical Analysis of the "Acta Thomae"* (London, 1905), can still be consulted with profit.

185 Bede *Martyrologia* (*PL* 94.965-66, 1137): July, translation to Edessa; for December, Jerome's data are repeated. The copies of Bede's Martyrology show fidelity to the original in what concerns Thomas's feast, as well as the diffusion of the text. See L. Delisle, "Mémoire sur d'anciens sacramentaires," *Mémoires de l'Académie des Inscriptions et Belles-Lettres* 32, pt. 1 (1886): 313 (fragment of a Merovingian calendar, July: "v nonas. Translatio Thome apostoli in Edisa"), 353 and 360 (calendar of the Sacramentary of Saint-Vaast and Corbie, July: "v non. Translatio corporis sancti Thomae apostoli ab India in Edissa civitate"; December: "xii kl. Natalis sancti Thomae apostoli. Solstitium"). A calendar from Freising cele-

brates Thomas on 20 and 21 December; cf. A. LECHNER, *Mittelalterliche Kirchenfeste und Kalendarien in Bayern* (Freiburg im Breisgau, 1891), p. 23.

186 ALDHELM *Carmina ecclesiastica* 4.6 in *MGH: Auctores Antiquissimi*, vol. XV, ed. R. EHWALD, pt. 1 (1913), pp. 24-25 ("In sancti Thomae apostoli").

187 METLITZKI, *The Matter of Araby in Medieval England*, pp. 7 ff. In addition, this book supplies a wealth of information on what was known in England, in the twelfth century and after, about all aspects of the Muslim world.

188 MEDLYCOTT, *India and the Apostle Thomas*, p. 82. Florence of Worcester reproduces an item found in the *Anglo-Saxon Chronicle*; cf. DEVOS, "Le miracle posthume de saint Thomas l'Apôtre," p. 255.

189 WILLIAM OF MALMESBURY *Gesta regum Anglorum* 2.122 (*PL* 179.1082); having restored peace to his kingdom, Alfred sent large gifts to Rome and to St. Thomas in India: "Legatus in hoc missus Sigelinus, Scirebarnensis episcopus, cum magna prosperitate, quod quivis hoc seculo miretur, Indiam penetravit; inde rediens, exoticos splendores gemmarum, et liquores aromatum, quorum illa humus ferax est, reportavit."

190 On the veneration of St. Thomas by the people of Edessa, see DEVOS, "Le miracle posthume de saint Thomas l'Apôtre," pp. 249 ff.

191 Ibid., pp. 231-32: Odo, abbot of Saint-Remi in Rheims before 1137, and an anonymous author who report the coming of a patriarch from India during the reign of Pope Callistus II (1119-24), are responsible for launching this "revival."

192 The most remarkable of these new story elements seems to be an inversion of the text by Gregory of Tours. He related that water was plentiful at Edessa during the annual commemorative feasts. Now the phenomenon is reversed: Thomas's tomb in India is surrounded by water all year long, but once a year, during the pilgrimage which draws the faithful to the tomb, the water recedes to allow them free access [are we to imagine that it rises simultaneously at Edessa by way of compensation?] and flows back at the end of the ceremonies. I cannot resist making a comparison of this miraculous event with one mentioned by Bernard, a Frankish monk, in the ninth century: "In festivitate autem sancti Michaelis non conjungitur mare in redundando in circuitu illius montis, sed stat, ad instar murorum, a dextris et a sinistris. Et in ipso die solemni possunt omnes, quicunque ad orationem venerint, omnibus horis adire montem, quod tamen aliis diebus non possunt" (BERNARDUS MONACHUS *Itinerarium* 21 in TOBLER, *Descriptiones Terrae Sanctae*, p. 98). Another theme taken from Gregory of Tours and enhanced: henceforth the lamp at the tomb is miraculously fed with precious balsam.

193 DEVOS, "Le miracle posthume de saint Thomas l'Apôtre," pp. 242-43: the author studies at length the story, made up out of whole cloth, of a certain Eliseus, "in India natus et nutritus." *Prester John is already involved in this tale.*

194 The theme of the annual pilgrimage to the Indian tomb stayed very much alive in Western Europe although blacks were not an essential element in its iconography. A fifteenth-century Flemish manuscript (Brussels, Bibliothèque Royale Albert Ier, MS. 9278-80: *Débat sur l'honneur et autres œuvres*, translated by Jean Miélot, fol. 45^r^) represents the pilgrimage of the patriarch of the Indias to the tomb of St. Thomas: two darker personages, who, however, have no clear "Negroid" characteristics, wear a white bandeau on their foreheads and follow the cortège of white horsemen at a distance. The imaginary geography of the tomb is exploited by the painter.

195 An effort to gain credence for the idea that Thomas, like Mark, Nicholas, and Bartholomew, had finally been delivered from the hands of the Infidels, did not succeed; cf. a letter from Gui de Blond, analyzed in C. KOHLER, "Documents inédits concernant l'Orient latin et les Croisades (XIIe-XIVe siècle), "*Revue de l'Orient latin* 7 (1899): 1-9. A countess in Edessa is alleged to have handed over the saint's relics to the Western Europeans.

196 At that time the geographical notions inherited from antiquity still left the Indias outside of Africa; cf. J. RICHARD, "L'Extrême-Orient légendaire au Moyen Age: Roi David et Prêtre Jean," *AdE* 2 (1957): 226. Three Indias were already distinguished early in the twelfth century: one this side of the Ganges *(India inferior)*, one beyond the Ganges *(India superior)*, and one closer to the Red Sea *(India ultima)*. These details are essential for the understanding of the myths upon which the Occident built its vision of the Orient.

197 Mount Athos, Monastery of Iveron, Codex 463, *Life of Barlaam and Joasaph* (late twelfth to early thirteenth century), fol. 3^r^: land of the Indians; cf. S. DER NERSESSIAN, *L'illustration du Roman de Barlaam et Joasaph* (Paris, 1937), vol. I, pp. 23-25; vol. II, *Album*, pl. II, 2.

198 MONNERET DE VILLARD, "La fiera di Batnae," pp. 100-103, has noted the usefulness of calendars for this study. He points to two mentions frequently found in them: at 21 December, "Passio Thomae apostoli in India et in Mesopotamia civitate Edessae translatio corporis ejusdem," and on 3 July, "In Edissa Mesopotamiae translatio corporis sancti Thomae apostoli qui passus est in India."

199 Lunel, Bibliothèque municipale, MS. 1, *Psalter*, fol. 5^r^: month of December. This psalter is thought to have been written in eastern England during the first half of the twelfth century.

200 Ibid., fol. 3^r^. We note, along with H. STERN, *Le calendrier de 354: Etude sur son texte et ses illustrations*, Institut français d'archéologie de Beyrouth: Bibliothèque archéologique et historique, vol. 55 (Paris, 1953), p. 365, that the custom of placing a human figure, often a young servingman, in the months of June and December goes back to antiquity.

201 Avignon, Musée Calvet, G 202 A, thirteenth-century relief from Caissargues; see P. PRADEL, "Vestiges d'un zodiaque-calendrier nîmois du XIIIe siècle," *Monuments et Mémoires publiés par l'Académie des Inscriptions et Belles-Lettres, Fondation Eugène Piot* 55 (1967): 105-13.

202 Odilo records as follows the acclamation spoken to Otto III at his coronation: "May the *Slav* grumble and the *Hungarian* gnash his teeth; may the *Greek* be stricken with confusion, the *Saracen* be troubled and take flight; may the *Africans* pay tribute and *Spain* beg for help. May *Burgundy* revere and cherish the emperor and may *Aquitaine* run joyously to greet him. Let all *Gaul* say, 'Who has heard the like?' And the *Italian* people, arms raised high, will cry out, 'By God! This is the only son of Caesar Otto the Great!'" (text quoted by PACAUT, *Frédéric Barberousse*, p. 22). These are allusions to concrete situations, and easier to resolve at the level of words than at that of action; but a century and a half later these situations left no more than the memory of ancient splendor, and it is hard to know whether or not it embraced a lived reality. Already Widukind of Corvey, speaking to the daughter of Otto I, says of the emperor: ". . . quamquam in Affricam Asiamque patris tui iam potestas protendatur" (WIDUKIND OF CORVEY *Rerum gestarum saxonicarum libri tres* 1, ed. G. WAITZ and K.A. KEHR, 5th ed., in *MGH: Scriptores rerum Germanicarum in usum scholarum*, vol. 60 [Hannover, 1935], p. 61).

203 PACAUT, *Frédéric Barberousse*, p. 79.

204 Ibid., p. 122.

205 Ibid., e.g., pp. 151-52.

206 PETER OF EBOLI *De rebus siculis carmen*, p. 202, shows the peoples ready to render homage to the imperial power by payment of tribute:

> Hic grave pondus Arabs missi deliberat auri,
> Hic Melechinas exhibet Indus opes
> Et decus et precium, gemmas dat Persis et aurum,
> Materiam superans mittit Egyptus opus.

207 M.-D. CHENU, *La théologie au douzième siècle*, Etudes de philosophie médiévale, vol. 45 (Paris, 1957), pp. 77 ff.

208 Otto of Freising's culture was really remarkable. In Paris he followed the teachings of Hugh of St.-Victor, Abelard, Thierry of Chartres, and Gilbert de la Porrée; cf. Folz, "Otton de Freising: Témoin de quelques controverses intellectuelles de son temps," pp. 70-89. He also became acquainted with the "new Aristotle" which was beginning to be known and worked on in Paris. Moreover, it is not impossible that, through this learning or through the traditions then current in the empire, Otto had come into contact with the Judeo-Hellenistic Apocrypha, which prefigured this new organization of History in successive ages.

209 Chenu, *La théologie au douzième siècle*, p. 78, shows how Otto of Freising seized on the Augustinian idea that the Roman Empire was predestined to welcome the birth of Christ, while at the same time Ordericus Vitalis and other European thinkers neglected this idea and, on the contrary, enlarged upon the "nations" that were in the process of being born.

210 The Germanic Empire, heir to the Roman, was, like the latter, subject to the *mutatio rerum*. One of the favorite themes of philosophic meditation at the time was that of the millstone, the circular symbol of the changeableness of things, which, for the theologians, contrasted with the squared stone on which Christ had built the Church. On this theme see Rauh, *Das Bild des Antichrist*, pp. 123 ff., 305 ff.

211 A poetic play, *Ludus de Antichristo*, was composed about 1178 at the Abbey of Tegernsee in Bavaria, no doubt at the instigation of the imperial court. The emperor's role as protector of Christendom is of course made much of in this work. On the text see E. A. F. Michaelis, "Zum Ludus de Antichristo," *Zeitschrift für deutsches Altertum und deutsche Litteratur* n.s. 42 (1913): 61-87, which gives a detailed analysis. The prototype of the *Ludus* is the work of a tenth-century author, Adso, abbot of Montier-en-Der, who wrote a Dialogue on Antichrist for Gerberga, wife of Louis IV d'Outremer. Adso, who was remembered for his learning, had a good personal library, which was catalogued by monks in 992, after Adso left for Palestine: he never got there, by the way; cf. H. Omont, "Catalogue de la bibliothèque de l'abbé Adson de Montier-en-Der (992)," *BiblEcChartes* 42 (1881): 157-60. For the cultural history of Western Europe it is interesting to note that the list of Adso's books is closely related to the much larger catalogue of the library of the archdiocese of Rheims under Hincmar (see J. Devisse, *Hincmar Archevêque de Reims 845-882*, Travaux d'histoire éthico-politique, no. 29 [Geneva, 1976], vol. III, pp. 1467-1514); note also that Adso's text is indirectly dedicated to a Carolingian. We have been able to demonstrate that Bavaria gathered in both the heritage of the Rhemish libraries and that of the royal tradition expressed in these texts.

It is well to note, in passing, the richness and complexity of the Antichrist theme which was rampant in Germany in the second half of the twelfth century; cf. Rauh, *Das Bild des Antichrist*. In the north the Antichrist was thought of as being associated with the pagans—therefore, in the twelfth century, with the Slavs and perhaps also in part with the Scandinavians—with the color black, and with the mandrake. This is a whole foisoning universe into which we have not wished to enter.

212 Otto was eleven years old in 1122 when a laborious compromise put a temporary end to the conflict between the empire and Rome, a conflict which had been going on for nearly fifty years. For him the empire and the papacy of necessity coexist in the Church.

213 Returning from the East in 1149-50, Otto of Freising passed through France and met St. Bernard. Bernard entrusted him with a peace mission—to reestablish harmony between the empire and Roger II of Sicily; cf. Folz, "Otton de Freising: Témoin de quelques controverses intellectuelles de son temps," p. 89, n. 92.

214 Ibid., pp. 71-72.

215 When he speaks about the Muslims, he is more impressed by the diplomatic and military role of the Turks than by the unity of Islam, which was not evident in his time. In the only passage describing Muslims as believers, Otto notes that they believe in one God, have books of law, practice circumcision, and do not deny the existence of Christ and the Apostles; they deny the divinity of Christ but recognize him as a great prophet and venerate him; cf. Otto of Freising *Chronica* 7.7, pp. 510-11.

216 Otto of Freising *Chronica* 4.14, pp. 328-29.

217 Otto of Freising *Chronica* 7.3, pp. 502-5.

218 Otto of Freising *Chronica* 1.1, pp. 60-61: Africa is a small continent surrounded by vast seas.

219 Otto of Freising *Chronica* 2.23, 32, 34, 38, 41, 42, 50 (pp. 144-45, 162-63, 166-67, 174-75, 180-83, 200-201); 3.43 (pp. 282-83, 286-87); 4.22, 24, 29 (pp. 350-53, 362-63); 5.4, 13 (pp. 382-85, 400-401); 6.4 (pp. 438-39).

220 Otto of Freising *Chronica* 1.8, pp. 72-73.

221 Otto of Freising *Chronica* 1.17, pp. 82-83.

222 The author uses the term *denigrati*. While in the Latin of the Christian writers (cf. A. Blaise, *Dictionnaire latin-français des auteurs chrétiens* [Strasbourg, 1954], p. 254), the word *denigrare* maintains the strictly "technical" meanings 'to blacken the skin', one of its meanings in classical Latin passed into the French *dénigrer* and the English *denigrate*—words that unconsciously convey a burden of rather contemptuous implications.

223 Otto of Freising *Chronica* 8.12, pp. 608-11.

224 Otto of Freising *Gesta Frederici* 1.66, pp. 270-71.

225 Otto of Freising *Chronica* 3.43, pp. 284-85.

226 This phrase, taken from Oriental sources, was to furnish an important commonplace: the Orient is overpopulated, and its bishops, like its powerful provinces, are too numerous to be counted. We will find this notion tacked on to the personage of Prester John.

227 Otto of Freising *Chronica* 7.32, pp. 554-57.

228 On this prelate see P. Pelliot, *Mélanges sur l'époque des Croisades*, Académie des Inscriptions et Belles-Lettres: Extrait des Mémoires de l'Académie, vol. 44 (Paris, 1951), pp. 24-40.

229 Thus begins the turning of the Prester John theme to the profit of the empire, a process that characterizes the first stage of the whole affair.

230 The combining of two functions in one and the same person constituted a basic stumbling block for medieval Western political theory, but the idea was abroad in the East. We find it in the thirteenth-century *Chronicle* by Abu Ṣāliḥ; cf. Devos, "Le miracle posthume de saint Thomas l'Apôtre," p. 245: in Abyssinia, a country contiguous to India, every king is a priest. This confusion sat badly with a Western Christian. At least since Charlemagne's era the accepted idea was that after Christ no one could be priest and king at the same time. The two functions had been deliberately vested in two distinct persons, and the life of the Christian people depended entirely on the close and trustful cooperation of the two holders of power. Otto of Freising *Chronica* 7, pp. 496-99, insists on the duality of powers in Christianity. The return to the joining of the two powers in a single head certainly was a major influence (which has not yet been sufficiently studied) in Frederick Barbarossa's imperial pretensions as opposed to those of the popes.

231 J. Richard ("L'Extrême-Orient légendaire au Moyen Age") has said all there is to say on this point and said it very well.

232 The recent work by Sivan, *L'Islam et la Croisade*, pp. 50 ff., has shown that the hopes of the northern Muslim princes paralleled exactly those of the Occidental Christians after the fall of Edessa. The emirs looked for help from the powerful ally in Cairo—an encircling alliance against the Christians—as the Christians, later on, were to aspire to such an alliance with Prester John.

233 Otto of Freising *Chronica* 7.33, pp. 556-59.

234 It is not by accident that Otto of Freising repeats the account of an embassy from Byzantium to the king of India, in 567, when Chilperic I and Justin II were reign-

ing: "Huius diebus pax inter Romanos et Persas rumpitur. Imperator vero ad Aretham Indorum regem Julianum misit. Qui, ut postmodum retulit, eum pene nudum, circa lumbos tantum cincturam et linea vestimenta auro contexta et circa ventrem indumenta scissa, margaritis preciosis conserta, in brachiis quinos circulos et armillas aureas, in capite pannum gemmis ornatum, in collo torquem aureum habentem, super quatuor elefantes rotis quatuor curru excelso innitente stantem, scutum parvissimum deauratum cum duabus lanceolis aureis tenentem, invenit" (OTTO OF FREISING *Chronica* 5.5, pp. 386-87). This comes close to the descriptions contained in the letter of Prester John: the myth of an Orient abounding in gold is launched.

235 V. SLESSAREV, *Prester John: The Letter and the Legend* (Minneapolis, 1959), pp. 32-54, gives a very interesting study of the letter in its Latin version and of its sources. The text appeared in the Latin version between 1165 and 1177.

236 M.-P. Jabinet-Caire has embarked upon an overall study (first as a *mémoire de maîtrise*, then as a *thèse de troisième cycle*) of the manuscript tradition of this text. An interpolation (dating from the thirteenth century at the earliest: its origin is difficult to determine) attributes the Latin translation of the letter to Christian I, archbishop of Mainz from 1160/61 to 1183 and archchancellor of the empire. Thus the document is formally connected with the entourage of the imperial court. Mme Jabinet-Caire's study also shows the extent to which the forgery was always taken over by lay political circles, both in the empire and, for a brief period, by people in the court of St. Louis.

237 If we connect the myth of Prester John with the description (furnished by OTTO OF FREISING *Chronica* 7.28, pp. 548-49) of what the bishop of Jabala said and did, it becomes clear that the latter prelate was just as anxious to block seizure of his see by the Byzantines as he was to oppose the Muslim threat. Prester John constituted what, in the diplomatic language of the seventeenth century, would have been called an *alliance de revers*, a kind of encirclement: the distant Oriental potentate would serve as a counterbalance almost equal to the pressure of Islam and Byzantium on the Latin colonies in the East.

238 Prester John lives in a palace built by Thomas. The letter mentions the tomb of the apostle.

239 From this point of view, the decisive phase is Prester John's "passage to Africa"; he had certainly been an Asiatic for a century or two at least. As Western diplomatic and military efforts were thwarted time after time in Asia, Ethiopia drew increasing attention in the hunt for the providential but vainly sought ally against Islam.

240 F. RÖHRIG, *Der Verduner Altar* (Vienna and Munich, 1955). The ambo was severely damaged by a fire in 1330, but was restored immediately and transformed into a triptych altarpiece; cf. M.-M. GAUTHIER, *Emaux du moyen âge occidental* (Fribourg, 1972), pp. 167-75 and esp. pp. 364-67, ill. 118.

241 J. DANIÉLOU, *Sacramentum futuri: Etudes sur les origines de la typologie biblique*, Etudes de théologie historique (Paris, 1950).

242 SUGER *Liber de rebus in administratione sua gestis* 32 (*PL* 186.1237), tells us how in the stained-glass windows of the Abbey of Saint-Denis, New Testament scenes are placed in relation to the most appropriate corresponding Old Testament scenes. This is the beginning of what we call *typology*.

243 COSMAS INDICOPLEUSTES *Topographie chrétienne* 2.50 (ed. and trans. W. WOLSKA-CONUS, S. C., no. 141 [Paris, 1968]), vol. I, pp. 358-59: "From the Lord's words it can also be concluded that he regarded these regions as the ends of the earth, when he said this: 'The queen of the South will arise at the judgment with this generation and condemn it; for she came from the ends of the earth to hear the wisdom of Solomon'" — implying that she did not understand a word of it!

244 ISIDORE OF SEVILLE *Quaestiones in Vetus Testamentum: In Regum tertium* 5 (*PL* 83.417).

245 Regarding the important influence of Rupert of Deutz on iconography, see R. HAACKE, *Programme zur Bildenden Kunst in den Schriften Ruperts von Deutz*, Siegburger Studien, vol. 9 (Siegburg, 1974).

246 RUPERT OF DEUTZ *De Trinitate et operibus ejus libri XLII: In libros Regum* 3.30 (*PL* 167.1175-76). He is commenting on the verse (3 Kings 10:1) that tells how the queen came to Solomon "to try him with hard questions": "Hoc modo actum est, ut veniret ad regem istum, regina Saba, id est dives et insignis de gentibus Ecclesia; non quia prius regina erat, quippe quae daemonum potius erat ancilla, sed quia veniendo ad Christum regina facta est, credendo in Christum regio diademate coronata est, ornata bonorum operum, vestibus deauratis, cunctarumque virtutum lapidibus pretiosis. . . . Venit haec regina in Hierusalem, cum multo comitatu, id est, non jam cum una gente tantum, scilicet Judaeorum, sicut prius Synagoga solos habebat Hebraeos, *sed totius mundi gentibus diversisque nationibus* [italics ours]. Venit ergo exhibens munera digna Christo, aurum et gemmas pretiosas, *et hoc camelis portantibus, id est ex gentili populo venientibus* [italics ours]. . . ." The iconographic interest of this passage is considerable, as we shall see.

247 CHENU, *La théologie au douzième siècle*, p. 78.

248 On the legend of the Queen of Sheba and its medieval iconography, see A. CHASTEL, "La légende de la Reine de Saba," *Revue de l'histoire des religions* 119, nos. 2-3 (1939): 204-25; 120, no. 1 (1939): 27-44; 120, nos. 2-3 (1939): 160-74; idem, "La rencontre de Salomon et de la Reine de Saba dans l'iconographie médiévale," *GBA*, 6th ser. 35 (February 1949): 99-114.

249 Canterbury, cathedral, stained-glass window in the north choir aisle, late twelfth century; cf. J. BAKER, *English Stained Glass* (New York, [1960]), p. 61 and black and white pl. 8; M. H. CAVINESS, *The Early Stained Glass of Canterbury Cathedral, circa 1175-1220* (Princeton, 1977), pp. 53, 91 and fig. 44.

250 Herrad of Landsberg's *Hortus deliciarum*, miniature 221, shows the queen, also designated a Sibyl (*Sibylla regina Austri*: more about this further on), arriving on a palfrey with a camel loaded with gifts alongside, but the queen is white; cf. HERRAD OF LANDSBERG *Hortus deliciarum*, ed. J. WALTER (Strasbourg and Paris, 1952).

251 Chartres, Cathedral of Notre-Dame, north portal, right bay, embrasure on the left (about 1230): console of the statue of the Queen of Sheba, surrounded by those of Balaam and Solomon.

252 Strasbourg, Musée de l'Œuvre Notre-Dame, MAD. LVII.5, panel of a stained-glass window from the Church of St-Thomas in Strasbourg; cf. *L'Europe gothique: XIIe-XIVe siècles*, Exhibition catalogue, Paris, Musée du Louvre, Pavillon de Flore, 2 April-1 July 1968 (Paris, 1968), pp. 120-21, no. 200.

253 The glass in the Chapel of St. Stephen in Cologne Cathedral came from the former Dominican Church of the Holy Cross. On these stained-glass windows, see H. RODE, *Die mittelalterlichen Glasmalereien des Kölner Domes*, Corpus vitrearum medii aevi: Deutschland, vol. IV 1: Köln, Dom (Berlin, 1974), p. 53, no. 4a and pl. 3, fig. 3 and pl. 8, fig. 12; p. 87, no. 3a and pl. 57, fig. 160.

254 On the story of the Magi, see the recent excellent exposition by M. ELISSAGARAY, *La légende des Rois Mages* (Paris, 1965).

255 On Rainald of Dassel, see J. FICKER, *Reinald von Dassel: Reichskanzler und Erzbischof von Köln, 1156-1167* (Cologne, 1850); *Die Regesten der Erzbischöfe von Köln im Mittelalter*, Publikationen der Gesellschaft für rheinische Geschichtskunde, no. 21 (Bonn, 1901), vol. II, ed. R. KNIPPING, *1100-1205*; M. PACAUT, *Alexandre III: Etude sur la conception du pouvoir pontifical dans sa pensée et dans son œuvre*, L'Eglise et l'Etat au Moyen âge, no. 11 (Paris, 1956); idem, *Frédéric Barberousse*.

256 In 1159 Eckbert wrote Rainald of Dassel a letter congratulating him on his elevation to the seat of Cologne and reminding him that

they had known each other in youth; cf. *Die Regesten der Erzbischöfe von Köln*, vol. II, p. 114.

257 A Liège document states that these relics had been promised to Henri, bishop of Liège, by Frederick I, and that Rainald of Dassel had taken advantage of the bishop's death to lay hold of them. We see how valuable the bishops of the Rhine and Meuse areas considered these venerable bodies; cf. FICKER, *Reinald von Dassel*, p. 62. Frederick I, who had just dealt handsomely with Rainald in Italy, seems to have closed his eyes to this incident, perhaps because he was unaware of the value of these particular relics. The *Gesta Friderici*, quoted in *Die Regesten der Erzbischöfe von Köln*, vol. II, pp. 130-31, note, for 10 June 1164, that Rainald of Dassel set out for Cologne, taking with him the bodies of SS. Nabor and Felix, as well as "tria alia corpora, quae erant condita in archa, quae erat in ecclesia b. Eustorgii, et quae dicebantur esse Magorum trium...." However, other sources suggest that Rainald had not revealed the supposed identity of the rediscovered bodies to Frederick.

258 As time rolled on, innumerable legends were pinned to the story of the journey of the relics: probably they had no foundation but the claims made by many Swiss and German churches that they had venerated the holy bodies on the way; cf. H. CROMBACH, *Primitiae gentium seu Historia SS. Trium Regum Magorum evangelicorum et encomium* (Cologne, 1654). The author, a Jesuit, dedicated his work to the son of Emperor Frederick III; he spares the patient reader no detail, no legend. It is a golden book of forgeries, and more than one historian seems to have been taken in by it.

259 Perhaps without obtaining Frederick's consent. Shortly thereafter the emperor relieved Rainald of some of his duties.

260 Alexander III asked the archbishop of Rheims to halt the chancellor's march.

261 Consultation of the *Acts* of the archbishops of Cologne leaves no doubt about the authenticity of the itinerary described in 1850 by FICKER, *Reinald von Dassel*, p. 66, differing from so many less scrupulous historians, his successors. The only possible question concerns the date of Rainald's arrival—23 or 24 July.

262 *Die Regesten der Erzbischöfe von Köln*, vol. II, pp. 132-33.

263 G. VEZIN, *L'adoration et le cycle des Mages dans l'art chrétien primitif: Etude des influences orientales et grecques sur l'art chrétien*, Forme et style: Essais et mémoires d'art et d'archéologie (Paris, 1950).

264 Ibid., pp. 31-32. Vezin quotes PRUDENTIUS *Cathemerinon* Hymn 12: "De Epiphania": "The dust of myrrh foretells the tomb; the gold and the odor of Sabaean incense proclaim the king and God."

265 LEO I THE GREAT *Sermons* "Premier sermon pour l'Epiphanie" 2 (ed. and trans. J. LECLERCQ and R. DOLLE, S. C., no. 22 [Paris, 1949]), vol. I, pp. 190-93: the Magi "adore the Word in the flesh, wisdom in infancy, strength in weakness, and, in the reality of a man, the Lord of majesty. To show forth a sign of their faith and understanding, they bear witness by their gifts to what they believe in their hearts: they offer incense as to God, myrrh as to man, gold as to the king, conscious of honoring in unity the divine nature and the human nature."

266 There is a whole Greek tradition in the same sense, coming from the fourth century; cf. ELISSAGARAY, *La légende des Rois Mages*, pp. 23-24.

267 LEO I THE GREAT *Sermons* "Deuxième sermon pour l'Epiphanie" 2, 4, vol. I, pp. 196-97, 200-201.

268 LEO I THE GREAT *Sermons* "Troisième sermon pour l'Epiphanie" 2-3, vol. I, pp. 204-7.

269 BERNARD *In Epiphania Domini: Sermo II* (*PL* 185.52).

270 HUGH OF ST.-VICTOR *Sermones centum* 17, 36 (*PL* 177.932, 988-91).

271 ABELARD *Sermones* 4 (*PL* 178.409-17).

272 "Ac si jam in ipsis gentium primitiis, primi discipulorum Christi praesignarentur apostoli" (ABELARD *Sermones* 4 [*PL* 178.415]).

273 ABELARD *Sermones* 4 (*PL* 178.413). But the main theme of the commentaries is the Nativity; only the anecdote concerns the Magi.

274 RUPERT OF DEUTZ *De gloria et honore filii hominis super Matthaeum* 2 (*PL* 168.1333-34); idem *In Evangelium S. Johannis commentariorum libri XIV* 10 (*PL* 169.628); idem *In Apocalypsim Joannis Apostoli ad Fridericum* [Frederick was Rainald's predecessor] 9.16 (*PL* 169.1125).

275 "Videlicet corpora insignia beatissimorum trium Magorum ac Regum, qui primitiae gentium, in typum ac praesagium futurae ex gentibus Ecclesiae, jacenti adhuc Christo in praesepi munera pretiosa obtulerunt..." (*Acta Sanctorum*, Julii, vol. III [Antwerp, 1723], pp. 286-87); cf. *Die Regesten der Erzbischöfe von Köln*, vol. II, p. 131.

276 RAUH, *Das Bild des Antichrist.*

277 Frederick Barbarossa prohibited pressure and forced conversion; cf. PACAUT, *Frédéric Barberousse*, p. 122.

278 This is also the opinion of M. Elissagaray.

279 There may be some question as to how much the emperor participated in the ceremony of the translation of the relics. There is no doubt about the fact that afterward he fully supported the initiatives taken at Cologne. We note that one of the oldest mystery plays to put the Magi on the stage originated in Freising and probably dates from the eleventh century—and need we add that Freising had certain ties with the emperor! Cf. J. TORSY, "Achthundert Jahre Dreikönigenverehrung in Köln," in *Achthundert Jahre Verehrung der Heiligen Drei Könige in Köln, 1164-1964, Kölner Domblatt: Jahrbuch des Zentral-Dombauvereins* 23-24 (1964): 35.

280 We are frank to say that in this area we do not completely agree with the conclusions found in the copious German historical literature. There can be no doubt that in Germany analysis of the liturgy in its relation to the royal and imperial authority has been pushed much too far. This is particularly true, in our opinion, in the article by TORSY, "Achthundert Jahre Dreikönigenverehrung," p. 26. From seventeenth-century commentaries and from attitudes for which there is no proof before the fifteenth, the author draws hypotheses that go well beyond the premises, particularly for the twelfth and thirteenth centuries. Among other things, it is hard to see how a pope as jealous of his authority as Innocent IV could have granted an indulgence, even in 1247, to sinners who visited the miraculous tomb of the Magi in Cologne if the tomb was at the same time the symbol of the right to crown the emperor, claimed by the archbishop of Cologne, as our author supposes. However, we are happy to be able to glean useful information on other points from this work. We call attention here to the fine book by H. KEHRER, *Die Heiligen Drei Könige in Literatur und Kunst*, 2 vols. (1908-9; reprint ed. in 1 vol., Hildesheim and New York, 1976). On the spread of the Magi cult outward from Cologne and on the success of the pilgrimage itself, see *Achthundert Jahre Verehrung der Heiligen Drei Könige in Köln, 1164-1964, Kölner Domblatt: Jahrbuch des Zentral-Dombauvereins* 23-24 (1964), particularly the article by E. MEYER-WURMBACH, "Kölner 'Zeichen' und 'Pfennige' zu Ehren der Heiligen Drei Könige," ibid., pp. 205-92.

While we of course accept full responsibility for "daring" hypotheses and for errors which may have slipped into this part of our essay, we wish to acknowledge the information provided us by the remarkable preliminary study of the Magi theme written by Ladislas Bugner in 1970, and perhaps even more by the friendly conversations we have had, all during the preparation of this paper, on the Magi and many other matters. We ask Ladislas Bugner to accept our cordial thanks.

281 ELISSAGARAY, *La légende des Rois Mages*, p. 29; B. BISCHOFF, "Wendepunkte in der Geschichte der lateinischen Exegese im Frühmittelalter," *Sacris Erudiri* 6 (1954): 189-281. The author gives (pp. 216-17) the names used for the Magi before the ninth century in Western Europe: following the Hebrew: *Apellius, Arem, Damascus*; following

the Greek: *Malgalath, Galgalath, Saracin*; in Latin: *Humilis, Fidelis, Misericors*; following an apocryphal writing attributed to Isidore of Seville: *Melchio, Aspar, Patisarsa.*

282 Peter Comestor *Historia scholastica: In Evangelia* 8 (*PL* 198.1542); Elissagaray, *La légende des Rois Mages*, p. 30.

283 *Excerptiones Patrum* (*PL* 94.541); Elissagaray, *La légende des Rois Mages*, p. 28; Kehrer, *Die Heiligen Drei Könige in Literatur und Kunst*, vol. II, p. 223, still attributed this text to Bede.

284 On the life and visions of Elizabeth of Schönau, see *Acta Sanctorum*, Junii, vol. III (Antwerp, 1701), pp. 604-43; F.W.E. Roth, *Die Visionen und Briefe der hl. Elisabeth sowie die Schriften der Aebte Ekbert und Emecho von Schönau*, 2d ed., rev. and enl. (Brünn, 1886).

285 *Acta Sanctorum*, Junii, vol. III, p. 618.

286 Ibid., p. 624.

287 This text, *Historia de nativitate et infantia Salvatoris*, dates from the sixth century at the earliest; cf. Elissagaray, *La légende des Rois Mages*, pp. 19-20. It is impossible, except by long research, to learn how Elizabeth of Schönau could have known it, even by oral tradition; pure coincidence seems inadmissible to us.

288 Although she may have rallied to the support of the antipope Victor IV, perhaps at the instigation of her brother; cf. Roth, *Die Visionen und Briefe der hl. Elisabeth*, p. xcix.

289 This date seems admissible although F. W. E. Roth himself, basing his fixing of the date on a fifteenth-century text, acknowledges that some authors move it back a year (ibid., p. cii).

290 Ibid., p. xcvii.

291 K. Köster, "Elisabeth von Schönau: Werk und Wirkung im Spiegel der mittelalterlichen handschriftlichen Überlieferung," *Archiv für mittelrheinische Kirchengeschichte* 3 (1951): 243-315; idem, "Das Visionäre Werk Elisabeths von Schönau: Studien zu Entstehung, Überlieferung und Wirkung in der mittelalterlichen Welt," ibid. 4 (1952): 79-119.

292 "*Vita Eckeberti*," ed. Dr. Widmann, *Neues Archiv der Gesellschaft für ältere deutsche Geschichtskunde* 11 (1886): 447-54.

293 Ibid., pp. 452-53.

294 One author recently suggested the hypothesis that this prayer might go back to the twelfth century, whereas Roth, *Die Visionen und Briefe der hl. Elisabeth*, p. 176, holds that it belongs to the thirteenth, basing this conclusion on paleographic criteria; cf. H. Hofmann, *Die Heiligen Drei Könige: Zur Heiligenverehrung im kirchlichen, gesellschaftlichen und politischen Leben des Mittelalters*, Rheinisches Archiv, no. 94 (Bonn, 1975). In fact either date fits in with our argument. But we are wary of the tendency among Cologne historians to push back the date of certain texts for subjective, albeit perfectly honorable, reasons.

295 The passage devoted to Balthasar will suffice here: "Rex Baltasar, qui niger et rubea tunica indutus et calciamentorum varietate eadem stella dono dei securus et per miram ejus incarnationem ejus crucem et sanguinem figurasti, quem inmortalem, que divine nature, quem ineffabilis potentia cognovisti, te rogo pro peccatis et negligentiis meis" (H. Hofmann, *Die Heiligen Drei Könige*, p. 151).

296 *Thesaurus linguae latinae*, vol. VI, pt. 1 (Leipzig, 1912-26), cols. 1653-54, s.v. "fuscus": "Diff. gramm. VII 519, 18: fusco album opponitur, nigro candidum. Diff. ed. Beck 107, p. 40: fuscum est, quod neque album neque nigrum, sed medii est coloris. . . . Gloss. V 560, 13: affulvum: fuscum subnigrum. . . . Paulus Festus, p. 22: aquilus color est fuscus et subniger." The *Thesaurus* adds the detail that in the classical sources the word *fuscus* is applied to Indians, Ethiopians, and Egyptians: "Boethius (herm. pr. 1, 7, p. 89, 14) designat . . . 'homo albus non est' et rubri coloris esse et pallidi et fusci" (*Thesaurus linguae latinae*, vol. VI, pt. 1, col. 1654).

297 On the heritages from antiquity, see *The Realms of Colour. Die Welt der Farben. Le monde des couleurs*, ed. A. Portmann and R. Ritsema, Eranos-Jahrbuch, vol. 41 (Leiden, 1974).

298 The Magi became the patron saints of travelers (cf. A. Franz, *Die kirchlichen Benediktionen im Mittelalter* [Freiburg im Breisgau, 1909], vol. II, pp. 261 ff.), and then the guides of souls toward Salvation (A. Franz quotes [p. 268] a manuscript of 1466: "Caspar me ducat, Balthasar me regat, Melchior me salvet et ad vitam aeternam me perducant"). In the thirteenth century and thereafter they were credited with the power of curing epilepsy and many other diseases (idem, *Die kirchlichen Benediktionen*, pp. 300, 505).

299 Formerly in Berlin, Preussische Staatsbibliothek, MS. Quart. 700 (destroyed during the Second World War); W.W.S. Cook, "The Earliest Painted Panels of Catalonia (VI)," *ArtB* 10 (1927-28): 309-22 and fig. 16. The Catalan origin seems certain.

300 Vezin, *L'adoration et le cycle des Mages*, pp. 64-65.

301 In the seventeenth century H. Crombach (*Primitiae gentium*, pp. 214-15) raises the question whether or not the third Wise Man, Melchior in this case, came from India—"An tertius colore fusco ex India?"; then he establishes an affirmative answer. We find again this title: *Melchior Indorum rex triennio post adoratum Christum redit in Indiam, templum condidit Deiparae, cuius vestigia superant* (idem, *Primitiae gentium*, p. 534). In subsequent chapters the ties between Melchior and Thomas are examined. It is true that in the seventeenth century the conversion of India may have looked more important than that of Africa, especially to a Jesuit.

302 Cf. *supra*, pp. 72-80 and figs. 25-39, pp. 115-18, and p. 120, fig. 94.

303 Siena, cathedral, pulpit sculpted by Nicola Pisano, 1266-68: on one of the panels, Cortège of the Magi and Adoration of the Child; cf. E. Carli, *Il pulpito di Siena* (Bergamo, Milan, and Rome, 1943), pp. 18-19, pls. 32-37; M. Ayrton, *Giovanni Pisano: Sculptor* (London, 1969), pp. 157-84 and pls. 155-79.

304 Semur-en-Auxois, Church of Notre-Dame, north portal, tympanum: lower register.

305 See R. Bernheimer, *Wild Men in the Middle Ages: A Study in Art, Sentiment, and Demonology* (Cambridge, Mass., 1952), p. 26 and fig. 7.

306 William of Malmesbury was not the only one. In 1148 the Venetians boarded one of Manuel Comnenus's ships during the siege of Corfu, and a ceremony mocking His Majesty was organized. In a cabin hung with purple and gold fabric a black man was installed on a throne. His color was reminiscent of the swarthy complexion of the basileus, and the strange ceremonial was a mixture of ridiculous obeisances and insults; cf. W. Heyd, *Histoire du commerce du Levant au Moyen âge*, trans. F. Raynaud, French ed. rev. and enl. by the author, vol. I (Leipzig and Paris, 1885), p. 199.

307 William of Malmesbury *Gesta reg. Angl.* 4.377 (*PL* 179.1332), describing the capture of a town in the Holy Land, writes: "Caetera timore incolarum abrasa, praeter aliquantos Aethiopes, ferrugineam capillorum lanugine fuliginem praetendentes; quorum caedem nostri aestimantes infra virtutem suam, non eos ira, sed risu dignati sunt." Here the author expresses the feelings of a soldier from the West. Yet he notes that in the fortress of Jerusalem, when it fell, they found "quingentos quoque Aethiopas, qui . . . claves portarum, pollicita membrorum impunitate, tradiderant . . ."; the victors sent them off unharmed to Ashqelon, while the Turks were slaughtered (idem *Gesta reg. Angl.* 4.369 [*PL* 179.1321]).

308 On these matters the study of the *Chronicle of Spain* and the *General Chronicle*, composed on order of Alfonso X, is extremely rewarding. In them the French sources figure much more prominently than the Spanish, whether Christian or Muslim. In the *Chronicle of Spain* Muhammad is given a large amount of space, and Alexander makes an important appearance.

309 Chenu, *La théologie au douzième siècle*, pp. 80-81.

310 Medeiros, "Judaïsme, Islam et Gentilité," pp. 103 ff.

311 We are beginning to realize this through a systematic inquiry on the sources. F. de Medeiros notes (ibid., p. 104) that few works were copied as much in Europe as the *Disputatio Judaei et Christiani* by Gilbert Crispin, abbot of Westminster (1085-1117). In this work the Jew's arguments are carefully set forth, especially if they are embarrassing. To judge by the thirteenth-century Germanic sources we are talking about, the method appears to have been fully applied in the thirteenth century between the Rhine and the Danube, where there were powerful Jewish communities.

312 Berlin (GFR), Staatsbibliothek Preussischer Kulturbesitz, MS. lat. fol. 141, Rotulus: *Genealogia Christi*, about 1230, from Soest, Cathedral of St. Patroklus.

313 The Oriental Apocrypha go on at great length about Seth. His history was taken up again by Muslim and Jewish sources.

314 This indicates borrowing from outside sources. The word comes either from post-Ptolemaic Greek texts or from translated Arabic or Jewish writings.

315 "Aethiopia quae nunc Affrica." Never until now had so precise a detail been provided by a source coming from the imperial area.

316 This name probably comes from a Jewish source.

317 V. Nikiprowetzky, *La troisième Sibylle*, Ecole Pratique des Hautes Etudes, Sorbonne, Sixième section: Sciences économiques et sociales, Etudes juives, no. 9 (Paris and The Hague, 1970), pp. 36 ff.

318 On this point, cf. L. Poliakov, "Les idées anthropologiques des philosophes du Siècle des Lumières," *Revue française d'histoire d'outre-mer* 58, no. 212 (1971): 255-78.

319 From this point of view, the reduction of the genealogical ground to Jesse and his descendants, down to Christ, could have been seen in fifteenth-century France as a step toward this polygenistic theory.

320 P. Deslandres, *L'ordre des Trinitaires pour le rachat des captifs*, 2 vols. (Toulouse and Paris, 1903); R. von Kralik, *Geschichte des Trinitarierordens von seiner Gründung bis zu seiner zweiten Niederlassung in Österreich* (Vienna, [1918]).

321 This is no mean problem. After a military balance between Christians and Muslims became a reality in the tenth and eleventh centuries, their tactics consisted mostly of raids of pillage upon the enemy territory, in the course of which the largest possible number of resalable captives was taken. Thus to the immediate advantage of plunder was added the profit gained by exchange of prisoners and payment of ransom. The same war tactics, moreover, had long been used by Byzantines and Muslims. Until the Cluniacs intervened, Spanish Christendom accommodated itself to these customs more easily than did other European countries. A long-standing tradition in the West made it a duty for clergy to devote a part of their revenues to the eventual ransoming of captives. The Carolingian world concerned itself with the plight of those held in captivity and turned over sizable ransoms to the Normans in addition to the regular tribute paid them by the kings. It is known that both ransom and tribute affected the regional distribution of precious metals in Europe. This practice went on in Spain also in the eleventh century, although we still do not know much about the movement of currency and metals there.

322 In 1213 two merchants from Marseilles were excommunicated for selling children.

323 Kralik, *Geschichte des Trinitarierordens*, p. 30. The Rule was modified in 1217 and made less severe in 1263. In 1319 and 1421 it was replaced by two new statutes, which were reformed in 1576; in 1719 the statutes were changed once again. The order was thriving in the seventeenth and eighteenth centuries: it had 600 houses in thirteen provinces.

324 Deslandres, *L'ordre des Trinitaires*, vol. I, p. 319. These texts permit or command the diversion to the ransoming of captives of funds invested, for instance, in objects for church use.

325 One hundred eighty-six captives were first ransomed in Morocco in 1199 (ibid., p. 321). From then until the seventeenth century the activity of the Trinitarians and of other orders created for the same purpose (e.g., the Order of Our Lady of Mercy founded in 1228 in Provence) achieved conspicuous results through these highly specialized transactions. In 1315, for instance, at the request of Robert of Naples, they ransomed captives from Marseilles who were detained in Bougie (Bejaïa), Algeria (Deslandres, *L'ordre des Trinitaires*, vol. II, pp. 85-86, no. 59).

326 In Paris the Trinitarians were known as 'Mathurins'; cf. Kralik, *Geschichte des Trinitarierordens*, p. 24.

327 John of Matha died at S. Tommaso in Formis in 1213. This house was richly endowed. In the thirteenth century it was taken away from the order and then restored. At the end of the fourteenth century it was taken away for good.

328 G.B. de Rossi, *Musaici cristiani e saggi dei pavimenti delle chiese di Roma anteriori al secolo XV* (Rome, 1899), p. [163] and pl. XXXVI. The lower arch bears the following inscription: "Magister Iacobus cum filio suo Cosmato fecit ohc [hoc] opus." Jacopo and his son Cosma are also known for the works they executed in 1210 in another Roman church. See also W. Oakeshott, *The Mosaics of Rome from the Third to the Fourteenth Centuries* (Greenwich, 1967), pp. 298-99, 309; p. 308, fig. 193. W. Oakeshott dates this mosaic to 1218.

329 This was the insigne of the order decreed by the Rule of 1198. The cross itself was reproduced on a large scale above the medallion and on the arcature of the tabernacle.

330 "Signum ordinis sanctae Trinitatis et captivorum." Its authenticity is confirmed by an act passed in 1203 by the bishop of Marseilles.

331 L.-C. Douët d'Arcq, *Collection de sceaux*, Archives de l'Empire: Inventaires et documents (Paris, 1868), vol. III, pp. 233-36.

332 Ibid., pp. 233-34, nos. 9801 and 9802. Only in the latter example is the second captive identifiable as Saracen by his dress, but he is not black. Moreover, there are other scenes on certain thirteenth-century seals (Douët d'Arcq, *Collection de sceaux*, vol. III, pp. 234-35, nos. 9806-8).

333 Ibid., pp. 234-36, nos. 9803-16. This theme will be illustrated again, beginning in the late sixteenth century, in other forms.

334 Deslandres, *L'ordre des Trinitaires*, vol. II, p. 145:

> Angelus tenet in manus (sic)
> Viros binos: cristianus,
> Sarracenus sunt nomina;
> Dant signare quod paganus
> Et hic ordo Trinitanus
> Tractabunt mercamina.

335 Paris, Bibliothèque nationale, MS. lat. 9753, fol. 10v: here is described the vision which led John of Matha to found the order: ". . . vidit majestatem Dei et Deum tenentem in manibus suis duos viros habentes cathenas in tibiis, quorum unus niger et deformis apparuit, alter macer et pallidus" (quoted in Deslandres, *L'ordre des Trinitaires*, vol. II, p. 142).

336 Paris, Musée de Cluny: fragment from the lower register of the tympanum of the Last Judgment portal, west façade of the Cathedral of Notre-Dame in Paris.

III

A SANCTIFIED BLACK: MAURICE

1 The veneration of St. Maurice has had a vigorous life throughout the centuries at the Abbey of Saint-Maurice in Agaunum. Magnificently situated where the Valais opens out toward the Lake of Geneva, the monastery played an important role, at least until the thirteenth century, in the relations between the areas north and south of the Alps. In their work entitled *Vies des Saints et des Bienheureux selon l'ordre du calendrier avec l'historique des fêtes*, vol. IX, *Septembre* (Paris, 1950), p. 455, the Benedictines of Paris make the point that certain critics consider it probable that the names of Maurice and his companions are inventions: "Maurice" would stand for 'black', "Candidus" for 'white', "Exuperius" for 'raised on high', "Victor" for 'victorious'. They also note (p. 457) that in France sixty-two communes are named for St. Maurice.

2 Note that in our time the Swiss Confederation, which regards Maurice as a "national" saint, adopted his banner (white cross on a red ground, an inversion of St. George's red cross) as the federal emblem. L. Réau, *Iconographie de l'art chrétien*, vol. III, *Iconographie des saints*, pt. 2 (Paris, 1958), p. 936, remarks that Maurice was venerated at Angers where King René created the Order of the Crescent in his honor and where the cathedral was named for him. Réau also notes that the same King René had Maurice depicted as his patron saint in the *Triptych of the Burning Bush* housed in the Cathedral of St-Sauveur at Aix-en-Provence, a treatment we find repeated in the painting by the Master of Moulins in Glasgow, Glasgow Art Gallery and Museum. Tours also venerated Maurice's memory and dedicated its cathedral to him. Vienne, in the Isère, possessed relics, about which we shall see more later on, and rendered a devout cult to the martyr of Agaunum as early as the eighth century. Northern Italy created a military order in honor of St. Maurice. Poland and Riga in Latvia venerated him. Finally (we are still following Réau who put these details in no particular order), Maurice is often associated with other saints: first with his companions in martyrdom, then with other military saints (George, Demetrius, Mercurius), and sometimes with St. Erasmus, St. Lupinus, or St. Martin. We shall come back to most of these points to clarify them further.

3 The critical position is exemplified by J. Bernard de Montmélian, *Saint Maurice et la Légion thébéenne*, 2 vols. (Paris, 1888); despite its date this work is still important. Likewise critical is D. van Berchem, *Le martyre de la Légion thébaine: Essai sur la formation d'une légende*, Schweizerische Beiträge zur Altertumswissenschaft, no. 8 (Basel, 1956), who sternly repudiates the legend set down by Eucherius. Berchem points out that Agaunum has no tradition of its own and that the monks simply adopted the versions that came from Lyons and Vienne. In this author's opinion the body of the legend is of late origin, and he postulates a bishop of the end of the fourth century as its organizer; he insists on the political aspect of the localization of the legend pertaining to St. Maurice and his companions.

4 L. Dupraz, *Les passions de S. Maurice d'Agaune: Essai sur l'historicité de la tradition et contribution à l'étude de l'armée pré-dioclétienne (260-286) et des canonisations tardives de la fin du IVe siècle*, Studia Friburgensia, n.s., no. 27 (Fribourg, 1961). L. Dupraz has pursued this point further in idem, "Les rapports de l'archéologie et de l'histoire illustrés par les trouvailles de Saint-Maurice d'Agaune," *Jahrbuch der Schweizerischen Gesellschaft für Urgeschichte* 50 (1963): 26-32; this paper makes use in part of H. de Riedmatten, "L'historicité du martyre de la Légion Thébaine: Simples réflexions de méthodologie," *Annales Valaisannes*, 2d ser., nos. 2-4 (October 1962): 331-48.

5 For different editions of Eucherius *Passio Agaunensium martyrum*, see Bernard de Montmélian, *Saint Maurice et la Légion thébéenne*, vol. I, pp. 213-21; *CSEL* 31.1.165-72; *Monumenta Germaniae historica: Scriptorum rerum Merovingicarum*, vol. III, ed. B. Krusch (Hannover, 1896), pp. 20-41 (hereafter cited as *MGH*). The manuscripts are scarce: Paris has four, dating from the sixth-seventh, tenth, and thirteenth centuries; Saint-Gall has one dating from the ninth century; Leiden and Munich, one each from the twelfth century. We may note the curious coincidence that in the manuscript located in Paris, Bibliothèque nationale, MS. nouv. acq. lat. 453, the *Passion* of St. Maurice is accompanied by an apocryphal document relating to St. Thomas; cf. *Passio sancti Thomae Apostoli* in M. Bonnet, ed., *Acta Thomae*, Supplementum codicis apocryphi, vol. I (Leipzig, 1883), pp. 133-60. The Leiden manuscript contains a commentary by Sigebert of Gembloux on the Theban martyrs along with passages borrowed from Gregory of Tours and Venantius Fortunatus on the same subject.

6 Letter to Salvian, a friend of Eucherius (*CSEL* 31.1.173).

7 Marbod of Rennes *Passio sancti Mauritii et sociorum ejus* (*PL* 171.1625-30). Note that the author says nothing about St. Maurice's color—nor did the bishop of Lyons for that matter. The text had some circulation in the twelfth and thirteenth centuries, particularly in Germanic Europe.

8 E. Duemmler, "Sigebert's von Gembloux Passio sanctae Luciae virginis und Passio sanctorum Thebeorum," *Abhandlungen der königlichen Akademie der Wissenschaften zu Berlin: Philosophisch-historische Classe*, no. 1 (1893): 1-125.

9 L. Dupraz edited the text following two manuscripts: Paris, Bibliothèque nationale, MS. lat. 5301 and Einsiedeln, abbey, MS. 256 (461); cf. Dupraz, *Les passions de S. Maurice d'Agaune*, Appendixes II and III, pp. 8*-18*. A German translation of the Einsiedeln manuscript has been done by P. Müller, "Mauritius, Zeuge seines Glaubens: Die Einsiedelner Version X 2 der Passion des heiligen Mauritius," in F. Schrader, ed., *Beiträge zur Geschichte des Erzbistums Magdeburg*, Studien zur Katholischen Bistums- und Klostergeschichte, vol. 11 (Leipzig, 1968), pp. 179-91.

10 Dupraz, *Les passions de S. Maurice d'Agaune*, pp. 170 ff.

11 Ibid., pp. 196 ff.

12 Ibid., p. 241.

13 Ibid., pp. 295-96.

14 Gregory of Tours states that the relics of the martyrs buried at Agaunum were, in his time, the object of profound veneration; cf. Gregory of Tours *Historia francorum* 10 in *MGH: Script. rer. Mer.*, vol. I, ed. W. Arndt and B. Krusch (1885), p. 448.

15 Dupraz, *Les passions de S. Maurice d'Agaune*, p. 296.

16 Cf. J.-M. Theurillat, "L'Abbaye de St-Maurice d'Agaune des origines à la réforme canoniale, 515-830 environ," *Vallesia: Bulletin annuel de la Bibliothèque et des Archives cantonales du Valais, des Musées de Valère et de la Majorie* 9 (1954): 97 ff. The author places the scene of the martyrdom in the plain of Vérolliez two kilometers upriver from Agaunum. He thinks the bodies were buried in a common trench before Theodore, bishop of Octodurus, transferred them at the end of the fourth century. A modest monastery, he surmises, was erected over the tomb at that time. The author follows step by step the successive transformations of the buildings as the excavations at Agaunum have brought them to light.

17 Ibid.: remarkable study of the documents relating to the abbey. J.-M. Theurillat's conclusions agree fairly often with L. Dupraz's.

18 This was an Eastern custom, still unknown in the West as a whole (ibid., p. 32).

19 Sigismund founded the abbey before his accession to power. In this he followed the advice of Maximus, bishop of Geneva, in order to gain the protection of the martyrs for his Burgundian kingdom (ibid., p. 39), summoning monks from the region around Lyons and from the Jura (ibid., p. 57). Sigismund was martyred by the Franks after his

defeat, and himself became an object of veneration. In the Carolingian period a *Passion* was written about this Burgundian saint; see *Vitae sanctorum generis regii: Passio sancti Sigismundi regis* in *MGH: Script. rer. Mer.*, vol. II, ed. B. Krusch (1888), pp. 329-40. There would be good reason to study the cult of St. Sigismund himself. He was soon regarded as a protector against fevers; cf. Dijon, Bibliothèque municipale, MS. 448, from the Abbey of Saint-Bénigne, early eleventh century, fol. 8r: "Carmen ad febres. . . . Pro commemoratione sancti Sigismundi regis libera famulum vel famulam N. Domine Deus in nomine P. dico vobis febres. In nomine Filii contradico vos. In nomine SS. conivro vos febres. . . ." Sigismund was frequently invoked in areas where swamp fever was prevalent: the cartography of these invocations would therefore probably furnish some interesting medical information. We have come across invocations of this nature in the following manuscripts: Paris, Bibliothèque nationale, MS. lat. 816 (Angoulême, ninth century), fol. 115v: "Missa Si. Sigismundi regis que pro febribus cantari solet"; Orléans, MS. 105 (Winchcombe [Gloucester], tenth century), fol. 212r: "Missa in honore Si. Sigismundi regis et martyris et pro febricitantibus"; Tours, MS. 184, *Sacramentary of St. Martin* (late ninth century), fol. 284v: "Missa S. Sigismundi regis pro febribus"; Rheims, MS. 214 (late tenth century), fol. 119v: "Missa S. Sigismundi regis contra febres." Similar mentions are found in eleventh-century manuscripts from Reichenau, Metz, and Saint-Denis; cf. V. Leroquais, *Les sacramentaires et les missels manuscrits des bibliothèques publiques de France* (Paris, 1924), vol. I, pp. 8, 89-91, 43-53 (esp. p. 46), 91-94, 113-16, 118-19, 142-44. In the eleventh century Sigismund became the patron saint of Einsiedeln Abbey; in the fourteenth century his cult was still alive at Freising and in North Italy. Emperor Charles IV gave the devotion a new impetus when, in 1365, he bought relics of St. Sigismund for the Cathedral of St. Vitus in Prague; cf. Réau, *Iconographie de l'art chrétien*, vol. III, *Iconographie des saints*, pt. 3 (1959), pp. 1214-16.

It would also be of interest to study the variations—rather subtle, to judge by the surveys we have made—in the relations between the cult of St. Sigismund and that of St. Maurice in the fifteenth century. The commemoration of Sigismund in May no longer had the purely utilitarian aspect it had had previously.

20 M. Roblin, *Le terroir de Paris aux époques gallo-romaine et franque: Peuplement et défrichement dans la "Civitas" des "Parisii" (Seine, Seine-et-Oise)*, 2d ed., enl. (Paris, 1971), pp. 161-62, mentions a Church of St-Maurice at Rouen in 420, as well as chapels at Nanterre and Charenton in the fifth century.

21 Venantius Fortunatus *De sanctis Agaunensibus* (*PL* 88.108-9).

22 Beginning in the early Middle Ages, the manuscripts of the Hieronymian Martyrology generally include Maurice and his companions.

23 The Hieronymian Martyrology just referred to puts the figure at 6,585! Jacob of Voragine *La Légende dorée* (trans. J.-B. M. Roze [Paris, 1967]), vol. II, pp. 218-22, of course retains all the picturesque details of Maurice's career; he fixes the number of martyrs at 6,666 (p. 219) and the date as 280 (p. 220).

24 Berchem, *Le martyre de la Légion thébaine*, pp. 48 ff.

25 We are not sure we would be justified in including in the Merovingian documentation the testimony of the *Gesta Dagoberti I. regis Francorum* in *MGH: Script. rer. Mer.*, vol. II, p. 421, which describes Dagobert's devotion to SS. Denis, Maurice, and Martin. The date of this text is uncertain; in any case, it is from the eighth or more probably the ninth century.

26 B. Opfermann, "Das Messformular von Fest des heiligen Mauritius," in Schrader, *Beiträge zur Geschichte des Erzbistums Magdeburg*, pp. 192-213. We shall refer frequently to this study.

27 Ibid., pp. 193-94 (entire text given). See also F. Cabrol and H. Leclercq, *Dictionnaire d'archéologie chrétienne et de liturgie*, vol. X, pt. 2 (Paris, 1932), cols. 2724-25.

28 Opfermann, "Das Messformular," in Schrader, *Beiträge zur Geschichte des Erzbistums Magdeburg*, p. 195. The author gives all needed references to the single manuscript and to the most recent edition.

29 Ibid., pp. 195-96. Complete references to the single manuscript and to the most recent edition.

30 It would be advisable to check the ancient manuscripts of the Sacramentary before reaching a conclusion: for instance, a manuscript from Aachen dating from the end of the eighth century does not mention St. Maurice. He is also absent from the *Liber Sacramentorum*.

31 Opfermann, "Das Messformular," in Schrader, *Beiträge zur Geschichte des Erzbistums Magdeburg*, p. 196, with references. The burden of the prayers is still a plea for the martyrs' intercession in favor of sinners. Other trends, as we shall see, appear in the Carolingian world.

32 Ibid., pp. 197-98. According to the texts published by Opfermann, the Fulda Sacramentary (tenth-eleventh century) reproduces the prayer over the offerings from the Angoulême Sacramentary. The same prayer appears again in a Niederaltaich compilation (Vatican, Biblioteca Apostolica Vaticana, MS. Ross. lat. 204, eleventh century) and in the Lateran Missal (eleventh-twelfth century). The prayers of Compline also went from Angoulême to the Lateran, and the Preface from Angoulême to Fulda.

33 Ibid., p. 197. There are numerous copies found in the following compilations: Niederaltaich (eleventh century), Lateran (tenth-eleventh century); also in a missal from Brandenburg (1494) but probably by way of a relay that we have not discovered.

34 An examination of the sequences relating to St. Maurice (ibid., pp. 209-10) confirms our analysis. For the tenth century, besides two sequences whose locations are unknown, there are one in France, one at Reichenau, and two at Saint-Gall. Then a long silence—one example each for the eleventh, twelfth, and thirteenth centuries—before the sequences reappear in the fourteenth century.

35 Ibid., pp. 197-98. References and text (tenth-eleventh century).

36 See L. Delisle, "Mémoire sur d'anciens sacramentaires," *Mémoires de l'Académie des Inscriptions et Belles-Lettres* 32, pt. 1 (1886): 57-423; Leroquais, *Les sacramentaires et les missels manuscrits*, vol. I; H. Quentin, *Les martyrologes historiques du moyen âge: Etude sur la formation du martyrologe romain*, Etudes d'histoire des dogmes et d'ancienne littérature ecclésiastique (Paris, 1908); A. Lechner, *Mittelalterliche Kirchenfeste und Kalendarien in Bayern* (Freiburg im Breisgau, 1891); A. Schröder, *Das Bistum Augsburg*, vol. I, *Die ältesten Heiligenkalendarien des Bistums Augsburg* (Augsburg, 1909-11); P. Miesges, *Der Trierer Festkalender: Seine Entwicklung und seine Verwendung zu Urkundendatierungen*, Trierisches Archiv, supp. no. 15 (Trier, 1915).

37 Mentions in the Sacramentaries of Senlis, Amiens, Saint-Vaast, Corbie, Rheims. *De Liturgia Gallicana libri tres* 3.64 (*Missale Gothicum*: "Missa sancti ac beatissimi Mauricii cum sociis suis") (*PL* 72.302-3).

38 Cf. the Sacramentaries of Gellone (second half of the eighth century), Saint-Amand, Senlis, Amiens.

39 Usuard *Le martyrologe d'Usuard: Texte et commentaire* (ed. J. Dubois, Subsidia hagiographica, no. 40 [Brussels, 1965], p. 307).

40 Quentin, *Les martyrologes historiques du moyen âge*, p. 33, studies one example of a copy of Bede's Martyrology with such interpolations. The text, he says, came from Le Mans, and the manuscript was written in Italy at the end of the tenth or beginning of the eleventh century. The same author shows that additions relating to St. Maurice were made to the Martyrology of Florus.

41 They are always associated in the ninth and tenth centuries and celebrated on 22 September. Later the cult of St. Maurice tends to be restricted to him alone.

42 We have been able to follow to some extent the way the situation evolved in the province of Rheims. This province was not at all favorable to the development of the cult of St. Maurice, being extremely careful, at least from the mid-ninth century on, to guard the regional primacy of St. Remigius. Yet the Abbey of Saint-Thierry, near Rheims, seems to have maintained a resolute independence when faced with pressure from the bishops. A ninth-century, liturgical manuscript from Saint-Thierry (Rheims, Bibliothèque municipale, MS. 213, fol. 107[r]) includes for 22 September a mass in honor of St. Maurice and his companions; at Compline the celebrant prays for the protection of the community by Maurice and the other martyrs: "Caelestibus refecti sacrosanctis, . . . supplices te rogamus, omnipotens deus, ut quorum gloriamur triumphis protegamur auxiliis. Per. . . ." The same office is found in a tenth-century manuscript originating at Saint-Thierry (Rheims, Bibliothèque municipale, MS. 304, fol. 21[v]). The other provincial, liturgical manuscripts which we have consulted are infinitely more noncommittal.

Other codices of the eleventh and twelfth centuries show that the Maurician cult had not disappeared. At Laon (Bibliothèque municipale, MS. 261, fols. 102[v]-109[v]), a manuscript contains the *Passion*. At Rheims itself (Bibliothèque municipale, MS. 300, fols. 127[r]-128[v]), eight lessons taken from the *Vita* are all that survives of the cult; there is no longer a special mass. Finally, a Rhemish manuscript (Rheims, Bibliothèque municipale, MS. 235, fol. 221[r]), written in the fifteenth century for the province of Trier, contains no more than a simple mention of SS. Maurice and Gatian.

43 On this specific point we are preparing a supplementary study which will be published at a later date.

44 Alcuin *Carmina* in *MGH: Poetae Latini aevi Carolini*, vol. I, ed. E. Duemmler (Berlin, 1881), p. 314: a purely literary text with no religious or liturgical import. Theodulf *Carmina* in *MGH: Poetae*, vol. I, p. 559 ("Versus in die Palmarum"), gives Maurice only a minor and purely conventional mention. The same is true for the following: Rabanus Maurus *Carmina* in *MGH: Poetae*, vol. II, ed. E. Duemmler (1884), pp. 207, 218; Ermoldus Nigellus *Carmina* in *MGH: Poetae*, vol. II, p. 49; Wandalbert of Prüm *Carmina* in *MGH: Poetae*, vol. II, p. 594 ("Martyrologium: September"); *Carmina centulensia* 68, 152 in *MGH: Poetae*, vol. III, ed. L. Traube, pt. 2, fasc. 1 (1892), pp. 320, 358. A change comes with Walafrid Strabo *Carmina* 21 in *MGH: Poetae*, vol. II, pp. 367-69 ("Ymnus de Agaunensibus martyribus"): he exhorts his readers to admire St. Maurice and his companions. This work must have been very popular, judging by the number of manuscripts found in the same geographic area we have seen defined by mentions in the liturgy. A Rhemish Martyrology in verse (Paris, Bibliothèque nationale, MS. lat. 9432), dating from the second half of the ninth century, mentions the saint and his companions, but only briefly; cf. Quentin, *Les martyrologes historiques du moyen âge*, pp. 120-30.

45 One index of the influence of the Maurice cult among the people at large is the use of the patronymic. This was very rare at least until the thirteenth century, judging by the surveys we have made.

46 F. Piper, *Karls des Grossen Kalendarium und Ostertafel aus der Pariser Urschrift* (Berlin, 1858). If what follows is to be understood, Maurice's new status as a model of the soldierly virtues and then as the perfect knight must be kept clearly in mind. Although he did not emerge as a spectacular literary figure like Roland, Percival, or Galahad, Maurice the knight is celebrated in an abundant and important iconography.

47 Eginhard *Vita Karoli Magni*, ed. G.H. Pertz and G. Waitz, 6th ed., in *MGH: Scriptores rerum Germanicarum in usum scholarum*, vol. 25 (Hannover and Leipzig, 1911), pp. 46-47 (*Litania Karolina*): "Pipino rege Longobardorum vita! Sancti Mauricii, tu lo juva!" A. Prost, "Caractère et signification de quatre pièces liturgiques composées à Metz en latin et en grec au IXe siècle," *Mémoires de la Société nationale des Antiquaires de France*, 4th ser. 7 (1876): 174, points out a late eighth-century psalter (Paris, Bibliothèque nationale, MS. lat. 13159, fol. 163[r]), which strikes this note in the prayers of Lauds:

> Exaudi Christe. R/. *Omnibus judicibus vel cuncto exercitui Francorum vita et victoria.*
> Se Hilari. R/. Tu illos adjuva.
> Se Martine. R/. Tu illos adjuva.
> Se Maurici. R/. Tu illos adjuva.
> Se Dionisi. R/. Tu illos adjuva.
> Se Crispine. R/. Tu illos adjuva.
> Se Crispiniane. R/. Tu illos adjuva.
> Se Gereon. R/. Tu illos adjuva.
> Christus vincit....

Another text, probably originating in Saint-Gall and written between 858 and 867, contains the same official prayer, with St. Alban inserted between St. Denis and St. Crispin (idem, "Caractère et signification de quatre pièces liturgiques," pp. 175-76). The Metz Lauds (second half of the ninth century) repeats the same prayer, but Crispin and Crispinian have disappeared (idem, "Caractère et signification de quatre pièces liturgiques, " pp. 237-40). In a text from Beauvais dated 1002, St. Maurice's name has been dropped both from the prayer for the king and from the prayer for the army: the Capetians left the patronage of St. Maurice to the emperors (idem, "Caractère et signification de quatre pièces liturgiques," pp. 180-82).

48 The confraternities and guilds played an important role in England at that time; see E. Coornaert, "Les ghildes médiévales (V[e]-XIVe siècles): Définition. Evolution," *Revue historique* 199 (1948): 35-41. Their activity in the Carolingian Empire has not yet been closely studied.

49 The royal acts mentioning St. Maurice became increasingly rare. The Acts of Philip I cite a donation in which a Church of St-Maurice at Compiègne is involved, the presence of another church at Villemeux (Eure-et-Loire), and a place dedicated to St. Maurice in the Haute-Loire; cf. M. Prou, ed., *Recueil des Actes de Philippe Ier, roi de France (1059-1108)*, Chartes et Diplômes relatifs à l'histoire de France publiés par l'Académie des Inscriptions et Belles-Lettres (Paris, 1908), pp. 319-20 (donation of 7 March 1092), p. 166, n. 3 (donation of 21 May 1073), and p. 43 (confirmation of a donation to the Church of St-Philibert in Tournus). The *Gallia christiana* contains very little relative to St. Maurice: in the eleventh century, donation of a church near Forcalquier (in empire territory) and foundation of a church at Carnoët; in the twelfth, acquisition of the church at Rians by the diocese of Aix, but also the disappearance of St. Maurice's name at Sens in favor of St. Remigius, who rarely tolerated Maurice on Rhemish soil. In the thirteenth century, it is again a parcel of empire land that the bishop of Riez grants to Templars of St. Maurice, while at Senlis relics of the saint are installed in a chapel, dedicated to Maurice and the martyrs of Agaunum (1264), close to the royal palace. This last event is evidence of St. Louis's devotion to Maurice, about which we shall speak further. Except for the mention of an abbey near Amiens, the *Gallia* gives us no other references. At Tours the cult of St. Maurice seems to have waned after the twelfth century. A council held by Alexander III at the Cathedral of St-Maurice in Tours in 1163 did nothing to change this, nor did the dedication of a church to Maurice at Dijon by Paschal II in 1107 revive popular piety to any extent; cf. L. Duchesne, ed., *Le Liber Pontificalis*, Bibliothèque des Ecoles françaises d'Athènes et de Rome, 2d ed. (Paris, 1955), vol. II, p. 310. Similar observations could be made about Italy which was not directly subject to imperial authority. Anagni and Canossa seem to have been centers of veneration, but we have not come across others. The situation is quite different, as we shall see, when we cross the western limits of imperial control.

50 On Charlemagne's gifts to Agaunum, see A. Grabar, "L'archéologie des insignes médiévaux du pouvoir," *Journal des Savants*, January-March 1956, pp. 5-19; April-June 1956, pp. 77-92; January-March 1957, pp. 25-31. Charles the Bald visited Agaunum several times, and the abbey continued to be of great political importance in the ninth century.

51 Ado, archbishop of Vienne, in his *Chronicle*, speaks of the construction of a small vaulted building in honor of St. Maurice (860-75).

52 Sacramentary destined for the Abbey of Winchcombe. St. Maurice and his companions come into the Martyrologies of Bede which are of Anglo-Saxon origin only at a late date; cf. F. PIPER, *Die Kalendarien und Martyrologien der Angelsachsen, so wie das Martyrologium und der Computus der Herrad von Landsperg* (Berlin, 1862). But the calendar of St. Willibrord mentions the martyr, with 6,666 companions, on 22 September; see H.A. WILSON, ed., *The Calendar of St. Willibrord from MS. Paris. Lat. 10837: A Facsimile*, Henry Bradshaw Society, vol. 55 (London, 1918).

53 H.A. WILSON, ed., *The Missal of Robert of Jumièges*, Henry Bradshaw Society, vol. 11 (London, 1896). This missal contains an office for 22 September which has little that is original except for Compline.

54 Of course our investigations may be partly responsible for some lacunae, but we have found nothing of real importance south of the Loire and the Alps. It is difficult to say anything final about the Rome manuscript, MS. Casanatense 719 (B.I. 4), dating from the end of the eleventh century, which mentions the *Passion* at fols. 138[r] ff.: its origin is unknown.

55 In the eleventh century, a commemoration of SS. Maurice and Exuperius and their companions was interpolated in a sacramentary from Senlis (about 880), fol. 21[v]. In the twelfth, a mass in honor of St. Maurice is added to a ninth-century sacramentary from Amiens; a tenth-century sacramentary from Saint-Denis contains, at fol. 41[v], a marginal note: "oration for the mass of St. Maurice." In a late tenth-century sacramentary from Angers, at fol. 53[v] "Laurentio intercedente beato" is replaced by "Mauricio, martyre tuo," and at fols. 90[r]-91[v] the passages relating to St. Maurice look to be by another hand than the rest of the manuscript. This information is taken from LEROQUAIS, *Les sacramentaires et les missels manuscrits*, vol. I, pp. 32-33, 38-43, 64-68, 85-89. See also H. MÉNARD, ed., *Divi Gregorii Papae . . . Liber Sacramentorum . . . ex Missali ms. Sancti Eligii* (Paris, 1642), p. 180: later additions relating to St. Maurice in the Codex of Ratoldus, abbot of Corbie at the end of the tenth century. Such additions were made only rarely in the twelfth century.

56 At Freising, from whence the movement seems to have spread, at Salzburg, and at Saint-Gall.

57 R. POUPARDIN, *Le Royaume de Provence sous les Carolingiens (855-933?)*, Bibliothèque de l'Ecole des Hautes Etudes, Sciences philologiques et historiques, fasc. 131 (Paris, 1901), pp. 357-68 (app. X: "L'Obit de Boson et le Reliquaire de Saint-Maurice de Vienne").

58 Cf. PROST, "Caractère et signification de quatre pièces liturgiques," pp. 177-80. The author presents a text from the Limoges area of the tenth century (between 923 and 936) which reproduces a slightly earlier liturgy from Arles.

59 BERCHEM, *Le martyre de la Légion thébaine*, mentions frequent donations between 888 and the middle of the tenth century. The abbey at Agaunum, destroyed in 939 in a raid by Muslims based on the coast of Provence, was rebuilt and the pilgrimage resumed with the help of gifts made by Rudolf III of Burgundy.

60 Boso ordered the making of a reliquary in gold or gilded silver for the head of Maurice; see "Versus Bosonis" in *MGH: Poetae*, vol. IV, fascs. 2-3, ed. K. STRECKER (1923), p. 1054:

> Rex decorando Boso gemmis vestivit et auro
> Mauricii sancti hoc in honore caput

The king included in his epitaph a reminder of the devotion he had helped to promote; see "Epitaphium Bosonis regis" in *MGH: Poetae*, vol. IV, fascs. 2-3, pp. 1027-28:

> Regis in hoc tumulo requiescunt membra Bosonis.
> Hic pius et largus fuit, audax, ore facundus.
> Sancti Mauricii capud ast [et] circumdedit auro,
> Ornavit gemmis claris . . .
> . . . .
> Munera multa dedit patrono carmine dicto.

On this reliquary, see POUPARDIN, *Le Royaume de Provence*, pp. 357-68. This author studies not only Boso's generosity but also that of his successors in Provence and of the archbishops of Vienne.

61 A. J. HERZBERG, *Der heilige Mauritius: Ein Beitrag zur Geschichte der deutschen Mauritiusverehrung*, Forschungen zur Volkskunde, no. 25/26 (Düsseldorf, 1936). This very detailed book makes it possible to follow the transformations of the cult in Germany. Unfortunately we have no comparable study for the other countries. The oldest group of places dedicated to St. Maurice was located in the region of Trier and Saarbrücken; the church at Tholey, named for him in 920, is the oldest in Germany so identified. In the eleventh century there were some thirty places dedicated to the saint in the dioceses of Trier, Mainz, and Speyer, all tracing their origin to Tholey. Prüm adopted Maurice as a second patron saint at the end of the ninth century; an altar was dedicated to him in 862. It seems that from the beginning at Echternach there were relics of this saint; in the eleventh century St. Maurice had his altar. We find another group of places in Saxony in the tenth century. An abbey dedicated to SS. Maurice and Victor was founded near Bremen toward the middle of the century. A third group sprang up in Bavaria, starting at Niederaltaich, which was established in 741 by monks who came from Reichenau. Niederaltaich also received the liturgy of St. Maurice from Reichenau, probably in the ninth century. Herzberg raises a question which would be worth studying: how much did the tradition of the Bavarian dynasty have to do with these foundings, and how much is due to purely monastic initiative? In any case, Niederaltaich played a leading role in the spread of the Maurician cult and was repeatedly endowed by the Germanic kings and emperors.

In all the instances cited, the decision to propagate the cult of St. Maurice originated principally in monastic circles. But the influence of the aristocracy was also a factor in these foundations. The seal of the Abbey of Tholey shows Maurice as a knight, mounted, carrying a triangular shield decorated with a cross (idem, *Der heilige Mauritius*, pp. 48-70). This is a typical representation of a military saint. Herzberg notes (p. 56) that the role of the German nobility in the spread of the cult increased until the fourteenth century—one example in the eleventh century, three in the twelfth, eight in the thirteenth (especially in the second half, a fact probably traceable to imperial initiative, to which we shall return later on), eight in the fourteenth, then three in the fifteenth, two in the sixteenth, and one in the seventeenth. In the eleventh century, according to Herzberg, St. Maurice was one of the three saintly protectors of the armies whose intercession was prayed for in the ceremony of the dubbing of a knight: SS. George and Sebastian were the others. Herzberg further notes that the Maurician cult, which sometimes sprang up in the Rhineland during the eighth century (he is thinking principally of St. Firminus), suffered an eclipse from the ninth to the eleventh century and then enjoyed a brilliant resurgence. His conclusions might be still further refined. Judging by what we have just seen, the diffusion of the cult in Germany must have gone through three phases: (1) early tenth century, the western group, (2) Saxon and Ottonian enterprises, and (3) reaction of the old Alemannic and Bavarian substrata to these royal initiatives.

62 *Die Urkunden der deutschen Karolinger* in *MGH: Diplomata regum Germaniae ex stirpe Karolinorum*, vol. I, ed. P. KEHR, fasc. 1 (Berlin, 1932), p. 2 (diploma dated 6 October 830: the abbey is founded by Gauzbald "sacri palatii nostri summus cappellanus et abba monasterii quod dicitur Altaha, quod est constructum in honore sancti Mauricii martyris Christi . . ."); pp. 64-65 (diploma of 8 March 848?); pp. 80-81 (diploma of 22 March 851); p. 113 (diploma of 24 March 857). The abbey owned Slav serfs; privileges in 857 (cf. pp. 123-24), 860, 863, 864, 883, and 905. Later, other diplomas in 1040, 1045, 1048. See also G. STADTMÜLLER and B. PFISTER, *Geschichte der Abtei Niederaltaich 741-1971* (Augsburg, 1971).

63 We have found no trace of a major development of the Maurice cult at Cologne, even

at a time when, as we have seen, the transfer of the relics of the Magi gave the city an unprecedented religious quickening. It is as if in medieval times each town or region, while trying to acquire the relics of saints "foreign" to its area and of good reputation, sought to retain a kind of exclusive right to its own "specialty" in the matter of holy relics—a right tacitly admitted by other towns and regions, which did exactly the same thing for themselves. The cult of St. Maurice became a specialty of Magdeburg, and Cologne did not try to outdo the metropolis on the Elbe in this regard.

64 This subject has had ample treatment. See R. Poupardin, *Le Royaume de Bourgogne (888-1038): Etude sur les origines du Royaume d'Arles* (Paris, 1907); R. Folz, *Le Souvenir et la Légende de Charlemagne dans l'Empire germanique médiéval*, Publications de l'Université de Dijon, n.s., vol. 7 (Paris, 1950); Herzberg, *Der heilige Mauritius.* These authors furnish the best accounts and interpretations.

65 A. Brackmann, *Magdeburg als Hauptstadt des deutschen Ostens im frühen Mittelalter* (Leipzig, 1937), p. 3, thinks that Rudolf II was compelled to turn over the relics at Worms as a warranty of good faith, at a time when Henry I had been disturbed by the marriage of the Burgundian's daughter to the duke of Swabia in 922.

66 Grabar, "L'archéologie des insignes médiévaux du pouvoir," pp. 78-79. P. E. Schramm, *Herrschaftszeichen und Staatssymbolik: Beiträge zur ihrer Geschichte vom dritten bis zum sechzehnten Jahrhundert*, Schriften der Monumenta Germaniae historica (Deutsches Institut für Erforschung des Mittelalters), no. 13/II (Stuttgart, 1955), vol. II, pp. 492-537. Schramm thinks the lance was the emblem of power and authority among the ancient Germans. About the year 1000 the throne, the crown, and the scepter replaced it as symbols. But Poland, Bohemia, and Hungary kept the lance as a regal insigne for a long time.

67 Folz, *Le Souvenir et la Légende de Charlemagne*, p. 53.

68 W. Schlesinger, "Zur Geschichte der Magdeburger Königspfalz," in Schrader, *Beiträge zur Geschichte des Erzbistums Magdeburg*, pp. 9-43, shows that Otto's immediate successors gave much attention to the city, but that the Salians, after 1025, were far less interested in it.

69 Brackmann, *Magdeburg als Hauptstadt*: this book is somewhat dated, but the documentation given in it is clear. More recently, the collective study edited by Schrader, *Beiträge zur Geschichte des Erzbistums Magdeburg*, to which we have referred frequently, furnishes precise and scientifically reliable information. Finally, the work by D. Claude, *Geschichte des Erzbistums Magdeburg bis in das 12. Jahrhundert*, 2 pts., Mitteldeutsche Forschungen, vols. 67/I, 67/II (Cologne and Vienna, 1972-75), contains several passages with precise and very useful data on the Maurician cult.

70 H. Kunze, "Der Dom Ottos des Grossen in Magdeburg," *Geschichtsblätter für Stadt und Land Magdeburg* 65 (1930): 1-72, with excellent archeological maps; L. Grodecki, *Au seuil de l'art roman: L'architecture ottonienne*, Collection Henri Focillon, no. 4 (Paris, 1958), pp. 95 ff.; H.-J. Mrusek, *Drei deutsche Dome: Quedlinburg, Magdeburg, Halberstadt* (Dresden, 1963). Despite the efforts made, the buildings of the Ottonian period are still not well known. See W. Götz, "Der Magdeburger Domchor: Zur Bedeutung seiner monumentalen Ausstattung," *Zeitschrift des deutschen Vereins für Kunstwissenschaft* 20 (1966): 97-120, esp. p. 102. This excellent article is a clear commentary on the results to date of research on Magdeburg construction in successive periods.

71 Götz, "Der Magdeburger Domchor," p. 102, n. 24: a bull of Pope John XIII conferring on Magdeburg the rank of primatial see in Germany.

72 The translation of the relics was carried out with the utmost solemnity. The bishop of Basel took part; cf. Poupardin, *Le Royaume de Bourgogne*, p. 313. A detailed account is given by Thietmar of Merseburg *Chronicon* 2.17 in *MGH: Scriptores rerum Germanicarum*, n.s., vol. IX, ed. R. Holtzmann (Berlin, 1935), p. 58.

73 Folz, *Le Souvenir et la Légende de Charlemagne*, pp. 56-60. The lance acquired this title by decision of Otto the Great after 961. The first known mention dates from 1007.

74 Ibid., pp. 58, 457-60.

75 Schlesinger, "Zur Geschichte der Magdeburger Königspfalz," in Schrader, *Beiträge zur Geschichte des Erzbistums Magdeburg*, pp. 32-33.

76 "A Merseburg tunc exiens, sancti Mauricii apud Deum intercessionem itinerisque prosperitatem Magadaburg peciit" (Thietmar of Merseburg *Chronicon* 6.3 in *MGH: Script. rer. Germ.*, n.s., vol. IX, p. 276). Expedition of 1004.

77 "In nativitate sancti Johannis baptistae, quae tunc proxima erat, ad Gosleri cesar veniens, Ernasti ducatum nepti suae et filio ejus dedit; et inde ad Magathaburg proficiscens, interventum Cristi militis Mauricii ad exsuperandam hostis Bolizlavi contumatiam suppliciter rogavit" (Thietmar of Merseburg *Chronicon* 7.16 in *MGH: Script. rer. Germ.*, n.s., vol. IX, p. 416).

78 It is not possible to follow the advance of the Maurician cult east of the Oder through the materials so far published. It may be that all that happened in Poland was receipt of a copy of the "Lance of St. Maurice."

79 "Quomodo conveniunt Zuarasi vel diabolus et dux sanctorum vester et noster Mauritius? Qua fronte coeunt sacra lancea et, qui pascuntur humano sanguine, diabolica vexilla?" cited in Claude, *Geschichte des Erzbistums Magdeburg*, pt. I, p. 246.

80 Ibid., p. 247.

81 Ibid., p. 247: in June 1015 in Magdeburg, Henry II besought Maurice's help against the Poles.

82 Ibid., pp. 254 ff. As early as 997, Magdeburg men-at-arms killed in battle near Arneburg were called *milites sancti Mauricii.* In the twelfth century, a *ministerialis* of Magdeburg called himself, in his epitaph, a *miles sancti Mauricii.* Also in the twelfth century, the archbishops of Magdeburg could readily muster more than one thousand *milites sancti Mauricii*, fully equipped mounted men.

83 Ibid., p. 254.

84 Cf. H.D. Rauh, *Das Bild des Antichrist im Mittelalter: Von Tyconius zum deutschen Symbolismus*, Beiträge zur Geschichte der Philosophie und Theologie des Mittelalters, n.s., vol. 9 (Münster, 1973), pp. 263-64.

85 The practice of connecting the vicissitudes of life with dominant winds goes back to Greek antiquity, as we see from the works of philosophers and physicians, and perhaps even to ancient Egypt. This concept was part of a theory, still widespread, on the influence of the climates.

86 Cf. Rauh, *Das Bild des Antichrist im Mittelalter*, p. 264, who quotes Gregory the Great: "Per aquilonem vero gentilitas figuratur, quae diu in perfidiae suae frigore torpuit."

87 E. Neuss, "Die Gründung des Erzbistums Magdeburg und die Anfänge des Christentums im Erzstiftischen Südterritorium (Saalkreis)," in Schrader, *Beiträge zur Geschichte des Erzbistums Magdeburg*, pp. 45-86.

88 Before 1300, out of ninety-eight parishes checked only three were dedicated to St. Maurice; of five monasteries only one was his. At Halle only one of eleven churches bore his name. For the same period St. George has four parishes and one abbey. The "Maurician royalty" was not yet won around Magdeburg.

89 With the support of Henry III, the cathedral at Minden was dedicated to St. Maurice between 1042 and 1045; cf. H.A. Erhard, comp., *Regesta historiae Westfaliae*, vol. I (Münster, 1847), p. 180, no. 1030. It is to Frederick, bishop of Münster after 1064, that we owe the *Liber rubeus* of Minden, which mentions the possessions of the cathedral. In 1090 the new Collegiate Church of St. Maurice in Münster was opened for worship. Its properties were promptly inventoried by order of Bishop Erpho (1024-97); cf. M. Lapp, *Die Verfassung der Grundherrschaft*

St. Mauritz im Mittelalter (Borna and Leipzig, 1912). In the mid-twelfth century the cathedral already had about thirty altars. The work by F. DARPE, *Die Heberegister des Klosters Ueberwasser und des Stiftes St. Mauritz*, Codex traditionum Westfalicarum, no. 3 (Münster, 1888), completes the work cited above by M. Lapp and shows the growth of the riches of Münster's Collegiate Church of St. Maurice in the ensuing centuries.

90 In 1152, on the feast day of St. Maurice, Landgrave Louis II summoned the troops he hoped to employ in putting down a local war; cf. *Die Reinhardsbrunner Briefsammlung* in *MGH: Epistolae selectae*, vol. V, ed. F. PEECK (Weimar, 1952), pp. 48-49, no. 52.

91 *Die Urkunden der deutschen Könige und Kaiser* in *MGH: Diplomatum regum et imperatorum Germaniae*, vol. V, ed. H. BRESSLAU and P. KEHR, 2d ed. (Berlin, 1957), pp. 129-31, 573, etc. These texts interest us insofar as, for instance, Henry III confirms privileges relating to churches or abbeys dedicated to St. Maurice in northern and central Italy.

92 An Evangelistary from Mainz dating from the first half of the eleventh century shows a white St. Maurice, armed with the Holy Lance; cf. A. BÜHLER, "Die Heilige Lanze: Ein ikonographischer Beitrag zur Geschichte der deutschen Reichskleinodien," *Das Münster: Zeitschrift für christliche Kunst und Kunstwissenschaft* 16 (1963): 85-116, esp. p. 88. Henry II and Conrad II considered possession of the Holy Lance a major sign of their legitimacy (idem, "Die Heilige Lanze," p. 89). In Henry II's time the Holy Lance (by then called the "Lance of St. Maurice"), first mentioned by Bruno of Querfurt, received wide and favorable publicity from Benzo of Alba as well as from French authors, Suger among them.

93 C. ERDMANN, *Die Entstehung des Kreuzzugsgedankens*, Forschungen zur Kirchen- und Geistesgeschichte, vol. 6 (Stuttgart, 1935), p. 77: the consecrating priest blesses the banner, lance, sword, and shield, then the knight himself, invoking particularly the three military saints. Another interesting mention (p. 254), from the eleventh-century Pontifical of Cologne. For ORDERICUS VITALIS *Historia ecclesiastica* 6.1 (*PL* 188.451-52), Demetrius and George, Theodore and Sebastian, Maurice and Eustace prefigure the knight. A. FRANZ, *Die Kirchlichen Benediktionen im Mittelalter* (Freiburg im Breisgau, 1909), vol. II, pp. 295-97: "Ordo ad armandum ecclesiae defensorem vel alium militem.... *Oratio*: Domine deus, qui conteris bella ... et per merita sanctorum martyrum tuorum et militum Mauritii, Sebastiani, Georgii . . . ." HERZBERG, *Der heilige Mauritius*, lays great stress on this aspect of the matter. See also STADTMÜLLER and PFISTER, *Geschichte der Abtei Niederaltaich*, p. 62.

94 *Gallia christiana*, vol. III (Paris, 1725), p. 781: an order of women dedicated to St. Maurice was created at Cologne in 1140 by a patrician and his wife. T. KLAUSER and R.S. BOUR, "Un document du IXe siècle: Notes sur l'ancienne liturgie de Metz et sur ses églises antérieures à l'an mil," *Annuaire de la Société d'Histoire et d'Archéologie de la Lorraine* 38 (1929): 497-639; this article notes that a chapel of St. Maurice was put at the disposal of the Templars in Metz in 1133. We have not been able to find any solid connection between the Maurice cult and the military orders in general. The question would be worth studying, at least for Europe. In the East St. Maurice was not regarded as very important, to judge by the slight mention given him by WILLIAM OF TYRE *Historia rerum in partibus transmarinis gestarum* 19.8 in *Recueil des historiens des Croisades: Historiens occidentaux*, vol. I (Paris, 1844), pt. 2, p. 894.

95 BENZO OF ALBA *Gesta romanae aecclesiae contra Hildebrandum* Ep. 2.11 (ed. K. FRANCKE) in *MGH: Libelli de lite Imperatorum et Pontificum. Saeculis XI. et XII. Conscripti*, vol. II (Hannover, 1892), p. 380.

96 BENZO OF ALBA *Gesta romanae aecclesiae* Ep. 3.4 in *MGH: Libelli*, vol. II, p. 382.

97 HONORIUS OF AUTUN *Summa Gloria* 24 (ed. I. DIETERICH) in *MGH: Libelli*, vol. III (1897), p. 74: "Sic et Mauritius cum exercitu suo eisdem imperatoribus auxilium contra hostes regni prebuit; cum vero contra religionem christianam agere ab eisdem cogeretur, facere renuit . . . ."

98 The text, *Das Annolied* v. 102 (ed. M. ROEDIGER) in *MGH: Deutsche Chroniken und andere Geschichtsbücher des Mittelalters*, vol. I (Hannover, 1895), pt. 2, p. 117, records that St. Maurice is the protector of the empire. The *Saxon Chronicle* (*Sächsische Weltchronik* 73 in *MGH: Dt. Chron.*, vol. II, ed. L. WEILAND, fasc. 1 [1876], p. 113), stresses the point that the saint and his companions refused to go against the Christian religion. This theme certainly runs throughout the imperial propaganda.

99 HERZBERG, *Der heilige Mauritius*, p. 116.

100 OPFERMANN, "Das Messformular," in SCHRADER, *Beiträge zur Geschichte des Erzbistums Magdeburg*, p. 212.

101 HERZBERG, *Der heilige Mauritius*, p. 106: liturgy of the twelfth and thirteenth centuries: "Henrico a Deo coronato . . . Sce. Maurici, Tu illos adjuva. / Sce. Dionysi, Tu illos adjuva."

102 England unfortunately is poorly represented in the material we have been able to assemble to date. No doubt that country will bring us valuable data in the future. England is particularly interesting because of her relations during the twelfth and thirteenth centuries with the empire and especially with the Germanic milieus.

103 *Epistola CCXIII* (*PL* 207.497-98): probably written in England. The text of this letter is preserved in the following manuscripts: Oxford, St. John's College, MS. 115; Vienna, Österreichische Nationalbibliothek, Cod. 8457, fol. 18[r]. Eighteenth-century copies exist in Paris, Bibliothèque nationale, MS. fr. 9062, fols. 66[r] and 242[r].

104 ". . . ambas Aethiopias, Maurithumanam, Parthiam, Syriam, Persiam, . . . Arabiam, Chaldaeam, ipsamque Aegyptum" (*Epistola CCXIII* [*PL* 207.498]).

105 M. PACAUT, *Frédéric Barberousse* ([Paris], 1967), p. 102.

106 J.C. VON DREYHAUPT, *Pagus Nelecti et Nudzici, oder Ausführliche diplomatisch-historische Beschreibung des zum ehemaligen Primat und Ertz-Stifft* . . . (Halle, 1755), pt. I, pp. 743-44.

107 Ibid., pp. 9-13.

108 Details in CLAUDE, *Geschichte des Erzbistums Magdeburg*, pt. II, pp. 94 ff.

109 Ibid., pp. 109 ff. On this point two important hypotheses could be considered. On the one hand, the appeal for colonizing settlers sounded far toward the west: in the thirteenth century Flemings established themselves in the Jüterbog region, and it is possible that at that time Maurice's name became known in the Low Countries and the lower Rhine Valley. On the other hand, it may be that the archbishops of Cologne were not sufficiently alert to the efforts being made to recruit a labor force in their province—there are traces of such efforts—and that the "hostility" to the saint of Magdeburg had its roots in this twelfth- and thirteenth-century conflict of interest. (Later on we shall pick up the forms taken by this hostility.) Both of these hypotheses would be worth verifying.

110 Ibid., p. 115.

111 *Germania sacra*, fasc. I, *Die Bistümer der Kirchenprovinz Magdeburg*, vol. III, *Das Bistum Brandenburg*, pt. 2, ed. F. BÜNGER and G. WENTZ (Berlin, 1941), p. 337.

112 CLAUDE, *Geschichte des Erzbistums Magdeburg*, pt. II, p. 170.

113 P. DOLLINGER, *La Hanse (XIIe-XVIIe siècles)*, rev. ed., Collection historique (Paris, 1970), pp. 24 ff.

114 We must not neglect the economic aspect of this policy of conquest and colonization, for its authors were certainly mindful of this aspect. At Jüterbog, Archbishop Wichmann relieved the local market of all taxes in order to foster exchanges with the Slavs to the east and north, while simultaneously Albert the Bear granted the same exemptions to Halle, Magdeburg, Calbe, and Burg, as well as to Stendal.

115 The cult of St. Nicholas spread in Germany even before the translation of his relics to Bari; cf. Claude, *Geschichte des Erzbistums Magdeburg*, pt. II, pp. 479-80 and p. 374. As early as the tenth and eleventh centuries, Meissen, Halberstadt, and Quedlinburg venerated this distant saint, probably due to the influence of the Empress Theophano. In the eleventh century there was also a monastery dedicated to St. Nicholas in Magdeburg. The Baltic mariners were quick to adopt the saintly protector of sailors; cf. Dollinger, *La Hanse*, p. 342. Stendal may have served as a relay point in the transmission of this cult toward the north.

116 Claude, *Geschichte des Erzbistums Magdeburg*, pt. II, p. 112.

117 Ibid., pp. 100, 104. Brandenburg, destroyed at the end of the tenth century, is rebuilt in 1170.

118 We think it of interest to underscore the degree to which Maurice was always tied to the class in power. Consultation of the important lists of names from the twelfth, thirteenth, and fourteenth centuries contained in *Germania sacra* reveals that the use of the name Maurice was almost nonexistent. We have come across two abbots and one monk who bore this patronymic at Kloster Zinna in the twelfth century. A single bourgeois of Magdeburg, who died on 16 June 1520, was named after Maurice.

119 Dollinger, *La Hanse*, pp. 29 ff.

120 J. Leitzmann, "Die Bracteaten mit dem heiligen Moritz," *Numismatische Zeitung* 27 (1860): 49-52, 62-64, 73-76, 84-88, 89-92, 97-101, 105-10; T. Stenzel, "Moritzpfennige des Gross-Rosenburger Bracteatenfundes," *Archiv für Bracteatenkunde* 1 (1886-89): 281-84; F. Friedensburg, "Drei merkwürdige Pfennige von Magdeburg," *Blätter für Münzfreunde* 60 (1925): 273-75; *Magdeburg in der Politik der deutschen Kaiser: Beiträge zur Geopolitik und Geschichte des ostfälischen Raums* ([Heidelberg and Berlin], 1936); R. Schildmacher, *Magdeburger Münzen*, Magdeburger Kultur- und Wirtschaftsleben, no. 5 (Magdeburg, [1936]); H.-D. Kahl, *Slawen und Deutsche in der Brandenburgischen Geschichte des Zwölften Jahrhunderts: Die letzten Jahrzehnte des Landes Stodor*, Mitteldeutsche Forschungen, vol. 30/I (Cologne and Graz, 1964), vol. I, pp. 301 ff.

121 One of the oldest of these dates from Henry III. There are many other coins like those from Magdeburg, but little is known about where they were minted before the middle of the eleventh century.

122 Schildmacher, *Magdeburger Münzen*, p. 4.

123 Ibid., p. 6: the name comes from *bractea* which means 'thin sheet of metal'. That some of the pfennigs are badly stamped is probably due to the fact that they were struck out of unevenly hammered sheets of metal.

124 There are a great many of these *Moritzpfennige* dating between 1124 and 1152, but the best ones were coined during the reign of the very active Archbishop Wichmann (1152-92).

125 A thirteenth-century chronicle (about 1270) states that Maurice is the titled protector of Magdeburg; cf. *Braunschweigische Reimchronik* 14 in *MGH: Dt. Chron.*, vol. II, fasc. 1, p. 475.

126 The *Gesta archiepiscoporum Magdeburgensium* mentions for 1278: "Egressi autem omnes viri bellatores cum archiepiscopo electo et cum vexillo sancti Maurici viriliter contra hostes pugnaverunt, et auxiliante Deo et sancto Mauricio, gloriose triumphaverunt" (Herzberg, *Der heilige Mauritius*, pp. 81-82). R. Folz, *Le Souvenir et la Légende de Charlemagne*, thinks that as early as the tenth century Otto the Great ordered a banner representing St. Maurice to be carried in battles against the Hungarians. On the types of representation, see Leitzmann, "Die Bracteaten."

127 Several of the authors cited stress that the Magdeburg coinage is one of the most remarkable in medieval Germany, but archeology has furnished no information on the circulation of the pieces in question, whether coins or medals. It might be thought that the Slavic and Baltic lands, where Magdeburg played a large role, received pfennigs and bracteates representing St. Maurice, but we have not found the shadow of an allusion to any interesting discoveries on this point. The whole inquiry regarding the geographic distribution of Magdeburg coinage is still to be undertaken.

128 M. Buchner, "Pseudo-Turpin, Reinald von Dassel und der Archipoet in ihren Beziehungen zur Kanonisation Karls d. Gr. (Forschungen über Quellen, Tendenz, Abfassungszeit und Autor der *Historia Karoli Magni* Pseudo-Turpins und des *Liber S. Jacobi*)," *Zeitschrift für französische Sprache und Litteratur* 51 (1928): 1-72. Buchner (p. 24) gives the background of the "canonization" of Charlemagne. In the *Historia Karoli Magni* certain themes, in themselves worthy of further study, make their appearance in the Occident. Among them is the theme of the crown that awaits the king in heaven if he helps to free Santagio de Compostela (p. 26), and that of the "mass mobilization of the West" to expand Christianity. The Crusades, of course, already exemplified this latter theme, but it took on greater importance in the eastward thrust of the empire, whereas the *Historia Karoli Magni* anticipates it for the deliverance of Santiago de Compostela.

129 Roland became fashionable; the East is copiously represented in the German version, the text of which was composed between 1130 and 1170, probably in close connection with the Second Crusade; cf. H. Szklenar, *Studien zum Bild des Orients in vorhöfischen deutschen Epen*, Palaestra: Untersuchungen aus der deutschen und englischen Philologie und Literaturgeschichte, vol. 243 (Göttingen, 1966), pp. 210-16 ("Das Rolandslied des Pfaffen Konrad").

130 See, once again, Claude, *Geschichte des Erzbistums Magdeburg*, pt. II, pp. 176 ff.

131 *Regesta archiepiscopatus Magdeburgensis*, ed. G. A. von Mülverstedt, pt. II (Magdeburg, 1881). Several acts show that the archbishop scrupulously carried out his mission.

132 Dollinger, *La Hanse*, pp. 50-51.

133 Ibid., pp. 48-49.

134 F. Salles, *Annales de l'Ordre Teutonique ou de Sainte-Marie-de-Jérusalem depuis son origine jusqu'à nos jours*, Ordres religieux de chevalerie (Paris and Vienna, 1887).

135 Letter from Father Bernhard Damel, dated 18 August 1969, to Ladislas Bugner: the Teutonics' patron saint was St. George. The Order celebrated the Feast of the Holy Lance annually from the thirteenth century until 1965, but no reference to St. Maurice occurred in this liturgy.

136 A painted manuscript from the mid-fifteenth century, *Banderia Prutenorum* (now in Cracow, Biblioteka Jagiellońska), contains the banners used by the Teutonic Knights in the battles of Tannenberg (1410) and of Nakel (1431). The banner of the master of Livonia is at fol. 44^v. A critical edition of this manuscript has been done by S. Ekdahl, ed., *Die "Banderia Prutenorum" des Jan Dlugosz, eine Quelle zur Schlacht bei Tannenberg 1410*, Abhandlungen der Akademie der Wissenschaften in Göttingen, Philologisch-historische Klasse, 3d ser., no. 104 (Göttingen, 1976), p. 276 and fig., p. 277.

137 H. de Ziegler, *Vie de l'empereur Frédéric II de Hohenstaufen*, 5th ed., Les lettres et l'histoire ([Paris], 1935), pp. 40-44.

138 M. Tumler, *Der deutsche Orden im Werden, Wachsen und Wirken bis 1400 mit einem Abriss der Geschichte des Ordens von 1400 bis zur neuesten Zeit* (Vienna, [1955]), pp. 154 ff.

139 Ibid., pp. 54-55, n. 1. They acquired a church there in 1235.

140 Ibid., p. 54, n. 1.

141 Albert was a friend of Frederick II, who manifested his confidence in him in many ways and entrusted him with important missions in 1222, 1223, and 1224. As early as 1215-20, he was put in charge of the county of Romagna, extending from Forli to Rome and from the sea to the mountains; from 1223 on, he was appointed imperial legate in Lombardy; cf. *Regesta archiepiscopatus Magdeburgensis*, pt. II, pp. 305-39. Yet he refused to take Frederick's part when the emperor was censured by Rome perhaps in 1224: in that year, acting as the legate of

Innocent IV, he is said to have excommunicated the bishop of Halberstadt, who sided with Frederick (*Regesta archiepiscopatus Magdeburgensis*, pt. II, p. 339, par. 734). In 1225 Albert was officially designated as papal legate, and once the feud between the papacy and Frederick II was patched up, he was restored to full favor with the emperor. He is frequently mentioned in the imperial acts in 1226 and 1227, and later was equally favored by the son of Frederick II (*Regesta archiepiscopatus Magdeburgensis*, pt. II, p. 396, par. 854).

142 Götz, "Der Magdeburger Domchor," pp. 103 ff.

143 Ibid., pp. 111 ff.

144 *Regesta archiepiscopatus Magdeburgensis*, pt. II, p. 277, par. 599 and p. 284, par. 618.

145 Herzberg, *Der heilige Mauritius*, p. 82.

146 *Regesta archiepiscopatus Magdeburgensis*, pt. II, p. 317, par. 691: papal indulgence dated 18 July 1223 encouraging the development of a pilgrimage which will continue to hold our attention.

147 Ibid., p. 459, par. 985: letter dated 30 January 1233.

148 Herzberg, *Der heilige Mauritius*. Miesges, *Der Trierer Festkalender*, rightly notes this revival of the Maurician cult in the old western nucleus around Trier. The movement, moreover, continued in the fourteenth and even in the fifteenth century. Lechner, *Mittelalterliche Kirchenfeste*, pp. 255, 184: the breviaries of the thirteenth and fourteenth centuries note that for the feast of 22 September nine lessons were of obligation, which gave this feast the same rank as that of St. Thomas and placed it just below the feasts of the Four Evangelists. At Augsburg the commemoration of St. Maurice and his companions was a major feast in the thirteenth and fourteenth centuries. Sometimes, as at Passau, in that same period the obligation of twelve lessons shows that the liturgy still honored the saint whose office Rome had ruthlessly suppressed almost two centuries before.

149 Albert II's brother Wilbrand, archbishop from 1235 to 1254, sought to encourage popular devotion to Maurice, which, as we have seen, had not been strong; he issued a proclamation to this effect in May 1236 (cf. *Regesta archiepiscopatus Magdeburgensis*, pt. II, p. 488, par. 1063).

150 We have consulted the *Acts* of Frederick II (see J.-L.-A. Huillard-Bréholles, ed., *Historia diplomatica Friderici secundi sive Constitutiones, privilegia, mandata, instrumenta quae supersunt istius imperatoris et filiorum ejus...*, 7 vols. in 12 pts. [Paris, 1852-61]), the texts relating to his entourage (idem, *Vie et correspondance de Pierre de La Vigne, ministre de l'empereur Frédéric II, avec une étude sur le mouvement réformiste au XIIIe siècle* [Paris, 1865]), and the various studies concerning him (cf. Ziegler, *Vie de l'empereur Frédéric II*; A. de Stefano, *La cultura alla corte di Frederico II imperatore*, 2d ed. [Bologna, 1950]; F. Maurer, *Die politischen Lieder Walthers von der Vogelweide* [Tübingen, 1954]), but we have found no positive evidence.

151 Ziegler, *Vie de l'empereur Frédéric II*, p. 44. Bühler, "Die Heilige Lanze," p. 90, makes much of the *Ordo* of Cencius Camerarius (papal chamberlain, 1192-98), which notes the Germanic emperor's wish to be crowned in the future before the altar of St. Maurice, not at the altar of St. Peter.

152 Herzberg, *Der heilige Mauritius*, p. 31: in 1215 the Chapel of St. Maurice in the Cathedral of Aachen was also called the Chapel of Charlemagne. This was where the future king spent the night in prayer before his sacring, and where the royal insignia, including the "sword of St. Maurice," were kept. On this last point, R. Folz (*Le Souvenir et la Légende de Charlemagne*, p. 460), disagrees with A. J. Herzberg. In Folz's opinion the sword appears as a theme in the middle of the eleventh century, but was not used in the coronation ceremony until 1350, taking the place of the Lance from then on. The Lance, says Folz (p. 200), was connected in the thirteenth century with Charlemagne's triumphs over the enemy and continued to be the most prestigious emblem of power; he also says (p. 365) that for thirteenth-century authors, Charlemagne was thought to have received the Holy Lance in 800. Folz holds (cf. pp. 459-60) that in the second half of the thirteenth century the Lance lost its connection with St. Maurice and once more became the Holy Lance.

153 Ziegler, *Vie de l'empereur Frédéric II*, p. 38. At first sight this literature does not speak of St. Maurice, and this is rather surprising. On the contrary it is Roland who made a strong showing in Germany at that time, and who in the fifteenth century took the lead over Maurice, particularly in the field of iconography, as the image of the knight. Folz, *Le Souvenir et la Légende de Charlemagne*, p. 512 and n. 112, remarks that at Magdeburg, in the fifteenth and sixteenth centuries, Roland looks much like St. Maurice in his posture and the way he carries his lance. See also Götz, "Der Magdeburger Domchor," pp. 111 ff.

154 Huillard-Bréholles, *Vie et correspondance de Pierre de La Vigne*, p. 204: transfer of the relics of "St. Charlemagne"; p. 205: praise in honor of St. Elizabeth of Hungary; pp. 205-6: further examples.

155 Ibid., pp. 207-8: Frederick II writes to his son, "divine race of the blood of the Caesars," and speaks of his mother as "diva mater nostra."

156 The weakening of the empire seems to have occasioned, in France in the thirteenth and early fourteenth centuries, a marked increase of interest in the ideological signs of imperial power. A study by M.-P. Jabinet-Caire, "La tradition manuscrite de la Lettre du Prêtre Jean" (M. A. thesis, Université de Paris VIII, 1970), has shown how strong interest in this text was in France at that period. The fact is that so far we have only scattered inklings of this trend, and the work undertaken by Mme Jabinet-Caire will undoubtedly give us more information on the subject.

157 Bernard de Montmélian, *Saint Maurice et la Légion thébéenne*, vol. I, p. 315. Thus a liturgy and a veneration reappeared in the French-speaking area. We shall not, however, have occasion to follow this development since the iconography of Maurice, in this tradition, always represents him with the features of a white man. When these questions have been answered, it will no doubt be time to make a comparative study of the ideology of power in the thirteenth and fourteenth centuries in France, in Europe, and probably also in England.

158 We may here refer again to the pseudo-letter of Frederick Barbarossa to Saladin (cf. *supra*, n. 103).

159 Frederick, like many other Crusaders, learned that Turks and blacks did not get along with each other at all well, especially in Egypt. In these circumstances to adopt a black as a hero of Christian knighthood might well have seemed a stroke of genius.

160 We should not forget that in Byzantine manuscripts of the twelfth and thirteenth centuries the painters depicted some of the Egyptians as black. Why not, then, a "Theban"? Could not the "Theban" origin be brought back to life after centuries of neglect?

161 The fine essay by Szklenar, *Studien zum Bild des Orients*, provides a clear insight here; see particularly pp. 105 ff. (Alexander and the Candaces).

162 F. de Medeiros, "Recherches sur l'image des Noirs dans l'Occident médiéval (XIIIe-XVe siècles)" (Ph. D. diss., 3e cycle, Université de Paris VIII, 1973).

163 Ibid., pp. 276-81.

164 A systematic study of the representations of St. Maurice as a black has been inaugurated by the Menil Foundation. The outcome of this research, which is being carried out by Dr. Gude Suckale-Redlefsen and Dr. Robert Suckale of Munich, will be the publication of a catalogue raisonné. In the pages that follow, the iconographic references are taken from the inventory in course of production.

165 It is regrettable that no good monograph on Charles IV is available. Some writers see him as a weakling manipulated by the priests, while others exalt him as a new

Frederick II; in other words, practically nothing is known about the motives behind his actions or the importance of his decisions. Further on we shall have occasion to point out that this precise and scrupulous man left no detail to chance.

166 J. J. Morper, "Ein Mauritiuskopf vom Bamberger Dom," *Pantheon* 19 (1937): 18-20, attributes the head of a white warrior to St. Maurice. This attribution, and also the provenance, have recently been questioned by W. Sauerländer in *Bayern: Kunst und Kultur*, Exhibition catalogue, Munich, Münchner Stadtmuseum, 9 June-15 October 1972, 2d ed. (Munich, 1972), pp. 315-16, no. 76. On the other hand, J. J. Morper has drawn up an interesting list of representations of a white, bearded Maurice dating from before the middle of the thirteenth century.

167 D. Schubert, *Von Halberstadt nach Meissen: Bildwerke des 13. Jahrhunderts in Thüringen, Sachsen und Anhalt* (Cologne, 1974), pp. 293-95, no. 115. W. Paatz, "Die Magdeburger Plastik um die Mitte des XIII. Jahrhunderts," *JPKS* 46 (1925): 91-120. Note also that another St. Maurice, shown as a white man and probably executed a few years earlier, also figures in the choir. See Mrusek, *Drei deutsche Dome*, p. 48.

168 E. Wenzel, "St. Mauritius im Dom zu Magdeburg und die Entwicklung des Kriegskleides zur Zeit der Kreuzzüge," *Der Burgwart: Jahrbuch der Vereinigung zur Erhaltung deutscher Burgen* 32 (1931): 36-41.

169 E. Schubert, *Der Magdeburger Dom* (Vienna and Cologne, 1975), pp. 202-6 and pls. 2, 3, 104.

170 In Naumburg in the twelfth century there was a monastery dedicated to St. Maurice of which nothing remains; the present church was rebuilt in the sixteenth century. The inscriptions found in the Naumburg district include no references to St. Maurice; cf. E. Schubert, ed., *Die Inschriften des Landkreises Naumburg an der Saale*, Die deutschen Inschriften, vol. 9, Berliner Reihe, vol. 3 (Berlin and Stuttgart, 1965). Inscriptions in the city itself contain only very rare mentions of Maurice's name, and there is no sign of a special veneration of the saint; cf. idem, *Die Inschriften der Stadt Naumburg an der Saale*, Die deutschen Inschriften, vol. 7, Berliner Reihe, vol. 2 (Berlin and Stuttgart, 1960).

171 The first mention of a standard *(vexillum)* of St. Maurice seems to be one that appeared in 1278; cf. G. Sello, "Dom-Altertümer," *Geschichtsblätter für Stadt und Land Magdeburg* 26 (1891): 139, n. 1. But the saint was mentioned earlier, about 1250, in the Magdeburg calendar of feasts; cf. E. Rosenstock, "Zur Ausbildung des mittelalterlichen Festkalenders," *Archiv für Kulturgeschichte* 10 (1912): 276. I thank Professor R. Folz for his kindness in letting me have these items of information.

172 See Maps pp. 270-71.

173 Prague became an archdiocese in 1344. A university was created there four years later.

174 Bühler, "Die Heilige Lanze," pp. 90-91.

175 Folz, *Le Souvenir et la Légende de Charlemagne*, p. 453.

176 Bernard de Montmélian, *Saint Maurice et la Légion thébéenne*, vol. I, p. 342.

177 L. Neubert and B. Černý, *Karlštejn* (Prague, 1973); G. Schmidt, "Malerei bis 1450: Tafelmalerei, Wandmalerei, Buchmalerei," in K. M. Swoboda, ed., *Gotik in Böhmen: Geschichte, Gesellschaftsgeschichte, Architektur, Plastik und Malerei* (Munich, [1969]), pp. 201-4; A. Kutal, *L'art gothique de Bohême*, trans. M. Vanèk (Prague, 1971), pp. 61-63.

178 J. Pfitzner, *Kaiser Karl IV.*, Bilder aus dem deutschen Leben: Deutsche Könige und Kaiser (Potsdam, 1938), p. 95. Each year the paraphernalia of the coronation were to be put on display there, and the public invited to admire them.

179 V. Dvořáková and D. Menclová, *Karlštejn* (Prague, 1965), pp. 108-9.

180 See, e.g., Paris, Bibliothèque nationale, MS. lat. 1052. *Breviary* of Charles V, decorated in France, second half of the fourteenth century, fol. 513r: Maurice is white and his executioners black.

181 A. Matějček and J. Pešina, *La peinture gothique tchèque, 1350-1450*, trans. J. Delamain and L. Dostálová (Prague, 1955), esp. pp. 24-28, 62-64; A. Friedl, *Magister Theodoricus: Das Problem seiner malerischen Form*, trans. R. Messer (Prague, 1956); idem, *Počátky Mistra Theodorika* (Prague, 1963).

182 According to Friedl, *Magister Theodoricus*, p. 44, a sort of oil receptacle is seen in the picture and is the painter's real signature.

183 Matějček and Pešina, *La peinture gothique tchèque*, p. 26.

184 Gerona, Museo Diocesano de Gerona, 273. *Martyrology*, Bohemia, about 1402, fol. 94v: martyrdom of St. Maurice and his companions. Cf. part 2 of this volume, pp. 36-37 and p. 269, nn. 180-82.

185 Kroměříž (Czechoslovakia), Uměleckohistorické Muzeum, P 11; cf. V. Tomášek, *Obrazárna Kroměřížského Zámku* (Kroměříž, 1964), p. 38, no. P 11.

186 We know this mural painting only through a poor photograph and therefore cannot comment on it.

187 This is not surprising, in view of the promotion of the cult of St. Wenceslas, and also because of the "anti-Slav" character given to Maurice's presence as protector of the Germanic armies in preceding centuries.

188 Lechner, *Mittelalterliche Kirchenfeste*: a fifteenth-century calendar from Freising no longer mentions St. Maurice in September, but at 2 May (p. 110) carries a mention of St. Sigismund, who evidently replaced the other. At Passau the calendar of the St. Nicholas Monastery also introduces the feast of St. Sigismund on 2 May, but keeps that of St. Maurice and his companions on 22 September. At Ratisbon (Regensburg) St. Maurice is no longer celebrated on 22 September, St. Emmeram alone remaining. It seems to us that the cult of St. Maurice was abandoned deliberately in the old Bavarian province, except perhaps at Passau, which was still too close to Niederaltaich to escape its influence. We have been able to establish the fact of this development, but not discover its cause. It may be that quite apart from liturgical and Roman influences, a new political situation affected the changing status of the Maurician cult: from the fourteenth century onward, the House of Savoy accorded great prominence to St. Maurice, and it seems that a new shift in the geography of the cult, this time toward the south, was the result.

189 Vienna, Stefansdom, double-winged altarpiece coming from Wiener Neustadt: Maurice is pictured between two bishops on the reverse of the outer right-hand wing. Here the saint's historiated arms are composite: the party-colored, red-and-white Latin cross brings this Maurice closer to the northern representations than to those of Bohemian inspiration. However, the headdress closely resembles that of the Kroměříž bust and, particularly, that of a polychromed wood statue (about 1470) now in the Church of St. Maurice in Breslau (Wroclaw). For the Wiener Neustadt altarpiece, cf. *Österreichische Kunsttopographie*, ed. D. Frey, vol. XXIII, *Geschichte und Beschreibung des St. Stephansdomes in Wien* (Vienna, 1931), pp. 273-81, and *Friedrich III. Kaiserresidenz Wiener Neustadt*, Exhibition catalogue, Wiener Neustadt, St. Peter an der Sperr, 28 May-30 October 1966 (n.p., n.d.), pp. 401-3, no. 234.

190 Brandenburg, cathedral, choir: carved and painted altarpiece, about 1370-80; cf. *Die Kunstdenkmäler der Provinz Brandenburg*, vol. II, pt. 3, *Die Kunstdenkmäler von Stadt und Dom Brandenburg* (Berlin, 1912), pp. 271-73; R. Nissen, "Die Plastik in Brandenburg a. H. von ca. 1350 bis ca. 1450," *Jahrbuch für Kunstwissenschaft* (1929): 61-99.

191 Brandenburg, cathedral: painted altarpiece, dated 1465; cf. *Die Kunstdenkmäler der Provinz Brandenburg*, vol. II, pt. 3, *Stadt und Dom Brandenburg*, p. 273; J. Fait, "Die Baugeschichte des Domes und seine Kunstschätze," in J. Henkys, ed., *800 Jahre Dom zu Brandenburg: Im Auftrage des Domkapitels Brandenburg* (Berlin, 1965), pp. 45-46.

192 L. Köhler, *Dietrich von der Schulenburg, Bischof von Brandenburg (1365-1393)* (Halle, 1911), pp. 34 ff. On Charles IV's relations with the Hansa, cf. Dollinger, *La Hanse*,

pp. 140-44. Charles IV was the only emperor who was really interested in the trade with the north and the Hansa; he had a "northern policy" after acquiring the Marches of Brandenburg and Lusatia.

193 E. Fidicin, *Kaiser Karl's IV Landbuch der Mark Brandenburg* (Berlin, 1856); C. Brinkmann, *Die Entstehung des Märkischen Landbuchs Kaiser Karls IV* (Berlin, 1908).

194 True, a very fine alabaster statue made in 1467 represents him with the features of a white man; cf. J. Braun, *Tracht und Attribute der Heiligen in der deutschen Kunst* (Stuttgart, 1943), col. 530, fig. 284. In this case, the nature and quality of the material probably dictated such a return to the old conceptions.

195 E. Schubert, *Der Magdeburger Dom*, p. 36 and pl. 35.

196 The investigation in progress reveals the multiplication of paintings on wood in the early sixteenth century around Halle and Leipzig.

197 Halle, Moritzkirche: statue executed by Conrad von Einbeck and dated 1411 (the polychromy is recent, and the features are not very "Negroid"); the other statue was done a little earlier by an unknown artist. Cf. G. Schönermark, *Die Stadt Halle und der Saalkreis*, Beschreibende Darstellung der älteren Bau- und Kunstdenkmäler der Provinz Sachsen und angrenzender Gebiete, n.s., vol. 1 (Halle, 1886), p. 111; B. Meier, "Die Skulpturen am Chor der Moritzkirche in Halle a.d.S.," *Thüringisch-Sächsische Zeitschrift für Geschichte und Kunst* 3 (1913): 50-56.

198 Stendal, cathedral, stained-glass window located in the north side of the choir, executed about 1430-40.

199 Halberstadt, Moritzkirche: side of a stall, about 1470-80; cf. O. Doering, *Die Kreise Halberstadt Land und Stadt*, Beschreibende Darstellung der älteren Bau- und Kunstdenkmäler der Provinz Sachsen, no. 23 (Halle, 1902), pp. 384-85.

200 Halberstadt, cathedral: statue standing against a pillar on the north side of the central nave, dated 1513 (gift of Sebastian von Ploto). Maurice's shield shows the eagle of Albert of Brandenburg, and the bracket on which the statue stands is decorated with two Negro heads. Cf. ibid., p. 264; J. Flemming, E. Lehmann, and E. Schubert, *Dom und Domschatz zu Halberstadt* (Vienna and Cologne, 1974), pp. 51-52 and pl. 101.

201 Medingen, abbey: silver statuette of St. Maurice which, according to the abbess, Dame von Bülow, came from Magdeburg; another, more recent statuette (about 1506) by Hermen Worm, who also made an abbatial crosier with St. Maurice and the Virgin and Child back to back in the volute.

202 Ebstorf, abbey: pyx in gilded silver with a St. Maurice atop the cover; fragment of an altarpiece, now in very bad condition, in which Maurice's blackness is still visible; burse embroidered with the image of the black saint.

203 Wienhausen, abbey, chapter room: triptych in polychromed and gilded wood, about 1450-1500, with SS. Antony, Maurice, and James on the left wing; cf. *Die Kunstdenkmale des Landes Niedersachsen*, vol. XXXIV, *Die Kunstdenkmale des Landkreises Celle im Regierungsbezirk Lüneburg: Textband* (Hannover, 1970), p. 121; H. G. Gmelin, *Spätgotische Tafelmalerei in Niedersachsen und Bremen* (Munich and Berlin, 1974), pp. 377-78, no. 119. Another triptych, in the nun's choir, presents eight saints, including a black Maurice, on its painted predella. The black Maurice appears again, with shield and standard marked with a cross, on a separate altarpiece fragment, which was added later above this same altarpiece; cf. idem, *Spätgotische Tafelmalerei*, pp. 457-66, no. 152.

204 Refer to the map (see *infra*, p. 270) of the representations of the black St. Maurice at the present stage of the research. The catalogue raisonné now being prepared will give the full list.

205 Delitzsch, Church of SS. Peter and Paul: carved altarpiece, left wing: St. Maurice and a deacon; cf. G. Schönermark, *Kreis Delitzsch*, Beschreibende Darstellung der älteren Bau- und Kunstdenkmäler der Provinz Sachsen und angrenzender Gebiete, no. 16 (Halle, 1892), pp. 37-38.

206 Frankenhain, church: carved altarpiece, central panel: Virgin and Child between St. Maurice and St. Sebastian; cf. R. Steche, *Amtshauptmannschaft Borna*, Beschreibende Darstellung der älteren Bau- und Kunstdenkmäler des Königreichs Sachsen, no. 15 (Dresden, 1891), p. 83.

207 Rottenbach, church: altarpiece from the studio of Valentin Lendenstreich, central panel: Virgin and Child flanked, on the right, by St. Catherine and St. Maurice; cf. *Bau- und Kunst-Denkmäler Thüringens*, ed. P. Lehfeldt, vol. I, *Fürstenthum Schwarzburg-Rudolstadt* (Jena, 1894), p. 213; G. Voss, *Die Thüringer Holzschnitzkunst des Mittelalters insbesondere die Werke der Saalfelder Bildschnitzschule*, Heimatbilder der Vergangenheit aus Saalfeld und Umgegend, no. 1 (Magdeburg, 1911), pp. 20-21.

208 Braunsdorf, church: carved altarpiece, right wing: St. Maurice; cf. R. Steche, *Amtshauptmannschaft Chemnitz*, Beschreibende Darstellung der älteren Bau- und Kunstdenkmäler des Königreichs Sachsen, no. 7 (Dresden, 1886), p. 6; W. Hentschel, "Ergänzung des spätgotischen Schnitzaltars von Bräunsdorf," *Deutsche Kunst und Denkmalpflege* 1-2 (1940-41): 195-96.

209 Teterow, church: carved altarpiece, lower register of left wing: black St. Maurice, half length; cf. *Die Kunst- und Geschichts-Denkmäler des Grossherzogthums Mecklenburg-Schwerin*, vol. V, *Die Amtsgerichtsbezirke Teterow, Malchin, Stavenhagen, Penzlin, Waren, Malchow und Röbel*, 2d ed. (Schwerin i. Mecklenburg, 1902), pp. 11-12.

210 H. Ludat, *Deutsch-slawische Frühzeit und modernes polnisches Geschichtsbewusstsein* (Cologne and Vienna, 1969), p. 56.

211 Wismar, Nikolaikirche: carved altarpiece (Krämeraltar), central panel: Virgin and Child between St. Michael and St. Maurice; cf. *Die Kunst- und Geschichts-Denkmäler des Grossherzogthums Mecklenburg-Schwerin*, vol. II, *Die Amtsgerichtsbezirke Wismar, Grevesmühlen, Rehna, Gadebusch und Schwerin*, 2d ed. (Schwerin i. Mecklenburg, 1899), p. 37; K. H. Clasen, *Der Meister der Schönen Madonnen: Herkunft, Entfaltung und Umkreis* (Berlin and New York, 1974), p. 98.

212 Roskilde, Domkirke, chapel called Chapel of Christian I or of the Three Magi; cf. *Danmarks Kirker udgivet af Nationalmuseet*, vol. III, *Københavns Amt*, ed. E. Moltke and E. Møller (Copenhagen, 1951), pp. 326-32 and p. 327, fig. 262.

213 See Dollinger, *La Hanse*, pp. 341-42.

214 Originally in Riga, House of the Black Heads; cf. W. Neumann, *Werke Mittelalterlicher Holzplastik und Malerei in Livland und Estland* (Lübeck, 1892). At the moment we do not know what finally became of this statue.

215 E. Thomson, *Die Compagnie der Schwarzhäupter zu Riga und ihr Silberschatz*, Schriftenreihe Nordost-Archiv, vol. 6 (Lüneburg, 1974).

216 Ibid., p. 6.

217 Ibid., p. 15.

218 Lübeck, cathedral, mural painting: epitaph of the Morum family, early fifteenth century.

219 W. Neumann, *Das Mittelalterliche Riga: Ein Beitrag zur Geschichte der norddeutschen Baukunst* (Berlin, 1892), pp. 54-56 and pls. XXV-XXVI.

220 Thomson, *Die Compagnie der Schwarzhäupter zu Riga*, p. 27.

221 As late as the seventeenth century an altar was dedicated to St. Maurice in the crypt of the cathedral at Cologne; cf. *Die Kunstdenkmäler der Rheinprovinz*, ed. P. Clemen, vol. VII, fasc. 1, *Die Kunstdenkmäler der Stadt Köln*, vol. II, fasc. 1, *Die Kirchlichen Denkmäler der Stadt Köln*, ed. H. Rahtgens (Düsseldorf, 1911), p. 64. Maurice is not black; only one Theban soldier—is it Gregory?—has the features of a black.

222 For references concerning the iconography of St. Gregory the Moor, see part 2 of this volume, p. 38 and p. 270, nn. 190-94.

223 Munich, Bayerische Staatsgemäldesammlungen, Alte Pinakothek, 1474, 1475. Anton Woensam, two wings from an altarpiece, from Cologne, Church of St. Gereon; cf. G. GOLDBERG and G. SCHEFFLER, *Altdeutsche Gemälde: Köln und Nordwestdeutschland*, Bayerische Staatsgemäldesammlungen, Alte Pinakothek/München: Gemäldekataloge, vol. 14 (Munich, 1972), *Textband*, pp. 506-14; *Tafelband*, pls. 155-56.

224 Brussels, Bibliothèque Royale Albert Ier, MS. 9786-90. *Missal* of the priory of Bilzen (Limburg); cf. J. VAN DEN GHEYN, *Catalogue des manuscrits de la Bibliothèque Royale de Belgique*, vol. I, *Ecriture sainte et Liturgie* (Brussels, 1901), pp. 257-64, no. 435.

225 On the subject of Maurice and his companions, we have found the following in the catalogue cited *supra*, n. 224: eight liturgical texts, twenty-eight readings of different types and levels (one by Albertus Magnus), twelve poems, three hymns, two prayers (one by Albertus Magnus), one sequence, and one martyrology.

226 Brussels, Bibliothèque Royale Albert Ier, MS. 9786-90, fol. 15[r]: martyrdom of the Theban Legion. The miniature on this folio, closely connected with the text, unquestionably represents whites as the victims.

227 Ibid., fol. 99[r]: martyrdom of the Holy Moors. The identification of the scene is the one given by GHEYN, *Catalogue des manuscrits*, vol. I, p. 260. The context relates the Holy Moors to the Theban martyrs, but in no way confuses them.

228 Fröndenberg, collegiate church: polychromed and gilded wood statue, about 1400; cf. R. FRITZ, *Fresken, Altäre, Skulpturen: Kunstschätze aus dem Kreis Unna* (Cologne and Berlin, 1970), pp. 76-77.

229 G. DE MANTEYER, *Les origines de la Maison de Savoie en Bourgogne (910-1060)* (Rome, 1899); further information in F. HAYWARD, *Histoire de la Maison de Savoie*, vol. I, *1000-1553* (Paris, 1941), and vol. II, *1553-1796* (1943).

230 MANTEYER, *Les origines de la Maison de Savoie*, pp. 525-26.

231 In the departments of Saône-et-Loire and Ain, in Savoy, and in the canton of Valais, there are villages named for St. Maurice and churches dedicated to him. Without giving exact chronological references, G. de Manteyer enumerates at least fifteen such churches (ibid., pp. 380-81).

232 D. PROMIS, *Monete dei Reali di Savoia*, 2 vols. (Turin, 1841).

233 ". . . a parte pile infra circulum medium unum militem armatum armis et ad imaginem sancti Mauritii appodiantem se ad ensem . . ." (ibid., vol. I, p. 93).

234 F. MUGNIER, *Les manuscrits à miniatures de la Maison de Savoie* (Moutiers-Tarentaise, 1894). The manuscript is in Paris, Bibliothèque nationale, MS. lat. 9473 Réserve (between 1440 and 1445). The relevant illustrations are at fol. 180[v]: six scenes, in addition to the central figure, which embellish the *Vita* as freely as those in Jüterbog. One or two of these scenes probably allude to the organization of the Order of the Knights of St. Maurice, granted by Pope Eugenius IV to Duke Amadeus VIII of Savoy in 1434; cf. idem, *Les manuscrits à miniatures*, p. 94.

235 On this occasion Amadeus VIII withdrew from the world with five of his counselors, forming the first group of the Knights of St. Maurice.

236 *L'Ordine dei Santi Maurizio e Lazzaro* (Milan, 1966), p. 12.

237 In 1420 an attack on the region by the Pomeranians was repulsed, but was resumed in 1425.

238 B. HENNIG, *Die Kirchenpolitik der älteren Hohenzollern in der Mark Brandenburg und die päpstlichen Privilegien des Jahres 1447: Kapitel IV: Besetzung der Bistümer Brandenburg, Havelberg und Lebus* (Leipzig, 1906).

239 A town hall was built in 1380 and reconstructed between 1450 and 1506. The first mention of a Church of St. Nicholas, a dependency of the Cistercian monastery founded by Wichmann in the twelfth century, dates from 1307: important donations were made to this church in 1350 and 1371; cf. *Germania sacra*, fasc. I, *Die Bistümer der Kirchenprovinz Magdeburg*, vol. III, *Das Bistum Brandenburg*, pt. 2, pp. 321-60. A Franciscan church was built toward the end of the fifteenth century.

240 Jüterbog, Church of St. Nicholas: fragment of the altarpiece of the old high altar (about 1425), reverse of the painted exterior wing: life and martyrdom of St. Maurice. Reading from bottom left to top right, following the conventions adopted for stained-glass windows and ivories in the Middle Ages, we see the saint's baptism, appearance before the emperor, refusal to renounce the Christian faith and to sacrifice to idols, and his martyrdom. Cf. C. GIESE, "Zur Rekonstruktion des ehemaligen Hochaltares der Nikolai-Kirche in Jüterbog," *Die Denkmalpflege: Zeitschrift für Denkmalpflege und Heimatschutz* (1931): 190-92; H. BETHE, "Ein niedersächsischer Altar um 1430," *Zeitschrift für bildende Kunst* 65 (1931-32): 22-24.

241 This point of view will be developed more fully in the first chapter of part 2.

242 Characteristic of the last decades of the fourteenth century and the early years of the fifteenth in Germany were a new, serious, and lasting weakening of the imperial power, and the divergence, which continually grew deeper, between the northern and the southern area of that part of Europe. The disturbances that beset Bohemia, southern Germany, and Hungary had no counterparts in the north. Brandenburg stood somewhat outside of the general course of events; hence, it is not unreasonable to see a degree of originality and a discreet, anti-imperial aloofness in Hohenzollern policy.

243 Kloster Zinna, former Fürstenhaus, second floor, north wall.

244 L. ACHILLES, ed., *Zehn Jahre Denkmalpflege in der Deutschen Demokratischen Republik* (Leipzig, 1959), p. 213.

245 A letter from Mrs. G. Fink, curator of the Kreis-Heimatmuseum in Jüterbog, dated 21 August 1969, informs us that the painting, now carefully restored, had for several centuries been covered with layers of paint and varnish which preserved its original colors. Maurice's face is reddish brown; his standard is white with a black cross (also the cross of the Teutonic Order); on the shield is a black eagle on a white ground.

246 A prominent personage in his own right, Ernest of Saxony was elected archbishop at the age of eleven but was not consecrated until he was twenty-five years old.

247 F. W. HOFFMANN, *Geschichte der Stadt Magdeburg*, rev. G. HERTEL and F. HÜLSSE (Magdeburg, 1885), vol. I, p. 252. As we know, the exposition of the relics was already traditional in the thirteenth century. Albert of Brandenburg later broadened its scope.

248 A. SCHMIDT, "Der Magdeburger Dombau und die St. Mauritiusbruderschaft," *Geschichtsblätter für Stadt und Land Magdeburg* 62 (1927): 102 ff.; text of the archbishop's letter, pp. 105-8.

249 Magdeburg, cathedral, Ernstkapelle; provenance, Johanneskapelle.

250 A. SCHMIDT, "Der Magdeburger Dombau und die St. Mauritiusbruderschaft," p. 102; text of 1491, pp. 109-13.

251 The pastoral letter sets down in detail the methods of collection, counting the money, and preparation of the bags before witnesses.

252 OPFERMANN, "Das Messformular," in SCHRADER, *Beiträge zur Geschichte des Erzbistums Magdeburg*, pp. 192-213.

253 Magdeburg Missal, edition of 1486, revised in 1493 and 1503; cf. W. H. J. WEALE and H. BOHATTA, *Bibliographia liturgica: Catalogus Missalium ritus latini ab anno 1474*

impressorum (London, 1928), pp. 100-101. Opfermann, "Das Messformular," in Schrader, *Beiträge zur Geschichte des Erzbistums Magdeburg*, used manuscripts of Dresden (1493) and Wolfenbüttel (1486), which contain these texts.

254 Although he did not emphasize it particularly, the clarity of B. Opfermann's edition (Opfermann, "Das Messformular," in Schrader, *Beiträge zur Geschichte des Erzbistums Magdeburg*), brings out the relationships among the several liturgical compilations of Halle (1486, 1494, 1500), Fulda (1493), Kassel (fifteenth century), Beuron (1485-1523), Mainz (1507-90), Bautzen (1485-95), and Speyer (1487), in the case of manuscripts studied, and the Missals of Bursfelde (1498) and Brandenburg (1494), at the level of texts cited. The Magdeburg Missal (see B. Opfermann, "Das Magdeburger Missale des späten Mittelalters," in Schrader, ibid., pp. 276-89, esp. pp. 282-83), definitively fixes, as of the end of the fifteenth century, not only the prayers in honor of St. Maurice, but also the calendar of commemorations at Magdeburg; this text is still in use in our day. The following days are commemorated: 25 February, arrival of the saint's relics; 3 June, feast of St. Erasmus; 22 September—principal feast day, with octave—martyrdom of Maurice and his companions; 28 September, reception of the martyr's head; 10 October, SS. Gereon and Victor and their companions; 16 October, SS. Gall and Lupus, and St. Sigismund, confessor of the faith; 19 October, the Moorish martyrs.

255 Folz, *Le Souvenir et la Légende de Charlemagne*, p. 513, n. 113.

256 Magdeburg, cathedral, Ernstkapelle: bronze funerary monument of Archbishop Ernest of Saxony (died 1513) by Peter Vischer the Elder; the statuette of St. Maurice, beneath a multifoil arcature, is the only figure on the head side of the base of the tomb; cf. E. Schubert, *Der Magdeburger Dom*, pp. 211-12 and pls. 147-52.

257 Other difficulties arose when the people of the city were called upon to make contributions for the towers of the cathedral; cf. A. Schmidt, "Der Magdeburg Dombau und die St. Mauritiusbruderschaft," pp. 100-113.

258 E. Neuss, ed., *Das alte Halle: Aus den Schriften von Siegmar von Schultze-Galléra* (Leipzig, 1965), p. 31.

259 Ibid., p. 30 and see *supra*, p. 174 and n. 197.

260 The statue is now in Halle, Staatliche Galerie Moritzburg; see R. Hünicken, *Halle in der mitteldeutschen Plastik und Architektur der Spätgotik und Frührenaissance, 1450-1550* (Halle, 1936), p. 14; E. Neuss, *Kunstwerke des gotischen Gewölbes in der Moritzburg zu Halle* (Halle, 1955), p. 15.

261 Hoffmann, *Geschichte der Stadt Magdeburg*, vol. I, pp. 255 ff.

262 Ernest of Saxony endowed the Moritzburg, after 1503 the residence of the archbishops of Magdeburg in Halle, with a chapel dedicated to St. Maurice in 1509. The residence was badly damaged in the seventeenth century.

263 Berlin (GFR), Staatliche Museen, Gemäldegalerie, 603 A. Triptych, right wing: St. Maurice (reverse: St. Agnes). Cf. *Staatliche Museen Berlin: Verzeichnis der Ausgestellten Gemälde des 13. bis 18. Jahrhunderts im Museum Dahlem* (Berlin, 1962), p. 10, no. 603 A; K. Oettinger and K.-A. Knappe, *Hans Baldung Grien und Albrecht Dürer in Nürnberg* (Nuremberg, 1963), pp. 119-20, pls. 6, 8-15, and c. pls. IV, V.

264 Halle, Moritzkirche, large altarpiece from the high altar, with triple wings dated 1511; cf. Schönermark, *Die Stadt Halle und der Saalkreis*, pp. 139-50.

265 We owe the fixing of these dates to information furnished by Gude and Robert Suckale.

266 Sebastian Weynmann, *Libellus de sanctis reliquiis*, quoted in Sello, "Dom Altertümer," p. 138. I also owe my acquaintance with this text to the kindness of R. Folz.

267 "Et referunt, qui prospexerunt, de serico albo factum esse, ymaginem Christi salvatoris . . . in se habere" (ibid., p. 139).

268 Albert, younger brother of Prince Elector Joachim I of Brandenburg, was elected archbishop of Magdeburg at the age of twenty-three. In 1513 he was entrusted with the administration of the diocese of Halberstadt; in 1514 he became administrator of the archdiocese of Mainz and the diocese of Erfurt, prince elector, and primate of Germania; in 1518, when he was twenty-eight, Leo X made him a cardinal. His election, however, cost 24,000 florins, which his brother had to borrow from the Fuggers, and Albert's need of money continued to grow.

269 G. von Térey, *Cardinal Albrecht von Brandenburg und das Halle'sche Heiligthumsbuch von 1520: Eine kunsthistorische Studie* (Strassburg, 1892), p. 9.

270 The very valuable essay by E. Wind, "Studies in Allegorical Portraiture—I (2): Albrecht von Brandenburg as St. Erasmus," *Journal of the Warburg Institute* 1 (1937-38): 142-62, provides a harvest of new and essential information on this subject. It is his opinion—and his demonstration is convincing—that the introduction of the cult of St. Erasmus at Halle, decided upon by Albert, was intended to attract the good will of the Rotterdam scholar and the humanistic public.

271 P. Wolters, "Ein Beitrag zur Geschichte des Neuen Stiftes zu Halle (1519-1541)," *Neue Mittheilungen aus dem Gebiete historisch-antiquarischer Forschungen* 15 (1882): 7-41, esp. pp. 7-8. See also A. Wolters, *Der Abgott zu Halle, 1521-1542* (Bonn, 1877), p. 21.

272 P. Redlich, *Cardinal Albrecht von Brandenburg und das Neue Stift zu Halle, 1520-1541: Eine kirchenkunstgeschichtliche Studie* (Mainz, 1900), p. 15.

273 P. Wolters, "Ein Beitrag zur Geschichte des Neuen Stiftes zu Halle," p. 7.

274 Before 1520 Erasmus, by decision of the archbishop, became the third patron saint of Halle, along with Maurice and Mary Magdalene. Wind's argument is well buttressed, and one is tempted to accept his interpretation, however much fluttering this may cause in the dovecotes of tradition—the tradition certainly being no better guaranteed than Wind's solution.

275 Wind, "Studies in Allegorical Portraiture," esp. pp. 144-53.

276 W. K. Zülch, *Grünewald: Mathis Gothardt-Heithardt*, 2d ed. rev. (Munich, 1949), p. 51, dates the work as of 1525. Zülch's argument in favor of this date does not strike us as very solid. He states that Grünewald took as the model for his figure of Maurice a silver statue of the saint, cast by order of the cardinal in 1520, but melted down in 1540 when Albert needed the metal for his coinage (idem, *Grünewald*, p. 52). There is no irrefutable proof that it was not the other way around, Grünewald being copied in the 1520 statue.

277 L. Réau, *Iconographie de l'art chrétien*, vol. III, *Iconographie des saints*, pt. 1 (1958), pp. 437-38.

278 Wind, "Studies in Allegorical Portraiture," pp. 154-55, shows that the introduction of the cult of St. Erasmus, whose remains were transferred to Halle with great pomp and ceremony in 1516, modified the planning for the iconography in the collegiate church at Halle.

279 Halle painters seem to have had an excellent reputation in the fifteenth century; cf. R. Hünicken, "Grünewald in Halle," *ZfK* 5 (1936): 220. Yet Albert called upon a young painter who was a stranger to the city.

280 Munich, Bayerische Staatsgemäldesammlungen, Alte Pinakothek, 1044; cf. C. A. zu Salm and G. Goldberg, *Altdeutsche Malerei*, Alte Pinakothek München, Katalog 2 (Munich, 1963), pp. 93-96 and fig. on p. 269; U. Steinmann, "Der Bilderschmuck der Stiftskirche zu Halle: Cranachs Passionszyklus und Grünewalds Erasmus-Mauritius-Tafel," *Staatliche Museen zu Berlin: Forschungen und Berichte* 11 (1968): 92-104.

281 The crown on the reliquary bust of Maurice, reproduced in the Aschaffenburg manuscript (see *infra*, fig. 167), presents a problem: is it earlier than Grünewald's painting, hence possibly used by him as a model, or vice versa?

282 Note that the theme of the baptism of St. Maurice appeared once in Jüterbog.

283 L. Grote, *Matthias Grünewald (Mathis Gothardt-Neithardt): Die Erasmus-Mauritius-Tafel*, Werkmonographien zur bildenden Kunst in Reclams Universal-Bibliothek, no. 17 (Stuttgart, 1957).

284 Zülch, *Grünewald*, p. 52.

285 Aschaffenburg, Hofbibliothek, MS. 14. *Liber Ostensionis*, fol. 227v: drawing of a reliquary statue of St. Maurice in the Collegiate Church of St. Maurice and St. Mary Magdalene in Halle.

286 Halle, Marktkirche (Marienkirche): double-winged altarpiece dated 1529, left wing: St. Maurice, attributed to the Master of the Mass of St. Gregory by M. J. Friedländer and J. Rosenberg, *Die Gemälde von Lucas Cranach* (Berlin, 1932), p. 96. A replica of this painting was sold in New York in 1946; see *Old Masters and XIX Century Paintings*, Auction catalogue, New York, Parke-Bernet Galleries, Villarosa sale, 15 May 1946, no. 36B.

287 Aschaffenburg, Hofbibliothek, MS. 10. *Missal* of Cardinal Albert of Brandenburg, fol. 437v; see *Aus 1000 Jahren Stift und Stadt Aschaffenburg*, Exhibition catalogue, Aschaffenburg, Museum der Stadt, 15 June-30 September 1957 [Aschaffenburg, 1957], p. 29, no. 93; A. W. Biermann, "Die Miniaturenhandschriften des Kardinals Albrecht von Brandenburg (1514-1545)," *Aachener Kunstblätter* 46 (1975): 15-20, 152-79, and 166, fig. 223.

288 Aschaffenburg, Hofbibliothek, MS. 10, fols. 369r, 381v; Biermann, "Die Miniaturenhandschriften," pp. 172-73.

289 Aschaffenburg, Hofbibliothek, MS. 10, fol. 7v; Biermann, "Die Miniaturenhandschriften," p. 157 and p. 156, fig. 198. Note that fol. 32v of this manuscript presents a full-page painting of the Adoration of the Magi in which the black King occupies a predominant place; idem, "Die Miniaturenhandschriften," p. 157 and p. 158, fig. 202.

290 Halle, Collegiate Church of St. Maurice and St. Mary Magdalene; cf. E. Ruhmer, "Der Meister der Hallischen Dom-Skulpturen," *ZfK* 21 (1958): 209-29 and fig. 4; more recently, I. Lühmann-Schmid, "Peter Schro, ein Mainzer Bildhauer und Backoffenschüler," *MZ* 70 (1975): 1-62, esp. p. 58 and pl. 13.

291 Halle, Collegiate Church of St. Maurice and St. Mary Magdalene: this plaque was long attributed to a pupil or assistant of Backoffen; cf. J. L. Sponsel, "Flötner-Studien," *JPKS* 45 (1924): 133-44 (chap. II: "Die Ausstattung der Stiftskirche in Halle"), 144-63 (chap. III: "Der Hallische Domschatz"). This excellent study has been usefully completed by H. Volkmann, "Die Weihetafeln des Kardinals Albrecht von Brandenburg in der Stiftskirche zu Halle," *Wissenschaftliche Zeitschrift der Martin-Luther-Universität Halle-Wittenberg: Gesellschafts- und Sprachwissenschaftliche Reihe* 12, nos. 9-10 (1963): 757-63. Recently, Lühmann-Schmid, "Peter Schro," pp. 52-55 and pl. 18, attributes the work to Peter Schro.

292 See an attempted restoration in Volkmann, "Die Weihetafeln des Kardinals Albrecht von Brandenburg," p. 761.

293 Ibid., p. 758.

294 Eichstätt, cathedral: epitaph of Canon Bernhard Arzat (died 1525).

295 Cf. the map, p. 271.

296 G. Suckale's research has already located a dozen representations of St. Maurice as a black, and other examples will come to light. This is the largest concentration we have found in any one time and place. The works are related either to the new type of Maurice wearing a large hat, or to older types.

297 Jüterbog, Kreis-Heimatmuseum: statue of St. Maurice, from the façade of the *Rathaus* ("town hall"), dated 1508; see R. Bergau, *Inventar der Bau- und Kunst-Denkmäler in der Provinz Brandenburg* (Berlin, 1885), p. 431. See also G. Dehio, *Handbuch der Deutschen Kunstdenkmäler*, vol. II, *Nordostdeutschland*, 3d ed. (Berlin, 1926), p. 215; in this book the statue is dated as of 1508.

298 There are fewer examples here, but they too show that the diffusion from Halle went in all directions.

299 Lüneburg, Museum für das Fürstentum Lüneburg, H 75. Painted and carved triptych, from the chapel at Gross-Wittfeitzen; right wing (painted), upper register: St. Maurice, surrounded by his companions, carries a gonfalon with the cross pattée and a shield with a giant face. Here we are out of the zone of the official Magdeburg iconography under Albert, yet the type of the Maurice wearing a hat was kept; cf. H. Busch, *Meister des Nordens: Die Altniederdeutsche Malerei 1450-1550* (Hamburg, 1940), pp. 82-83; Gmelin, *Spätgotische Tafelmalerei*, pp. 165-68, no. 23.

300 Schleswig, cathedral, large altarpiece from the high altar by Hans Brüggemann, completed in 1521, from the abbey church of Bordesholm. A statuette in natural wood representing St. Maurice with "Negroid" features is seen in the predella.

301 Marienburg, castle, Collection of H. R. H. the Prince of Hannover, altarpiece called "Calenberger Altar," attributed by Gmelin, *Spätgotische Tafelmalerei*, pp. 442-48, no. 148, to the Master of the Goslar Sibyls, about 1515; left wing: St. Maurice and his companions. We note, although we cannot pursue it here, that in the central panel of the altarpiece among the women in the lady donor's suite, kneeling at the feet of the Virgin and Child, is a black.

302 Consult the map, p. 271. When the repertory is completed, it will probably increase the number of locations presently inventoried.

303 Wing of an altarpiece now lost, originally from Schwaigern, formerly (before 1926) in Stuttgart, Württembergisches Landesmuseum, 13254; cf. J. Baum, *Kataloge der Kgl. Altertümersammlung in Stuttgart*, vol. III, *Deutsche Bildwerke des 10. bis 18. Jahrhunderts* (Stuttgart and Berlin, 1917), p. 262, no. 314.

304 Nuremberg, Germanisches Nationalmuseum, Gm. 285/286.

305 Limbach, church, "Ritteraltar" by Hans von Kulmbach; cf. *Meister um Albrecht Dürer*, Exhibition catalogue, Nuremberg, Germanisches Nationalmuseum, 4 July-17 September 1961 (Nuremberg, 1961), p. 110, no. 174, which gives a bibliography on this work.

306 Opfermann, "Das Messformular," pp. 200 ff.

307 On the gifts that flowed into Halle, see Térey, *Cardinal Albrecht von Brandenburg*, pp. 15 ff. In 1520 Leo X awarded the intrepid cardinal the Golden Rose in recognition of his effort to reconquer Germany for Roman Catholicism.

308 Ibid., pp. 7-8. The author establishes, for the years of Ernest of Saxony and Albert, totals of over 100 antependia, over 600 gold and silver objects, more than thirty-two silk and damask flags, and over thirty-five gold-embroidered, silk tapestries—all collected at Halle, without counting any other objects used in worship services.

309 In the early sixteenth century Halle boasted of the fact that it possessed 8,133 relics and forty-two complete bodies. That was a collection unique in Europe and perhaps in all of Christendom; cf. Wind, "Studies in Allegorical Portraiture," p. 145.

310 One could hardly overstress the dialectical and dramatic aspects of the clash between the cardinal and Luther. Once swords were crossed, each of them pushed to excess the logic of his position. It is obvious that this cynical trading on popular credulity in order to obtain money in return for a look at relics and the promised indulgences was not Albert's sole motive. However, it was the weak point in his position, and Luther attacked it savagely on every occasion, first by de-

nouncing the "idolatry" *(Abgötterei)* being organized in Halle (letter of 7 October 1521 to Albert). Luther denounced the cardinal's taking advantage of the pilgrimage to get money and implied that Albert's motive was greed. This conflict of ideas was to divide the German Christian community for hundreds of years; cf. A. WOLTERS, *Der Abgott zu Halle*.

311 The following paragraphs are based on the excellent study by P. WOLTERS, "Ein Beitrag zur Geschichte des Neuen Stiftes zu Halle." The breviary is still in Bamberg.

312 Folio 187[r] of this breviary begins the inventory of the relics exposed at the high points of the liturgical year in the Collegiate Church of St. Maurice and St. Mary Magdalene.

313 TÉREY, *Cardinal Albrecht von Brandenburg*, pp. 37 ff., describes seven of them. The first, a very old one, presents an image of St. Paul; the second pictures the Last Judgment; the third consists of an ivory crucifix on black silk. The fourth has a gilded cross at the top and bears images of the Virgin, St. John, St. Benedict, and other saints, plus the Four Evangelists; the fifth represents the Nativity; the sixth includes a bust of Christ and the Four Evangelists; the seventh shows the Annunciation.

314 P. WOLTERS, "Ein Beitrag zur Geschichte des Neuen Stiftes zu Halle," pp. 17-18.

315 Epiphany, anniversary of the dedication of the Collegiate Church of Halle, the solemn feast of St. Erasmus, Pentecost, nativity of St. John the Baptist, feast of SS. Peter and Paul, Visitation, feast of St. Mary Magdalene, Assumption, feast of St. Maurice, All Saints' Day, Christmas.

316 The anniversary of the translation of St. Maurice's relics was marked by a limited exposition—seven *Plenaria* and no lateral tables. The same arrangement was followed for the feasts of St. Gregory the Great, St. Joseph, St. George, the Coronation of the Virgin, the Invention of the Cross, the anniversary of the transfer of the head of St. Stephen, etc. In every case, the days after the feast itself saw the progressive withdrawal of the relics, again following a strict order. It may be of some interest to reproduce here the notice regarding the anniversary of the arrival in Halle of the head of Maurice; cf. P. WOLTERS, "Ein Beitrag zur Geschichte des Neuen Stiftes zu Halle," pp. 30-31:

Adventus capitis sancti Mauritij. Plenaria ut supra [i.e., twelve] Epiphanie domini. Vexillum sancti Mauritij. Das silbern sanct Moritz brustbilde. Der ubergult sargk mit dem Engel. Der ubersilberte Sargk, mit dem B. gezceichnet. [Das silbern Pulpitum.] Der lengelich, vorgult sargk mit dem leyden christi. Der lengelich silbern sargk mit der hystoria der X.[m] ritter. Das gross silbern sanct Victors Brustbilde. Der silbern armme mit dem schwert. Das silbern ubergult haupt sanct Gereonis. Die perlen mutter in silber gefasset und ubergult, auff der decken eyn gewapnetter mit eynem schilt. Der silbern sargk mit eyteln sanct Moritz bildern. [Die silberne monstrantz, in dem tabernackel eyn vorgult sanct Augustins bilde.] Den grossen cristallen becher yn silber gefasset, ubergult und mit Perlen getzyrett. Die Greiffes clawe in silber gefasset, ubergult, uff der decke sanct Moritz bilde, *et sanguinem dominj miraculosum*.

317 Ibid., pp. 38 ff.

318 This arrangement explains the use of the word *Gang* for the description of the relics that we will find in the *Heiltumsbuch*.

319 P. WOLTERS, "Ein Beitrag zur Geschichte des Neuen Stiftes zu Halle," pp. 8-9.

320 A. WOLTERS, *Der Abgott zu Halle*, pp. 35 ff.

321 An incomplete, unpaged copy of this work is in Nuremberg, Germanisches Nationalmuseum, Post. Inc. K 1603, *VOrtzeichnis und zceigung des hochlobwirdigen heiligthumbs der Stifftkirchen . . . zu Halle*; cf. *Meister um Albrecht Dürer*, p. 219, no. 393. A complete copy is in Stuttgart, Württembergische Landesbibliothek, R 16 Vor I.

322 This work, the so-called *Hallesche Heiltumsbuch* or *Hallesche Heiltum*, is now in Aschaffenburg, Hofbibliothek, MS. 14; see *Aus 1000 Jahren Stift und Stadt Aschaffenburg*, pp. 29-30, no. 96. Several studies of this work have been published. The first task was to find the pages that had been torn out. TÉREY, *Cardinal Albrecht von Brandenburg*, was the first to make a careful analysis of the contents, but three important drawings and several pages were missing from the manuscript he used. F. SCHNEIDER, "Wiedergewinnung von Miniaturen aus dem Aschaffenburger Prachtcodex des Halleschen Heiligtums, einer Stiftung des Kardinals Albrecht von Brandenburg," *Hohenzollern-Jahrbuch* 1 (1897): 176-86, found some of the missing folios. E. NEEB, "Die letzten drei fehlenden Blätter, vom Aschaffenburger Prachtcodex des Halleschen Heiligtums aus der Zeit des Erzbischoffs Albrecht von Brandenburg," *MZ* 17-19 (1921-24): 35-40, completed the work of showing the original makeup and appearance of the codex. The detailed study is in REDLICH, *Cardinal Albrecht von Brandenburg*. The *Heiltumsbuch* was edited by P. M. HALM and R. BERLINER, eds., *Das Hallesche Heiltum: Man. Aschaffenb. 14*, Jahresgabe des deutschen Vereins für Kunstwissenschaft, 1931 (Berlin, 1931).

323 H. BÖSCH, "Die kirchlichen Kleinodien des Kardinals Albrecht, Erzbischofs und Kurfürsten von Mainz, Markgrafen von Brandenburg," *Mitteilungen aus dem germanischen Nationalmuseum* 2 (1887-89): 123-52.

324 We have not been able to do more than outline the study that should be made, comparing the Breviary of 1532 with the available inventories. This would reveal the details of these liturgical spectacles and would enable us to form a concrete idea of the demonstrations of religious feeling in the sixteenth century.

325 In this same manuscript there are also representations of St. Maurice as a white; cf. HALM and BERLINER, *Das Hallesche Heiltum*, p. 37, no. 111b and pl. 60 (silver triptych, one wing of which has a St. Maurice), and p. 47, no. 179 and pl. 101b (reliquary in silver and vermeil, on which are several busts, one representing Maurice without "Negroid" features).

326 Aschaffenburg, Hofbibliothek, MS. 14, fols. 110[v], 284[v], 288[v]; see HALM and BERLINER, *Das Hallesche Heiltum*, p. 35, no. 99 and pl. 58b; p. 52, nos. 221, 225 and pls. 126a, 129.

327 Aschaffenburg, Hofbibliothek, MS. 14, fol. 283[v]; see HALM and BERLINER, *Das Hallesche Heiltum*, p. 52, no. 220 and pl. 30b.

328 Aschaffenburg, Hofbibliothek, MS. 14, fol. 427[v]; see HALM and BERLINER, *Das Hallesche Heiltum*, p. 66, no. 339 and pl. 180.

329 Aschaffenburg, Hofbibliothek, MS. 14, fol. 100[v]; see HALM and BERLINER, *Das Hallesche Heiltum*, p. 34, no. 89 and pl. 45.

330 Aschaffenburg, Hofbibliothek, MS. 14, fol. 292[v]; see HALM and BERLINER, *Das Hallesche Heiltum*, p. 53, no. 229 and pl. 134a.

331 Aschaffenburg, Hofbibliothek, MS. 14, fol. 94[v]; see HALM and BERLINER, *Das Hallesche Heiltum*, p. 33, no. 83 and pl. 41a.

332 Aschaffenburg, Hofbibliothek, MS. 14, fol. 335[v]; see HALM and BERLINER, *Das Hallesche Heiltum*, p. 57, no. 265 and pl. 131b.

333 Aschaffenburg, Hofbibliothek, MS. 14, fol. 291[v]; see HALM and BERLINER, *Das Hallesche Heiltum*, p. 52, no. 228 and pl. 132.

334 Cf. p. 194 and fig. 150. This large silver statue was in the choir at Halle (TÉREY, *Cardinal Albrecht von Brandenburg*). A text dating from 1535 seems to allude to it again; cf. REDLICH, *Cardinal Albrecht von Brandenburg*, app. 26, p. 112*, vv. 75-78.

335 Aschaffenburg, Hofbibliothek, MS. 14, fol. 376[v]; see HALM and BERLINER, *Das Hallesche Heiltum*, p. 61, no. 295 and pl. 110a.

336 Aschaffenburg, Hofbibliothek, MS. 14, fol. 228[v]; see HALM and BERLINER, *Das Hallesche Heiltum*, p. 46, no. 175 and pl. 98.

337 These goblets have been studied by A. VON SALDERN, *German Enameled Glass: The Edwin J. Beinecke Collection and Related Pieces*, The Corning Museum of Glass Monographs, no. 2 (Corning, 1965), pp. 128-29, 348-52. Here we mention four of them whose dates seem

sure (there exist a number of late copies): Cleveland, Cleveland Museum of Art, 48.232 (dated 1568); Corning, The Corning Museum of Glass, 57.3.82 (dated 1593), 57.3.83 (dated 1594); Leipzig, Museum des Kunsthandwerks, 56.56 (dated 1594).

338 Magdeburg, cathedral, pulpit by Christof Kapup, about 1595-97; cf. E. Schubert, *Der Magdeburger Dom*, pp. 215-16 and pl. 131.

339 Refer to Maps, pp. 270-71.

340 Algermissen, Moritzkirche, statue, recently polychromed, which may have been part of an ensemble. Münster, cathedral, statue backed against a pillar, dated 1613.

341 Hildesheim, Moritzstift, large altarpiece of the high altar, late seventeenth to early eighteenth century.

342 Langenweddingen, Church of St. George, monumental altarpiece by Michael Helwig, dated 1710.

343 Münster, cathedral, monumental tomb of Jodocus Droste (died 1594).

344 Cf. *supra*, p. 164.

LIST OF ILLUSTRATIONS

1 Eulogia ampulla: St. Menas between two camels. From Egypt. V-VII century. Terracotta. Diam: 10 cm. Marseilles, Musée Borély, 1214.

2, 3 Eulogia ampulla. Side A: profile of St. Menas; side B: invocation formula. From Alexandria. V-VI century. Terracotta. H: 10 cm. Paris, Musée du Louvre, Département des Antiquités grecques et romaines, MNC 140.

4 St. Menas on horseback. Illustration of a text relating one of the saint's miracles. From Edfu. Between 950 and 1050 (?). Parchment. 17 fols., 165 × 100 mm. London, British Library, Department of Oriental Manuscripts and Printed Books, MS. Oriental 6805, fol. 10^r.

5 Marriage of Isaac (detail): meeting of Eliezer and Rebecca. *Ashburnham Pentateuch.* VI-VII century (?). Parchment. 142 fols., 375 × 330 mm. Paris, Bibliothèque nationale, Département des Manuscrits, MS. nouv. acq. lat. 2334, fol. 21^r.

6 Joseph receives his brothers in Egypt (detail): Hebrews and Egyptians at table. *Ashburnham Pentateuch.* VI-VII century (?). Parchment. 142 fols., 375 × 330 mm. Paris, Bibliothèque nationale, Département des Manuscrits, MS. nouv. acq. lat. 2334, fol. 44^r.

7 Crossing the Red Sea (detail): the pharaoh's army. *Ashburnham Pentateuch.* VI-VII century (?). Parchment. 142 fols., 375 × 330 mm. Paris, Bibliothèque nationale, Département des Manuscrits, MS. nouv. acq. lat. 2334, fol. 68^r.

8 Tenth plague on Egypt and the deliverance of the children of Israel. *Ashburnham Pentateuch.* VI-VII century (?). Parchment. 142 fols., 375 × 330 mm. Paris, Bibliothèque nationale, Département des Manuscrits, MS. nouv. acq. lat. 2334, fol. 65^v.

9 *Oikoumenē* of Strabo. Reprinted from E.H. Bunbury, *A History of Ancient Geography* (London, 1879), vol. II, p. 238, pl. III.

10 Facsimile reconstruction (made in 1844) of al-Idrīsī's planisphere, 1140-50, after a thirteenth-century copy (now in Paris, Bibliothèque nationale, Département des Manuscrits orientaux, MS. arabe 2221). Paper. 329 × 134 cm. Paris, Bibliothèque nationale, Département des Cartes et Plans, Ge AA 2004.

11 Ethiopians. *De rebus ex Oriente mirabilibus.* Winchester, second quarter XI century (?). Parchment. 147 fols., 260 × 210 mm. London, British Library, Department of Manuscripts, MS. Cotton Tib. B.V. (part 1), fol. 86^r (detail).

12 *Exultet* roll (detail). South Italy, late XII century. Parchment. Overall dims: 6430 × 255 mm. Troia, cathedral, Archivio capitolare.

13 Combat between Fel and Fol. Mosaic fragment. From the Collegiate Church of Sta. Maria Maggiore in Vercelli. XI century. 154 × 183 cm. Vercelli, Museo Camillo Leone.

14 Forces of evil and the "second death." *Apocalypse.* IX century. Parchment. 40 fols., 270 × 200 mm. Valenciennes, Bibliothèque municipale, MS. 99, fol. 37^r (detail).

33 Judgment of Solomon. Relief. Late XIII or early XIV century. Stone. Auxerre, Cathedral of St-Etienne, west façade.

34 Stoning of St. Stephen. *Images de la vie du Christ et des saints.* Hainaut (?), about 1280-90. Parchment. V-107 fols., 185 × 130 mm. Paris, Bibliothèque nationale, Département des Manuscrits, MS. nouv. acq. fr. 16251, fol. 76r.

35 Betrayal of Judas. *Sarum Missal.* Salisbury, XIII century. Manchester, John Rylands Library, MS. Lat. 24, fol. 150v.

36 Carrying of the Cross. *Images de la vie du Christ et des saints.* Hainaut (?), about 1280-90. Parchment. V-107 fols., 185 × 130 mm. Paris, Bibliothèque nationale, Département des Manuscrits, MS. nouv. acq. fr. 16251, fol. 37v.

37 Executioner's head. Fragment from the archivolts of the north door of the west façade of Rheims Cathedral. 1247-55. Stone. Rheims, Palais du Tau.

38, 39 Scenes from the life of St. Catherine (detail): executioner near Emperor Maxentius (before and after restoration). Stained-glass window. XII century. Angers, Cathedral of St-Maurice, nave.

40 Yaḥyā al-Wasīṭī. Ship crossing the Persian Gulf. Al-Ḥarīrī, *Maḳāmāt (The Assemblies).* 1236-37. 167 fols., 370 × 280 mm. Paris, Bibliothèque nationale, Département des Manuscrits, MS. arabe 5847, fol. 119v.

41 Yaḥyā al-Wasīṭī. Slave market. Al-Ḥarīrī, *Maḳāmāt (The Assemblies).* 1236-37. 167 fols., 370 × 280 mm. Paris, Bibliothèque nationale, Département des Manuscrits, MS. arabe 5847, fol. 105r (detail).

42 Abū Sa'īd a guest at supper with a group of savants. Al-Ḥarīrī, *Maḳāmāt (The Assemblies).* Syria or Mesopotamia, 1222-23. 187 fols., 300 × 230 mm. Paris, Bibliothèque nationale, Département des Manuscrits, MS. arabe 6094, fol. 16r (detail).

43, 44 Conquest of Majorca by James I of Aragon. Mural painting. From Barcelona, Palacio Aguilar. XIII century. 176 × 530 cm. Barcelona, Museo de Bellas Artes de Cataluña, 71447.

45 *Chessbook* of Alfonso X the Wise. 1283. 97 fols., 400 × 270 mm. Escorial, Real Monasterio, Biblioteca, Cod. T. I, 6, fol. 55r.

46 Astrological symbol for the stone *Zebech. Lapidario* of Alfonso X the Wise. XIII century. Parchment. 118 fols. Escorial, Real Monasterio, Biblioteca, Cod. H. I. 15, fol. 95v (detail).

47 *Chessbook* of Alfonso X the Wise. 1283. 97 fols., 400 × 270 mm. Escorial, Real Monasterio, Biblioteca, Cod. T. I, 6, fol. 22r.

48 Muslim expedition on Christian soil and taking booty. *Las Cántigas de Santa Maria* of Alfonso X the Wise. Second half XIII century. Parchment. 256 fols., 490 × 326 mm. Escorial, Real Monasterio, Biblioteca, Cod. T. I, 1, *Cantiga* XLVI (detail).

49 Expedition at sea: kidnapping a Christian count. *Las Cántigas de Santa Maria* of Alfonso X the Wise. Second half XIII century. Parchment. 256 fols., 490 × 326 mm. Escorial, Real Monasterio, Biblioteca, Cod. T. I, 1, *Cantiga* XCV (detail).

50 Story of a woman accused of committing adultery with a Moor. *Las Cántigas de Santa Maria* of Alfonso X the Wise. Second half XIII century. Parchment. 256 fols., 490 × 326 mm. Escorial, Real Monasterio, Biblioteca, Cod. T. I, 1, *Cantiga* CLXXXVI.

51 Story of a Moor's conversion. *Las Cántigas de Santa Maria* of Alfonso X the Wise. Second half XIII century. Parchment. 256 fols., 490 × 326 mm. Escorial, Real Monasterio, Biblioteca, Cod. T. I, 1, *Cantiga*, CXCII.

52 Two black captives on trial. Historiated initial. *Fueros del Reino de Aragon*, fol. 244r. From Barcelona (?). About 1260-80. Parchment. 277 fols., 363 × 243 mm. Aachen, Dr. Peter and Irene Ludwig Collection.

70 Joseph sold to Putiphar by the Ishmaelites. *Octateuch.* Constantinople, XI century. Parchment. 260 fols., 360 × 285 mm. Vatican, Biblioteca Apostolica Vaticana, MS. Vat. gr. 747, fol. 59^{v} (lower scene).

71 Sixth plague on Egypt: boils. *Octateuch.* Constantinople, XI century. Parchment. 260 fols., 360 × 285 mm. Vatican, Biblioteca Apostolica Vaticana, MS. Vat. gr. 747, fol. 82^{r} (upper scene).

72 Sarah is brought to Pharaoh; Pharaoh gives Sarah back to Abraham. *Octateuch.* Constantinople, XI century. Parchment. 260 fols., 360 × 285 mm. Vatican, Biblioteca Apostolica Vaticana, MS. Vat. gr. 747, fol. 35^{r} (two upper scenes).

73 Apostles· teaching the nations. *Tetraevangelion.* Constantinople, mid-XI century. Parchment. 215 fols., 255 × 200 mm. Paris, Bibliothèque nationale, Département des Manuscrits, MS. gr. 74, fol. 20^{r} (detail).

74 Pentecost (detail). Mural painting. Early XIV century. Peć, Church of St. Demetrius.

75 Preaching of the Apostles. *Psalter.* From Constantinople, Studion Monastery. 1066. Vellum. 108 fols., 230 × 195 mm. London, British Library, Department of Manuscripts, MS. Add. 19352, fol. 20^{r}.

76 Pentecost. Enameled plaque. From Constantinople. XII century. Pala d'Oro, upper part, second panel from the right. 30.7 × 30 cm. Venice, Basilica of St. Mark, high altar.

77 Pentecost. Gregory of Nazianzus, *Homilies.* Constantinople, XII century. Parchment. 295 fols., 262 × 210 mm. Paris, Bibliothèque nationale, Département des Manuscrits, MS. Coislin 239, fol. 28^{r} (detail).

78 Pentecost. Enameled plaque. Before 1105. Pala d'Oro, frame of the upper part, fourth panel from the right. 13 × 13.4 cm. Venice, Basilica of St. Mark, high altar.

79 Satan's fall, illustration of the verse, "I saw Satan fall... from heaven" (Luke 10:18). Margin decoration. *Tetraevangelion.* Constantinople, mid-XI century. Parchment. 215 fols., 255 × 200 mm. Paris, Bibliothèque nationale, Département des Manuscrits, MS. gr. 74, fol. 131^{r} (detail).

80 Chancellor Matthew of Ajello treating his gout in a black man's blood. Peter of Eboli, *Liber ad honorem Augusti.* Palermo (?), between 1195 and 1197. Parchment. 148 fols., 330 × 200 mm. Berne, Burgerbibliothek, Cod. 120, fol. 127^{r}.

81 Pantaleone. "Ascension" of Alexander. Mosaic (detail). 1163-65. Otranto, cathedral, central nave, western part, south side.

82, 83 Pantaleone. Queen of Sheba and Solomon. Mosaic (details). 1163-65. Otranto, cathedral, lower part of the choir.

84 Abba Moses swimming across the Nile. *Vitae Patrum.* Italy, XIV century. Parchment. 129 fols., 390 × 275 mm. Vatican, Biblioteca Apostolica Vaticana, MS. Vat. lat. 375, fol. 54^{v} (detail).

85, 86 Episcopal throne supported by three atlantes. 1098. Marble. Bari, Church of St. Nicholas.

87 Scenes from the life of Abba Moses. *Vitae Patrum.* Italy, XIV century. Parchment. 129 fols., 390 × 275 mm. Vatican, Biblioteca Apostolica Vaticana, MS. Vat. lat. 375, fol. 55^{r} (detail).

88 Ethiopian cutting wood. Historiated initial. *Vitae Patrum.* Italy, XIV century. Parchment. 129 fols., 390 × 275 mm. Vatican, Biblioteca Apostolica Vaticana, MS. Vat. lat. 375, fol. 112^{v} (detail).

89, 90 Capital decorated with four heads. From South Italy. About 1212-20. Limestone. H: 36 cm. New York, Metropolitan Museum of Art, The Cloisters, 55.66.

112 Workshop of the Cosmati. Christ between two captives. Mosaic. About 1212. Rome, former Trinitarian convent of S. Tommaso in Formis (now Stazione Chimico Agraria Sperimentale).

113 Head of the black in the Resurrection of the Dead. Fragment of a carved tympanum. From the central portal of the west façade of the Cathedral of Notre-Dame in Paris. About 1220-30. Stone. 112 × 115 cm. Paris, Musée de Cluny, Cl. 18643.

114-116 Statue of St. Maurice. About 1240-50. Sandstone (traces of polychromy). H: 112 cm. Magdeburg, Cathedral of St. Maurice and St. Catherine, choir.

117 Master Theodorik. St. Maurice. Painted panel. Before 1367. 114 × 90 cm. Karlštejn, castle, Chapel of the Holy Cross, east wall of the choir, right side of the lower register.

118 Reliquary bust of St. Maurice. Bohemia, about 1440. Polychromed wood. H: 47.5 cm. Kroměříž, Uměleckohistorické Muzeum, P 11.

119 St. Maurice and a Benedictine pope. Painted panel from an altarpiece. Bohemia (?), about 1420-30. 99.5 × 71 cm. Quittelsdorf, evangelical church.

120 Coronation of the Virgin (detail): martyrs and confessors. Central panel of a painted altarpiece. Dated 1465. 146 × 142 cm. Brandenburg, Cathedral of SS. Peter and Paul.

121 St. Maurice. Detail of a painted panel from the outer right-hand wing of a polyptych. From the Abbey of Wiener Neustadt. 1447. Dims of the wing: 370 × 137 cm. (H of the detail: approx. 80 cm.). Vienna, Stefansdom.

122 St. Maurice. Detail of the painted reverse of the right wing of an altarpiece. About 1370-80. Overall H of the wing: 166 cm. H of St. Maurice: approx. 40 cm. Brandenburg, Cathedral of SS. Peter and Paul, choir.

123 Statue of St. Maurice. About 1360-70. Stone. Magdeburg, Cathedral of St. Maurice and St. Catherine, gable over the west portal.

124 St. Maurice. Side of a stall, upper part. About 1470-80. Wood. H of the detail: 58 cm. Halberstadt, Church of St. Maurice.

125 St. Maurice. Stained-glass window (detail). About 1430-40. Stendal, Cathedral of St. Nicholas, choir, north side.

126 Statue of St. Maurice. Before 1411. Stone. H: 116 cm. Halle, Church of St. Maurice.

127 Statue of St. Maurice standing against a pillar on the north side of the central nave. 1513 (gift of Sebastian von Ploto). Stone. Halberstadt, Cathedral of St. Stephen.

128 Silver statuette of St. Maurice. From Magdeburg (?). About 1470-80. H: 16 cm. Medingen, abbey.

129 Virgin and Child between St. Maurice and St. Sebastian. Central panel of a carved altarpiece. About 1500. Polychromed and gilded wood. 164 × 149 cm. Frankenhain, church.

130 St. Maurice (detail). Right wing of a carved triptych dated 1517. Polychromed and gilded wood. 160 × 51.5 cm. Braunsdorf, church.

131 Studio of Valentin Lendenstreich. St. Maurice and St. Catherine. Detail of the central panel of a carved triptych dated 1498. Wood. H of St. Maurice: approx. 80 cm. Rottenbach, church.

132 St. Maurice. Detail of the left wing of a carved altarpiece. About 1450-1500. Polychromed and gilded wood. Dims of the wing: 125 × 65 cm. H of St. Maurice: approx. 65 cm. Wienhausen, abbey, chapter room.

133 St. Maurice. Detail of the left wing of a carved altarpiece dated 1492. Polychromed and gilded wood. Dims of the wing: 230 × 121 cm. H of St. Maurice: approx. 150 cm. Delitzsch, Church of SS. Peter and Paul.

134 Bust of St. Maurice. Lower compartment of the left wing of an altarpiece. About 1430-40. Polychromed wood. H of St. Maurice: approx. 35 cm. Teterow, church.

135 St. Maurice. Detail of the central panel of a carved altarpiece. About 1430-40. Polychromed wood. Dims of the central panel: 202 × 185 cm. Wismar, Church of St. Nicholas.

136 St. Maurice. Mural painting (detail). About 1464. Roskilde, Domkirke, so-called Chapel of Christian I or of the Three Magi, south wall.

137 Statue of St. Maurice. Early XV century. Polychromed wood. Formerly in Riga, House of the Black Heads. Present whereabouts unknown.

138 Virgin and St. Maurice beneath the heraldic bearings of the city and the Black Heads. 1522. Stone. Reliefs on the door jambs of the House of the Black Heads in Riga.

139 Statue of St. Maurice from the altarpiece of the old high altar. About 1425. Polychromed wood. H: 85 cm. Jüterbog, Church of St. Nicholas.

140 Scenes from the legend of St. Maurice. Painted fragments of the altarpiece of the old high altar. About 1425. Wood. Approx. 190 × 175 cm. Jüterbog, Church of St. Nicholas.

141 St. Maurice. Mural painting (detail). Second half XV century. Kloster Zinna, former abbatial guesthouse, second floor, north wall.

142-144 Peter Vischer. Funerary monument of Archbishop Ernest of Saxony. Overall view and details: statue of St. Maurice on the base of the tomb; figures of St. Maurice and St. Stephen on the bishop's mitre. 1495. Bronze. H of St. Maurice: 55 cm. Magdeburg, Cathedral of St. Maurice and St. Catherine.

145 Altarpiece of the high altar, wings closed. Late XV-early XVI century. Halle, Church of St. Maurice.

146 St. Maurice. Statue from a niche in the central panel of the altarpiece of the high altar. 1480-90. Wood. H: approx. 75 cm. Halle, Church of St. Maurice.

147 Hans Baldung Grien. St. Maurice and St. George. Altarpiece wings. From the collegiate church at Halle. 1507. Wood. Dims of each wing: 121 × 28 cm. Berlin (GFR), Staatliche Museen Preussischer Kulturbesitz, Gemäldegalerie, 603 A.

148 St. Maurice. Left wing of an altarpiece dated 1529. Wood. Overall width of the altarpiece: 460 cm. Halle, "Marktkirche."

149 Nikolaus Glockendon. St. Maurice and his companions. *Missal* of Cardinal Albert of Brandenburg. 1524. Parchment. 572 fols., 385 × 280 mm. Aschaffenburg, Hofbibliothek, MS. 10, fol. 437^v.

150 Reliquary statue of St. Maurice. *Heiltumsbuch.* 1525-27. Parchment. 428 fols., 350 × 250 mm. Aschaffenburg, Hofbibliothek, MS. 14, fol. 227^v.

151, 152 Matthias Grünewald. St. Erasmus and St. Maurice. From Halle, collegiate church. About 1520-24. Painting on wood. 226 × 176 cm. Munich, Bayerische Staatsgemäldesammlungen, Alte Pinakothek, 1044.

153 Jehner von Orlamünde. Three companions of St. Maurice. Interior of the first wing on the right of the altarpiece of the high altar, dated 1511. Halle, Church of St. Maurice.

154 Peter Schro. Statue of St. Maurice standing against a pillar in the nave. 1525. Stone. H: 196 cm. Halle, Collegiate Church of St. Maurice and St. Mary Magdalene.

155 Peter Schro. Plaque commemorating the dedication of the collegiate church at Halle by Cardinal Albert of Brandenburg. 1523. Stone. 208 × 150 cm. H of St. Maurice: 92 cm. Halle, Collegiate Church of St. Maurice and St. Mary Magdalene.

156 Statue of St. Maurice. From the façade of the town hall in Jüterbog. 1508. Stone. H: 185 cm. Jüterbog, Kreis-Heimatmuseum.

157 St. Maurice and his companions. Upper half of the right wing of a triptych. From the chapel at Gross-Wittfeitzen. About 1520. Wood. Dims of the wing: 168 × 84 cm. Lüneburg, Museum für das Fürstentum Lüneburg, H 75.

158 St. Maurice. Altarpiece fragment. From Schwaigern. About 1520. Wood. 88 × 45 cm. Formerly in Stuttgart, Württembergisches Landesmuseum, 13254.

159 Master of the Goslar Sibyls (attrib.). St. Maurice and his companions. Left wing of the so-called Calenberger Altar. About 1515. Wood. 99 × 65.6 cm. Marienburg, castle, Collection of H. R. H. the Prince of Hannover.

160, 161 Hans von Kulmbach. St. Maurice. Stationary left wing of the so-called Ritteraltar. About 1518. Wood. 157 × 65 cm. Limbach, church.

162 Covered ciborium topped with a bust of St. Maurice. *Heiltumsbuch.* 1525-27. Parchment. 428 fols., 350 × 250 mm. Aschaffenburg, Hofbibliothek, MS. 14, fol. 335^{v}.

163 Drinking horn decorated with a statuette of St. Maurice. *Heiltumsbuch.* 1525-27. Parchment. 428 fols., 350 × 250 mm. Aschaffenburg, Hofbibliothek, MS. 14, fol. 291^{v}.

164, 165 Wolf Traut. Reliquary busts of Fidis and Maurice. Woodcuts from the *Heiltumsbuch* printed in 1520. 76 fols. Nuremberg, Germanisches Nationalmuseum, Post. Inc. K 1603.

166 Reliquary bust of Fidis. *Heiltumsbuch.* 1525-27. Parchment. 428 fols., 350 × 250 mm. Aschaffenburg, Hofbibliothek, MS. 14, fol. 376^{v}.

167 Reliquary bust of St. Maurice. *Heiltumsbuch.* 1525-27. Parchment. 428 fols., 350 × 250 mm. Aschaffenburg, Hofbibliothek, MS. 14, fol. 228^{v}.

168 Enameled glass goblet decorated with a figure of St. Maurice and the armorial bearings of the canons of Magdeburg. 1568. H: 26 cm. Cleveland, Cleveland Museum of Art, 48.232.

PERMISSIONS

AACHEN Sammlung Ludwig, Aachen: *52, 53*
ASCHAFFENBURG Hofbibliothek Aschaffenburg: *149, 150, 162, 163, 166, 167*
AVIGNON Musée Calvet: *98*
BARCELONA Museo de Bellas Artes de Cataluña: *27, 28, 43, 44*
BERLIN (GFR) Gemäldegalerie, Staatliche Museen Preussischer Kulturbesitz, Berlin (West): *147*
Staatsbibliothek Preussischer Kulturbesitz, Berlin: *108, 109*
BERNE Burgerbibliothek Bern Cod. 120 (Petrus de Ebulo): *80*
BOULOGNE-SUR-MER Bibliothèque municipale: *20*
BOURG-EN-BRESSE Bibliothèque municipale, 65, bd de Brou, 01000 Bourg-en-Bresse: *22*
BURGO DE OSMA Museo de la Catedral: *15*
CLEVELAND The Cleveland Museum of Art, Gift of Mrs. Henry White Cannon: *168*
ESCORIAL Biblioteca de El Escorial: *17, 45, 46, 47, 48, 49, 50, 51, 54, 55*
JÜTERBOG Kreis-Heimatmuseum: *156*
KLOSTERNEUBURG Emailaltar von Nikolaus von Verdun, 1181, Chorherrenstift Klosterneuburg: *103*
KROMĚŘÍŽ Umĕleckohistorické Muzeum: *118*
LAON Bibliothèque municipale: *21, 29*
LEÓN Colegiata San Isidoro: *23*
LONDON By permission of the British Library: Department of Manuscripts, *11, 75*; Department of Oriental Manuscripts and Printed Books, *4*
LÜNEBURG Museum für das Fürstentum Lüneburg: *157*
LUNEL Bibliothèque municipale: *97*
MANCHESTER The John Rylands University Library of Manchester: *35*
MARIENBURG Courtesy of Ernst-August, Prince of Hannover: *159*
MARSEILLES Musée Borély: *1*
MUNICH München, Alte Pinakothek: *151, 152*
NEW YORK The Cloisters, The Metropolitan Museum of Art: *89, 90*
NUREMBERG Germanisches Nationalmuseum, Nürnberg: *164, 165*
PARIS Bibliothèque nationale, Doc. Bibl. nat., Paris: *5, 6, 7, 8, 10, 18, 19, 24, 25, 34, 36, 40, 41, 42, 59, 60, 61, 67, 73, 77, 79*
Musée de Cluny: *110, 111, 113*
Musée du Louvre, Département des Antiquités grecques et romaines: *2, 3*
RHEIMS Palais du Tau Trésor de la Cathédrale: *37*
ROME Istituto sperimentale per la nutrizione delle piante (former Convent of S. Tommaso in Formis), courtesy its director Professor Luciano Tombesi. Courtesy Soprintendenza al Monumenti del Lazio: *112*
STRASBOURG Musée de l'Œuvre Notre-Dame: *102*
TROIA Cathedral, Archivio capitolare: *12, 16*
VALENCIENNES Bibliothèque municipale: *14*
VATICAN Biblioteca Apostolica Vaticana: *56, 57, 58, 64, 65, 66, 68, 69, 70, 71, 72, 84, 87, 88, 95*
VENICE Biblioteca Nazionale Marciana: *62, 63*
Procuratoria di San Marco: *76, 78*
VERCELLI Museo Camillo Leone, Courtesy Istituto di Belle Arti: *13*

PHOTO CREDITS

BARCELONA MAS: *15*
BELGRADE Izdavački Zavod "Jugoslavija": *74*
BERLIN (GFR) Foto: Jörg P. Anders: *147*
Staatsbibliothek Preussischer Kulturbesitz, Berlin: *108, 109*
BERNE Burgerbibliothek Bern: *80*
CLEVELAND The Cleveland Museum of Art, Gift of Mrs. Henry White Cannon: *168*
COLOGNE Rheinisches Bildarchiv: *53*
COPENHAGEN The National Museum Copenhagen: *136*
DACHAU Wolf-Christian von der Mülbe: *160, 161*
FLORENCE G. C. Sansoni Editore Nuova S.p.A.: *76*
KROMĚŘÍŽ Umĕleckohistorické Muzeum: *118*
LONDON By permission of the British Library: Department of Manuscripts, *11, 75*; Department of Oriental Manuscripts and Printed Books, *4*
Photograph by courtesy of the Courtauld Institute of Art: *52*
MANCHESTER The John Rylands University Library of Manchester: *35*
MARBURG Bildarchiv Foto Marburg: *137, 138*
MARSEILLES Musée Borély: *1*
Menil Foundation/Mario Carrieri: *12, 13, 16, 56, 57, 58, 62, 63, 64, 65, 66, 68, 69, 70, 71, 72, 78, 82, 83, 84, 85, 86, 87, 88, 91, 95, 105, 112, 119, 129, 130, 131, 133*
Menil Foundation/Hickey & Robertson: *2, 3, 14, 17, 20, 21, 22, 23, 26, 27, 28, 29, 30, 31, 32, 33, 37, 43, 44, 45, 46, 47, 48, 49, 50, 51, 54, 55, 89, 90, 92, 93, 94, 97, 98, 100, 101, 102, 106, 107, 110, 111, 113, 114, 115, 116, 120, 122, 124, 125, 126, 127, 128, 132, 139, 140, 141, 142, 143, 144, 145, 146, 148, 149, 150, 153, 154, 155, 156, 157, 159, 162, 163, 166, 167, jacket illustration*
MUNICH München, Alte Pinakothek: *151, 152*
NUREMBERG Germanisches Nationalmuseum, Nürnberg: *164, 165*
PARIS Archives photographiques: *38, 39*
Phot. Bibl. nat., Paris: *5, 6, 7, 8, 10, 18, 19, 24, 25, 34, 36, 40, 41, 42, 59, 60, 61, 67, 73, 77, 79*
PRAGUE L. Neubert: *117*
ROME Gabinetto Fotografico Nazionale: *81*
ROSTOCK E. Fischer: *134, 135*
SALONICA Archive of Patriarchal Institute for Patristic Studies, Thessaloniki, Greece: *96*
STUTTGART Ltd. Direktor Dr. Hans-Peter Geh, Württ. Landesbibliothek, Stuttgart: *158*
VIENNA Bundesdenkmalamt: *121*
Photo Ritter, 1180 Wien: *103*
WEIMAR Klaus G. Beyer: *123*
WESTON TURVILLE Photograph by Sonia Halliday & Laura Lushington: *99*
Reprinted from E.H. Bunbury, *A History of Ancient Geography* (London, 1879), vol. II, p. 238, pl. III: *9*
Reprinted from W. W. S. Cook, "The Earliest Painted Panels of Catalonia (VI)," *The Art Bulletin* 10 (1927-28): fig. 16: *104*

BLACK SAINT MAURICE. Geographical Diffusion

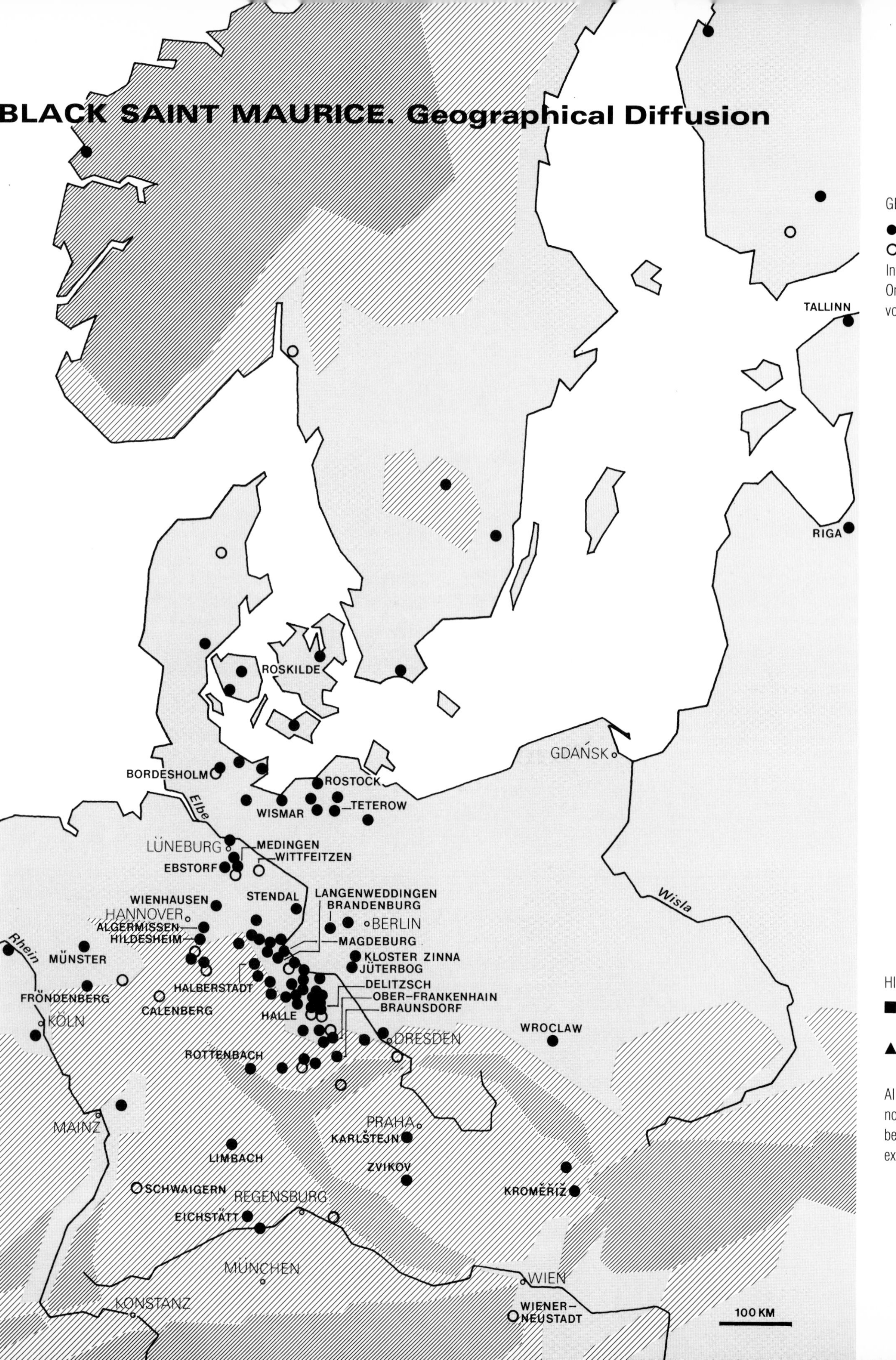

GEOGRAPHICAL DIFFUSION

● Work(s) in place

○ Work moved elsewhere or missi

Inventory made in 1978

Only localities cited in this volume are mentioned.

HISTORICAL DIFFUSION

■ 1200-1360 ▌1361-1460

● 1461-1540

▲ 1541-1640 ★ 1641-1800

○ very inexact date

All the works located in the northern part of the map belong to the period ● except Riga ▌●

cartography M. C. LAPEYRE

Historical Diffusion

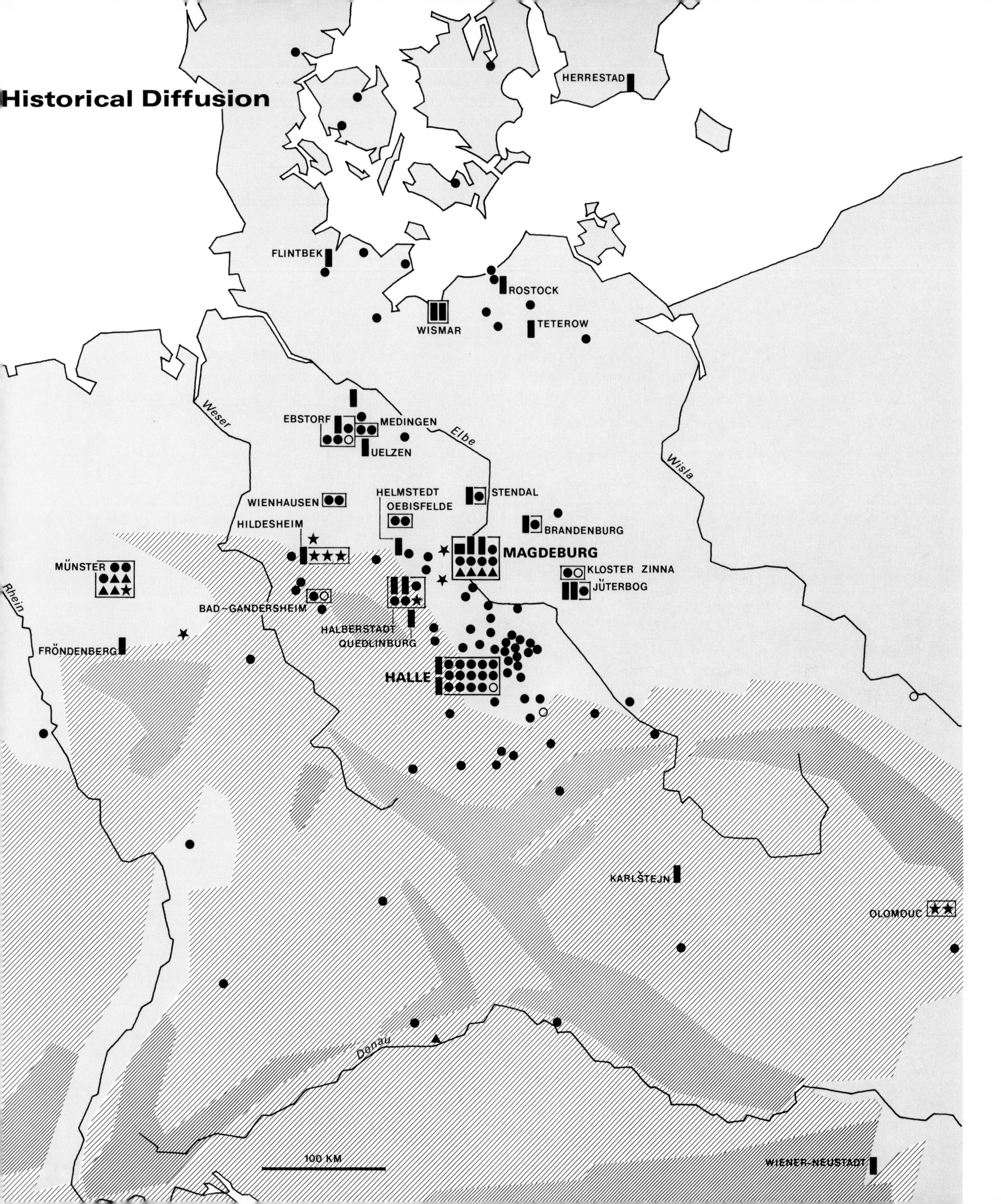
HERRESTAD
FLINTBEK
ROSTOCK
WISMAR
TETEROW
EBSTORF
MEDINGEN
UELZEN
Weser
Elbe
Wisla
WIENHAUSEN
HELMSTEDT
OEBISFELDE
STENDAL
BRANDENBURG
HILDESHEIM
MAGDEBURG
MÜNSTER
KLOSTER ZINNA
JÜTERBOG
Rhein
BAD-GANDERSHEIM
HALBERSTADT
QUEDLINBURG
FRÖNDENBERG
HALLE
KARLŠTEJN
OLOMOUC
Donau
100 KM
WIENER-NEUSTADT

INDEX OF PROPER NAMES

Printed in Switzerland

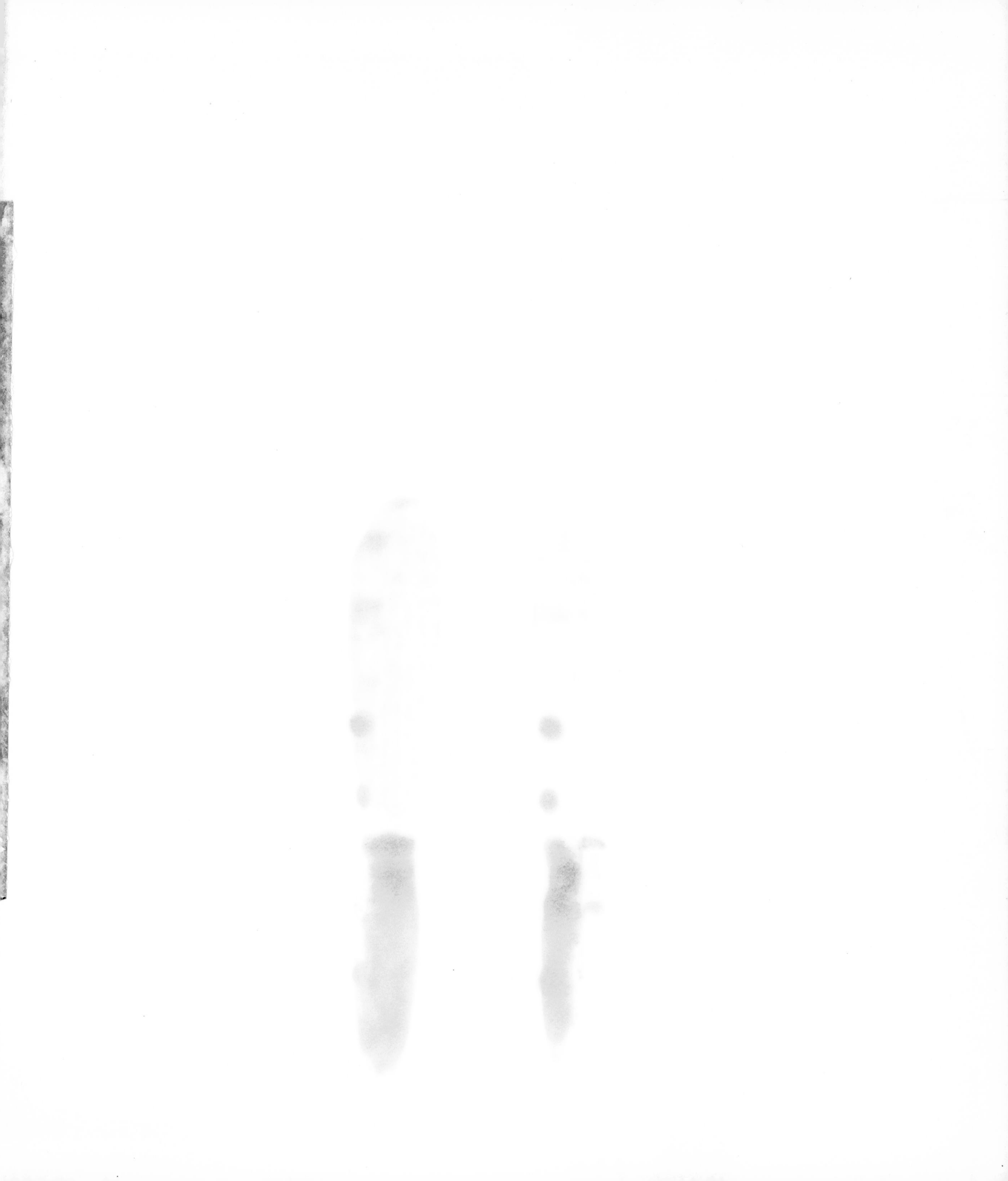

DATE DUE
